ART / WOMEN / CALIFORNIA
1950–2000

ART / WOMEN / CALIFORNIA
1950–2000

Parallels and Intersections

EDITORS
DIANA BURGESS FULLER and
DANIELA SALVIONI

POETRY EDITOR
GAIL TSUKIYAMA

EDITORIAL ASSISTANT
DEBORAH MUNK

Published in association with the San Jose Museum of Art

UNIVERSITY OF CALIFORNIA PRESS

Berkeley / Los Angeles / London

University of California Press
Berkeley and Los Angeles, California

University of California Press, Ltd.
London, England

© 2002 by Diana Burgess Fuller
and Daniela Salvioni

Library of Congress Cataloging-in-
Publication Data
Art, women, California 1950–2000 : parallels
and intersections / Diana Burgess Fuller and
Daniela Salvioni, editors ; Deborah Munk,
editorial assistant ; Gail Tsukiyama, poetry
editor.

     p.   cm.

  "Published in association with the San Jose
Museum of Art."

  Includes bibliographical references and
index.
ISBN 0–520-23065-5 (cloth : alk. paper)—
ISBN 0–520-23066-3 (pbk. : alk. paper)

  1. Women artists—California. 2. Minority women artists—California. 3. Art,
American—California—20th century—Social
aspects. 4. Feminism and art. I. Fuller,
Diana Burgess. II. Salvioni, Daniela.

N8354 .A73 2002
704'.042'0979409045—dc21   2001027674
Printed in Hong Kong
10 09 08 07 06 05 04 03 02
10 9 8 7 6 5 4 3 2 1

The paper used in this publication meets the
minimum requirements of ANSI/NISO
z39.48–1992 (R 1997) (Permanence of Paper). ♾

DESIGNER
Nicole Hayward

COMPOSITOR
Integrated Composition Systems, Inc.

INDEXER
Margie Towery

TEXT
Filosofia

DISPLAY
Akzidenz Grotesk

PRINTER + BINDER
Asia Pacific Offset, Inc.

This book is dedicated to the gift of vision
To our children, and to theirs
Vita
Anthony, Joanna, Mia, Brien, Whitney, and Antonia

The *Rosie the Riverter Memorial* honoring women's contribution to World War II was constructed on the site of the former Kaiser Shipyard, Richmond, California, and conceived as a mnemonic walkway recalling the 441 ft. length of a liberty ship. The memorial links the prefabrication process of building ships with the process of human recollection. Elements include stainless steel sections, hull, stack, and overlook; porcelain enamel and etched stainless steel image panels; granite pavers with sandblasted text and concrete walkway; forehatch (rockrose garden), afthatch (seagrass garden).

CONTENTS

PREFACE

The acknowledgment of perspective is a key to wisdom. *Art/Women/California 1950–2000: Parallels and Intersections* presents a forum for comparing perspectives on the definition of art and its role within society. The essays provide a basis from which to consider interpretations of parallel experiences in California's major cultural communities and to examine points of intersection in the artists' themes and practices.

We chose to concentrate on California because after World War II the state had become a new frontier and a gateway to waves of immigrants, particularly from Pacific Basin and Latin American countries. We focused on women working as artists in California during the second half of the twentieth century because sociopolitical and economic factors during and after the war fostered a radical activism, especially during the late 1960s and the 1970s, which attracted and encouraged talented and powerful women. We invited twenty scholars from different cultural backgrounds to investigate how the vast changes of the postwar era affected these women, how the ensuing events influenced the art that they produced, and how their art in turn affected society and its understanding of art.

The essays in this book reveal a multiplicity of vision and reflect the cultural fermentation of the period by contrasting and comparing the artists and their varied artistic practices in relation to the larger sociological context. Exploring the conjuncture between place and artistic activity from multiple perspectives, *Art/Women/California 1950–2000: Parallels and Intersections* stands as testament to the rich diversity that is contemporary California culture.

FOREWORD

When it was first suggested that we present an exhibition based on *Art/Women/California 1950–2000: Parallels and Intersections*, we immediately recognized the tremendous opportunity to examine the contribution of women artists working in California during the second half of the twentieth century.

Art/Women/California 1950–2000, the first survey of its kind, delves into subject matter that mainstream art history has neglected, not least of which is the effect of post–World War II sociopolitical conditions on the themes, issues, and practices reflected by these artists. In nearly every case the contributors to the book have taken a non-mainstream approach. While methodologies vary, art historian Whitney Chadwick announces the general tack in her introductory essay. Chadwick begins by asking, "How is it possible to generalize about the experiences of women who have, in many cases, located their social, political, and cultural identity in a recognition of difference?" Her solution is to focus on individual contributions rather than to make generalities. This approach is more akin to a roving telescope than a wide-angle lens, making for an exciting treatment of artists who are individuals first and foremost.

In covering such untrammeled terrain, Diana Fuller and Daniela Salvioni provide a significant forum for further discussion and an investigation of landmark art by a selection of artists who have worked in California during the past fifty years. Presenting this exhibition has proved to be a formidable task that has been at once exhausting and exhilarating. An exhibition of this scope and scale requires the time and attention of many people. Here at the San Jose Museum of Art, deserving thanks should be given to our associate curator Merrill Falkenberg and to JoAnne Northrup, the coordinating curator for the exhibition. I would like to thank the entire museum staff, particularly Lisa McDermott, who secured the loans of art-work, and Rich Karson, who designed the installation. In addition, the exhibition would not have been possible without the cooperation of the numerous lenders who have so graciously agreed to part with their works. The museum is very grateful to AT&T and The Myra Reinhard Family Foundation, which are major sponsors of *Art/Women/California 1950–2000: Parallels and Intersections*, and to Adaptec, which is a sponsor of the exhibition. And finally, I would like to acknowledge the artists who are no longer with us as well as those who continue to provoke, delight, and inspire us.

Susan Landauer
Katie and Drew Gibson Chief Curator
San Jose Museum of Art

PROJECT SPONSORS

 AT&T

The Myra Reinhard Family Foundation

ⓐadaptec

ACKNOWLEDGMENTS

In 1997 the kernel of an idea was first proposed to a group of wise friends and has evolved over a four-year period from a point of view to a symposium and finally to this publication, *Art/Women/California 1950–2000: Parallels and Intersections*.

We are profoundly grateful to Theresa Harlan, Phyllis J. Jackson, Carole Ann Klonarides, Amalia Mesa-Bains, Tere Romo, and Moira Roth for their wisdom and commitment throughout the early development of this project and for their subsequent contributions to this book. Special thanks go to Whitney Chadwick, a valued contributor and member of the original advisory group, whose generous counsel has continued to serve us at every level, and to Ann Chamberlain and Jeanie Weiffenbach, whose constant support helped us to persevere. Thanks are also due to Karla Malette and Marcia Tanner, who helped to shape the project at its onset, and to Regina Mouton, who created the language and structure which became the building blocks for our further discussion. The variety of perspectives we encountered early in the project indicated that this would be a mapping adventure with little precedent—would we be able to find the storyline, identify the landmarks, and determine the guideposts along the way, or decide where the varying perspectives interfaced and where they differed?

We will be forever grateful to Lorrie Greene of the Northern California Council of the National Museum of Women in the Arts (NCC/NMWA), whose faith and enthusiasm convinced her organization's national office to be our fiscal sponsor. They have supported our efforts from the beginning. We would also like to express our appreciation to the current director, Hanna Regev, for her support and vision; she is revitalizing the local organization and is using our project to spur new educational outreach programming.

In turn, we want to thank Henry Hopkins, Walter Hopps, and Alberta Mayo for their early advice and recommendations; and Steven Nash, Associate Director and Chief Curator, and Tim Burgard, Department Head and Ednah Root Curator of American Art, of the Fine Arts Museums of San Francisco, for their initial encouragement. We also wish to thank Phil Linhares, Chief Curator at the Oakland Museum of California, for his efforts on behalf of the exhibition, as well as Susan Sterling, Chief Curator at the National Museum of Women in the Arts in Washington, D.C.

Gradually the key questions in our search crystallized, and the issues emerged. During our three years of research, Jeff Gunderson, Director of the Anne Bremer Library at the San Francisco Art Institute, gave unstintingly of his time in locating historical information. Additional thanks are due to Steve Seid, Video Curator at the University of California, Berkeley Art Museum and Pacific Film Archive, as well as Gail Silva, Director of the Film Arts Foundation; Steve

Anchor, Director of Cinematheque, San Francisco; and film scholar and critic Ruby Rich for their cinematic expertise. Sharon Bliss generously continues to this day with enormous ability to structure and organize the many grant proposals submitted on behalf of the project.

Gratitude is owed to Mark Johnson, Professor of Art and Director of the Art Department Gallery at San Francisco State University, and to his staff for hosting and producing the symposium *Articulating California*, which took place in early 1999 and led to the further refinement of the thinking presented in this book. Special thanks go to Dean Keith Morrison, Sylvia Solochek Walters, Paul Dorn, Sharon Spain, and to Deborah Munk, without whose patience and organizational skills we would not have been able to continue. Thanks also to the panelists at the symposium, including, in addition to our original advisors, Jennifer Gonzalez, Allucquere Rosanne Stone, and Judith Wilson, who also subsequently became brilliant contributors to this book. Thanks to Eungie Joo, whose participation on the panel provided a much appreciated fresh perspective.

Other writers who came to the project after this juncture were Nancy Buchanan, Angela Davis, Karin Higa, Suzanne Lacy, Pam Lee, Laura Meyer, Sandra Phillips, Jolene Rickard, and Rosa Linda Fregoso. We would like to express our deep gratitude to them for their immediate response and energetic cooperation through the many edits and revisions. Thanks also to Amelia Jones, who made time for an extensive interview, book and baby pending. Profound thanks also go to Gail Tsukiyama for her understanding and thoughtful research as well as to JoAnn Hanley for her healing presence and expert counsel and advice concerning women's history in technology.

Last, but not least, we would like to thank Susan Landauer, Katie and Drew Gibson Chief Curator, who responded instantly and with enthusiasm to the possibility of hosting an exhibition at the San Jose Museum of Art; Daniel T. Keegan, Oshman Executive Director, for keeping the exhibition on course; and especially Senior Curator JoAnne Northrup, as well as the entire museum staff. Their efficiency and positive manner under stress have allowed us to look forward with pleasure to finalizing the exhibition, which opens at the San Jose Museum of Art in the summer of 2002. Our thanks also to Merrill Falkenberg and to Cathy Kimball, Director of the San Jose Institute of Contemporary Art (ICA), who gave encouragement when it was needed.

We would like to express our personal thanks to John Kreidler, formerly Program Executive with the San Francisco Foundation, now Executive Director of Cultural Initiatives Silicon Valley; to Drew Talley, Registrar of the California African American Museum, and to Leah Levy for helping us in our research; Ed Gilbert at Gallery Paule Anglim, who was always ready to respond to a question; Kimberly Shuck, whose wisdom and experience provided much needed help and direction; to Claire Aquilar, Manager Broadcast Programming, KCET, Los Angeles; Larry Thomas, Dean at the San Francisco Art Institute; Stephanie Barron, Senior Curator of Modern and Contemporary Art at the Los Angeles County Museum; to Paule Anglim, Rosamund Felsen, Brian Gross, and Jeremy Stone, for knowledgeable counsel; and to Annette Goldman, Cecilia Dougherty, Tony Labat, Grace Welty, and Ari Rosa. Finally, we wish to express our gratitude to Dilva and Daniele Salvioni, Paola Salvioni, Allan and Charlotte Jolly, and the Blecker and Symanovich families, who helped us out during moments of crisis. Immense appreciation goes to Jim Clark, Director of the University of California Press, for his willingness to take our preliminary concept to fruition, and for the meticulous help and sainted patience provided by our editor, Kathleen MacDougall. We would also like to gratefully acknowledge the assistance of Senior Editor Sue Heinemann, Mari Coates, and the rest of the Press's editorial and design staff.

This project would not have been possible without the crucial and generous support provided by the following individuals and organizations:

Paule Anglim
Cris and Paul Carter
Enrique Chagoya

Georgiana Ducas

Ann Hatch

Elizabeth Lawson

Anne MacDonald

Lenore and Rich Niles

Becky Tamblyn Pence

Mary and Carter Thacher

Jeremy Stone

Eileen Sullivan

ArtSpace, San Francisco/New York

The California Council for the Humanities

LEF Foundation

National Endowment for the Arts

The Bernard Osher Foundation, San Francisco

San Francisco Foundation

The Zellerbach Family Fund, San Francisco

We would like to extend our appreciation to the museums, galleries, film archives, arts organization, individual collectors and collections as well as publishers that contributed images for this publication.

California African American Museum, Los Angeles

California Afro-American Museum Foundation, Los Angeles

The Fine Arts Museums of San Francisco

Armand Hammer Museum of Art and Cultural Center, Los Angeles

Nora Eccles Harrison Museum, Logan, Utah

Kemper Museum of Contemporary Art, Kansas, Missouri

Los Angeles County Museum of Art

Mexican Museum, San Francisco

The Museum of Contemporary Art and The Geffen Contemporary, Los Angeles

The Museum of Modern Art, New York

National Museum of American Art, Smithsonian Institution, Washington, D.C.

University of California, Berkeley Art Museum and Pacific Film Archive

Whitney Museum of American Art, New York

ACA Galleries, New York

George Adams Gallery, New York

American Indian Contemporary Arts, Oakland

Blum and Poe Gallery, Los Angeles

Ronald Feldman Fine Arts, New York

Rosamund Felsen Gallery, Los Angeles

Brian Gross Fine Art, San Francisco

Gallery Paule Anglim, San Francisco

Paul Kasmin Gallery, New York

Sean Kelly Gallery, New York

Koplin Gallery, Los Angeles

Margo Leavin Gallery, Los Angeles

Karyn Love Gallery, Los Angeles

David McKee Gallery, New York

Mark Moore Gallery, Los Angeles

Pilkington Olsoff Fine Arts, Inc., New York

Regen Projects, Los Angeles

Michael Rosenfield Gallery, New York

Acknowledgments

Daniel Saxon Gallery, Los Angeles

Brent Sikkema Gallery, New York

Sperone Westwater Gallery, New York

Steinbaum Kraus Gallery, Miami Beach

Allan Stone Gallery, New York

Steven Wirtz, San Francisco

Frameline, San Francisco

Moongift Films, New York

Women Make Movies, New York

Xochitl Films, San Francisco

ARS (Artists Rights Society), New York

Bi-State Development, Arts in Transit, St. Louis,
    Missouri

Pat Rodriguez and Las Mujeres Muralistas,
    California

SPARC, Los Angeles

Through the Flower, New Mexico

Alexa Young, California

Paula Maciel Benecke and Norbert Benecke,
    Los Angeles

Collection of Dr. Walter O. Evans, Michigan

Collection of Lorrie and Richard Greene, California

Hatch-Billops Collection, New York

Collection of Drs. James W. and Caryn Hobbs,
    California

Richard "Cheech" Marin, San Francisco

Janice Mirikitani, San Francisco

Diane di Prima, California

Arte Publico Press, University of Houston, Texas

Celestial Arts Publishing, Berkeley, California

New Directions Publishing, New York

W. W. Norton and Company, New York

John F. Crawford and West End Press, New Mexico

And to all the artists who permitted the use of
images of their work for this publication.

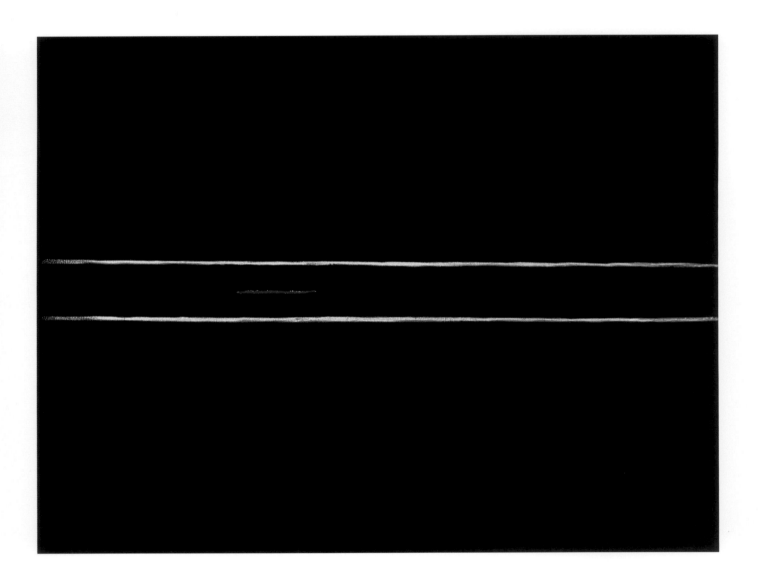

Mary Lovelace O'Neal, *Untitled, Plenum Series*, 1968–72. Charcoal and pastel on canvas, 7 x 14 ft. Photo: John Brain. Collection of the artist.

DANIELA SALVIONI

INTRODUCTION

Art in Context

Art/Women/California 1950–2000: Parallels and Intersections is a comprehensive survey of women artists working in California in the second half of the twentieth century who have contributed in dynamic and innovative ways to broadening the definition of art. We seek to reveal the richness of this period by contrasting and comparing these artists and their varied artistic practices in relation to the larger sociopolitical context. We present five parallel perspectives on this history, which reflect the distinct experiences of California's major ethnic and cultural communities, and investigate the points of intersection in shared themes and practices. We examine how women artists have been affected by the vast sociopolitical changes of the post–World War II era, which in California had a very distinct character, and how the ensuing events influenced the art they produced. Moreover, we trace the impact that these artists and their work have had on shaping both the California profile and the larger culture into what they are today.

We explore the conjuncture between place and artistic activity from multiple perspectives: thematic and formal, as well as social and historical. The California context has heuristic value both because of the set of factors that make the state unique and, conversely, because of the ways in which California functions as a microcosm of national and global sociopolitical developments.

In California, place is indexed to space. Poised at the edge of the continent, before

1

the earth's largest body of water, the land that is California offers a very palpable sense of exterior space. Physical space, the land's very physicality, presses itself on its inhabitants because there is simply more room out west, because the land has been subjected to obvious geophysical and man-made stress, because of the economic value of land due to California's robust agricultural and industrial sectors, and because it is the ground upon which so many of its immigrants toil. Space may also be seen as the locus of the body; that is, the corporeal as the place from which to move out into the world, which the feminist movement defined and which had a particularly significant impact on feminist art in California. Space may also be considered as interior, an inner sanctum, a site of personal freedom and introspection. In part this conception derives from the forms that spirituality takes in the non-European cultures that have been absorbed into California culture, and in part from the drive toward active spiritual self-definition forged in those idiosyncratic and unorthodox ways with which California is associated. And finally there is the newest definition of space, interactive and creative, but devoid of geographical space and unhinged from the limitations of the physical body, which comes to us via the Internet frontier, largely developed in California. In this volume, Jennifer Gonzalez, Amelia Jones, Pamela Lee, and Allucquere Rosanne Stone show how

the theme of space—physical, corporeal, spiritual, and virtual—reverberates throughout the art produced in California in the later half of the twentieth century.

The California art world—the real life structures within which its artists operate—has its own specificity. During the second half of the twentieth century, California became a mecca for art students because of its wealth of excellent art schools and its tuition assistance programs (by the 1990s greatly slashed). The schools encouraged the exploration of new artistic practices, rendering California an experimental hotbed populated by scores of young, ambitious artists. California's trove of nonprofit exhibition spaces, which arose in the 1970s, gave artists opportunities to show their work without commercial pressures. Its hitherto relatively undeveloped art market (this too began to change in the 1980s) rendered it an art environment that was underdetermined by exclusionary commodifying forces, compared to other art centers. These factors freed up artists to be as experimental as they wished, regardless of how commodifiable the results would be.

But, for all its specificity, California is also a place that epitomizes national and global trends, and indeed, often presages them. Deep demographic changes, the shift toward ever greater diversity and complexity with all its concomitant sociopolitical implications, are accelerated and exacerbated in California but similarly are under way elsewhere in the United States as well as abroad. While California is at the vanguard of the information technology revolution, the technology is quickly adopted everywhere, radically altering the ways in which we all work and play. The state's extreme politics, and its late twentieth-century governors ranging from Jerry Brown to Ronald Reagan, were at first viewed as Californian oddities but no longer, particularly after Reagan captured the nation as president. Hollywood has made California into the engine of mainstream popular culture, while freedom of expression and the willingness to experiment in lifestyles and ideas have fostered a global "alternative" culture with a distinct Californian bent. California's role as sociopolitical crystal ball of the nation and its near-mythic role in the global cultural imagination are reflected in much of the work made there and in the influence art made-in-California has on art generally.

The artists presented in this book form a heterogeneous group—diverse in age, ethnic background, cultural milieu, and formal artistic training. They are painters, sculptors, photographers, performance artists, installation artists, filmmakers, video artists, artists using new technologies, and graphic artists. Their works employ different artistic styles, content, modes of address, target audiences, and sites of interventions. When focusing on artists who may have little or nothing

in common aesthetically or culturally except for the fact that they are all women, there is the risk of over-determining the importance of gender. But, we eschew a single privileged optic and the search for a oneness of artistic vision whose homogenizing effects distort the complexity of reality. Rather, we examine the work in the larger context, taking into account how California history, politics, and economics have affected the artists' cultural formation and their artistic production. For instance, Amalia Mesa-Bains and Terezita Romo discuss how some Chicana/Latina artists critically address the structure of Chicano/Latino gender relations in their imagery and in the way they work. Similarly, while so much art of the 1980s addressed issues of cultural and sexual identity, which early feminist art had thematized in the 1960s and 1970s, we recognize its roots in historical developments running parallel to and/or preceding feminism (such as the Civil Rights movement, and anticolonial movements abroad) as well as in profound economic shifts.

From whence did the developments that fostered this artistic fermentation arise? World War II was a historic watershed for the United States because it marked the beginning of a profound economic and social upheaval that unleashed far-reaching demographic and cultural changes. The war effort spurred economic growth and social independence for both working-class and middle-class European American women and to a lesser extent for men and women of color as well, who suddenly found themselves filling jobs previously reserved solely for white males. California was an important center of the military industrial complex, which drew workers from across the rest of the nation. At the same time, California's agricultural and industrial economies were burgeoning, which renewed immigration trends from Asia and both Central and South America. The sociopolitical and economic landscape that emerged in California after World War II stimulated a radical social activism, particularly during the 1960s and 1970s, which triggered an enormous response by scores of women of all cultural backgrounds, prompting them to make art that reflected their personal experiences and/or often was politically charged.

What was the artistic climate women artists faced in the period covered by this book? By the 1950s, the institutionally sanctioned art world was no longer exclusively the province of well-to-do white men and recent emigrés from Europe but was, instead, becoming more diversified in terms of class. The postwar GI Bill of Rights afforded unprecedented numbers of middle-class and working-class veterans the luxury of training to become professional artists. By the 1950s American artists had established new ways of making and perceiving art that was no longer derivative of European art—the unbound expres-

sivity of abstract expressionism and subsequently the ironic complicity of Pop art were the cornerstones of a newfound autonomy. But, because they conceived of expressivity abstractly, these artists did not thematize personal subject matter or content as such. Moreover, until the feminist art movement, the sociological profile of the artists, while broadened, was still staunchly European-American and male. The rare exceptions in the earlier part of the postwar period were artists such as Louise Bourgeois, Louise Nevelson, and Lee Bontecou, who explored ways for making art unfettered by the male-dominated aesthetics of the time. But their work was marginalized and relegated to the status of curious asides in the official histories. Artists who did fit the dominant mold, like Helen Frankenthaler, were often dismissed as feminized versions of the "real" thing. Eva Hesse stands out for having incorporated a "feminized" aesthetic into postminimalism and having been highly acclaimed by the mainstream art world. But she is the exception that proves the rule, for very few other women artists at the time achieved such recognition.

The social changes that swept the nation in the postwar era introduced "new" protagonists— women, peoples of color, gays and lesbians—onto the social stage. Against the background of the postwar economic boom and coupled with California's cultural openness toward the new, California became an environment where people from diverse backgrounds were emboldened to create their own artistic vocabularies. The advent of the feminist explosion, which itself was born of the Civil Rights and antiwar movements of the 1960s, was especially felt in California, particularly Los Angeles, which became a principal epicenter for a variety of feminist art practices, particularly performance.

Feminism forcefully made content, instead of abstraction, art's essential and critical component. Although the feminist movement was limited in its support of women of color, its ripple effect was to render personal experience acceptable subject matter for art. Moreover, it made women artists—whether overtly feminist or not—more visible en masse, bringing them greater public and institutional attention.

The struggle for civil rights and empowerment of people of color, which peaked in the 1960s and 1970s, also inspired women of color to exercise their role as artists and to develop art practices that reflected and addressed their own specific concerns and interests centered on the issue of identity. But it was not until the latter part of the 1980s that the effects of these struggles were finally absorbed by the mainstream art world, and the excellence of the artistic reality promulgated interest and response. The issues and themes elaborated by artists of color began to be acknowledged; their opportunities for exhibiting increased; and they received greater critical attention, though here, too, biases were not entirely expunged. Nevertheless, today the art world has been compelled to realize that seemingly neutral categories and distinctions ordinarily taken for granted in the hegemonic discourse on art were actually often exclusionary and restrictive.

The unique confluence of distinct energies and traditions of this period resulted in multiple challenges to the formal European modernist aesthetic that had dominated artistic creation, theory, and discourse. In their challenge to the established discourse, women artists employed strategies that had hitherto been downplayed, if not outright exorcised, from modernist art. With rising concerns over a host of issues—from environmental hazards to threats to community cohesiveness within the urban context—the notion that artists might have the ability to initiate social change suddenly became relevant again (after lying dormant since the 1920s). This radical new awareness must have been especially compelling to women artists, who had so much to gain from changes to the white male-dominated bastion of art.

Women artists started to break away from established formalist theory and to develop new styles, strategies, and goals which put personal experience at the center of the work, invoked narrative, incorporated folk and craft elements, critically appropriated media images, impelled attention from the media, performed concrete bodily enactments, and made activism a viable art strategy. The art practices spawned by women artists anticipated and laid the foundation for contemporary art through the close of the century and beyond.

Issues of personal and/or collective identity have dominated much of the work produced in the period covered by this book. They are a constant theme, from the visceral performance-based work centered in Los Angeles's Woman's Building and the fictional personae developed in enduring performances sometimes lasting a year by artists such as Lynn Hershman Leeson and Linda Montano in San Francisco in the 1960s and 1970s, to the plethora of 1980s and 1990s artists wrestling with the subject, including artists as different as Tran T. Kim-Trang, Kara Walker, Laura Aguilar, Jean LaMarr, and Diana Thater.

What is less obvious is the pervasiveness of identity issues lying beneath the surface. For instance, art involving new technologies raises identity issues on an interstitial level of the work. Free of prescribed frames of reference dictating the making and viewing of the art, art that employs new technologies is open to preoccupations that are excluded from the art historical cannon. It raises questions about the nature and the role of the collective and/or individual viewer and issues of what is deemed public and private. By contrast, traditional media tend to beg already prescribed responses by the artists and the tradi-

tional art viewer alike. Of course, this is not always true. Painters like Kim Dingle are finding subtle and provocative ways to use the traditional medium of painting that unsettle the traditionally conceived relation between art and viewer. And we can imagine a time, perhaps in the immediate future, when the "old new technology," like video, will become ossified and formulaic. Indeed, video is now on the verge of becoming technologically obsolete as new equipment and software become available, constantly challenging the artist with ever broader potential.

Exploding onto the art world in the 1960s, new technologies ushered in an array of new responses and new interlocutors which concretely shifted the identity of the targeted audience away from the circumscribed parameters of the past and engaged viewers who had hitherto been un- or under-addressed. "New technology" is a historical category that changes with time, but in the last four decades of the twentieth century it included video, computers and proto-computers, and communications technologies. California—with its culture of experimentation, its role in innovative technology and in generating popular media, and its wealth of new media facilities—has been a hub for new technology-based art. JoAnn Hanley, Nancy Buchanan, and Allucquere Stone discuss the conditions that first prompted women artists to use the new medium of video to document feminist performance-based work of the 1970s, and then challenged them to explore new ways to create, to communicate, and to travel in the potentially infinite world of cyberspace.

Some women artists in California in the 1960s and 1970s turned their backs on "high art" by pursuing art's capacity to affect the status quo through directly intervening into society, rather than speaking only from within its established venues. As creative agents for social change, artists such as Bonnie Sherk, Suzanne Lacy, Judith Baca, Helen and Newton Harrison and, more recently, Reiko Goto, Ann Chamberlain, and Susan Schwartzenberg have stretched the boundaries of art beyond the traditional and commodified confines, blazing a trail for art as a socially responsible activity. Curiously, during this period there were few comparable male artists developing art forms that intervened directly into society; German artist Joseph Beuys is the lone brilliant exception.

Social interventionist artists or, artists making social sculpture, like those mentioned above, create projects designed to initiate fundamental and concrete urban, social, and/or environmental change through social interactions that draw laypeople, the media, and/or government officials into the process. They take aim at specific governmental policies and social and ecological practices by targeting the source of the problem, often in dramatic and highly visible ways. More-

Kim Yasuda, detail from *The Canyon That Took the Place of a Couch*, 1999. Mixed media installation (foam, fabric, plastic, porcelain, cast plaster, resin, video projection), 12 x 18 x 30 ft. Art in General, New York.

over, instead of merely critiquing objectionable aspects of modern society, the most ambitious interventionist projects actually instantiate microcosmic examples of the changes they seek. Bonnie Sherk's "Farm" project, for instance, was a living example of an alternative form of community space which fostered creative and democratic interaction between people amidst environmental soundness. The notion of "retraditionalization" that Jolene Rickard discusses in this volume, referring to the political import of Indigenous artists' work, bears significant affinities to the "instantiating" aspect of social interventionist art. Some younger artists, such as Catherine Opie and Hulleah Tsinhnahjinnie, insert interventionist/instantiating modes back into the traditionally bounded art sphere by making discrete art objects that are metonymic of their communities. They "take over" pieces of the visual (art) domain by placing in it a lesbian and an Indigenous presence, respectively.

Political art is traditionally divided between art that is closely linked to grassroots organizing and that self-marginalizes itself from the art world, on the one hand, and art that functions exclusively from within the art world, relying on illusion and representation to affect political consciousness, on the other. Social sculpture marks a third way: it extends art into society, targeting policy and institutional practices directly, while remaining firmly committed to participating in the discourse on art. The extension of art into society is the inverse of, for instance, Hans Haacke's art-based activism. While he performs an incisive critique of the vested corporate interests that underwrite art institutions, rather than dwell on the negative moment of critique, social sculpture concretely instantiates utopian alternatives.

The novel and audacious ways in which social sculpture has expanded the definition of art informs much of the most interesting work produced in the United States and abroad in the 1990s. But, what is perhaps most impressive is the fact that some of the interventionist artists discussed in this book have seen their work successfully and concretely affect public policy and institutional practice. In surveying the landscape of women artists working in California in the second half of the twentieth century, we find that issues of identity and social sculpture (cultural reflection upon and active intervention into the environment and the community) are among the areas where women artists have been their most experimental, ambitious, and innovative.

When planning a book, one never fully foresees all that the book will be. A text holds its own surprises, even for the editors. Unexpected parallels and intersections emerged in the course of the making of this book. One sub-theme that surfaced in a number of the essays is that of mentoring. JoAnn Hanley notes how women artists who took up new technologies in the 1960s and 1970s sought each other out, freed as they were by working in a field devoid of "father figures." Mentoring is also a persistent subtext in Theresa Harlan's discussion of the struggle faced by Native artists. Judith Wilson invokes the importance of mentoring as a weapon against invisibility imposed on African American women artists. On the other hand, Allucquere Stone describes the Web as overrun by grrrl guerrilla artists who reject both "mother" and "father" figures.

Our project has three goals: (1) to consider the effects of sociopolitical forces on culture at large, on the artists, and on their communities of origin and/or choice; (2) to investigate commonalities of themes, issues, and practices among these artists, as well as the differences between their experiences; and (3) to examine how art by women in the last half century expanded the critical dialogue and aesthetic practices with new concepts, approaches, and perspectives.

Contributions to this book by twenty distinguished cultural figures document and assess the artistic responses by women artists to the shifting conditions of the post–World War II era and to California as a global microcosm of cultural innovation. Their voices are individual, distinct, unique, often complementary, and at times discontinuous, reflecting the complexity and variety of the art and the artists discussed.

The book opens with two overviews, one art

historical and the other political. Whitney Chadwick writes an art historical "anti-overview," to borrow her term, that highlights five artists from the five dominant ethnic groups of California, who are considered as individual instances of their subcultures rather than as representative of a community. Angela Davis contributes a political perspective in which she provocatively suggests how labor struggles and aesthetic values might combine.

The book is organized into two main sections, "Parallels" and "Intersections," which establish a grid of historical perspectives for placing the art within relevant sociopolitical trajectories.

The essays in the "Parallels" section, subtitled "Reconsidering the Terrain: Five Historical Perspectives," examine how women artists from the five major ethnic communities in California—African American, Asian American, Chicana/Latina, European American, and Native American—in parallel fashion are historically influenced by their separate experiences within the California context, and how they in turn have left their distinct mark upon it.

Phyllis Jackson shows how the art of African American women, who she describes as multiply oppressed, sheds light on white bias in the media, art, and art history, as well as actively promoting positive Black imagery. Karin Higa discusses the work of Asian American women artists in light of their historical travails and experiences, while at the same time commenting on the shortcomings of the homogenizing term "Asian American." Laura Meyer looks at the peculiar predicament of European American women artists, at one and the same time relatively privileged because they belong to the dominant cultural group, and yet subordinate because their interests and concerns are still devalued. Artist and scholar Amalia Mesa-Bains illuminates how art making and the struggle for recognition and dignity are deeply intertwined for Chicana and Latina artists. Jolene Rickard examines how Native artists, as key agents in sovereignty building by Indigenous nations, break down the borders between art and life or community, which dovetails in interesting ways with similar efforts to break down the barrier between art and life undertaken by non-Native artists since the 1960s.

The "Intersections" part of the book opens with a section called "Ley Lines." Ley lines are alignments of ancient sites stretching across the landscape. We took this as our metaphor for the deep-seated differences and unresolved issues that persist. They are the product of the specificities of particular histories, which is not to suggest that these conditions are self-caused, but that, once in place, they follow their own track. The "Ley Lines" section is not exhaustive; rather it merely gives a sense of the ongoingness of those issues that continue to agitate, even though seemingly absorbed into contemporary culture.

Amelia Jones discusses how feminist principles greatly influenced women's artistic practices and the content of their work, but notes that feminist art is still barely acknowledged by academics and critics. This exemplifies the propagation of feminism's unresolved issues. Terezita Romo analyzes the path-breaking course pursued by Las Mujeres Muralistas, the Latina artist collective, against the background of Latino culture's specific gender biases. Theresa Harlan gives a poignant picture of the very real barriers uniquely confronted by Native artists to this day. Judith Wilson shows how the unique invisibility of black women artists has been fabricated and imposed.

The second part of "Intersections" is called "Themes and Practices"; in it we trace some of the more compelling points of contact between the work of various artists, in terms of the themes they raise and the artistic practices they employ. In surveying the field, we found that there tends to be more overlap among artists engaging in nontraditional art practices than traditional ones, and this is reflected in the type of work discussed in this section. Place, space, and technology enter into the field as legitimate "canvases."

Jennifer Gonzalez discusses artists who metonymically engage land in their work as culturally laden subject matter, in contrast to the dumb primary material it has been for 1960s male Earth Artists. Sandra Phillips points out how the suggestion of narrative is effectively mined by artists whose work is indexed to the notion of photograph as documentation, from Jay DeFeo to Carrie Mae Weems. Film scholar and critic Rosa Linda Fregoso's tour de force essay rounds out our discussion of women artists' contribution to visual culture by taking a panoramic view of women's film in California in this period. Pamela Lee discusses the quasi-spiritual vein that traverses the art of some women artists in California, and how this aligns with the concept of space as redefined in the technology of the Internet. In a recorded e-mail conversation, scholar Moira Roth and artist Suzanne Lacy illustrate how West Coast women's performance art enacts a paradigm shift from the 1960s "postmodern" variant associated with New York, toward a more activist form. JoAnn Hanley clearly demonstrates the pioneering role of women artists in the history of technology-based art, against mainstream assumptions to the contrary. Similarly, Nancy Buchanan explodes the myth that video art is a white bastion, revealing it to be at the forefront of critiques of the Other in art.

The epilogue by Allucquere Rosanne Stone looks into the future with a tantalizing discussion of the creative and freeing aspect of the construction of gender, opening up the definition of woman to womyn. She underscores how woman/womyn is a mutable political construct, a battleground, and the basis for creative acts,

especially in relation to new technology's ability to spawn entirely new interactive communities unattached to physical locus and the constraints that come with it.

The method adopted in this book combines the use of updated art historical criteria with a sensibility that identifies and cherishes differences. We seek to locate the social forces underpinning the relations of power that are infused in society at large and the art world in particular, in an effort to expose—and undermine—the hidden biases lurking beneath tacit assumptions about "the norm" or "ground zero" in art. In many ways, the artworks presented here perform similar critical dialogues.

To achieve a comprehensive survey, we adopted a three-pronged strategy—by our selection of the writers, the artists, and the work: (1) We invited writers who are prominent in their fields and who write from different positions of ethnicity, sexual orientation, and class. They come from California's five dominant ethnic communities—African American, Asian American, Chicana/Latina, European American, and Native American—and this is reflected in the structure of the "Parallels" section of the book, where the writers discuss work from their own communities of origin. In addition, Davis's overview provides a class perspective, and Stone's epilogue speaks from a position of defined sexuality and gender. (2) The artists come from a wide array of cultural and ethnic backgrounds and exist within different artistic, political, sexual, and cultural communities. (3) The work presented in this volume includes all contemporary genres of visual art. It is varied in form and content. We went beyond the mainstream galleries, exhibition spaces and art publications, to the streets, local communities and independent initiatives to find work for inclusion. As a result, the book contains institutionally sanctioned art alongside art that lies outside of mainstream circuits, without placing one over the other.

We sought to identify work for inclusion in the book that has affected the greater collective discourse of art and, in the process, has transformed our perceptions, disrupted stifling norms, and/or revitalized art's connection to its surrounding community. Our desire to be comprehensive does not sacrifice quality in the art. But in order to accommodate the gamut of artistic practices employed in the latter half of the twentieth century, we needed a notion of quality that is not reducible to the restrictive traditional formalist criteria of Western Modernism. Our notion of quality had to take into account content, process, practice, and the context of the artist's self-defined community—aspects that contemporary art has raised as important to our evolving notion of what constitutes art. But, at the same time, we do not do away with formal art historical criteria. Rather, we underscore the importance of the

aesthetic dimension in rendering the work appreciable to those outside of specific traditions and/or experiences. In this collection of essays, we document and critically evaluate the strength and importance of these artists' work, not all of which has received adequate critical attention.

In selecting artists for inclusion in the book, our criteria had to be both elastic enough to accommodate vastly different art projects, yet strict enough to be useful in defining artistic value. For us this meant that the work needed to signal an important stage of development, a cultural turning point, and/or an achievement that reflects the unique experience of each artist. The field of potential artists for consideration was limited, of course, to artists who have worked in California for some time, but also included artists who have made work there which has had significant ramifications for the art public, for the artists' own work, and/or for other artists (as is the case, for instance, with Ann Hamilton and Faith Ringgold). We only considered artists who reference their work to an art context, even if antagonistically. We had no wish to "import" makers of artisanal or ritualistic objects into a Western-conceived art context—which we deem replete with problems. (However, in some cases, especially with some Native American artists, the work may also function in ritualistic or artisanal ways, as well as referring to an art context.) But, the flexibility of some of these criteria means that their application is neither conclusive nor infallible, and undoubtedly there are deserving artists who have been overlooked. For this, we are sorry.

Certain themes recur throughout much of the work presented and discussed here. They include: reclamation and affirmation of the artist's particular heritage, experience and identity; (re)presentation and deconstruction of objectification, stereotyping, sexuality and the body; political resistance and protest; appropriation and subversion of hegemonic cultural icons; cultural critique, particularly of Eurocentric art historical traditions and masculinist media imagery; personal and autobiographical narrative and/or the elaboration of fictitious personae; preservation and reclamation of the urban and natural environment; ideas of public vs. private spheres; exploration of the expressive potential of new or previously devalued forms, materials and techniques; and reconsideration and reconfiguration of our relationship to space. A comprehensive look at contemporary art in California reveals to us new criteria for evaluating and classifying art that counter the prejudices of Eurocentric Modernism. It prompts us not to limit ourselves to the physical object—which is

the basis of both Western formalism and craft-oriented practices, but also not to discard traditional art historical criteria entirely. Rather, it prompts us to combine those criteria with a consideration of the extended context of each work and the perspective (whether individual or collective) of each viewer—thus expanding the critical discourse.

In the second half of the twentieth century, California became a supportive environment for artists. California's culture of experimentation, its proximity to centers of technology and media, its role as gateway for a myriad of immigrants, its history of social activism and alternative institutions—all contributed to a climate of unprecedented openness in which sizable numbers of women from diverse cultural groups found ways to establish new aesthetic practices of their own. In multifaceted ways, individual strands of autobiographical discovery have been recast as part of the identity of an entire culture. In the context of great social transformations, the artists discussed in this book have enhanced our appreciation of California as a global cultural and sociopolitical microcosm, and have helped to empower us to imagine future possibilities for the new millennium.

CULTURAL OVERVIEW

I am walking rapidly through striations of light and dark thrown
under
an arcade.

I DREAM I'M THE
DEATH OF ORPHEUS

Adrienne Rich

I am a woman in the prime of life, with certain powers
and those powers severely limited
by authorities whose faces I rarely see.
I am a woman in the prime of life
driving her dead poet in a black Rolls-Royce
through a landscape of twilight and thorns.
A woman with a certain mission
which if obeyed to the letter will leave her intact.
A woman with the nerves of a panther
a woman with contacts among Hell's Angels
a woman feeling the fullness of her powers
at the precise moment when she must not use them
a woman sworn to lucidity
who sees through the mayhem, the smoky fires
of these underground streets
her dead poet learning to walk backward against the wind
on the wrong side of the mirror

WHITNEY CHADWICK

REFLECTING ON HISTORY AS HISTORIES

I was thirteen years old and in love with the Beach Boys and Annette Funicello when my best friend moved to California. Homesick at first, she sent long letters back East describing what seemed to me unimaginable freedoms played out in a vast and exotic landscape: fast cars, boys, walks across the Golden Gate Bridge, dinners in Chinatown, more boys, trips to beaches and mountains. From the perspective of my mostly white, mostly middle-class suburban life in western New York, California glowed with promise, offering a shimmering vision of escape from everything conservative, tradition bound, and limited.

In 1965, when I graduated from college and made the first of several westward treks, other realities appeared to mediate those earlier, more unproblematic images: antiwar marches, rallies in support of the United Farm Workers strike in the San Joaquin Valley, political street performances by El Teatro Campesino and the San Francisco Mime Troupe, jazz clubs, and gay bars. The California I inhabited in 1965 and 1966 was less mythic, more humbled by social and political realities, with its history, or histories, increasingly obscured by waves of seekers more interested in the future than the past.

By 1978 I had become a permanent resident, with job and family in the Bay Area. Today, contemplating the challenge of providing an introduction to the histories (for the lives of women do not reduce to a monolithic or essentialized set of experiences) and contributions of women artists in California since 1950, I find myself drawn back again to the unresolved, perhaps unresolvable, tensions between mythologies of westward expansion and manifest destiny, and the realities of the complex, multifaceted society that confronts us today.

The years from 1950 to the present roughly encompass a historical era that extends from the end of World War II to the millennium. It is a period marked by postwar social transformations, Cold War politics, rapid demographic change, and far-reaching shifts in consciousness. These years saw the emergence of a succession of movements, several of which originated in California, that challenged traditional social hierarchies. In the wake of the Civil Rights and anti–Vietnam War movements came Black Power, Red Power, Chicano, Gay Liberation, and women's movements. Many of their ideologies moved beyond political rights, redefining political debate to include cultural struggles and the politics of identity. They were succeeded in the 1980s by powerful conservative attacks on social diversity and liberation, and by growing economic constraints for many Californians.[1]

As we move into a new century, older concepts of history, geography, and gender—not to mention race, ethnicity, and sexuality—have come under increasing scrutiny. It is difficult today to think in the linear patterns that have traditionally marked our historical narratives. But if California's social and political history and its art history are categories that demand rethinking, so also does the category "women artists"—for how is it possible to generalize about the experiences of women who have, in many cases, located their social, political, and cultural identity in a recognition of difference?

This book, part of a major project of definition and representation, is designed to recognize the vital roles that women in California have played in shaping contemporary visual culture. Thinking about the implications of a project such as this, I worry about whether California can be examined through the lenses of geography, history, and gender without the results leading us back into the fanciful myths that seem to cling to every mention of the state in the mass media.

These musings return me to an earlier dilemma. What has California—understood as a geopolitical entity and a set of cultural and social ideologies—contributed to the national cultural debate since World War II? And how has that debate been shaped by and through issues mediated by gender, class, race, and ethnicity? To explore the roles of women artists in California is also to explore the histories and roles of the institutions unique to California: our art schools and museums, our alternative cultural institutions, like the Galeria de la Raza and Crossroads Community (known as The Farm) in San Francisco, the Women's Graphic Arts Center and the Lesbian Art Project in Los Angeles, the Women's Building in San Francisco and the *Womanhouse* project in Los Angeles. And it requires rethinking issues of regionalism and of the relationship between cultural centers and margins.

The generous provisions of the GI Bill of Rights encouraged record numbers of young men to resume their education after World War II. Significant numbers of them chose to study the fine arts; art schools from the California School of Fine Arts (now the San Francisco Art Institute) to the Chouinard School and the Otis Art Institute in Los Angeles found themselves inundated with students who were more mature, more idealistic, and more highly motivated than those of previous generations. By the 1950s, the influx of art students included a number of the young women who would make up the first generation of postwar women artists in California; among them were Deborah Remington, Joan Brown, Ruth Asawa, Bernice Bing, Jay DeFeo, and Sonia Getchoff in San Francisco, and June Wayne and Joyce Treiman in Los Angeles.

The following decade, the social protest movements that led to the first demonstrations against racism and sexism in the art world reached California. The founding in New York of groups like Women Artists in Revolution within the Art Workers Coalition, Women Students and Artists for Black Art Liberation, and the Ad Hoc Women Artists' Committee had parallels on the West Coast in the project *Womanhouse*, the Los Angeles Council of Women Artists, and the first feminist studio programs at California State University, Fresno, and CalArts (the short name for California Institute of the Arts, located in Valencia).[2]

By the 1970s, liberation movements—women's, Chicano, Native American, gay, and lesbian—had begun to emerge in California, as elsewhere, bringing with them a set of issues about the intersection of representation and identity. At the same time, visual culture in California remained strongly inflected by the land: by the agricultural labor of field workers as well as the more romantic interventions of artists influenced by the 1970s preoccupation with earthworks, environmental and ecologically oriented art, and by notions of community that differed from those of older, eastern cities.

While some women chose to work in public places in order to reach audiences outside the closed confines of the art gallery and museum worlds, others continued working in more traditional media. Among both groups, however, a new attention to issues of family and personal or cultural histories, both real and imagined, is apparent. In San Francisco, women contributed significantly to the contemporary mural movement, as well as to other collective and community-based projects. In Los Angeles and San

Francisco, women played pioneering roles in the new media and emerging genres of a period later characterized by critic Moira Roth as "the amazing decade."[3] In Los Angeles, Judy Chicago, Miriam Schapiro, and others began their recuperation of women's histories and images in paintings, sculpture, and collages. The task of summarizing and encapsulating these stories within the categories produced through an intersection of space and time poses a challenge and risks essentializing women by burying their very real differences under an arbitrary linkage of artists and generations. Contemporary women artists in California, using a wide range of materials, forms, and strategies, have produced their own "histories," histories which intersect with and challenge dominant narratives. They have drawn attention to the margins of culture and knowledge, and to the repressed in hegemonic cultural discourse. Working within patriarchal social and institutional structures, and drawing from a dizzying variety of sources, these artists have challenged established meanings and destabilized fixed gender and racial categories. Rather than offer an "overview," a synthetic and totalizing account of women artists in California, I would like to propose rethinking the questions of women artists and California histories by focusing on five specific works of visual art produced between 1969 and 1994 that engage in different ways with issues of gender, race, class, ethnicity,

and California history. By doing this I hope to put the focus on the ways that women artists themselves have written and rewritten the historical narrative.

Eleanor Antin, *California Lives* (1969)

A spindly-legged metal tray table sits in the corner of a gallery. Sitting on its stenciled surface are a melamine cup and saucer, an unlit king-sized filter cigarette, a plastic hair curler, and a matchbook from Bully's Prime Rib restaurant. A panel of text accompanies the objects:

> She worked nights, late. Liked to watch the surf in the mornings. She didn't get much sleep then but she didn't really care about that. She worried about her little girl. Maybe her mother would send money from Idaho but she never did. Twice a week the lifeguard with the moustache would visit and they went inside the house. Later he came out alone and trotted back down to the beach. Much later she became a masseuse and her mother sent the granddaughter a red Camaro. She smashed it up on the freeway but she wasn't hurt.[4]

The fictive character identified only as "Jeanie" is evoked through the text and objects exhibited at the Gain Ground Gallery in New York in 1970. She, and other invented personalities, people *California Lives*, the first series produced by

1
Eleanor Antin, *California Lives*,
1969. Installation (dimensions
variable). Photo: Peter Moore.
Collection of the artist, courtesy
Ronald Feldman Fine Arts,
New York.

2
Eleanor Antin, *The Murfins*,
detail from *California Lives*,
1969. Installation (dimensions
variable). Photo: Steve Oliver,
Los Angeles County Museum
of Art. Collection of the artist,
courtesy Ronald Feldman Fine
Arts, New York.

Eleanor Antin after she arrived in Southern California with her husband and son at the end of 1968.

Antin came to California as an adult. Her idea of inventing a life, or a personal history, grew out of the narrative conceptual works with which she had already begun to experiment in New York. *California Lives* marked both a new stage in her own artistic development and a highly personal response to her initial encounter with Southern California culture. A series of assembled "portraits" of individuals, both real and imagined, the characters who made up *California Lives* were described through a combination of narrative texts and consumer goods and other household artifacts, many of these characterized by the glossy surfaces and bright colors of Southern California "pop" culture.

Antin arrived in California bearing a set of mythologies constructed around the notions of dispossession and reinvention not unlike those that had long accompanied earlier waves of European immigration. From Sir Francis Drake's landing in northern California in 1579 to the entry of North Americans into the burgeoning West Coast fur trade at the end of the eighteenth century, settlement was shaped by an ethos of so-called "discovery" mixed with fantasies of redemption and economic windfalls. By the late 1840s a belief in Manifest Destiny, the conviction that North America was destined to stretch from

sea to sea, was bringing new settlers west and, after the discovery of gold, by the thousands to California. Antin's Jeanie, like most of the characters in *California Lives*, was an inheritor of the belief that California offered a better life. An unsophisticated woman, Jeanie was a working-class single mother struggling to survive in a materialistic and hedonistic culture that seemed to promise everything, but often delivered little. Her fictional antecedents can be seen in the rootless men and women who inhabit the sterile modern apartments of Raymond Chandler's and Ross MacDonald's novels, and populate Joan Didion's edgy freeway culture.

For Antin, these were iconic figures, some known, others entirely made-up, who "inhabited" a world of what was increasingly being identified nationally as "California pop culture":

Remember, in those days there was a kind of trailer-park look to California—sleepy little towns and stoned-out surfers. These were the days of the Vietnam War, and I was very anti-war, but this was, like, *America.* I fell in love with it. I couldn't stop listening to country music. I mean, I loved it—white trash, white soul voices, breaking at every phrase. I still do, even though I've been living here for years—longer than I ever lived in New York, I'm so old already—it's still exotic to a New York Jewish commie like me.[5]

California Lives also introduced an intuitive, personal, domestic content into the cool geometries and slick surfaces associated with Los Angeles Pop art and post-painterly abstraction. Critic Howard Fox suggests that Antin's growing "feminine" approach to her practice be understood in relation to her reading in women's issues, an activity perhaps stimulated by the emergence of the contemporary women's movement in Southern California at around the same time. "She saw in the feminist movement an ideological and ethical corroboration of her fundamentally artistic belief that the range of content in contemporary art could, and should, be expanded to include modes of personal exploration, biography and autobiography (both true and fictional), narrative, and fantasy."[6]

Antin's move to California, and her growing interest in women's narratives, coincided with other early feminist developments. In 1969, painter Amy Goldin was appointed a visiting critic at University of California, San Diego. Her courses in criticism and aesthetics influenced several young painters to question the Eurocentric focus of North American culture, with its hierarchic ordering of the so-called "fine" and "applied" arts, and to begin to define the roles of decoration, patterning, and embellishment in visual art.

By 1970, Los Angeles sculptor Judy Chicago was encouraging women students at California State University, Fresno to explore the sources of their work in the specific experiences of growing up female. Chicago's pioneering women's studio, together with work being done by women artists and critics in New York, Los Angeles, and San Francisco, launched a movement that spread quickly. Within the next few years Chicago and her collaborator, New York painter Miriam Schapiro (then living in Southern California), had moved her feminist art program to the California Institute of the Arts (1971); Kim MacConnel and Robert Kushner mounted the exhibition *Decorations* at the University of California, San Diego (1972), inaugurating the pattern and decoration movement; and the Los Angeles Woman's Building opened at the Chouinard School (1973).

During the early 1970s women, for the most part white and middle class, were organizing consciousness-raising groups to share experiences under the slogan "the personal is political." Often these groups included artists. Antin became friends with Schapiro and Chicago, as well as with Suzanne Lacy, Pauline Oliveros, Linda Montano, and Ida Horowitz (later Applebroog), and formed a women artists' group. Also in Los Angeles, Barbara Haskell, Vija Celmins, Alexis Smith, Joyce Kozloff and others joined women's groups. In 1971 Miriam Schapiro and Judy Chicago visited the San Francisco Bay Area and met with the members of the three women artists' consciousness-raising groups active there. Among the Bay Area artists attending those sessions were Judith Linhares, Phyliss Ideal, M. Louise Stanley, and Donna Mossholder.

The desire to locate a female self, and to reinvent the feminine as subject rather than object, motivated Antin and other women to use their artistic practices as means of exploration and self-discovery. "I am interested in defining the limits of myself, meaning moving out to, in to, up to, and down to the frontiers of myself," Antin noted in 1974. "The usual aids to self-definition—sex, age, talent, time and space—are merely tyrannical limitations upon my freedom of choice. . . ."[7]

While the women's movement legitimized many women artists' interest in forming their practices around the matériel of their personal lives, and focused attention on this aspect of women's production, it was not the only force shaping the new consciousness. Increasingly women would fuse issues of self-identity with new attitudes toward materials and process.

Betye Saar, *Spirit Catcher* (1976–77)

A scarecrow-like form, part anthropomorphic figure and part cross, appears to rise from the center of a crude woven basket to which has been fastened a spiny armature of wooden sticks. Woven grasses and rattan link the forms to nature. Triangular shapes, beaded amulets, and feathers hang from the form's horizontal "arms,"

giving the impression of a persona or a deity (the form is, in fact, based on a Tibetan spirit trap, a straw and string structure empowered by a shaman and placed on a roof to trap, or perhaps frighten away, various spirits).[8]

Unlike Eleanor Antin, Betye Saar was born and raised in Southern California. *Spirit Catcher*, produced during the years of her travels to Haiti and Mexico, is one of several pieces from this period that refer to the spiritual traditions of Haiti, Mexico, and Africa, while also drawing on deep resources of personal memory and experience.

For Saar, a woman of mixed African, white, and Native American ancestry, those memories include visiting her grandmother's house in the Los Angeles neighborhood of Watts and watching the Italian visionary Simon Rodia at work in his yard on his 100-foot spiraling towers. A rich assemblage of discarded pottery, glass, tiles, mirrors, and other salvaged scrap materials, the towers emerged between 1921 and 1954. They would become a monument to a personal vision that resonated with allusions to nature and the spirit, and that evoked both domestic space and the spiritual grandeur of Gaudi's Church of the Holy Family in Barcelona. Saar remembers that

> It all began when I was a child in California. My mother and father would go on holiday, and I would spend that time with my grandmother

in Watts. It was rural then, back in the early 3os, very country. I'd go out in the back yard and find bits of glass and stones in the dirt. Sometimes we'd go to the beach and I'd collect little shells and even bits of dirt.[9]

She credits Rodia with what she calls "mother wit," a special kind of intuition that she identifies with her own clairvoyant powers as a child, as well as with the traditions of African American spiritual vision and belief.

Rodia's monument speaks to one aspect of California history: to immigrant dreams, rugged individuality, and personal vision. Saar's first assemblages appeared in the 1960s and centered on the evocative power of found objects and their potential to contain and convey spiritual energy. They drew upon a wide range of artistic sources and a search for spiritual roots and enduring traditions amidst a transient and mobile society that was widely shared by many in the African American community in Los Angeles in the period after World War II.[10]

African Americans returned from that war as heroes abroad but second-class citizens at home. Racism, segregation, unemployment had left their marks. Ten years later, in 1955, after the end of the Korean War, the Montgomery bus boycott in Alabama initiated the Civil Rights movement. A decade later in California the community of Watts exploded in frustration at the slow

3
Betye Saar, *Spirit Catcher*, 1976–77.
Mixed-media assemblage, 45 × 18 ×
18 in. Collection of the artist.

pace of promised social change. The art that resulted from these upheavals in Los Angeles stands in direct relationship to the literary and artistic goals laid out during the Harlem Renaissance of the 1920s: to define an aesthetic based in African American consciousness and identity.

In the 1960s expressions of this desire would be shaped by civil rights laws passed during the Kennedy and Johnson administrations, by a rise in African American consciousness fueled by the Black Power movement (and corresponding rises in social consciousness among Mexican Americans and Native Americans), and by the Vietnam War.[11]

The visual culture that emerged from these tangled threads was an art of figuration, social commentary, and historical consciousness. Often community-based, its adherents sought inspiration in the social movements of the day—the Black Panthers (the party founded by Bobby Seale and Huey Newton in Oakland in 1966), black nationalism, and pan-Africanism—and in the forceful social critique and rhetoric of emerging heroes like Angela Davis, a young philosophy professor at the University of California, Los Angeles. The 1960s cultural movement in Southern California began with the formation of the Black Arts Council at the Los Angeles County Museum at the end of the decade and culminated in the 1976 exhibition *Two Centuries of Black American Art*, organized by black scholar David

Driscoll for the Los Angeles County Museum of Art.

Saar's work, like that of Los Angeles black artists David Hammons, Noah Purifoy, John Outterbridge, and John Riddle, emerged out of liberationist politics and a political and social consciousness that embraced both African and African American traditions and rejected abstraction in favor of assemblage and a funk aesthetic. The latter owed much to the traditions of jazz, as well as to the presence in California of underground white artists like George Herms, Edward Kienholz, Bruce Conner, and early Joan Brown, whose work of the early 1960s had also embraced urban salvage, collage, and assemblage.

Saar's embrace of cast-off and recycled materials was shared by other African American artists working in Los Angeles in the years after the Watts uprising. Noah Purifoy and the artists connected with the Towers Art Center in Watts joined others interested in working with objects and materials salvaged from within the black community after the uprising. Purifoy's *66 Signs of Neon* derived its title from the sixty-six pieces of sculpture created from rubble that included melted neon signs and chunks of charred wood and twisted metal.[12]

A major exhibition of Joseph Cornell's boxes at the Pasadena Art Museum in 1968 also proved to be a major influence on Saar, as did the publication of Arnold Rubin's article "Accumulation:

Power and Display in African Sculpture" in the May 1975 issue of *Artforum*.[13] Her attraction to collage, her use of salvaged materials, cloth, and other scraps, and her interest in patterning and surface embellishment have multiple sources, including women's histories. Their roots lie in both African American traditions of quilt-making, and in the contemporary pattern and decoration movement that appeared in the work of artists influenced by Amy Goldin at UC San Diego. In the late 1960s Saar also began incorporating stereotypic images of blacks in collages and constructions with strong political content. During those same years, and influenced by the collective anger of black Americans during the years of the Civil Rights protests, she produced amulets containing explicit references to African and black folklore as part of a wider desire by black artists to project an African American identity in their work.[14]

In 1974 her Aunt Hattie, who had raised Saar's mother, died and Saar found her own work moving in a more intimate, autobiographical direction. This direction also coincided with a more general shift toward the personal and autobiographical in the work of many women artists influenced by the growing women's movement in California

As the 1970s progressed, Saar's earlier more militant and socially critical work gave way to works based in family and personal history, and in magic and spiritual transformation. She continued to employ found materials. As critic Lucy Lippard noted, Saar works "in the long and satisfying tradition of women making something out of nothing, reclaiming and reintegrating lost parts—the tradition of quilt making, which may have been brought to America by Africans. . . . the collage aesthetic by which women so often transfer to their art the sense of patched time in which they live their lives."[15]

Saar's interest in ritual and symbol incorporates psychic traditions that she understands as an integral part of African American history and the glue that binds that community to the world's non-Western cultures. Many of her collages and boxes used old wallpaper, postcards and greeting cards, fragments of quilts, old lace and other fabrics, photographs of her grandmother's house and of other family members, flowers, little bits of glass, and beads. Nostalgia is there, as is a powerful feeling of familial continuity projected into the forms of contemporary art. "My concerns, however," she notes, "remain the same: the recycling and transformation of materials, the quality of texture, form, pattern, a sense of beauty and mystery."[16]

Yolanda M. Lopez, *Guadalupe* Triptych (1978)

Three generations of women are depicted in Yolanda Lopez's *Guadalupe* triptych (1978), which follows the traditional form of the Catholic

4

Yolanda M. Lopez, *The Virgin of Guadalupe Series*, 1978. Oil pastel on paper, triptych, 22 × 30 in. each. Photo: Bob Hsiang. Collection of the artist.

Left
Margaret F. Stewart:
Our Lady of Guadalupe

Center
Portrait of the Artist
as the Virgin of Guadalupe

Right
Victoria F. Franco:
Our Lady of Guadalupe

church altarpiece. The painting is one of a number of works that explore the dichotomies and complexities of the Chicano/Chicana community's historically and culturally dual relationship with Mexican and Anglo culture. It represents three female members of the artist's family: her grandmother, her mother, and her-self, through the iconography of Mexico's most cherished female saint, Our Lady of Guadalupe. Through a dialogue that reaches across generations, cultures, and geographies, Lopez both celebrates the women of her family and offers a pointed critique of cultural relations between Mexico and the United States.

Recognized as both a woman of color and an incarnation of the Virgin Mary, the Virgin of Guadalupe is simultaneously the patroness of Mexico and the Blessed Virgin, mother of the Americas. Lopez's own relationship to the image is a complex one; she places her family images within the specifics of the Chicana cultural con-text in the United States, and also reads them against an ethnic, national, and religious heritage that goes back to Mexico.

An image of the artist herself appears in the triptych's center panel. Depicted as an athlete, a jogger in running shoes wrapped in the Virgin of Guadalupe's familiar cloak (a blue-green mantle dotted with golden stars), she carries in one hand a serpent, a sign of the goddess's power. Refusing popular culture's construction of the Chicana as passive and domestic, Lopez's well-muscled legs, determined gaze, and brown skin produce an image of powerful femininity that links the archetypal with the individual.

In the triptych's lefthand panel, the artist's mother is shown bent over a sewing machine stitching the Virgin's starry cloak. As children in San Diego, Lopez and her three younger sisters lived with their mother and grandmother. Lopez recognizes the dignity and importance of women's labor through her image of her mother, Margaret F. Steward, who worked with industrial sewing machines in a dry cleaners and laundry. The third panel depicts the artist's grandmother, Victoria F. Franco, a mestiza or mixed-blood Mexican, seated on a stool covered by the now-familiar starry mantle. She holds the rattlesnake she has just finished skinning. In all three panels, the women's body types, coloring, and postures are carefully delineated. These are portraits, not generalized or idealized images, and Lopez's choice of a large-scale format emphasizes the women's personal dignity and import. "We are all creatures of the society and culture from which we emerge," Lopez has written. "As a woman, as a Chicana and as an artist, my years of involvement with the Chicano movement have, among other things, made me aware of my family's unique story: a story rich in tradition and history."[17]

Lopez's triptych was exhibited at UC San Diego in 1978 as part of her master's thesis and again the following year at the Galeria de la Raza in San Francisco's Mission District; these public exhibitions identified her work with that of other Chicano/Chicana artists committed to providing positive visual representations of Latin Americans while, at the same time, countering the stereotypic representations common in Anglo culture. Prominent among those stereotypes was that of the passive, long-suffering wife/mother.

The Virgin Mary is said to have appeared in Guadalupe in December 1531, ten years after the political and economic conquest of Mexico by the Spanish. Her appearance to an Indian who had changed his name to Juan Diego became an important factor in the conversion of the decimated indigenous population. As an icon, the Virgin of Guadalupe carries complicated emotional, psychological, and historical significance for Mexicans and, by extension, for the Mexican American community in the United States. Linked to the rise of Mexican nationalism through her appearance on Padre Hidalgo's banner of rebellion, her image has been displayed as a symbol of national identity and pride by Chicano activists from Cesar Chavez's United Farm Workers to the Committee of Chicano Rights. That Lopez's appropriation of the image was not without controversy when it first appeared underscores the double nature of her practice: at once affirming and critical.[18]

The isolation and oppression of Chicanos in the Southwest and California date to the Treaty of Guadalupe Hidalgo and its ratification by the U.S. Senate in 1848. Although the treaty officially ended the war between the two countries (and Mexico ceded more than half her territory, including California, to the United States in exchange for $15 million), treaty provisions to protect land titles and water rights and to safeguard the rights of Mexican citizens were quickly ignored or overturned. A century later in California, the Chicano political movement of the 1960s allied farmworkers struggling to unionize, dispossessed land-grant owners, and a growing student movement. It emerged in tandem with a rich visual culture that began with the creation of the performing company Teatro Campesino by Luis Valdez in 1965 in Delano, California. After touring the country to publicize the strike, the company established El Centro Cultural and an independent farmworkers' cultural center in Del Ray. There they developed their *History Happenings*, theatrical performances using puppets and music to spread knowledge of the community and its struggle.

Culture and politics also came together in the mural movement of the later 1960s. In San Francisco, Las Mujeres Muralistas, the first women's mural collective, produced stunning public murals that fused the rich tradition of the Mexican muralists with contemporary history.[19] In Los Angeles in 1976, after completing murals at a state women's prison and at a religious convalescent home, Judy Baca began a monumental history painting. Still an ongoing project, *The Great Wall of Los Angeles*, the longest mural in the world, runs half a mile along a flood control channel in the San Fernando Valley. Made possible through the collaboration of 40 ethnic scholars, 450 multicultural neighborhood youths, 40 assisting artists, and over 100 support staff, the mural depicts a history in images that include the 1781 founding of Los Angeles, the coming of the railroad, scenes of the deportation of Mexican Americans in the 1930s and Japanese Americans the following decade, and the 1984 Olympic Games in Los Angeles.

Like many Chicano artists, it was through her activism that Lopez first found her voice as an artist. She dates her own feminist and cultural activism to the early 1970s. While a student at San Francisco State University, before going on to UC San Diego, Lopez became part of the Chicano movement. She joined other students who went on strike in January 1968, in part to demand that the university establish an ethnic studies program. In 1969 Lopez superimposed an image of the American flag over images of Los Siete, seven young Latinos accused of killing a plainclothes policeman:

I remember the thrill of seeing my art everywhere on walls, telegraph poles, and in demonstrations. I discovered my gallery—it was the streets. One of the most electrifying experiences was when the women in the Los Siete organization took a Greyhound bus to Canada for a conference to hear Indo-Chinese women. When we got back, an incident of domestic violence within our organization led to the creation of male and female discussion groups. That was the first time that I had really experienced the issue of women's oppression within the larger struggle of racism and imperialism. By 1972, I was doing paintings and drawings of my mother and grandmother, now understanding them within a bigger historical context.[20]

Although the movement to end the colonial oppression of Chicanos had its roots in the liberationist spirit of the 1960s, it was only gradually that Chicanas began to focus on issues of gender and on their triple marginalization—as women, as Chicanas, and as people of color. Lopez's art also exposes the contradictions of California's (and the United States') complicated relationship with its southern neighbor, as well as with the descendants of the Mexican community in the Southwest and a more recent immigrant population. Consumed by mass culture with its endless appropriation of Mexican images and foods and excoriated by politicians as illegal aliens and

a drain on the North American tax base, the Chicano community in California has, like other immigrant communities, struggled to produce a cultural identity out of diversity and oppression.

Hulleah Tsinhnahjinnie, *Metropolitan Indian Series* (1984)

A black-and-white photograph depicts a young Native American woman in traditional dress. Posed on a grassy hill next to a towering tree trunk, she contemplates the Bay Bridge and the city of San Francisco at dusk. In the distance, the towers of the bridge and the city beyond appear as indistinct shapes seen through a scrim of haze that magnifies the lights into glowing orbs. Removed to the edge of the frame, this Native American is in the picture and also at its edge, its margin; we look both at her and at what she sees.

In his book on photography and the Navajo, James Faris has argued that "not much can be understood about Navajo from photographs of them. But certainly something can be understood of photographers. . . ."[21] Looking at a history of photographic representations of the Navajo, Faris was forced to conclude that photography had become a "perverse asset" in denying Navajo a history and turning them into little more than subjects of the West's history.[22]

Yet Tsinhnahjinnie, a Seminole/Creek/Navajo who divides her time between Arizona and the

5

Hulleah J. Tsinhnahjinnie,
*Metropolitan Indian Series
#2*, 1984. Yerba Buena Island,
Calif. Silver print, 5 × 7 in.
Photo © 1984 Hulleah J.
Tsinhnahjinnie. Collection of
the artist.

San Francisco Bay Area, and other contemporary Native American artists have developed artistic practices that represent and compensate for both the genocidal history of the West vis-à-vis the Native American, and also the racism and sexism that continue to structure social relations between white and Native communities.

In her *Metropolitan Indian Series*, Tsinhnah-jinnie has appropriated the soft focus and Whistlerian values of pictorialist photography from the end of the nineteenth century, and used them to develop a contemporary Native American perspective on issues of history, geography, and identity. "Identity has been a constant and some-times unwelcome companion to me for the past forty years, all of my life," Tsinhnahjinnie has remarked.[23] The *Metropolitan Indian Series*, like much of Tsinhnahjinnie's photographic work, challenges anthropological and popularized representations of Native American women.[24] Drawing on European American Edward Curtis's ethnological project, *The North American Indian*

1907–1930, Tsinhnahjinnie uses parody, irony, and appropriation to tease out issues of Native American identity as they are tied to Native American history and European American notions about art and popular representation.[25] Peeling away the representational layers that construct the category "American Indian" (in both Native and European American eyes), Tsinhnahjinnie exposes a dense tangle of ideological assumptions, historical awareness, and neglected or obscured realities.

Curtis's mammoth project, published as twenty volumes of illustrated text and twenty portfolios of large-size photogravures drawn from the thousands of photographs of Native Americans in the western states that he began taking in the 1890s, set out to "capture" Native American culture through romantic portraits in which visual imagery is constructed around European American stereotypes of the stoic, noble, primitive, nature-loving Indian. Replacing the specificities of culture and history with universalized stereotypes, Curtis produced images of the "noble savage" in a timeless "nature."[26]

Tsinhnahjinnie has appropriated well-known Curtis images, like *The Mother* and *Hopi Woman*, in which Native Americans are displaced to the photograph's edges, where they gaze silently across vast western territories from which, by the time these photographs were made, they had been expelled. It is not surprising, given modernism's embrace of an "art for art's sake" ethos of aesthetic purity, that Curtis's work has been widely praised for its formal surface qualities while the troubling history of European conquest and genocide that underlies his images has been pushed outside the frame.[27]

In 1901, Arnold Genthe, probably the best-known pictorialist on the West Coast and a photographer who was himself in the midst of an extensive visual documentation of San Francisco's Chinatown, offered his own appraisal of Curtis's work:

> E. S. Curtis's Indian studies occupy quite a place by themselves. They are of immense ethnological value as an excellent record of a dying (*sic*) race, and most of them are really picturesque, showing good composition and interesting light effects. . . . "The three Chiefs" just misses being great. If the head of the foremost horse could have been turned so as to break the straight line formed by the three horses the composition would have been perfect. But, even as it is, the photograph is a very beautiful rendition of the picturesque phase of Indian life.[28]

The "picturesque phase of Indian life" to which Genthe refers becomes brutally ironic once one unravels the more specific histories referenced in Tsinhnahjinnie's photographs. Beginning in the early 1520s, when Hernando Cortés sent ships north along the Pacific coast in search of the fabled Strait of Anian, waves of European explorers, profiteers, and military personnel landed on California shores. These voyages led in 1769 to the first European landing in San Francisco Bay itself. If the progress of Spanish settlement was slow and halting, the destruction of pre-existing Native cultures was swift and irreversible (it has been estimated that in 1846 there were about 98,000 Indians left out of an original population of some 250,000; twenty-five years later there were about 30,000 left, and by 1900 about 16,000).[29]

Between 1792 and the discovery of gold in 1848, a wave of early visitors left published accounts of their impressions of what is now San Francisco (then Yerba Buena) and the mission settlement with its community of Native Americans. Tsinhnahjinnie's photograph, stripped of its pictorialist haze, offers an ironic view of the sight that defines the city for many contemporary tourists—the two great bridges that span the bay. Marking the entrance to the bay was the fort where early travelers to the city first went after leaving their ships. After leaving the military compound at the presidio, many of them took an overland route to Mission Dolores, where in many cases they recorded their impressions of the life of San Francisco's Native population under Christian domination. These first-person accounts, recording the enslavement and ill-treatment of the Native population, for the most part follow a depressingly familiar path, reiterating the cultural stereotypes that define the first encounters between European and Native peoples.[30]

Lying between the Golden Gate Bridge and the Bay Bridge is another contemporary tourist monument, the significance of which for the Native American community has often been erased from contemporary guidebooks. The political movement called Red Power, which arose in 1969 out of a pan-Indian consciousness in the West, emerged through an occupation of the abandoned federal prison on Alcatraz Island. The occupiers, many of them students at California's universities and colleges, subsequently inspired the radicalization of the activist American Indian Movement (AIM) and rallied support to force an end to the federal program of termination and related destructive federal policies of the postwar period with regard to Native Americans.[31]

By the 1970s, San Francisco had become a hub of urban Indians uprooted by World War II and the wars in Korea and Vietnam. Many returning veterans funneled through Bay Area ports and the federal relocation program of 1958 brought thousands more to the area. For Tsinhnahjinnie and many other Native American artists, this history demands retelling, and it forms a part of her reframing of the geography of San Francisco Bay and the Golden Gate.[32]

Hung Liu, *Jiu Jin Shan: Old Gold Mountain* (1994)

The name given to San Francisco in the nineteenth century by Chinese immigrants was *Jiu Jin Shan*, which translates as Old Gold Mountain, an expression of the hope, shared with so many other new arrivals on these shores, to find material prosperity in the new world. *Jiu Jin Shan: Old Gold Mountain* is one of several large-scale installations by Hung Liu, an artist born in Changchun, China, and educated at the Central Academy of Fine Art in Beijing as well as the University of California at San Diego, where she received her master's in fine arts degree in 1986. Now living and working in the Bay Area, Liu produced the multipart work as an installation at the M. H. de Young Memorial Museum in San Francisco in 1994. As exhibition curator Steven A. Nash observed, the installation, while dealing "specifically with the largely unwritten story of early Chinese immigration to California . . . expands metaphorically to embrace the more universal theme of cultural migration in general."[33]

In the center of the gallery, a conical mountain

of fortune cookies (themselves an American invention) rose from the floor. Symbol of the fabled mountain of gold that drew the original immigrants to northern California, the fortune cookie, with its carefully concealed message of hope and good fortune, has become a sign of cultural hybridization and globalization.

A series of shaped canvases, paintings of junks based on historical photographs of the vessels commonly used by the Chinese—both on the passage from China to California and (in a smaller version) as a means of transport on local bays, rivers, and deltas—were hung against a sober gray background. Four sundials in the gallery symbolized the four points of the compass, navigation, and passing time. Satellite photographs of different continents covered the faces of the sundials, suggesting that geographic directions and points of origin are relative and depend on cultural and physical perspectives.

Seventy feet of railroad track intersected and led in different directions across the gallery. Representing a crucial chapter in the history of Chinese labor in North America, the railroad track signified both opportunity and defeat. Though a means of transport to the fabled gold mines in the Sierra foothills, the railroad also became a terminus for the dreams of the many immigrants who perished while working to complete the Sierra Nevada stage of the transcontinental railroad. In 1870, one newspaper account

reported the shipment of 20,000 pounds of bones, representing some 1,200 individual railroad workers, back to China for proper burial.[34]

To underscore the motif of sacrifice, and to pay homage to the thousands of Chinese laborers who perished while working on the transcontinental railroad, Liu fashioned a schematic image of a temple on one wall from hundreds of individually folded bits of paper colored inside with silver or gold that are known as temple money. Traditionally burned as offerings or prayers for the dead, Liu's temple money projects "the dual meaning of ritual blessings for departing craft and homages to those who have lost their lives on the perilous journey."[35]

Liu's work evoked the long and complicated history of the Chinese community in California, a history that intersects with that of other Asian American groups. While Liu herself was born in China, California is home to many generations of Asian Americans. Although there was early immigration from Korea and the Philippines, the bulk of immigrants from Asia before 1965 were Chinese or Japanese. Strong anti-Asian feeling and restrictive legislation in the United States are reflected in the frequent lumping together of peoples of Chinese or Japanese ancestry.

The internment of Japanese Americans during World War II shattered the Issei-dominated (or Japan-born) family structure, and postwar federal relocation policy encouraged both greater assimilation and the further weakening of family ties by dispersing many Japanese Americans away from the West Coast and into the Mountain West. Low immigration quotas, a pattern established in 1943 with the revocation of the Chinese Exclusion Act, were somewhat ameliorated by Cold War policies that contributed to a greater diversification of Asian immigrants.

Later immigration patterns, particularly those for immigrants from Southeast Asia—including Vietnamese, Cambodians, and Laotians—were also shaped by recent political and military history. Thus there is no single "Asian American" entity in California; indeed, the work of artists from Asian ethnicities often reflects a concern with both a culture of origin and the experience of growing up in California, where tensions between assimilationist and exclusionary ideologies and social policies remain evident.[36]

Policies on immigration, assimilation, and education that date back to the end of World War II, combined with more recent patterns of immi-

gration sparked by political unrest and changing economic conditions, continue to shape demographics in California in ways that have produced a dizzying range of positive steps toward a more diversified and multicultural society (by early in the twenty-first century, whites will be the minority population in California), while at the same time fueling legislative setbacks for immigrants (Propositions 187 and 189, for example). If the history of California continues to emerge more fully through processes of retelling and revision, so also does the history of women artists' contributions to contemporary visual culture. The women discussed here have developed artistic practices that draw upon both the formal legacies of twentieth-century art and the specificities of personal and cultural history and identity. While their work continues to shape and enrich a cultural dialogue that intersects with California histories, it also stands as a testament to the rich diversity that is contemporary California culture.

Notes

1   For a discussion of these changes, as they were shaped by the historical and cultural conditions of the post–World War II period, see Kevin J. Fernlund, ed., *The Cold War American West, 1945–1989* (Albuquerque: University of New Mexico Press, 1988).

2   Recent feminist histories include discussion of these women-centered organizations and studio programs; see, for example, Norma Broude and Mary D. Garrard, eds.,

The Power of Feminist Art: The American Movement of the 1970s, History and Impact (New York: Harry N. Abrams, 1994).

3   The term was used by Roth as the title of her 1977 study of women and performance in California. See Moira Roth, ed., *The Amazing Decade: Women and Performance Art, 1970–1980* (Los Angeles: Astro Artz, 1983).

4   *Eleanor Antin* (exhibition catalogue), ed. Howard N. Fox

(Los Angeles: Los Angeles County Museum of Art, 1999), p. 26.

5 *Eleanor Antin*, p. 203.

6 Ibid., p. 32.

7 Ibid., p. 59.

8 Lucy R. Lippard, "Saphire and Ruby in the Indigo Gardens," in *Secrets, Dialogues, Revelations: The Art of Betye and Alison Saar* (Los Angeles: Wight Art Gallery, University of California, 1990), p. 10.

9 *Betye Saar* (exhibition catalogue) (Los Angeles: The Museum of Contemporary Art, 1984), p. 15.

10 Other pioneering black women artists working in Los Angeles in the years before the 1960s included Samella Lewis and Ruth G. Waddy.

11 This period formed the subject of the important exhibition *19 Sixties: A Cultural Awakening Re-evaluated 1965–1975* (Los Angeles: California Afro-American Museum, 1975). The accompanying catalogue contains essays by Lizzetta Le Falle-Collins and Cecil Ferguson.

12 Ibid., p. 25.

13 *Artforum* 13 (May 1975): 35–47.

14 *Rituals: Betye Saar* (exhibition catalogue) (New York: The Studio Museum in Harlem, 1980), p. 3.

15 Ibid., p. 13.

16 Ibid., p. 8.

17 *Yolanda M. Lopez Works: 1975–1978* (exhibition catalogue) (La Jolla: Mandeville Center for the Arts, 1978), n.p.

18 Lopez's interpretation of the imagery of the Virgin of Guadalupe was not without controversy. When the painting was first exhibited at the University of California at San Diego, the print shop's workmen refused to photograph it. And when the images appeared in the Mexican magazine *Fem*, vandals trashed several Mexico City kiosks and the magazine office received bomb threats. For a discussion of the work's reception, see "Yolanda Lopez's Art Hits Twitch Meter To Fight Stereotypes," *The Salt Lake Tribune Arts*, May 14, 1995, p. 4.

19 A two-panel mural by Antonio Bernal at El Centro Cultural is believed to be one of the earliest Chicano murals in California. For a more complete history of the mural movement, see Shifra Goldman and Tomas Ybarra-Frausto, "The Political and Social Context of Chicano Art," in *Chicano Art: Resistance and Affirmation* (Los Angeles: Wight Art Gallery, University of California, 1991), pp. 83–108, and the exhibition catalogue *Chicano Expressions: A New View in American Art* (Los Angeles: Otis Art Institute of Parson School of Design, 1986).

20 Cited in Broude and Garrard, *Power of Feminist Art*, p. 146.

21 James C. Faris, *Navajo and Photography: A Critical History of the Representation of an American People* (Albuquerque: University of New Mexico Press, 1996), p. 12.

22 Ibid.

23 Hulleah Tsinhnahjinnie, quoted in *Image and Self in Contemporary Native American Photoart* (exhibition catalogue) (Hanover, N.H.: Hood Museum of Art, Dartmouth College, 1995).

24 For a useful introduction to Tsinhnahjinnie's work, as well as that of other Native American women artists, see Theresa Harlan, "To Watch, To Remember and To Survive," in *Watchful Eyes: Native American Women Artists* (exhibition catalogue) (Phoenix: The Heard Museum, 1994), pp. 7–14. Two other important exhibitions (both with catalogues) devoted to the work of Native women were *Women of Sweetgrass, Cedar and Sage*, curated by Harmony Hammond and Jaune Quick-to-See Smith and held at the Gallery of the American Indian community house in New York City in 1985, and the *National American Indian Women's Art Show*, held at the Via Gambara Studio Gallery in Washington, D.C. in 1980. For a more general history of Native American photography, see Theresa Harlan, "A Curator's Perspective: Native American Photographers Creating a Visual Native American History," *Exposure* 29 (1993): 12–28.

25 Janet R. Skoda, "Image and Self in Contemporary Native American Photoart," *American Indian Art* 21 (Winter 1995): 48–57.

26 See Alex Nemerov, "Doing the 'Old America,' " in William H. Truettner, ed., *The West as America: Reinterpreting Images of the Frontier, 1820–1920* (exhibition catalogue) (Washington, D.C.: Smithsonian Institution, 1991), p. 311. Nemerov suggests that it is not enough to simply read these images as part of a wider cultural nostalgia. "They differ because they alone helped sanction the decimation they represented. By equating Indian cultures with the past they implicitly accepted a theory of social evolution that posited the disappearance of 'primitive' peoples before the inexorable advance of 'civilization.' Indians had no existence in the present" (p. 311).

27 See James Clifford, "Of Other Peoples: Beyond the Salvage Paradigm," in *Discussions in Contemporary Culture*, no. 1, ed. Hal Foster (Seattle: Bay Press), pp. 121–129.

28 Cited in Mick Gidley, *Edward S. Curtis and the North American Indian Incorporated* (Cambridge: Cambridge University Press, 1998), p. 59.

29 Most of the population loss was due to diseases—from measles to venereal infections—imported by the Europeans. Another 30 percent died of the effects of cultural dislocation as the swelling European-American population drove them from their ancestral food-producing regions. The remaining 10 percent were murdered; see T. H. Watkins, *California: An Illustrated History* (New York: Legacy Press, 1973; reprinted 1983), p. 129.

30 Occasionally, a fresh voice breaks the reiteration. In 1816, Otto von Kotzebue, a Russian traveler spending a month in San Francisco Bay while on the first of two around-the-world voyages of exploration, offered a scathing indictment of a European presence in California primarily devoted to religious propagation and conversion: "The pious Franciscans, who hold the missions in New California, are not skilled in the arts and trades which they ought to exercise and teach, nor in any of the languages spoken by the nations to whom they are sent. . . . All property belongs to the community of the mission, and is administered by the fathers. The savage Indian derives no immediate advantage from his labours. . . . He acquires no notion of property, and is not bound by it. We do not deny the mildness, the paternal anxiety of the missionaries, of which we have several times been witnesses. The relation still remains what is here represented; and, in our opinion, it would differ only in name, if the master of slaves kept them to work, and let them out at pleasure, he also would give them food." See Peter Browning, ed., *Yerba Buena/San Francisco: From the Beginnings to the Gold Rush 1769–1849* (Lafayette, Calif.: Great West Books, 1998), pp. 67–68.

31 Fernlund, *The Cold War*, p. 155 *passim*.

32 The federal relocation program of 1958 brought a steady stream of Native Americans to the Bay Area. Relocation was a program of assimilation and termination aimed at abolishing traditional Indian cultures; see Steve Fox, "From the Beat Generation to the Sanctuary Movement: Cold War Resistance Cultures in the American West," in Fernlund, *The Cold War*, pp. 139–166.

33 Steven A. Nash, "Hung Liu and Old Gold Mountain" (exhibition brochure) (San Francisco: The Fine Arts Museums of San Francisco, 1994), n.p.

34 John Kuo Wei Tchen, introduction to *Genthe's Photographs of San Francisco's Old Chinatown* (New York: Dover, 1984), p. 5.

35 Ibid.

36 See Karen Higa, "Some Notes on an Asian American Art History," in *With New Eyes: Toward an Asian American Art History in the West* (exhibition catalogue) (San Francisco: San Francisco State University Art Gallery, 1995), pp. 11–14.

KOPIS'TAYA, A GATHERING OF SPIRITS

Paula Gunn Allen

Because we live in the browning season
the heavy air blocking our breath,
and in this time when living
is only survival, we doubt the voices
that come shadowed on the air,
that weave within our brains
certain thoughts, a motion that is soft,
imperceptible, a twilight rain,
soft feather's fall, a small body dropping
into its nest, rustling, murmuring, settling
in for the night.

Because we live in the hardedged season,
where plastic brittle and gleaming shine,
and in this space that is cornered and angled,
we do not notice wet, moist, the significant
drops falling in perfect spheres
that are certain measures of our minds;
almost invisible, those tears,
soft as dew, fragile, that cling to leaves,
petals, roots, gentle and sure,
every morning.

We are the women of the daylight, of clocks
and steel foundries, of drugstores
and streetlights, of superhighways
that slice our days in two. Wrapped around
in plastic and steel we ride our lives;
behind dark glasses we hide our eyes;
our thoughts, shaded, seem obscure.
Smoke fills our minds, whiskey husks our songs,
polyester cuts our bodies from our breath,
our feel from the welcoming stones of earth.
Our dreams are pale memories of themselves
and nagging doubt is the false measure
of our days.

Even so, the spirit voices are singing,
their thoughts are dancing in the dirty air.
Their feet touch the cement, the asphalt
delighting, still they weave dreams upon our
shadowed skulls, if we could listen.
If we could hear.
Let's go then. Let's find them.
Let's listen for the water, the careful
gleaming drops that glisten on the leaves,
the flowers. Let's ride
the midnight, the early dawn.
Feel the wind striding through our hair.
Let's dance the dance of feathers,
the dance of birds.

ANGELA Y. DAVIS

OTHER LANDSCAPES

Exploring women's art practices in California over the last half of the twentieth century is a powerful way to consciously rethink and re-present our histories from the vantage of a present that shapes and is shaped by our relationship to the past. The attempt to construct multiple histories of California women artists should be a project not primarily of retrieving that which has been obscured by the racial and gender bias of the art world and of blending it with the work of women artists who may have achieved renown—or at least a footnote—in dominant art history. Rather, the challenge is to discover traces of the ways women have been imagined and how they have imagined themselves, their histories and their futures, drawing upon both the constraints and liberatory possibilities of California's social, economic, and cultural landscapes. If we try to take into account the rich, complicated, and conflictual fabric of these imagined worlds, the special and privileged place of women artists who have been able to materialize their imaginations must be envisioned in a cross-cutting relationship to those women—especially those who have evinced an awareness of their own social agency—who have expressed their fears and aspirations by other means.

We are dealing here with a number of problematic terms—"California," "women," "artists," all of which are replete with profound internal contradictions. California, for example, has been envisaged as a place of dreams and fantastic possibilities—of black amazons and gold mountains, of material prosperity and racial equality. Although the history of this state is often told as a story of renewal, hope, and utopian possibility, a parallel story of disaster and catastrophe—of a dystopia shaped by fires, earthquakes, war, and prisons—also informs the California imaginary.[1] In the 1992 work by California muralist Juana Alicia entitled *La Promesa de Loma Prieta: Que no se repita la historia*, women play a prominent and mediating role in a changing social landscape that dialectically incorporates these two narratives of dreams and disasters.

Juana Alicia's image evokes multiple racialized stories that commingle upon the fractured earth produced by the 1989 Loma Prieta earthquake. The seismic disturbances of nature, however, are not the most ominous dimension of California's history that the mural portrays; in discrete black-and-white segments, the mural confronts the even more cataclysmic violence of racism and war. At the center of the image is a utopian space merging past and future, watched over by an androgynous indigenous figure and rendered visible by the parting of two black-and-white panels capturing—as shades of the past—lynchings, Ku Klux Klansmen, police, and a helicopter of war. Behind both panels and located in the midst of the mural's realm of activity are static black-and-white strips—of masked riot police, skulls, chains, missiles, and two rows of television screens. The first row consists of images of George Bush, Oliver North, and Jesse Helms and

the second depicts scenes of the police beating of Rodney King and of Los Angeles burning in the aftermath of the King verdicts. When compared to the gruesome and frozen images of racist violence, the fissured earth represents release and liberation. In fact, in the foreground of the mural, the earthquake seems to have brought down the barbed wire of California's tightly closed borders, now easily parted by a ghostly figure of the future, permitting those on the other side to pass through. This wire evokes, of course, the shutting out of Central Americans and Asians but for some may also imply the growing presence of prisons *shutting in* men and women of color.

Women dominate this utopian California landscape, some recognizable—Maxine Hong Kingston, Ginny Lim, Dolores Huerta—and others anonymous participants in the social movements of this region. In inserting her own image into the mural, together with artists like Frida Kahlo, Juana Alicia gives women artists a central place and transformative role. Her mural suggests (as does the present book) that neither women's social history nor women's art history can be retrieved as a singular narrative, or as an assemblage of evidence that points to a story waiting to be told (and always according to an imaginary original order that reflects our appropriately gendered consciousness). Considering the troubled life of feminist retellings of history, with their sometimes unconscious emphases on the

7

Juana Alicia, *La Promesa de
Loma Prieta: Que no se repita
la historia/The Promise of Loma
Prieta: That History Not Repeat
Itself*, 1992. Acrylic on sheetrock,
30 × 30 ft. Mural by Juana Alicia,
© 1992, Oakes College,
University of California, Santa
Cruz. Photo: Marvin Collins.
Collection of the artist.

female dimension of dominant stories, the challenge here is to think about the ways our understandings of history might be transformed if we
took seriously women's participation in those
historical processes in California that have produced tremors in the social, economic, and political landscapes, which are also and importantly
aesthetic.

What would it mean, for example, to truly
respect the role of women in California's labor
history? And to try to think about the social
imagination and aesthetic practices of women
labor activists in a very different relationship
to artwork produced by women than is usually
assumed? If artworks are "evidence" of aesthetic
labor, what would count as evidence of women's
labor struggles, and how would we begin to value
the aesthetic dimension of these struggles? How,
for example, would we rethink the meaning of
the 1985 strike against the Watsonville Canning

Company by 1,000 cannery workers—primarily Chicana and Mexican women, who were members of Teamsters Local 91? As we consider today the declining access to health care for poor, working people and immigrant populations, and particularly in light of the corporatization of health care, the courageous act of the six women who initiated a hunger strike not only against Watsonville Canning but also against the union's failure to include medical benefits in the agreement ending the eighteen-month strike, has profound political and aesthetic "value." While their eventual success in forcing the union to obtain a new contract with medical benefits was celebrated as a victory for workers, women, and antiracists, these women also need to be remembered for the way they refused to surrender their *vision* of healthy lives for workers. Although the immediate impact of their political victory may have been felt only by the workers at Watsonville Canning, the aesthetic dimension of their struggle helped them and their supporters—workers and activists beyond the immediate strike situation—to imagine larger social possibilities. The world the hunger strikers imagined profoundly controverts prevailing assumptions that immigrant workers—and workers perceived as immigrants—have few human rights that deserve to be respected.

What would it mean to take seriously the work of Dolores Huerta, whose leadership of the United Farm Workers quite literally transformed California's agricultural landscape when she

pressed for the rights of those who labor in the fields? As the main negotiator during the Delano grape strike, Huerta not only helped produce the first health and benefit plans for California's farmworkers but also helped to teach Californians in general about the exploitation they so cavalierly enjoyed. Her labor activism has profoundly altered the way we imagine ourselves as consumers and has helped us to think critically about the food-production apparatus and the ideological obliteration of the human beings who do that work. But this struggle, primarily conducted by Chicanos and Mexicans, also offered solidarity to and received inspiration from the Civil Rights movement, a significant cross-racial intersection of social movements that allowed us a precious glimpse of a world beyond black and white.

What would be the further effect on our vision if we began to take account of the labor activism of Asian and Asian American women, who, even as they are represented in dominant ideologies as perpetual outsiders to U.S. history, have played pivotal roles in California's labor history? Consider the impact of the national boycott of the garment-making firm Jessica McClintock, conducted during the early 1990s by Asian Immigrant Women's Advocates (AIWA), after the sweatshop contracting with McClintock shut down and left the women workers with bad paychecks. This campaign helped to teach many young women—white as well as women of color—about the exploitation they unintentionally wore on their bodies as they danced at senior proms in dresses for which they paid McClintock close to two hundred dollars, but which brought a mere five dollars apiece to the workers. Looking good, *by other means*, turned out to be the best revenge.

In Juana Alicia's mural, a woman carries a picket sign bearing the words "La Mujer Presente en la Lucha," pointing to the continued necessity to document women's participation in struggles over labor and other social issues. The examples above, drawn from recent Chicana and Asian American women's labor activism, are but a few of an abundance of historical instances in California in which women have made extraordinary, yet often unrecognized and unimaged, contributions to the labor movement. But the significance of women's presence in social struggles is not primarily that they have inserted themselves into otherwise unaltered terrains of social conflict. Like this book, the mural should challenge us to think about women's presence not only as it has strengthened movements in defense of labor, immigration rights, and racial equality, but also as it has simultaneously shaken up those movements. In her analysis of the impact of globalization on women of color, California cultural theorist Lisa Lowe has noted that in

the complex encounters between transnational capital and women within patriarchal gender structures, the very processes that produce a racialized feminized proletariat both displace traditional and national patriarchies and their defining regulations of gender, space and work and racialize the women in relation to other racialized groups. These displacements produce new possibilities precisely because they have led to a breakdown and a reformulation of the categories of nation, race, class, and gender and in doing so have prompted a reconceptualization of the oppositional narratives of nationalism, Marxism, and feminism.[2]

Many of these transformations and reconceptualizations have taken place on California's public and private landscapes, both within and outside the labor movement. As Lowe points out, because the lives and histories of women of color attest to complex intersections of socially demarcated processes, mutations and transitions on one axis tend to create upheavals on other axes. Thus, in the mural, we not only see women actively engaged in social struggles; we also find the image of a lesbian embrace, indicating that breaks in the circuits of social and economic power intersect with the ways women negotiate, and sometimes propel renegotiations in, their personal lives.

World War II, for example, is often identified as a pivotal historical moment that prepared the socioeconomic terrain for the feminist consciousness of the 1960s and 1970s. And during the war, California, which attracted nearly 10 percent of all federal funds,[3] established major arenas of the military industrial complex in its northern and southern cities—aircraft plants in the south and shipbuilding operations in the north. While it is true that women (primarily white women, but black women to a significant extent as well) moved into the world of industrial production in a way that was without historical precedent, at the same time the political economy precisely resisted those structural changes—such as permanent subsidized childcare—that were necessary to the long-range support of the women who "manned" the defense plants. Of the many still pending questions about gender and World War II, we may ask in the present context how ideologies of racism prevented white women from understanding that if they did not support the right of their black, Latina, Native American, and Asian American sisters to work beside them on the assembly lines, they would in all likelihood find it even more difficult to consolidate their economic gains as *women*, and their daughters would be trapped inside racialized visions of women's liberation. In California's feminist cultural movements of the 1970s (in women's music and art, for example), white women still struggled, with varying degrees of success, to release themselves from this historical legacy.

During the war years, almost 350,000 black people migrated to California in search of the prosperity the state was expected to offer them. To whatever extent their labor might have been

needed in the defense industry, racial barriers were not easily eliminated. In fact, according to literary historian David Wyatt, "the resistance to hiring blacks and Mexican-Americans proved a boon to white women: by 1943, forty percent of the labor force in California aircraft was female."[4] Black and Chicana women did, however, find work in the service industry and, as historian Jacqueline Jones points out, "if black women did not achieve any long-lasting economic gains as a result of the war, they did test the limits of their own collective strength in ways that would reverberate into the future."[5]

One of the consequences of some black women's entrance into the public economy (after being confined largely to domestic work) was the diminishing economic importance of marriage. Jones quotes Huddie Ledbetter, whose "National Defense Blues" was inspired by the black migration to California during the war:

Just because she was workin', makin' so much dough,

That woman got to the place she did not love me no mo'.[6]

Commenting on his song, Leadbelly said, "The women are working on that defense and they's making lots of money, just quitting their husbands."[7] But the last lines give a different reading to the story:

Cultural Overview

That Defence [*sic*] has gone, just listen to my song,

Since that Defence has gone, that woman done lost her home.[8]

While vast numbers of white women (together with much smaller numbers of their counterparts, women of color) worked in Northern California's shipyards and in the aircraft plants of Southern California, many black, Mexican, and Chicana women relieved more prosperous white women of their domestic chores. In one section of a 1959 manual distributed in the Southwest entitled *Your Maid from Mexico*, its authors address Mexican women domestic workers and explicitly racialize the division of their labor: "By taking our place in the home and doing many of our jobs, you can give us free hours to do the things we enjoy—playing golf, sewing, playing the piano, attending club meetings, or working at a job we like."[9] As scholars like Mary Romero have pointed out, even the aspirations associated with the Women's Liberation movement of the 1960s and 1970s camouflaged the gendered racial sacrifice lurking behind demands for "women's" entrance into the public world of politics and economic production. Moreover, the discourse of separate private and public spheres tended to discount the relationship between changes in working-class women's economic lives and the restruc-

turing of their domestic arrangements, including the increasing vulnerability of poor, single mothers to the state's incursion into their lives via the welfare system. By the 1990s in California, the administration of Governor Pete Wilson combined its assaults on welfare mothers with its anti-immigrant strategies and succeeded in passing Proposition 187, barring undocumented immigrants access to welfare and other public services.

The failure, especially in California, to produce strong cross-racial alliances among black and Latina women opposing the assault on the welfare system during the 1990s demonstrated the extent to which dominant ideologies of race contravened the hopeful promise of the phrase "women of color." When *This Bridge Called My Back* was published in 1981, it attempted to excavate the aesthetic, analytic, and activist possibilities of including considerations of race, class, gender, and especially sexuality in the same conversations.[10] Feminist consciousness, still objectified by the media and in popular discourse as the property of middle-class white women, had entered clandestinely into nationalist movements within black and Chicano communities during the 1960s and 1970s, often under the banner of and simultaneously contesting those male nationalisms where it could therefore not be named.

As we reflect today on the racial fault lines[11]

and crossings of California, we see a profusion of untapped possibilities—no longer realizable in its original terms, but with threads that can be rewoven in our contemporary imagination. Black, Latina, and white women who came together under the leadership of community activists like Johnnie Tillmon and Alicia Escalante to build a Welfare Rights movement during the 1960s—despite sometimes irreconcilable tensions—implicitly theorized feminism quite differently from the Women's Liberation movement. In contesting government surveillance and control of AFDC recipients' sexual relationships and housing arrangements and other aspects of their "private lives," the Welfare Rights movement demonstrated that the private lives of poor women were not always primarily structured in accordance with the patriarchal power of husbands and fathers, but also of the state. By the 1990s, the force of the state was augmented and sometimes replaced by private and transnational corporations that further reconfigured patriarchal structures. Memories of what we may now recognize as the radical visions of welfare activists of the 1960s are sorely needed to inspire us to take more seriously efforts to support Mexican women working in the *maquiladoras* and generally to contest the impact on women of California's closed borders.

In the aftermath of the disestablishment of affirmative action programs in public education and employment, and with the rise of a prison industrial complex, symbiotically related to its military predecessor, California—like the larger world of global capital in which its economy is implicated—is becoming increasingly dangerous for working-class women. Ironically, however, what people tend to fear most is that earthquakes, fires, mudslides, and gang violence are ruining the promise of California. Perhaps by reflecting on the myriad ways California women artists and activists have urged us to disengage from those aspects of our lives that we tend to take most for granted and to imagine and strive for new social and psychic landscapes, we can begin to redefine the promise of California.

Notes

1. See David Wyatt, *Five Fires: Race, Catastrophe, and the Shaping of California* (New York: Oxford University Press, 1997) and Mike Davis, *Ecology of Fear: Los Angeles and the Imagination of Disaster* (New York: Vintage Books, 1998).

2. Lisa Lowe, *Immigrant Acts: On Asian American Cultural Politics* (Durham, N.C.: Duke University Press, 1996), p. 161.

3. Federal expenditures during the war years were $360 billion, approximately $35 billion of which was spent in California. Marilynn S. Johnson, *The Second Gold Rush: Oakland and the East Bay in World War II* (Berkeley: University of California Press, 1993), p. 8.

4. Wyatt, *Five Fires*, p. 163

5. Jacqueline Jones, *Labor of Love, Labor of Sorrow: Black*

Women, Work and the Family from Slavery to the Present (New York: Basic Books, 1985), p. 235.

6 Ibid., p. 254. I have used Paul Oliver's version of Leadbelly's verse, which seems to better catch the spirit of the song (in true, if accidental, deference to the form, no transcription of blues lyric is ever the same). Paul Oliver, *The Meaning of the Blues* (New York: Collier Books, 1960), p. 64.

7 Jones, *Labor of Love, Labor of Sorrow*, p. 254.

8 Oliver, *Meaning of the Blues*, p. 64.

9 Gladys Hawkins, Jean Soper, and Jane Henry, *Your Maid from Mexico* (San Antonio, Texas: Naylor, 1959); quoted in Mary Romero, *Maid in the U.S.A.* (New York: Routledge, 1992), p. 95.

10 See Cherríe Moraga and Gloria Anzaldúa, eds., *This Bridge Called My Back: Writings by Radical Women of Color* (New York: Kitchen Table Press, 1981).

11 This is the title of Tomás Almaguer's study: *Racial Fault Lines: The Historical Origins of White Supremacy in California* (Berkeley: University of California Press, 1994).

PARALLELS

RECONSIDERING THE TERRAIN:
FIVE HISTORICAL PERSPECTIVES

COAL

Audre Lorde

I   is the total black
being spoken
from the earth's inside.

There are many kinds of open
how a diamond comes
into a knot of flame
how sound comes into a word
coloured
by who pays what for speaking.

Some words are open
diamonds on a glass window
singing out within the crash
of passing sun
other words are stapled wagers
in a perforated book
buy and sign and tear apart
and come whatever wills all chances
the stub remains
an ill-pulled tooth
with a ragged edge.

Some words live in my throat
breeding like adders
others
know sun
seeking like gypsies
over my tongue
to explode through my lips
like young sparrows
bursting from shell.

Some words
bedevil me.

Love is a word, another kind of open.
As the diamond comes
into a knot of flame
I am Black
because I come from the earth's inside
take my word for jewel
in the open light.

PHYLLIS J. JACKSON

LIBERATING BLACKNESS AND INTERROGATING WHITENESS

The issue is really one of standpoint. From what political perspective do we dream, look, create, and take action? For those of us who dare to desire differently, who seek to look away from the conventional ways of seeing blackness and ourselves, the issue of race and representation is not just a question of critiquing the status quo. It is also about transforming the image, creating alternatives, asking ourselves questions about what types of images subvert, pose critical alternatives, transform our worldviews and move us away from dualistic thinking about good and bad. Making a space for the transgressive image, the outlaw rebel vision, is essential to any effort to create a context for transformation. And even then little progress is made if we transform images without shifting paradigms, changing perspectives, ways of looking.

bell hooks, *Black Looks: Race and Representation,* 1992[1]

Parallels and Intersections of "The Sisterhood"

Over the past fifty years, women artists in California have traversed a series of long and arduous roads in their inspirational journeys to aesthetic independence and artistic inventiveness. Across the ever-shifting and permeable boundaries of gender, race, ethnicity, culture, sexuality, and class, the most significant parallel among women art-makers in California is the exponential increase in the sheer number of women who now study, make, exhibit, sell, and teach art. The volume of work is phenomenal and extraordinarily diverse in form, content, and underlying aesthetic. Clearly, no single critical commentary or historical narrative can account for the art-making practices or experiences of all women in the most diverse and populous state on the "left coast." Thus, the notion of "parallels and intersections" emerges as a

59

useful way of characterizing artistic commonalities, as well as tensions and conflicts within a supposed sisterhood of artists. Necessarily, the search for creative expression by women artists of African descent has led them down paths that at some moments parallel and at other points intersect with the aesthetic and artistic journeys of Chicana, Asian American, Euro-American, and Native American women. The qualities that most sharply distinguish the work of Black women from other women artists are the valuing of their Blackness, and the simultaneous interrogation of the normalization of the construction of whiteness.

The roll call of Black visual artists who have lived, studied, worked, or exhibited in California in the last half of the twentieth century includes, but in no way is limited to, such visionaries as Phoebe Beasley, Camille Billops, Cheryl Dunye, Kira Lynn Harris, Mildred Howard, Margo Humphrey, Suzanne Jackson, Samella Lewis, O.Funmilayo Makarah, Evangeline J. Montgomery, Mary Lovelace O'Neal, Faith Ringgold, Sandra Rowe, Alison and Betye Saar, Ruth G. Waddy, Kara Walker, Pat Ward Williams, Carrie Mae Weems, and Gayle West. While all these artists draw creative energy from their shared experience of being Black and female in American society, the diversity of this select group's work is characteristic of the variety of form and subject matter employed by all Black women artists.

Consequently, "parallels and intersections" remains an effective metaphor when examining the range of artistic projects and aesthetics values among women artists of African descent.

Black women work in a broad range of media and styles, each exploiting the expressive potential of traditional and nontraditional materials in her own distinct way. The gamut runs from the colorful story quilts of Faith Ringgold to the black-and-white conceptual photography of Carrie Mae Weems through the site-specific installations of Sandra Rowe. Ringgold blends painting, pieced quilting, and autobiography, fashioning a unique, carefully stitched expressive form that pays homage to creative materials and techniques generally associated with women's crafts. Her large soft paintings enriched by hand-painted narratives are intended to hang on walls rather than cover bodies or beds. In *Change #3: Over 100 Pounds Weight Loss Performance Story Quilt* (1991), the artist explores how internalized racial oppression is compounded by the history of the objectification of women's bodies. In this way Ringgold transforms a utilitarian tradition and personal history into a poignant fine arts medium.

The juxtaposition of image and text in Weems's *As a child I loved the aroma of coffee . . .* (1988) suggests that seemingly benign objects, such as a percolator, a Formica countertop, and a coffee cup metaphorically and literally share an instrumental role in identity formation for some people

8
Faith Ringgold, *Change #3: Over
100 Pounds Weight Loss Performance
Story Quilt*, 1991. Acrylic on canvas, with
pieced fabric border, 53½ × 80½ in.
© 1991 Faith Ringgold. Collection of
the artist.

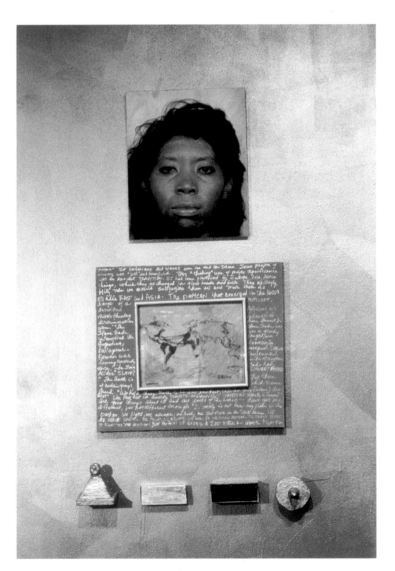

9
Sandra Rowe, detail from
Slave Series, 1992. Mixed-media
installation, 4 ft. × 30 in. × 4 in.
(overall size: 12 × 10 ft.). Photo:
Jan Blair. Collection of the artist.

of African descent in the United States. The text to the right of the image states, "As a child I loved the aroma of coffee. Smelling it drove me nuts cause it reminded me of cocoa, of chocolate, candy. Anyway, my parents rarely drunk coffee. But when they did I'd stand in the kitchen begging like a salivating dog for a lick. Momma and daddy would be sitting up, elbows on table, talking, sipping like white folk on T.V., shooing me away with, 'Ya don't need no coffee, coffee'll make you black.'" Weems abruptly ends a sentimental and humorous narration to tackle the difficult issue of African peoples' internalization of the white Western cultural devaluation of Blackness, i.e., self-hatred. Weems confronts the complex issue of "color hierarchy" by revealing how an intimate domestic space—the so-called haven in a heartless world—is also a site where the demonization of Blackness is internalized and passed on from one generation to the next.

Black women operate in a variety of intellectual and aesthetic arenas and find inspiration in disparate social, cultural, and political agendas. In addition, Black women embrace and espouse varying ideas about the role of artists, audiences, and the social implications of art. For instance, Sandra Rowe's *Slave Series* (1992) draws from the diverse intellectual traditions, cosmologies, spiritualities, values, aesthetics, artistic practices, cultures, and histories of African people on the African continent and in their diaspora. These

10

Varnette P. Honeywood, *Double Dare*, 1979. Acrylic on canvas, 36 × 48 in. *Double Dare* © Varnette P. Honeywood, 1979. Collection of Drs. James W. and Caryn Hobbs.

works describe the physical, mental, moral, and intellectual characteristics of people of African descent as they are employed in the construction of personal, public, and collective identities. In her work, Rowe re-codes Blackness and African-ness as strength, richness, power, beauty as well as infinite complexity. Varnette Honeywood creates culturally affirming paintings, such as *Double Dare* (1979), by celebrating the vitality of Black family life and the rich cultural texture of Black communities. Honeywood's canvases and prints are warm, stylized renderings that take viewers on nostalgic excursions through cherished aspects of daily life on school grounds, in churches, and domestic interiors.

In tone and content, this contrasts sharply with the historical and commemorative themes of muralist Noni Olabisi. Her mural inspired by the

11

Noni Olabisi, *To Protect and Serve,* 1995. Mural installed at Hair Expressions, Los Angeles. Acrylic on wall, 50 × 14 ft. Photo: Robin J. Dunitz. Courtesy of the artist and Social Public Art Resource (SPARC), Venice, Calif.

Black Panther Party, *To Protect and Serve* (1995), addresses the history of anti-Black lynching and police brutality that gave rise to the controversial Oakland-based organization and its community survival programs. Located on the exterior wall of a South Central Los Angeles barbershop, Olabisi's mural is one of dozens of outdoor murals that Black and Chicano artists have created to enhance the visual repertoire of their communities. Muralists bypass traditional galleries and art dealers, opting to create art that speaks directly to the residents of their distinct communities. These murals are such sources of inspiration and community pride that even in a graffiti-covered city like Los Angeles spray-paint bandits do not desecrate them. Other artists were inspired by movements outside the United States. For instance, in the visually stunning installation entitled *Ten Little Children Standing in a Line (one got shot, and then there were nine)* (1991), Mildred Howard joined an international call to end the violent practice of racial apartheid in South Africa.

These women also espouse varying ideas about the role of artists, audiences, and the social implications of art. Sometimes a critique of violence is lodged against image-makers, too. In the photographic assemblage entitled *Accused/ Blowtorch/Padlock* (1986; see fig. 71), Pat Ward

12
Mildred Howard, *Ten Little Children Standing in a Line (one got shot and then there were nine)*, 1991. Copper glove molds, wood, dirt bullet casings on rear word, text and photo mural (not shown), ambient light (dimensions variable). Photo: Lewis Watts. Collection of the artist, courtesy Gallery Paule Anglim.

Williams appropriated a mass-media photo of the ravaged body of a man who had been tortured and murdered. Ward Williams surrounds the picture with handwritten words that express not only her outrage with the lynch mob culture but also question photography's complicity with the crimes. She, thus, angrily interrogates both *Life* magazine's and the photographer's roles in perpetuating the ritual assault on Black lives. Betye Saar's *The Liberation of Aunt Jemima* (1972) was created almost thirty years before Kara Walker's Capp Street Project installation *"No Mere Words Can Adequately Reflect the Remorse This Negress Feels At Having Been Cast Into Such a Lowly State by Her Former Master and It Is With a Humble Heart that She Brings About Their Physical Ruin and Earthly Demise"* (1999). The two works seem to share a common theme focusing on the oppression and objectification of Black women. Nonetheless, Saar initiated an aggressive public campaign against Walker's visually seductive but graphically shocking art when Walker received a MacArthur Fellowship Award in 1997. Saar ignited tremendous and heated controversy in arts and academic communities about the propriety or impropriety of Walker's imagery and her responsibility as an artist. These types of polemic debates will surely continue well into the next century and attest to the variety of African American art.

Indebted to Political and Social Struggles

That so many women from all heritages now have the "liberty" to define themselves as artists, or aspire to be artists, is a direct inheritance of the political struggles and cultural wars that reached a zenith in the 1960s and 1970s, radically transforming our society. Obviously, the feminist-driven Women's Liberation movement challenged many patriarchal structures and male-centered

ways of thinking that had limited women's lives in the public and private spheres. For many, however, it is not as obvious that the Civil Rights and Black Power movements, that often served as models and points of reference for feminist activism, greatly expanded opportunities for all women, including artists. Activists recognized the pivotal role that "fine arts" and popular visual imagery plays in the maintenance of relationships of dominance and subordination. Women and men across the social spectrum theorized that the movements for social change had to embrace new aesthetic values, cultivate critical visual literacy, devise a nonoppressive visual language, and create more liberatory expressive arts traditions.

Social and cultural critics of the 1960s and 1970s challenged the authority of prevailing aesthetic philosophies, visual traditions, and arts institutions. They denounced them as abusive

instruments of oppression because, among other things, they rested on sexist and racist values that perpetuated racial and sexual objectification and stereotyping. Over the centuries, European and Euro-American artists have represented Black women in a litany of gross caricatures and demeaning visual clichés.[2] Black women have been pictured as female archetypes of a "race" of people at the bottom of some supposed "great chain of being": as personifications of a slumbering Africa, dutiful serving maids, stout and matronly caretakers, frightened needy slaves, impoverished mothers to tattered gangs of children, and wives to indolent husbands. It is alarming that, at the end of the twentieth century, so many of these visual clichés—originating in the artistic imaginations of the late eighteenth and nineteenth centuries' image makers—continue to have strong cultural currency. Even if cloaked in contemporary drag, they are prescribed visual codes not confined by any supposed boundaries between the so-called "fine arts" and "popular culture."[3]

A Black feminist critique maintains that no set of images so consistently devalues, defames, insults, and humiliates a specific group of people as viciously as do those by artists and image-makers of European ancestry representing women of African descent. This is not to say that other groups have not been the target of cruel stereotyping. Clearly they have. But, the ideologies of sexism, racism, and classism rely upon the notions of hierarchical and biological determinists that combine to consistently portray Black women in the least admirable of pictorial lights. In *Playing in the Dark: Whiteness and the Literary Imagination*, Nobel Prize–winning author Toni Morrison poignantly and profoundly explains her awakening to the reality that images such as Aunt Jemima tell us more about the white image-makers than about Black subjects:

> I came to realize the obvious: the subject of
> the dream is the dreamer. The fabrication of an
> Africanist persona is reflexive; an extraordinary
> meditation on the self; a powerful exploration
> of the fears and desires that reside in the white
> (writerly) conscious. It is an astonishing revela-
> tion of longing, of terror, of perplexity, of
> shame, of magnanimity. Once you realize this, it
> requires hard work not to see it.[4]

As a Black feminist reader and viewer who is theoretically prepared to encounter this intellectual hazing, it is still shocking to recognize that over the centuries so much energy and thought has gone into constructing concepts that either denied or devalued the humanity of African women and into developing visual practices that naturalized these disdainful ideas.

Conceptually, Morrison's approach to the interpretation of literary representations provides an important model for an analysis of visual "Africanisms" found in the works of white image-makers. It is an analytic strategy that moves beyond more conventional studies that only describe and evaluate one side of the proverbial coin—the black side—and in the analysis rarely move beyond the designation of "the negativity" of the image. It is an approach that not only focuses on the ways in which Black people are exploited and victimized by the American visual practices, but also takes into account the ways in which white Americans received advantage from and took comfort in the production and consumption of the hierarchies established by anti-Black images and ideas.

Works like Betye Saar's *The Liberation of Aunt Jemima* exemplify this poignant critique, stripping America's sacred icons of their mythic innocence, revealing them as shameless masks for social inequalities, ugly political ideas, and anti-Black practices. Saar's piece attacks "the most successful" advertising icon of the first half of the twentieth century. It was and continues to be a visual cliché that has plagued Black men, women, and children. Using an assemblage format, Saar's boxed construction creates a representational intervention that undermines the visual litany of maids, servants, mythic mammies, and Aunt Jemimas. In a humorous flipping of the script, Saar invests what is to whites a superficially comforting image of the Black caregiver with angry, confrontational content. She re-visions the "The Mythic Mammy" by endowing her with a pistol and a rifle, to go along with her broom. Saar's "Auntie" plans to "clean house," but not in her old role as symbolic caretaker to white America. Against the backdrop of repeated Aunt Jemima advertising icons, "The Legendary Mammy" assumes a new position as an urban guerrilla, ready to explode myths and disrupt routine expectations. Saar's work robs this established visual cliché of its widespread cultural currency, and in the process begins to pose new tests for our critical visual literacy. More often than not, through the skillful manipulation of form, artistic creations such as this push us to reevaluate what we think we know about Black women, what we think we know about the practice of making art, and what we think we know about the art historical tradition.

The core of what Black women have to say in their visual art, their sisters in other cultural

14

Betye Saar, *The Liberation of Aunt Jemima*, 1972. Mixed-media assemblage, 11¾ × 8 × 2¾ in. © Betye Saar, 1972. Photo: Colin McRae. Collection of the University of California, Berkeley Art Museum; purchased with the aid of funds from the National Endowment for the Arts (selected by The Committee for the Acquisition of Afro-American Art).

arenas have also been thinking and saying for many generations. Poets and novelists living and working in California, such as Octavia Butler, June Jordan, Alice Walker, and the recently deceased Shirley Anne Williams, or filmmakers like Camille Billops, Carroll Parrott Blue, and Zeinabu irene Davis also routinely mine the binary opposition between blackness and whiteness for poetic and narrative meaning. It is worth noting that literary artists have found a critical, academic, and popular reception that remains an elusive dream for most visual artists. Nonetheless, visual artists rank among the legions of incredibly resilient, courageous, and visionary Black women who acted on their beliefs that the life they wanted for *themselves* and *others* must be free of racial, sexual, economic, cultural, and visual barriers.

Thus, the Black women artists highlighted here shun the "cultural etiquette" that urges them just to "get over it" and forget the repressive aspects of the past, the present, and possible future that make many people uncomfortable.[5] Instead, they bring to the forefront debates on critical issues which serve to disrupt the post–Civil Rights mythology that we all live in harmony now that white supremacy has died with the abolition of de jure segregation and that anti-Black oppression ended with the birth of affirmative action programs.[6]

Foremost among their concerns is the use of the word "black." Since it serves as a common-place synonym, both adjective and noun, describing African people, the work of Black women artists usually rejects the use of "black," "blackness" or even "darkness" as descriptive and metaphorical signifiers of negativity or evil. This re-coding also requires a relinquishing of the beliefs and practices that position "blackness" as the symbolic and metaphorical negation, or antithesis of "whiteness" and all that it implies. Their work indicates sites where notions of white supremacy have become institutionalized in language and naturalized as accepted cultural values. Their re-coding of Blackness and valuing of Africanness provide a frame of reference that effectively undermines white supremacist thinking, language, and visual arts. A Black feminist art historical practice considers the interconnected notions and expressions of race, class, gender, and sexuality as central to any critical analysis of art and culture in the United States.[7]

Aesthetic Politics and the Normalization of Whiteness

"Parallels and Intersections" is a useful metaphor for discussing the art-world networks impacting career trajectories, collecting patterns, exhibiting opportunities, critical reviews, and the production of academic scholarship. Arts-related professions make up a complex web of patrons, dealers, critics, scholars, curators, and publishers. These interconnected and interdependent professions play pivotal roles in fostering individual developments as well as collective artistic trends. Until recently, the networks that support the making of art have not been friendly to women artists of any race or ethnicity. At the same time traditional systems of criticism and patronage such as art schools, museums, and galleries have been neither welcoming nor encouraging, especially to people of African descent and other people of color. More pointedly, the historic reality is that these networks have impeded rather than embraced the majority of creative Black women and their work.[8]

In California, de facto segregation, rather than Jim Crow segregation, shaped and continues to mold social, cultural, and political institutions. Custom, rather than the law, keeps segregation alive in churches, schools, residential housing patterns, and employment arenas. This effectively naturalizes cultural relations and social hierarchies that are, in fact, constructed. Likewise, the unconscious assumptions or subtle expressions of white superiority, as they surface in and also corrupt mainstream visual arts and art criticism, are a far more powerful and insidious phenomenon in contemporary society than the hateful expressions or violent practices of white supremacists or misogynists on the radical fringe. Indeed, the unwritten codes and unconscious assumptions are often more difficult to dismantle than the legally imposed ones.

The terms "unconscious" and "subtle" are used quite guardedly because, in many instances, notions of white superiority are not produced accidentally. Since they stand cloaked in the forgiving mantle of socially acceptable normalized whiteness, they are reproduced and embraced as the natural order of things or as beloved tradition. For many viewers and producers, regardless of race, the normalization of whiteness and Europeanness ends up working like a subliminal message, encoded below conscious awareness. These patterns are largely maintained by the public or private institutions that support the arts. For example, mainstream art networks and institutions traditionally privilege the art and aesthetics of European and Euro-American males, positioning their work as the objective and disinterested norm, the standard of quality, and the guideline for content by which others are measured. It is an assertion that allows those in positions of authority and decision making to dismiss all other artists and their art as everything from unimportant, derivative, "primitive," or female. Or, they use the ultimate and incredibly ironic quip of disdain, "it is merely art of special interest groups."[9]

Despite these odds, Black women continue to create, knowing that their modeling of clay, their handling of paint, stitching of cloth, or shooting of film can produce intriguing forms that express profound ideas, disturbing beliefs, or uplifting concepts. Maintaining, however, that the making of art is and should be about more than an exploration of the medium and its formal possibilities, does not mean that art is only about content. Art is about the artistry, the deftness of hand, the precision of eye, and/or the manipulation of materials and media. Undoubtedly, aesthetic debates should be more complex and nuanced than the simple either/or proposition that rhetorically distinguishes creative work as either "fine arts" or political propaganda. Yet, unfortunately, dichotomous arguments continue to limit the critical discourses surrounding the work of Black American artists in general and Black women in particular.

Black women's art rests on the assumption that Black people's dreams, memories, concerns, and lived experiences can inspire a robust art practice. They presume and visually assert that Black men, women, and children are legitimate and engaging subjects for art. This may seem self-evident. However, in a Eurocentric culture that deifies whiteness, the very act of choosing to represent the Black body in ways that do not demonize Blackness or ridicule Africanness instantly casts an artist's work into the middle of a long-standing debate centering on the politics of aesthetics. That the normalization of whiteness underpins Western aesthetic discourse reveals itself through the following formulaic assertion that holds widespread currency everywhere: If the subject of the artwork is of African descent or is Black, then the art is about "race" or racial issues, completely ignoring gender. Moreover, if the art is about "race," then it is art that delves into the realm of the political. In short, "Black" equals race, race equals politics, and politics does not equal Art.

Conversely, if the subject of a work involves figures that are white, or adopted into the European family, no commensurate political definition surfaces in traditional Western discourses. For instance, ancient Greek sculpture—replete with idealized, time-worn white marble figures—maintains cultural status as a depoliticized and privileged aesthetic category. Ironically, such a "disinterested" reading ignores the explicitly political (racially driven) import that classical sculpture has had since antiquity. Clearly, this formula for designating what is and what is not art, what are the appropriate subjects of art or what aesthetic values inform art criticism, rests on pernicious normalizing assumptions. Since the act of defining cultural phenomena is the exercise of power, using such normalizing definitions to forge dominating power relations is not merely cultural—it is Political. But, white critics and curators seldom see or acknowledge the absurdity of this disparity. They often note no contradictions as they celebrate a tradition that exploited and manipulated the authority of Western philosophy, aesthetics, social theory, and science to privilege "white European" over white European females and all people of color. Art by Black women artists and writing by Black critics, on the other hand, help to unmask the ideological underpinnings of propositions which claim that the best making, viewing, critiquing, collecting, and writing of the history of art emerge from some neutral aesthetic and are, therefore, apolitical and unraced.

These societal and cultural exclusions remind us that the realm of art making is enmeshed in the politics and culture wars at large. As a result, Black, Latino/a, Asian, Native American, and white women artists have had to work against dominant ideologies and hegemonic aesthetics. They also have had to struggle for inclusion and acceptance while building their own supportive communities, and with developing more healing and life-affirming aesthetic ideologies. The multifaceted and distinguished career of Samella Lewis provides an example of how one woman systematically confronted the exclusionary politics and aesthetics of the art world. Lewis is a celebrated artist and a pioneering scholar, educator, historian, and curator who has lived and worked in California during the past four decades. Recounting her trailblazing accomplishments can serve a dual purpose. The most apparent is to acknowledge and applaud her work. But the following brief synopsis also attempts to expand a historical narrative about artistic developments to include an examination of the social and cultural conditions that give rise to the production and critical reception of art.

Lewis recognized that artists seldom emerge and rarely thrive in the absence of vibrant and engaged arts communities which generate informed critical and historical attention, patronage, and exhibiting opportunities. Hence, Lewis inaugurated project after project to help build a supportive art network for herself and other Black artists and their audiences. Lewis founded the Museum of African American Art in 1979 in Los Angeles and served as curator on countless exhibits showcasing work by Black artists that mainstream institutions typically ignore. She continues to organize solo retrospectives and group shows, and has now expanded her coverage to include Caribbean artists.

Lewis produced a series of publications that filled a cultural void and were fundamental to the placement of modern Black American artists into the historical record. Her publications helped to establish new critical perspectives and voices of authority that drew on more than just European and Euro-American values. Lewis's two-volume *Black Artists on Art* (1969, 1971), co-authored with Ruth G. Waddy, is one of the major documents on the Black Arts Movement of the 1960s and early 1970s. Lewis also founded and for years was the editor of the longest-running periodical devoted to art by people of African descent in the United

States. Initially titled *Black Art Quarterly, Ltd.* (1976–1984), today it is published as *The International Review of African American Art*. It is an invaluable resource for Black artists, as well as patrons and historians interested their art. Although Lewis does not declare her approach as feminist, the historical studies she constructs always represent the artistic voices and visions of women as well as men.

In 1984, Lewis retired from her position as an art history professor at Scripps College in Claremont, California. When she began teaching there in 1969, she was one of a small group of scholars at any American academy to offer courses on African American and African art. In 1977 she published the survey *Art: African American*, which she subsequently revised, greatly expanded, and retitled *African American Art and Artists*. Until 1998, this book stood as the most comprehensive survey on Black artists and continues to be the most useful study from a biographical approach. Lewis's 1984 book on Elizabeth Catlett was the first, and for many years the only, full-fledged monograph on a Black woman artist. These are just a few examples of Lewis's long list of groundbreaking publications that keep Black artists and their art alive through the written text. Overall, her life's work charts a course that keeps us ever aware that the struggle to define and control the making, interpretation, and exhibiting of visual arts is a major political contest in our culture.

Liberating Darkness

The color black and notions of "blackness" carry such powerful metaphoric and symbolic meaning that they find routine expression at all levels of U.S. culture and society. It does not matter whether it is in an artist's canvas, a critic's review, a scientist's pie chart, a company's musical category, or a newscaster's report. It could be evoked by something as seemingly innocent as children's rhymes, as opportunistic as a politician's characterization of welfare, the mere description of a minister's sermon, as supposedly neutral as a journalist's article, as flippant as a designer's latest fashion, or as apparently clinical as the description of a newborn's skin tone. Whatever the purpose, the use of black as a visual element or a qualifying adjective dramatically influences the impact of an object or the implications of a description.

The images and connotations conjured by the color black and notions of blackness are by no means "universal" or uncontested. Quite the contrary, blackness or darkness can invoke such diametrically opposing sentiments, values, and behaviors that one person's chest may swell with pride while another person shivers with fear. Binary to black, the color white and notions of whiteness generally elicit sentiments and connotations that are black's polar opposite. Women artists of African descent, like many of their Black sisters working around the globe, create works that interrogate a multiplicity of issues regarding blackness/whiteness as conceptual and visual metaphors for beauty, intelligence, and character.

There is no universal notion of beauty. Our notions of the beautiful and our aesthetic sensibilities are culturally and socially constructed by the beliefs and values we consciously embrace and unconsciously imbibe. Therefore, we cannot depend on singular definitions of what constitutes good art, or even the appropriate subjects, materials, or techniques for making art. An artist can select paint or ink, marble or clay, film or videotape, found objects or manufactured supplies as the substance for creative expression. Whatever the form or content, artists' underlying aesthetics—what they think about art—are informed by the diverse value systems operating within our society. Since misogyny, the demonization of Blackness, and the wholesale devaluation of Africa are all hegemonic values, they inform our visual codes and representational language.

In this context the seemingly unifying rubrics of "women" or "gender" quickly reveal themselves as dangerously normalizing and potentially exclusionary when used too rigidly in art discourses. The ideas and definitions associated with women can and do differ dramatically when viewed through the prisms of race, ethnicity, sexuality, and economic class. For many Black women artists and other women of color,

the Anglophile version of white supremacy prevalent in the United States has been as formidable an obstacle as male supremacy. Some might suggest that racism presented and continues to present far more limitations than sexism, frequently uniting white women and men against people of color.

Black women do not experience racial and gender oppression separately, but simultaneously. Moreover, women of color are disproportionately clustered at the bottom of the economic scale, and as a result, all but a fortunate few experience the effects of class oppression concurrently. Those who are lesbians must also deal with homophobia and the presumptions of heterosexism. They encounter hostility not just because of their emotional and sexual intimacy with other women, but because they do not have visible intimate relationships with heterosexual men. Analogously, Black artists receive hostile or uninformed critical responses, not just because they take Black people as their subject, but because they do not celebrate whiteness. Thus, simple either/or dichotomies are weak analytic tools. Using liberation ideology, Black feminist theorist Deborah King labels approaches such as the Marxist contention that class oppression is primary as "monist" and less than adequate. They obscure more than they reveal, because gender is always raced and classed in the United States.[10] Deborah King goes on to maintain that the simultaneous experience of multiple oppressions places Black women in "multiple jeopardy." This holds true for other women of color, as well as poor, white women. Conceptually, "multiple jeopardy" avoids the tendency to universalize women's experiences. It also recognizes that oppressions are interlocking and impact women's lives in a multitude of ways. Necessarily, they contribute to the development of multiple perspectives on life in general, and art in particular. This does not mean that these disparate experiences and oppressions determine women's aesthetic and artistic concerns but rather that, quite obviously, they help shape them. Samella Lewis's print entitled *Field* (1968) foregrounds the ways in which gender, race, and social status intersect in the lives of Black women and informs their art.

Through the abstracted symbolism of the raised fist, *Field* is a black-and-white print that references Black women's experience as agriculture workers under the institution of slavery and after its demise. Clearly, slavery was a horrible experience for millions of African women, yet *Field* conveys their formidable strength to endure. It alludes to their historical role in fashioning powerful survival strategies, as well as in the building of the nation. The overwhelming majority of African women and girls in the United States were never restricted to the "domestic" or so-called "women's sphere." The vast majority performed grueling and highly public agricultural

field labor, while also working in the home space. By definition, working-class white women were not restricted to the "domestic sphere" either. An artwork like *Field* reminds us that cliché phrases such as "women were relegated to the domestic sphere" actually refers almost exclusively to the experiences and concerns of white, usually affluent women. The absence of the adjective "white" in the context of a phrase such as this is a glaring omission. What frequently distinguishes Black feminist discourses from the discourses of feminists who identify as white is that women of color foreground their "racial" and ethnic subjectivities. Conversely, women of European descent who don the homogenizing and normalizing mantle of white racial identity, routinely refuse to acknowledge or examine the racial aspects of their experiences or analyses.

Traditional writing about art marks the distinctive raised fist in *Field* as aggressively political, yet considers that in the ancient Greek sculpture Aphrodite of Cnidus, the figure's active gesture to cover her pubic area is a naturally modest reflex. Routinely, critics and scholars classify work like Lewis's abstracted figuration, her brilliant use of negative space, and her sensual manipulation of the material as primarily political, at best as political art. By the terms of late twentieth-century discourses, because *Field* is about Black people it is, therefore, about racial issues—ungendered. Conversely, all too frequently, traditional Western discourse positions the Aphrodite as a quintessential example of the supposed triumph of form over content, devoid of political inferences—gender neutral and unraced. Artists like Lewis urge viewers of all racial and ethnic backgrounds to ponder the multilayered significance of their constructions of Blackness and whiteness. To that end, they examine the ways in which racially gendered identities are constructed and "normalized," especially in the visual realm—and the many ways in which these notions find expression on the backs of Black women.

Ironically, as the twentieth century has now come to a close, many artists and art-world professionals seem to have forgotten that "power concedes nothing without a demand." The radical changes that have taken place were not negotiated at tea parties. Far too many suffer from a serious form of cultural amnesia that allows them to depoliticize the historical transformation of our society and its artistic communities. They slip dangerously close to embracing normalizing ideologies and elitist aesthetic arguments that originally catalyzed a generation to wage war against image-makers and their images. It is not merely petty arguments over who makes the prettiest pictures. It is a tense struggle for power to define the beautiful, the good, the worthy in art—and by extension in life.

15
Samella Lewis, *Field,* 1968.
Linocut, 26 × 20 in. Photo:
Armando Solis. Collection
of the artist.

Notes

1 bell hooks, *Black Looks: Race and Representation* (Boston: South End Press, 1992), p. 4.

2 For examinations on this history of representation see Michele Wallace, *Invisibility Blues: From Pop to Theory* (New York: Verso, 1990), p. 245; K. Sue Jewell, *From Mammy to Miss America and Beyond: Cultural Images and the Shaping of U.S. Social Policy* (London: Routledge, 1993); Hugh Honor, ed., *The Image of the Black in Western Art: From the American Revolution to World War One*, vol. 4, parts 1, 2 (Cambridge: Harvard University Press, 1989).

3 Movies as diverse as *Birth of a Nation, Gone with the Wind, Hannah and her Sisters, JFK* or *Forrest Gump*, along with dozens of television shows such as *ER, Ally McBeal* or *Time of My Life*, present Black women as handy sidekicks who provide the emotional/moral support and frequent sexual advice to the white lead roles (whether male and female).

4 Toni Morrison, *Playing in the Dark: Whiteness and the Literary Imagination* (Cambridge: Harvard University Press, 1992), p. 17.

5 F. James Davis discusses the customs and rituals of American "racial" etiquette: "The white person had to be clearly in charge at all times, and the black person clearly subordinate, so that each kept his or her place. It was a master-servant etiquette, in which blacks had to act out their inferior social position, much the same way slaves had done. The black had to be deferential in tone and body language, as portrayed by the actors who played the Sambo stereotype, and never bring up a delicate topic or contradict the white." See F. James Davis, *Who Is Black? One Nation's Definition* (University Park, Penn.: The Pennsylvania State University Press, 1991), p. 64.

6 See Farai Chideya, *Don't Believe the Hype: Fighting Cultural Misinformation About African-Americans* (New York: Plume Books, 1995).

7 See bell hooks, *Sisters of the Yam* (Boston: South End Press, 1993), particularly the chapters "Healing Darkness," "Dreaming Ourselves Dark and Deep Black Beauty," and "Walking in the Spirit," pp. 7–17, 79–97, and 183–190.

8 For a fuller discussion of this historical legacy, see Judith Wilson's essay in this volume; and Howardena Pindell, "Breaking the Silence: Art World Racism—the Glaring Omission," *New Art Examiner*, Part 1 (October 1990): 18–23, and Part 2 (November 1990): 23–51; Maurice Berger, "Are Art Museums Racist?" *Art in America* 78, no. 9 (September 1990): 68–77.

9 For an analysis of the rhetorical conventions used by "mainstream" art critics to discuss Black artists and their work, see the essays by Charles Gaines and Maurice Berger in Catherine Lord, ed., *Theater of Refusal: Black Art and Mainstream Criticism* (Irvine: Fine Arts Gallery, University of California, Irvine, 1993), pp. 9–53.

10 Deborah King, "Multiple Jeopardy, Multiple Consciousness, The Context of a Black Feminist Ideology," *Signs* 14, no. 1 (1988): 42–72.

YES, WE ARE
***NOT* INVISIBLE**

Janice Mirikitani

No, I'm not from Tokyo, Singapore or Saigon.

No, your dogs are safe with me.

No, I don't invade the park for squirrel meat.

No, my peripheral vision is fine.

No, I'm very bad at math.

No, I do not answer to Geisha Girl, China Doll, Suzie Wong,
  Mamasan, or gook, Jap or Chink.

No, to us life is not cheap.

I do not know the art of tea, and No,
  I am not grateful for all you've done for me.
  Friends of mine have died from AIDS.
  Another driven mad by P.T.S.D.
  Some of us were murdered, blamed for this economy.
  Another has od.'d.
  We've been jailed for mistaken identity.
  Incarcerated because of ancestry,
  And no, I am not the model minority.

No, I am from Stockton, Angel Island, Detroit,
  Waikiki, Los Angeles, Lodi, San Francisco,
  Delano, Chicago, Boston, Tule Lake, New York City,
  Anchorage, Jackson, Phoenix, Raleigh.

And Yes, I am alive because of memory,
  Ancestors who endured adversity,
  all our tongues breaking free,
  the strength of this diversity.

No, we are not Invisible

And Yes, I am from Tokyo, Singapore, Manila, Guam,
  Beijing, Cambodia, Thailand, Vietnam,
  India, Korea, Samoa, Hong Kong, Taiwan.

Yes, this strength like ropes of the sun

again lifts a new morning,

And Yes, we rise as always,

amidst you.

KARIN HIGA

WHAT IS AN ASIAN AMERICAN WOMAN ARTIST?

It must be odd
to be a minority
he was saying.
I looked around
And didn't see any.
So I said
Yeah
it must be.
> **Mitsuye Yamada,**
> *"Looking Out"*

With characteristic brevity and force, Mitsuye Yamada's poem "Looking Out" captures the complexity of identity and its dependence upon relative positioning and visible markers.[1] What appears simple and self-evident, subtly shifts and modulates depending upon one's position. In Yamada's poem, "he" sees her as what he is not: a minority, an Asian American woman. She, on the other hand, experiences the world through a different prism, as neither minor nor "odd." The poem prods us to consider what the names are that we call ourselves and whether it matters who does the calling. The fact that the poem characterizes the exchange as gendered—not surprising given Yamada's self-identification as a feminist woman of color—adds another element to the mix, underscoring the degree to which even casual contacts are fraught with complex assumptions and histories. It is within this matrix that an assessment of the term "Asian American woman artist" must begin. For what are the elements that characterize an Asian American, and how might a brief glimpse into the art and lives of some women illuminate our understanding of the term, its history, and its limits?

"Asian American" as a term emerged with its namesake movement in the late 1960s and 1970s and represented a new pan-Asian sensibility that jettisoned the then-common appellation "Oriental," both because of its association with European colonialism and its close connection to the stereotypic exoticism promulgated in the popular media. Inspired by the Civil Rights, Black Power, anti–Vietnam War, and women's movements, the Asian American movement consisted of a heterogeneous range of political, social, and cultural activity united by an overarching anti-racist stance but with varying degrees of leftist radicality, ranging from a generalized commitment to liberal social action to the revolutionary Red Guard Party, which, as its minister of information Alex Hing proclaimed, "[was] part of the Cultural Revolution that's going down in the United States."[2] The movement overwhelmingly consisted of young Chinese Americans and Japanese Americans, acculturated in an American context that, although racist in its treatment of Asian Americans, provided a shared set of experiences and a relationship to Asia that was indirect and mediated, largely through parents or grandparents, by the successive American military interventions in Japan, the South Pacific,

Korea, and Southeast Asia, or as some critics wryly noted "from the radio, off the silver screen, from television, out of comic books, from the pushers of white American culture . . ."[3]

The insufficiencies of the term "Asian American" have been acknowledged and challenged since its beginnings, as Yen Le Espiritu has documented.[4] Elaine Kim, writing in the introduction of her now-canonical study of Asian American literature, summarized the problems in using "Asian American," explaining that while "distinctions among the various national groups sometimes do blur after a generation or two, when it is easier for us to see that we are bound together by the experiences we share as members of an American racial minority . . . we are accepting an externally imposed label that is meant to define us by distinguishing us from other Americans primarily on the basis of race."[5] Hence, "Asian American" as an overarching political identity provided opportunities for mobilizing across communities, but did so with the recognition of its external origins. Today, demographic changes raise other issues. No longer does the term "Asian American" cover primarily Chinese Americans and Japanese Americans born and raised in the United States. The overhaul of discriminatory immigration laws in 1965 resulted in a massive shift in the profile of immigrants. Now Asian Americans may be identified with no fewer than 20 different ethnic subgroups and are more likely to be immigrants than American-born.[6] Asians, as a percentage of all immigrants to the United States, have steadily increased: 6 percent in the 1950s, 13 percent in the 1960s, 36 percent in the 1970s, and 42 percent in the 1980s.[7] They are (in order of largest to smallest group) Chinese, Filipino, Japanese, Indian, Korean, Vietnamese, Laotian, Thai, Cambodian, Hmong, Pakistani, and Indonesian. Most have a direct connection to Asia, with lingering sentiments, whether it be the political and cultural context of their country of origin or the experience of historical antagonism such as Japanese colonialism, that inform and shape their diverse identities in the United States. For some a pan-Asian identity is inadequate in the face of the post-1965 immigration patterns, which created even greater diversity among Asian Americans in terms of country of origin, experience, class, and identity.

The brutal murder of Vincent Chin, a Chinese American engineer, in 1982 dramatically demonstrated how the debates surrounding the political construction of a pan-Asian identity appear to have little relevance compared to entrenched racism against Asian Americans. Two European American men beat Chin to death with a baseball bat after getting into an argument with him at a strip club in suburban Detroit. The economic decline of the United States, especially as experienced in the American automobile sector, and the growing prosperity of Japan produced a climate of hostility toward "things" Japanese. Vincent Chin's assailants were laid-off autoworkers who reportedly fired racial epithets, including "Jap," at Chin before they retrieved a baseball bat, hunted the fleeing Chin down, and beat him unconscious. Days later, Chin died. The perpetrators were allowed to plead guilty to manslaughter, were sentenced to three years' probation, and fined less than four thousand dollars each. After a federal case charging violation of civil rights was heard in a U.S. district court, one of the European American men was sentenced to twenty-five years in prison. But the sense of justice was dashed when, on appeal in 1987, he was acquitted. Vincent Chin's murder and the ensuing struggles for legal justice were a rallying cry for many in the Asian American community and a brutal reminder of the struggles faced by Americans with an Asian face. The Chin case demonstrated how conceptual distinctions of ancestry, as well as political struggles and political gains, can evaporate into thin air when confronted by racial slurs and a baseball bat.[8]

In the 1960s and 1970s, a key strategy of the Asian American movement was to counteract the often negative and woefully inadequate representation of the Asian American experience in the mainstream media and to do so by documenting and interpreting the stories of individual and community struggles through oral histories, photography, films, publications, exhibitions, and the creation of art. The activity made a profound impact, still palpable over thirty-five years later. From the legendary journal *Gidra* to single issues produced by student collectives, or alternative publications, which made accessible the history of Asian American communities ignored by commercial publishers, the flurry of activity provided an arena for the voice and expression of an Asian American identity previously unheard. But the movement was not without its lacunae and omissions, most notably concerning women and the visual arts. Sexism was not uncommon, producing a milieu where challenges to male dominance were interpreted as treasonous to the cause.[9] At the same time, European American feminist organizations displayed a profound ignorance of the critical impact of race and class and its significance to women of color.[10] Thus, Asian American women were doubly excluded: by the male dominance of the Asian American movement and by the insensitive myopia of emergent feminism.

In the realm of the visual arts, the aesthetic advocated was one that emphasized a representational approach to documenting aspects of the Asian American experience and placed greater weight on accessible content that could be easily linked to political goals. Remarkable works of art were produced using this framework, such as the photography and films of individuals associated with the collective Visual Communications or the murals coordinated by Tomie Arai. A heady idealism and populist stance valorized work that challenged "high" art practices that had previously ignored (or so it seemed at the time) the art of Asian Americans. Murals situated in accessible public spaces and prints created in multiple editions replaced easel painting. Photography, in its infinite reproducibility, served to downplay the work of art as an autonomous and unique entity. Just as some have argued that what was revolutionary in the feminist art movement was its impact on content,[11] so a key legacy of the art of the Asian American movement was its unprecedented visualization of Asian Americans beyond the stereotypic representations that had freely circulated in both popular and high art forms. But unlike the activity in the nascent field of Asian American literature, little attention was paid to Asian American visual artists of previous generations. Writers such as Carlos Bulosan, Louis Chu, John Okada, Toshio Mori, and Hisaye Yamamoto were recognized for their pioneering work and were published alongside younger writers,[12] yet Asian American visual artists remained relatively hidden or ignored.

The cause of this absence is impossible to fix definitively. Whether it was the popular assumption that no Asian American artists had previously existed or the fact that extant works were more difficult to access, the specific history of art in an American context—its connection to elite and exclusionary cultural practices and its central identity as a commodity—undeniably impacted an Asian Americanist view of its own art history. The Asian American movement's emphasis on combating the cultural imperialism of the dominant society created blinders that made it impossible to see that although early Asian American immigrants struggled as farmers, laborers, and in small businesses to build a better life for themselves and their families, they were also painters and sculptors.[13] The fact that the work of these earlier artists was often more concerned with formal issues rather than content provided further obfuscation. Perhaps a painting by Miki Hayakawa (1904–1953) depicting the Japanese gardens at Golden Gate Park looked too much like the art collected by the San Francisco elite to be recognized as an ancestor, yet her vigorous activity and connection in the pre–World War II era with male and female painters of Asian American as well as European American heritage presents an intriguing story worthy of serious consideration.

Of course, within the last decade a very different situation emerged in which the recognition and interpretation of Asian American artists vastly improved, as recent exhibitions and studies attest. But the frameworks established during the 1960s and 1970s still shape the terms of the analysis. The relative weighting of race, ethnicity,

and gender with respect to artistic practice seems to continue in descending order, with the primacy of race taking utmost precedence. To gently question it is not to deny the profound and formative role that race and racism play in American acculturation or the undeniable fact that the movements of the 1960s opened up previously exclusive discourses and arenas. Indeed, the most provocative and successful strategies of the liberation movements of the 1960s have been those that challenged the structural hegemonies which served to perpetuate existing hierarchies, rather than only combat their effects. But rather, it argues for the need to consider what is gained and lost in such frameworks. To use the appellation "Asian American woman artist" to describe, for instance, this essay's grouping of important artists—Ruth Asawa (b. 1926), Hisako Hibi (1912–1991), Theresa Hak Kyung Cha (1951–1982), Rea Tajiri (b. 1956), and Hung Liu (b. 1948)—only explains part of their significance. Even a brief review of their art and biographies suggests the limits of this designation.

The existence of Asian American women artists working in the mid-twentieth century is astonishing given the political and social restrictions against them. Yet in 1943 Ruth Asawa managed to secure permission to attend college in Milwaukee, leaving the concentration camp in Rohwer where she and her family were incarcerated. She had been born and raised in Southern

California, had never visited Japan, and like two-thirds of those incarcerated, was an American citizen. While the violation of civil rights and due process of the 120,000 Japanese Americans living in the western states who were incarcerated during World War II has been recognized and redressed in recent years by the courts and legislature, in 1940s America, making the distinction between the Japanese nation and Japanese Americans seemed incredible. Nevertheless, in 1946 Asawa managed to transfer to Black Mountain College where she studied with Josef Albers and Buckminster Fuller, among others, in a provocative milieu of artistic experimentation that emphasized the process and conceptualization of art making as meaningful as the final art object. That Black Mountain College would become the most significant center for arts education during this period further complicates our understanding of mid-century limitations on women and Japanese Americans, given Asawa's access to and acceptance there. Asawa went on to break new boundaries outside the realm of art as well, with her work in childhood education that resulted in the Alvarado School in San Francisco, still thriving today.

For Asawa, the integrated approach to art making espoused by Albers provided the template for all subsequent practices. Work in the home, the public schools, and in specific sites replaced the need for a discrete studio art practice. In her early work of the 1950s and 1960s, Asawa was concerned with investigations of sculptural space, particularly through the manipulation of wire. The works evoked the process of crocheting and weaving—of women's work—at the same time as they evinced an interest in the abstract fashioning of organic form, suggestive of the body but clearly not representative of it.[14] This art challenged disciplinary boundaries—among some of the critical responses to her work were questions as to whether it was indeed sculpture, rather than craft or design[15]—at the same time it explored a number of binary relationships through its indeterminacy: movement vs. stasis, interior vs. exterior, form vs. space, art vs. craft. On the surface, Asawa's wire sculpture would seem to bear little connection to her experiences as a Japanese American woman, especially in light of later projects where she would take on this subject directly and representationally, such as her bronze public art sculpture commemorating the Japanese American incarceration installed in downtown San Jose in 1995. However, in their challenge to the then-current understanding of sculptural practice, her early work provides a conceptual analogy to aspects of her persona that defied conventional profiles. Asawa was a woman artist working at a time when men were predominant, a self-identified homemaker and a professional artist, and a representative of the United States in an international art arena just ten years after

Parallels

Japanese Americans were incarcerated because they were seen as un-American.[16] Could it be argued that Asawa's abstract work, which defies easy categorization, provides a more complex relationship to her status and experience, one that, ironically, is less present in her later, more direct work?

In examining the abstract paintings of Hisako Hibi, it is difficult to decode the trajectory of her long and at times tragic life. A generation older than Asawa and a Japanese immigrant to the United States, Hibi too had been incarcerated during World War II. Thirty-five years old at the time of incarceration, she was the mother of two young children and the wife of an accomplished painter twenty years her senior.[17] Her studies at the California School of Fine Arts (now the San Francisco Art Institute) in the 1930s had endowed her with some measure of training. In the camps she not only created an extensive body of paintings, she taught in the art schools established there by fellow Japanese American artists Chiura Obata and George Matsusaburo Hibi, her husband.[18] It wasn't until decades later—after the untimely death of her husband in 1947, followed by her years as a single mother supporting her family by working as a seamstress in New York City, and her return to California—that her work reached a level of formal and conceptual cohesion that demonstrates the emergence of a specific vision. Interestingly, Hibi appears to have been

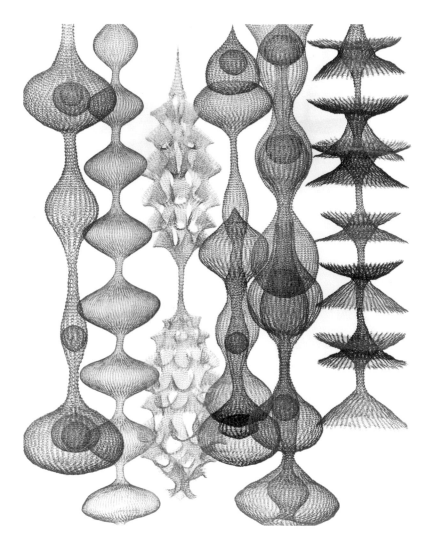

16
Ruth Asawa, *Group of Architectural Works*, 1955–65. Copper and brass wire (dimensions variable). Photo: Laurence Cuneo. Collection of the artist.

Japanese and their bath takes place in the concentration camp barracks. A reproduction of Cassatt's original painting from the collection of the Art Institute of Chicago is lovingly affixed to the back of the canvas.[19]

When Hibi was in her sixties and seventies, she began to merge abstraction and narrative content in a single canvas, incorporating both a calligraphic line and calligraphy itself with fragments and phrases of Japanese seemingly coming into and out of focus. The dynamic tension produced by this strategy is heightened by her interest in thinning the oil paint to create an effect similar to watercolor washes. Because they are on canvas, because the paint is *not* watercolor, because they vacillate between representation and abstraction, and because the finished works are left unvarnished, the paintings appear to breathe; they appear to be alive. But rather than conveying the feeling of being quickly executed, Hibi's paintings appear as though formed over time, with a durational quality that at once contrasts with the transparency and thinness of the paint. The incorporation of Japanese writing directly relates to Hibi's ethnic heritage, but Hibi's artistic interests were far wider, as she avidly and continuously made looking at art a central part of her life. She was interested in late nineteenth century European art[20] and, toward the end of her life, she became fascinated by German contemporary painting like that of Sigmar Polke, whose retro-

fully conscious of her status as a woman artist and looked for models. A 1943 painting, *Homage to Mary Cassatt*, created in the Topaz concentration camp reworks Cassatt's 1892 painting *The Bath*. In Hibi's canvas, the woman and child are

spective she saw at the San Francisco Museum of Modern Art.

While Hibi's art reached its pinnacle when she was in her sixties and seventies, Theresa Hak Kyung Cha produced mature and fully realized work in her twenties, which is all the more tragic given her death at age thirty-one. Cha was born in Korea to parents who had lived through the Japanese colonial occupation of Korea (1905–1945) and Manchuria (1932–1945), and immigrated with her family to the United States at twelve, making her part of what would be called the "1.5 generation," a name given to denote the in-between status of young immigrants who claim a birthright to Korea but whose acculturation as Americans places them between generations and identities.[21] A number of movements converged in the tumultuous milieu of San Fran-

cisco and Berkeley of the late 1960s and early 1970s. Although Cha was a student at San Francisco State when the Third World Liberation Front, a coalition of multiethnic students, staged a strike to force the university administration to establish, among other demands, a program in ethnic studies, her affinities appeared more connected to the radical changes affecting contemporary theory, conceptual art practice, and performance. Her studies at the University of California at Berkeley, where she received a B.A. in comparative literature (1973) and both a B.A. and M.A. in art (1975 and 1977), traversed a wide range of interests, including Korean poetry, European modernism, French film theory, and the feminism of Marguerite Duras and Monique Wittig, revealing a particular interest in the systems and play of language, semiology, and an

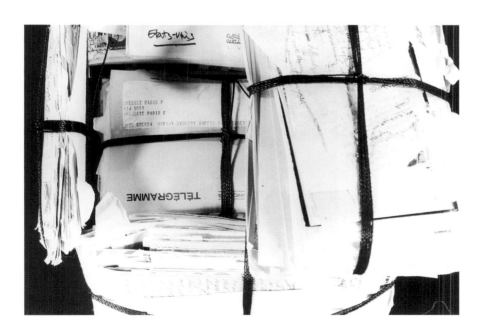

18
Theresa Hak Kyung Cha, *Passages Paysages*, 1978. Still from video. Distributed by University of California, Berkeley Art Museum; gift of the Theresa Hak Kyung Cha Memorial Foundation.

attempt to fragment and rupture existing narrative structures.

Cha found a voice in multiple forms. She created videos and video installations, artists' books, mixed media installations, performances, and performance documentation; edited an anthology of film theory, *Apparatus/Cinematographic Apparatus* (1980); and created *Dictée* (1982), a hybrid combination of autobiography, poetry, an artist's book, and biography whose form is a paperback. While the formal articulations of her art vary, it is characterized by a shared sentiment of evocative frailty and conceptual rigor. The 1977 performance "Reveillé dans la Brume" (Awakened in the mist), as described by Judith Barry, overlaid sound, slide projection, text, fire, light, movement, and Cha herself in an attempt to subvert traditional spectatorship by juxtaposing multiple narrative strands to make "an interstice through which we slip."[22] While French theory as well as the language (Cha first studied French at the Convent of the Sacred Heart High School in San Francisco) appear with great frequency in her art, Cha also liberally incorporates specifically Korean elements, whether it be the snapshots of a Korean woman and child or letters and phrases in Korean in the three-channel video installation *Passages Paysages* (1978) or the narratives of her mother and the Korean revolutionary Yu Guan Soon in *Dictée*. Although an old family photograph, letters, and spoken Korean may link the artist to a specific Korean identity, the fragmentary form of her work suggests both the necessity and inadequacy of that link as it challenges any conventionalized and simple relationship between story and meaning.

Over the last decade the number of Asian American women artists who are producing and exhibiting complex and engaging works of art has continued to increase. Many of them have taken questions of history, cultural identity, representation, and personal and collective memory as the subject of their art, and yet no one personal profile, formal approach, or discourse has proved dominant. Even when artists share a similar interest in visualizing Asian American women in their art, other factors come into play. Two women whose artistic content may have affinities in this regard are Rea Tajiri and Hung Liu. But there is a question as to whether Tajiri, who grew up as a third-generation Japanese American in Chicago and Los Angeles and trained as an artist at the California Institute of the Arts in the late 1970s and early 1980s, and Hung Liu, who was born in Changchun, China, trained in art in Beijing and later San Diego, experienced the Cultural Revolution's "re-education" (i.e., forced labor) at age eighteen, and immigrated to the United States in 1984, can be appropriately discussed in the same context. Both of their work engages in a conversation with historical models: Tajiri appropriates and reworks the conventional

19

Rea Tajiri, *Strawberry Fields*,
1997. Still from feature film
Strawberry Fields—left: Suzy
Nakamura (Irene), right: James
Sie (Luke). Distributed by
Phaedra Cinema. Cinemato-
grapher: Zack Winestine.
Collection of the artist.

forms of documentary film and road movies, while Liu pictorially conflates received images of Oriental commodities and Chinese prostitutes for Western consumption with traditional Chinese and Western painterly forms. Clearly, the form, the tenor, and the approach of their respective practices differ radically. Through her film and video projects, Tajiri has experimented with narrative and documentary forms to question the fabrications of history. Liu reprocesses traditional manifestations of China, both self-generated and externally generated, to explore the complex manufacturing of cultural identity. But if Tajiri's experiences as a third-generation

20

Hung Liu, *Mu Nu (Mother and Daughter)*, 1997. Oil paint on canvas, diptych, 80 × 140 in. Photo: Gamma One Conversions. Collection of the Kemper Museum of Contemporary Art, Kansas City, Mo., purchased with funds from the Kemper Museum of Contemporary Art.

Japanese American and Liu's experiences as a Chinese immigrant who was subjected to the harshness of the Cultural Revolution locate their production within specific historical circumstances, they only peripherally help the viewer unlock the meaning of their art.

What is the wisdom in grouping the diverse and divergent practices of these artists?

The parts that make up an individual's identity—the biography, circumstance, appearance, beliefs, and the practice—always exceed the sum, making categorical distinctions simultaneously more charged and less than adequate. So

to return to the question of what is an Asian American woman artist, we find that the term itself is so specific and yet so broadly encompassing as to render itself ambiguous and opaque, thereby relying on a situational context for meaning. Since contexts are ever changing, then a characterization like "Asian American woman artist" could be used to affirm, to delimit, to marginalize, or to valorize—all subject to slight (or major) differences in context. There is wisdom in identifying Ruth Asawa, Hisako Hibi, Theresa Hak Kyung Cha, Rea Tajiri, and Hung Liu as Asian American women artists, just as there is the need to explore the specific ways in which their own practices are shaped and formed through other frameworks. The "I" of Mitsuye Yamada's poem, which opens this essay, understood this. Proud of her position as an Asian American woman in other contexts—even if a minority in a world hostile to her—she knew that in this case, "he" used it to delimit her, to mark her world and her existence using his terms. The "I" in turn chooses another reality. Cha described one of her performances, citing Roland Barthes, as "a plurality of entrances, the opening of networks, and infinity of languages,"[23] a fitting way to characterize an approach to thinking and writing about artists, whether women or Asian American.

Notes

The author wishes to thank Yong Soon Min for her insight and assistance.

1   Mitsuye Yamada, "Looking Out," in *Camp Notes and Other Poems* (Latham, N.Y.: Kitchen Table: Women of Color Press, 1992), p. 39. See also Yamada's *Camp Notes and Other Writings* (Piscataway, N.J.: Rutgers University Press, 1998).

2   Neil Gotanda, "Interview with Alex Hing, Minister of Information of the Red Guard Army," *Aion* 1, no. 1 (Spring 1970): 32.

3   Frank Chin, Jeffery Paul Chan, Lawson Fusao Inada, and Shawn Wong, eds., *Aiiieeeee! An Anthology of Asian-American Writers* (Washington, D.C.: Howard University Press, 1974), p. vii.

4   See Yen Le Espiritu, *Asian American Panethnicity: Bridging Institutions and Identities* (Philadelphia: Temple University Press, 1992).

5   Elaine Kim, *Asian American Literature: An Introduction to the Writings and Their Social Context* (Philadelphia: Temple University Press, 1982), p. xii.

6   Stanley Karnow and Nancy Yoshihara, *Asian Americans in Transition* (New York: The Asia Society, 1992). The statistics cited derive from the U.S. Bureau of the Census, 1990.

7   Ibid., p. 17.

8   Renee Tajima-Peña and Christine Choy's groundbreaking film—*Who Killed Vincent Chin*—substantially impacted the understanding of the Chin case.

9   See Espiritu, pp. 47–49; Espiritu notes a number of instances where Asian American women, although active in the movement, were marginalized within both the debates of the movement and its leadership. It is interesting to note, however, that women leaders and a feminist agenda at times coexisted within a general milieu of sexism. This was made possible by the decentralized and constantly changing nature of the movement and the individuals involved. I am thinking here of the catalytic leadership of poet and activist Janice Mirikatani. See for instance Mirikitani's "Until the People Win . . ." and the accompanying photo-essay, which depicts North Vietnamese women in a variety of settings and situations: as health care providers and students, laboring in factories and construction sites, toting guns, and engaged in combat. *Aion* 1, no. 2 (Fall 1971): 30–51.

10 See Susie Ling, "The Mountain Movers: Asian American Women's Movement in Los Angeles" (M.A. thesis, University of California, Los Angeles, 1984). Yolanda M. Lopez and Moira Roth explore the intersections of women of color and feminist art practice in "Social

Protest: Racism and Sexism," in Norma Broude and Mary D. Garrard, eds., *The Power of Feminist Art* (New York: Harry N. Abrams, 1994), pp. 140–157.

11 Lucy Lippard, cited in Broude and Garrard, p. 10.

12 In *Aiiieeeee!*, the introductory essays and the anthology section are separated by a page that states, "Asian American Writers: We are Not New Here." That the writings of the earlier authors are integrated with those who came of age during the Asian American movement further emphasizes the direct relevance of the earlier work to contemporaneous practices.

13 Maxine Hong Kingston calls this a "terrible stereotype," in "One Hundred Beautiful Things," *With New Eyes: Toward an Asian American Arts History in the West* (exhibition catalogue) (San Francisco: San Francisco State University, 1995), p. 7.

14 While Asawa's work has been directly linked to her studies with Josef Albers, her relationship to Anni Albers, Josef's wife and an artist who made weavings, bears further scrutiny especially vis-à-vis the recent feminist recuperation and recasting of traditional women's work. For a examination of contemporary artists whose practice engages in domestic labors (Anni Albers's work is not included), see Lydia Yee, *Division of Labor: "Women's Work" in Contemporary Art* (Bronx: Bronx Museum of Art, 1995).

15 Gerald Nordland, *Ruth Asawa: A Retrospective View* (San Francisco: San Francisco Museum of Art, 1973), n.p. Nordland reviews the criticism of Asawa's early exhibitions of wire sculptures and notes that in 1953 and 1954 she exhibited with "craftsmen."

16 Asawa participated in the São Paulo Biennale in 1955. Her Japanese surname would have had specific resonance for the residents of São Paulo, which currently has the largest population of individuals of Japanese ancestry outside of Japan.

17 I am indebted to Kristine Kim and her exhibition brochure, *A Process of Reflection: Paintings by Hisako Hibi*, published on the occasion of an exhibition of Hibi's paintings at the Japanese American National Museum, July 1999–January 2000; and to Ibuki Hibi Lee.

18 For a detailed examination of Obata's art and activities of the Tanforan and Topaz art schools, see Kimi Kodani Hill, ed., *Topaz Moon: Chiura Obata's Art of the Internment* (Berkeley: Heyday Books, 2000).

19 Karin Higa, *The View from Within: Japanese American Art from the Internment Camps, 1942–1945* (Los Angeles: UCLA Wight Art Gallery, Japanese American National Museum, and UCLA Asian American Studies Center, 1992), pp. 27–28, 75.

20 Higa, p. 25.

21 Biographical information comes from Moira Roth, "Theresa Hak Kyung Cha 1951–1982: A Narrative Chronology," in Elaine H. Kim and Norma Alarcon, eds., *Writing Self, Writing Nation: Essays on Theresa Hak Kyung Cha's Dictée* (Berkeley: Third Woman Press, 1994), pp. 151–160. It is important to note that the actual term "1.5 generation" does not come into use until the years after Cha's death.

22 Judith Barry, "Women, Representation, and Performance Art: Northern California," in Carl E. Loeffler and Darlene Tong, eds., *Performance Anthology: Source Book of California Performance Art* (San Francisco: Last Gasp Press and Contemporary Arts Press, 1989), pp. 439–468. It was originally published in 1980.

23 Cited in Abigail Solomon-Godeau, "Theresa Hak Kyung Cha at the Matrix Gallery, University Art Museum," *Art in America* 73 (April 1985): 190–191.

From "THE POET IN THE WORLD"

Denise Levertov

Our age appears to me a chaos and our environment lacks the qualities for which one could call it a culture. But by way of consolation we have this knowledge of power that perhaps no one in such a supposed harmonious time had; what in the greatest poets is recognizable as Imagination, that breathing of life into the dust, is present in us all embryonically—manifests itself in the life of dream—and in that manifestation shows us the possibility to permeate, to quicken, all of our life and the works we make. What joy to be reminded by truth in dream that the Imagination does not arise from the environment but has the power to create it!

LAURA MEYER

CONSTRUCTING A NEW PARADIGM

European American Women Artists
in California, 1950–2000

Art in the post–World War II era comprises many histories, many media and thematic issues, and many ethnic and cultural traditions that have marked out separate paths, while simultaneously overlapping, in instances, to establish common ground. Women artists of European American descent occupy a uniquely intermediate position within the art establishment. During the years when Japanese American citizens in California faced imprisonment in internment camps, when African Americans began to organize the Civil Rights movement, and Latino farmworkers joined forces under the leadership of Dolores Huerta and Cesar Chavez, European American women experienced the benefits of membership in the dominant social group, including, for many, the expectation of attending a college or university. In California, their enjoyment of a certain degree of social and economic privilege was coupled with a comparatively undeveloped art context and a relatively permissive and experimental cultural milieu. As European Americans, additionally, white artists felt a greater degree of identification with the Eurocentric canon of modern art, claiming it as their own tradition, than did women of other ethnic groups. In short, they undeniably had concrete advantages not available to artists of color.

As women, however, white artists faced daunting obstacles to their creative freedom, as well as their professional survival. After World War II, they met with renewed opposition to their participation in the public realm, due both to the new postwar ideal

of feminine domesticity and the emergent tri-
umphalism of American art criticism which
idealized an implicitly "masculine" genius for
abstract thinking and transcendent action.
During the 1950s and 1960s, the few women who
gained a toehold in the art establishment hewed
closely to the formalist ideals of modernist
abstraction. The feminist art movement of the
1970s arose in response to such limitations,
introducing explicitly autobiographical subject
matter, body-based imagery, and traditionally
feminine craft media into the realm of high art.
In California's wide-open cultural arena, in contrast to New York's more institutionalized art
world, women artists placed less emphasis on
gaining parity with men in already existing institutions, and focused more on developing new art
strategies and separate networks for themselves.

By politicizing art, through an emphasis on
autobiography and community-building, the
feminist art movement in California in the 1970s
laid important groundwork for activism by artists
from many cultures outside the mainstream. At
the same time, the predominantly white movement was criticized for failing to consider the
diversity of women's experience. Since the
1980s, increased dialogue among women artists
of diverse ethnic and racial groups has led to
greater awareness, in turn enriching our visual
heritage. Poised on the verge of the new millennium, contemporary artists are revisiting the

themes of the last half-century with increased
flexibility and insight.

Women and Modernism: The 1950s and 1960s

In the wake of World War II, a groundswell of
artistic activity developed in the San Francisco
Bay Area, nurtured by the local art schools, newly
flush with students and GI Bill tuition monies,
and a regional tradition of political liberalism
and bohemian culture. Between 1945 and 1950,
with the critical ascendance of abstract expressionism, the center of the Western art world
shifted from Paris to New York. In San Francisco,
the California School of Fine Arts (now the San
Francisco Art Institute), under the leadership of
Douglas MacAgy, attracted as teachers nationally
known avant-garde abstract painters, including
Clyfford Still, Mark Rothko, and Ad Reinhardt;
and also employed a dynamic group of local
figurative painters, including David Park, Elmer
Bischoff, and Hassel Smith. The aesthetic culture of the California School of Fine Arts and
the larger Bay Area art community that orbited
around it was thus shaped equally by the some of
the finest early practitioners of abstract expressionism and some of its earliest dissidents.
Attitude was more important than style, as former students remember it; the most important
thing was to prove one's "seriousness" and dedication to one's work. Yet those who were taken
seriously were, for the most part, white men.

Nevertheless, several women, including Sonia Getchoff, Jay DeFeo, Deborah Remington, and Joan Brown, succeeded in negotiating this male-dominated institutional network to establish reputations for themselves.

Sonia Getchoff provided Bay Area women artists with a valuable link to the abstract expressionist avant-garde on the East Coast, where she was born and educated. After joining the faculty of the California School of Fine Arts in 1951, Getchoff soon became identified with the "California School" of abstraction, drawing critical accolades for her "openness to experience and the ability to project immediate sensations" into her work.[1] As an instructor and a successful practicing artist, Getchoff was an important mentor and role model for younger women artists.

Jay DeFeo took up the torch of avant-garde painting from Getchoff (the two were good friends and often painted together), but ultimately challenged the ideology of freedom and transcendence associated with abstract expressionism. DeFeo's radiant, mandala-like abstractions of the late 1950s replaced the abstract expressionist model of the creative individual defined through spontaneous action with a metaphor for the self developed over time, through the obsessive, almost devotional, repetition of simple gestures. Her legendary painting, *The Rose*, a tremendous, radiating, convex accumulation of more than two thousand pounds of oil paint, absorbed all of

DeFeo's efforts over a seven-year period between 1958 and 1965, coming to function as a palimpsest of her daily activity—each day's effort invisible in itself, yet contributing to a monumental sum.

Deborah Remington developed a clean, sensuous style of hard-edge abstraction more akin to abstract surrealism than the brushy abstraction and figurative painting taught at the California School of Fine Arts, where she studied from 1949 to 1952. The curvy, anthropomorphic forms of *Balaton* (1965), for example, simultaneously evoke the precision and complexity of machinery and the softness of flesh. With their rounded, open forms and central compositions, both Remington's and DeFeo's paintings might be considered prescient examples of "central core" imagery, or female sexual imagery, as it was later theorized during the feminist art movement in the 1970s.[2]

Joan Brown mastered the conventions of abstraction and then playfully remade them into a vehicle for a deeply personal, autobiographical body of work. In 1957, when she was still a student at the California School of Fine Arts,

Brown's abstract expressionist painting *Brambles* won second prize in a juried exhibition, edging out entries by better-established male painters Richard Diebenkorn, Nathan Oliveira, and David Park. The same year, Brown made some of the first "funk" assemblages in the Bay Area—dark, witty confabulations of scrap paper and cast-off junk, bundled and tied into animal forms—which she exhibited in a solo show at the Spatsa Gallery in 1958. Described by the artist as surrogates for her own fears and desires, animals continued to populate Brown's paintings over the next thirty years until her untimely death in 1990. Beginning around 1960, Brown made her family, her friends, and her own daily travails the explicit subject of her work. This break with abstraction cost Brown her affiliation with Staempfli Gallery, in New York, and ushered in a ten-year period of critical obscurity. In her mature paintings of the 1970s and 1980s, Brown subverted the modernist imperative toward "flatness" by exploiting the decorative (i.e., "feminine") and narrative possibilities of the flat picture plane, illustrating her travels, her memories, and her personal relationships in swift outline and broad blocks of unmodulated color.

In traditionally conservative Southern California, avant-garde art didn't gain significant institutional support until around 1960. Female mentors included painters Helen Lundeberg and Joyce Treiman, sculptor Claire Falkenstein,

23
Joan Brown, *The Journey #2*, 1976.
Enamel on canvas, 90 × 72 in.
Photo: courtesy of the San Francisco
Arts Commission. Collection of the
City and County of San Francisco,
San Francisco International Airport.

mixed-media artist Betye Saar, and printmaker June Wayne, all of whom had come of age before World War II and continued to be active afterward.[3] When the Los Angeles art boom of the 1960s did arrive, however, it ushered in a high-stakes commercial game that was even less hospitable to women artists than the more informal, bohemian atmosphere of the Bay Area art community in the previous decade. The now-legendary Ferus Gallery, founded in Los Angeles in 1957, became a showcase for objects made from shiny industrial materials developed for the aerospace industry and popularized in consumer products such as race cars, motorcycles, boats, and surfboards. As Pop art and minimalism began to challenge abstract expressionism's hegemony in the early 1960s, the cool, high-tech sensibility of this so-called "finish fetish" art attracted international acclaim to Southern California artists, and soon Los Angeles supported twenty-five or thirty commercially viable art galleries. Yet, women remained on the margins of the expanding art market. Galleries, critics, and collectors favored emotionally cool art and technological mastery, qualities traditionally associated with "masculine" rationality and prowess.

Two women artists who successfully navigated the Los Angeles art world in the 1960s, while introducing subtly feminist content into their work, deserve mention here. Vija Celmins was included in the 1966 anthology entitled *California*

Pop Art, drawing notice for her meticulously rendered oil paintings of heaters, hot plates, and other common household appliances. The essayist identified them as "warmly domestic pictures," going against the grain of Pop's cool irony.[4] Their laboriously handmade facture, as well as their subject matter, bespeak a homespun sensibility. Yet other critics detected a foreboding quality in Celmins's isolated subjects, which cast an eerie glow in an otherwise desolate field.

Maria Nordman, who is better known today in Europe than in the United States, helped pioneer the distinctively Southern California field of "light and space" art. Nordman extended the surface luminosity and optical effects of finish fetish art into new areas. While Robert Irwin, Douglas Wheeler, and James Turrell created luminous spectacles with fluorescent lights and scrim, or monumental constructions designed to intensify and channel natural light, Nordman created sculpture by subtraction. Drawing the viewer's attention to everyday light, she created contemplative environments that fostered a heightened awareness of the individual's relationship to the surrounding environment.

California women also founded and operated two important printmaking workshops during this period. June Wayne, with support from the Ford Foundation, opened the Tamarind Lithography Workshop in 1959. Designed to bring the art of lithography to a new level of excellence in the United States, Tamarind operated in Wayne's Hollywood studio until 1970, when it was transferred to the University of New Mexico in Albuquerque. Kathan Brown, an artist herself, started Crown Point Press in Oakland in 1962. In 1986 she relocated to San Francisco and in 1989 established a permanent base on Hawthorne Street. Crown Point specializes in reviving old techniques, including etching, intaglio, and Asian woodcut techniques, for application to new art ideas.

The Feminist Art Movement: The 1970s

The 1970s marked a watershed for California women artists. In previous decades, women had been tokens in the male-dominated art establishment, and their critical success depended upon adhering to the formalist values of the mainstream. While women artists often subverted viewers' expectations in subtle ways, they risked rejection if they directly challenged Clement Greenberg's dictum that modern art should "confine itself to what is given in visual experience and make no reference to any other orders of experience."[5]

Around 1970, the rising tide of the Women's Liberation movement began to spill over into the art world. Women artists across the nation organized activist groups, including the Los Angeles Council of Women Artists and the New York-based Women Artists in Revolution and the Ad Hoc Women Artists' Committee, to protest the dearth of work by women in museum and gallery exhibitions. Perhaps even more importantly, feminist artists, critics, and art historians began to challenge traditional art theory, attempting to redefine "high art" and its function in society. Artists in California played an especially important role in developing the concept of a unique "female sensibility" in art, a notion that came to characterize feminist art and art activism of the 1970s.

The most prominent figure in the West Coast feminist art movement was artist, educator, and activist Judy Chicago. A charismatic leader, as well as an inventive artist, Chicago galvanized a generation of young women to channel their personal experiences into politically charged art. In 1970, she founded the nation's first feminist art education program at California State University, Fresno, where she and her all-female students used feminist consciousness-raising techniques to explore potential themes for their artwork. The young women used unconventional and/or historically feminine media, including domestic crafts, costume, and performance, to explore their feelings about traditional gender roles, personal relationships, and sexuality. In this context, Chicago and her students began making images of the female sex organs, later theorized as "central core" imagery, as a symbol of pride in their identity as women. Artist Faith Wilding, who participated in the Feminist Art Program, describes the liberating sense of power associated with cunt art:

> [We were] defiantly recuperating a term that traditionally had been used derogatorily and thereby opposing the phallic imagery developed by men. We vied with each other to come up with images of female sexual organs by making paintings, drawings, and constructions of bleeding slits, holes and gashes, boxes, caves, or exquisite jewel pillows. Making "cunt art" was exciting, subversive, and fun, because cunt signified to us an awakened consciousness about our bodies and our sexual selves.[6]

Over the course of the decade, Chicago spread her message in increasingly public venues. In 1971, she collaborated with Miriam Schapiro to relocate the Feminist Art Program to the prestigious California Institute of the Arts. The ambitious project *Womanhouse* (1972), which grew out of the program, attracted national media attention. *Womanhouse* was a series of fantasy environments that explored the postwar ideal of feminine domesticity, with installations including Faith Wilding's room-sized, crocheted enclosure, *Womb Room* (or *Crocheted Environment*); Susan Frazier, Vicki Hodgett and Robin Weltsch's *Nurturant Kitchen*, where molded-foam fried eggs gradually transmuted into pendulous breasts; and Chicago's confrontational *Menstruation Bathroom*,

overflowing with bloodstained sanitary products. That same year, Chicago left CalArts and, with her colleagues the designer Sheila Levrant de Bretteville and art historian Arlene Raven, established the nation's first fully independent all-women's art school, the Feminist Studio Workshop. The culmination of Chicago's efforts to promote female imagery was her monumental 1979 installation, *The Dinner Party* (see fig. 47). Wrought collaboratively with hundreds of artists and non-artists, *The Dinner Party* consisted of an enormous triangular table of handmade porcelain plates decorated with central core imagery and laid out on hand-embroidered runners, honoring thirty-nine "great women" in history and myth.

Feminist artists in California pursued the notion of a female sensibility in a variety of media. By the early 1970s, Miriam Schapiro abandoned her earlier style of minimalist abstract painting for collages of fabric and lace, which she termed "femmage." In the words of Thalia Gouma-Peterson, Schapiro "did not wish to deal with domesticity 'minimally,' but with a Victorian abundance of both sentiment and ornament."[7] Her monumental 1983 collage, *Wonderland* (see fig. 45), is composed of hundreds of pieces of fabric and lace arranged in a quilt-like pattern around a central needlework image of a curtsying housewife. Others, including Judith Linhares in the Bay Area and Kim MacConnel and Robert Kushner in San Diego, helped

24

Judy Dater, *Self-Portrait with Stone*, 1981, Badlands, South Dakota. Gelatin silver print, 20 × 24 in. © Judy Dater 1981. Collection of the artist.

initiate a "pattern and decoration" movement that celebrated feminine decoration and non-Western pattern art.

De Bretteville, who, before the Feminist Studio Workshop, had founded the Women's Design Program at CalArts and later co-founded the Woman's Building in Los Angeles, sought to develop a democratic form of graphic design based on what she viewed as a feminine model of collaboration (as opposed to the more traditional, "masculine" emphasis on hierarchy). De Bretteville's famous poster, *Pink* (1974), initially designed as one-of-a-kind for a Whitney Museum exhibition on color, recorded the views of thirty-six women about the meaning of pink, leaving open spaces for viewers to add their own responses as well. She implemented a similar, egalitarian format in her design for *Chrysalis*, a journal of women's art and poetry published at the Woman's Building, honoring each contributor with her own two-page spread, and leaving empty pages for readers to add their own artwork and commentary.

Photographing herself nude in the wilderness, Bay Area artist Judy Dater created a series of powerful self-portraits evoking the figure of the "great goddess" popularized in feminist literature as a symbol of nature and the feminine

divine. In *Self-Portrait with Stone* (1981), for example, a woman is curled into a fetal, rock-like position, delicately juxtaposed and at the same time absorbed into the rough terrain. In *Self-Portrait with Sparkler* (1980), Dater stands on the rim of a volcanic crater with sparks flashing between her legs. Pictured without costume or makeup, often engaged in acts of physical strength or endurance, these figures emphasize the power and natural beauty of the female body, eschewing the cultural stereotypes of feminine frailty and artifice.

Performance developed into an especially important art form for women artists in the 1970s, providing a vehicle for personal catharsis, social critique, and community outreach. In Southern California, the most important venue for performance art was the Woman's Building, a cultural center in downtown Los Angeles that housed the Feminist Studio Workshop, several women's performance collectives, Womanspace Gallery, the Feminist Press, the Los Angeles chapter of the National Organization for Women, and other female-run galleries, cultural organizations, and businesses. The Woman's Building was the most influential and longest-running feminist cultural institution in the United States, remaining in operation for eighteen years, from 1973 to 1991. Steven Durland, former editor of *High Performance* magazine, credited feminist performance artists working at the Woman's

Building with reinventing the performance idiom:

> In performance art, most of what had come before was formal experimentation. Had feminist art not come along, the form would probably have died a natural death. Not only did they take the form and politicize it, but they [oriented it toward] autobiography. Now that's used by artists from cultures outside the mainstream for self- and group-affirmation. It's a way of letting people know that they aren't alone.[8]

Feminist Studio Workshop instructor Suzanne Lacy developed a community-based performance structure to address the issue of violence against women, eliciting participation from the media, the city government, and other local agencies. Lacy's *Three Weeks in May* (1977), for example, recorded daily rape reports during a three-week period on a twenty-five-foot map posted in a busy shopping center near the Los Angeles City Hall. The goal of the project was not only to raise public awareness, but to empower women to fight back and to transcend the sense of secrecy and shame associated with rape. Always concrete, Lacy made a second map charting the names, locations, and telephone numbers of community service centers for rape victims. Other events during the three-week performance period included a press conference, a rape "speak out," and self-defense demonstrations. The performance led to concrete policy changes, prompting the city government and police to publicize rape hotlines and speak openly about violence against women. By tackling issues of broad concern, Lacy and her collaborating partner Leslie Labowitz used performance art to unite women from different backgrounds around a common cause, demonstrating that through collaboration women could effect change in the structures of institutionalized power.

Many women artists in the 1970s used performance to challenge the traditional boundaries of feminine identity by elaborating multiple personas with separate histories, professions, and racial and sexual identities. Since 1972, performance artist Eleanor Antin has documented three highly developed alter egos, including an idealized masculine figure, The King of Solana Beach; an archetypal artist, the black ballerina Eleanora Antinova; and The Nurse, "a jaunty blend of servant and geisha, sharing features with many other women's service professions like secretaries, airline stewardesses and wives."[9] In the Bay Area, Linda Montano blurred the boundaries between art and life, inhabiting her characters, such as the Chicken Woman (1972), over extended periods. Lynn Hershman Leeson provided photographs, diary entries, psychiatrist's records, resumes, and so forth to track the life of her created persona, Roberta Breitmore, over a three-year period between 1975 and 1978, drawing

on her observations of the women around her.

In Los Angeles, performer Rachel Rosenthal, who was born in Paris between the world wars and worked with Antonin Artaud, Merce Cunningham, and John Cage before founding Instant Theater in Los Angeles in 1956, provided a link with an earlier era of modernist theater. Barbara Smith's early performances in Los Angeles, including *Ritual Meal* (1969) and *The Celebration of the Holy Squash* (1971), transformed the act of eating into a meditation on the relationship between humans and the plant and animal worlds, with its potential for either violence or harmony. The Feminist Art Workers, a performance group founded at the Woman's Building in 1976 by Nancy Angelo, Cheri Gaulke, Vanalyne Green, and Laurel Klick, took feminist performance on the road, traveling across the United States and sharing their message in coffee houses, restaurants, and college classes. The Waitresses, another performance group based at the Woman's Building, performed guerrilla actions in restaurants, in addition to appearing in more traditional venues. Nancy Buchanan combined autobiographical narrative with sociopolitical critique in performances such as *Fallout from the Nuclear Family* (1981), drawing on the personal papers of her nuclear physicist father.

Around the state, performance artist Bonnie Sherk established a working farm in 1974 on five acres of undeveloped land under a freeway inter-

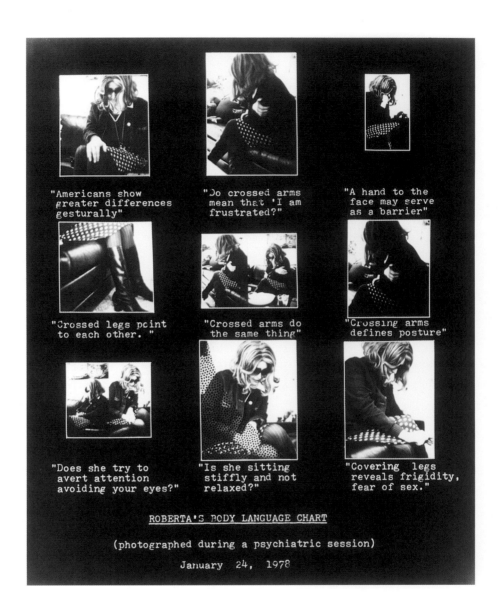

25
Lynn Hershman Leeson, *Roberta's
Body Language Chart (photographed
during a psychiatric session)*, 1977.
Gelatin silver print, 30 × 40 in.
Collection of the artist.

change in San Francisco, complete with crops and animals, as well as a performance center (The Raw Egg Theater) and art classes for children, senior citizens, and psychiatric patients (see fig. 64). Sherk's urban farm and art center, Crossroads Community, was the first of her "Life Frames," or models for social responsibility and integrated living. Martha Rosler, working in San Diego, criticized the dehumanization of the individual in bureaucratic, technological society in her 1974 performance, *Vital Statistics of a Citizen, Simply Obtained,* which was later made into a video (see fig. 96). Artists turned to video and film in the 1970s as a natural outgrowth of the desire to document performance. However, new media quickly developed into an exciting art practice in its own right. Today, in the work of Los Angeles artists such as Diana Thater, Jennifer Steinkamp, and Jessica Bronson, video has come full circle, reincorporating performance, only this time with the viewer as the performer by virtue of being placed within the image/installation.

Art publications proliferated in California beginning in the 1970s, nearly all of them founded or edited by women, including *Artweek* (Cecile McCann), *Visual Dialog* (Roberta Loach), *High Performance* (Linda Frye Burnham), *Umbrella* (Judith Hoffberg), *Visions* (Betty Ann Brown), *Chrysalis* (Kirsten Grimstad and Susan Rennie), *Shift* (Anne MacDonald), *Courant* (Leslie Wenger),

Newsletter (Judy Slotnick), and *West Art* (Jean Couzens).

Not all California women artists active in the 1970s worked under the auspices of feminist institutions. In addition to Nordman and Celmins, Alexis Smith, Karen Carson, and Helen Harrison, to name just a few, worked outside the educational and political apparatus established by the Feminist Art Program and the Woman's Building. However, these women's artistic strategies, as well as their critical successes, cannot be fully appreciated outside the context of the feminist art movement. Smith's and Carson's 1970s work exploited so-called feminine media that gained expressive power through their association with contemporary feminist theory. (Both artists participated in feminist consciousness-raising groups.) Smith's inclusion in a 1972 exhibition at the Los Angeles County Museum of Art, *Four Los Angeles Artists,* was the direct result of feminist activism on the part of the Los Angeles Council of Women Artists, which organized in the fall of 1970 to protest the near-total exclusion of women from the museum's highly publicized *Art and Technology* exhibition. And the Woman's Building sponsored the earliest environmentalist performances and installations created by Helen Harrison and her husband, Newton.

Alexis Smith's collages anticipated many of the deconstructionist strategies developed by feminist artists in the 1980s, highlighting the ways in

which seemingly fixed identities are cobbled together out of the transient "truths" provided by our media culture. Smith's first collages were assembled from the ordinary, ephemeral materials that teenage girls have long employed to create personal scrapbooks—typing paper, magazine photos, newspaper clippings, and the like. *Charlie Chan* (1973–74), for example, pairs an old Hollywood cliché about art and madness, credited to the outsider, Chan ("madman twin brother of genius: both live in world created by own ego"), with the results of a scientific study showing certain psychological similarities between schizophrenics and artists. While it is rife with cliché—a caricature of popular ideas about madness, artistic genius, gender, race, and identity—*Charlie Chan* balances skepticism with whimsy and affection, suggesting that we must sift through the many stories we are told to find our own truths.

Karen Carson created a series of monumental,

cubist-style "paintings" out of cotton duck and zippers for her 1971 master's exhibition at the University of California, Los Angeles. Her "zipper pieces" invited audience participation, allowing viewers to unzip and zip up the fabric to create different compositions. Thus, Carson playfully outdid traditional cubist painting by truly offering multiple perspectives to the viewer, rather than merely suggesting them, as cubism is believed to do. At the same time, the zipper pieces suggest a democratic attitude toward artistic creativity, incorporating degraded, "feminine" craft elements, and transferring artistic authority from the artist to the audience.

Helen Harrison, working in partnership with her husband, Newton Harrison, was among the first artists to make ecology the focus of her art. In 1970, the Harrisons began to document a dialogue between two mythological alter-egos, the Lagoonmaker (Newton) and the Witness (Helen),

drawing attention to the complex and sometimes conflicting ecological and philosophical issues involved in exploiting and safeguarding the environment. The Harrisons' projects have grown increasingly ambitious over time, including idealistic proposals for ecological interventions around the world, documented with photographs, maps, diagrams, and text. In many cases their artwork has led to tangible results. The World Bank decided to support the purification of the Sava River in Serbia and Croatia, for example, in response to one of their proposals.

Critiques of Representation: The 1980s

By the end of the decade, the idea of a feminine sensibility promoted by California women artists in the 1970s faced challenges from many quarters. Avant-garde critics deemed the notion of female imagery "essentialist," arguing that artwork focusing on women's bodies, women's

26
Alexis Smith, *Charlie Chan*, 1973–74. Mixed-media collage, two panels, 12 × 45 in. each. Photo: Paula Goldman. The Museum of Contemporary Art, Los Angeles, Gift of Frank and Berta Gehry, Santa Monica.

27
Karen Carson, *Untitled,* 1971. Cotton duck/zipper, 95 × 83 in. Photo: Douglas M. Parker. Courtesy of Rosamund Felsen Gallery.

crafts, or any subject matter traditionally associated with women only served to perpetuate sexual stereotypes and to prevent women artists from joining the mainstream. Drawing on poststructuralist linguistics, as well as Marxist theory and French psychoanalytic theory, feminists in many quarters, especially in New York and Great Britain, held that the best strategy for challenging the status quo was to resist the seductive power of beautiful images and familiar narratives through deconstruction or Brechtian distantiation.

Women of color and lesbian women also took white women and heterosexual women to task for failing to adequately address the variety of female experience and the multiplicity of challenges faced by women outside the dominant, heterosexual European American culture. Many of the tensions that began to develop among the women active in the feminist art movement came to a head at the Los Angeles Woman's Building in the late 1970s and early 1980s.

Racial imbalance was one of the most persistent obstacles to the goal of the Woman's Building, to create a community where all women artists could find support. Many felt that white women at the Woman's Building tried to impose their own narrow ideas about the nature of feminism and feminist art without trying to understand the experiences and values of women from different cultural backgrounds. As awareness of

the importance of race issues in the feminist movement developed in the 1980s, the Woman's Building responded by sponsoring increasing numbers of exhibitions, classes, readings, and other programming directed toward women of diverse ethnic backgrounds. Lesbian women at the Woman's Building also complained of feeling invisible in the early years. In the late 1970s and 1980s, however, lesbians increasingly played a leadership role, filling crucial administrative positions and spearheading large-scale projects such as *An Oral Herstory of Lesbianism* (1979), which was a series of workshops and performances directed and produced by Terry Wolverton, and the *Great American Lesbian Art Show* (1980).

The 1980s witnessed a broad shift in attitude on the part of women artists. While the importance of feminist institutions waned, the visibility of women in mainstream galleries and museums increased. Rather than attempting to create new, more "truthful" images of women, feminists critiqued the notion that there could be any essential feminine identity. Often employing irony and black humor, women artists focused instead on deconstructing the dominant cultural representations of sexual difference and identity.

The artist whose work best epitomizes the feminist spirit of the 1980s is, perhaps, Barbara Kruger, who has resided in Los Angeles since 1990. Her graphically striking image-text pieces, such as *Untitled (Your Gaze Hits the Side of My Face)* (1981), thwart the disembodied "male gaze" by destabilizing meaning through incongruent juxtapositions of image and text and by rendering ambiguous the implied interlocutors.

Conceptual artist Millie Wilson and photographer Catherine Opie transposed traditional representational codes for abjection and nobility into unfamiliar new contexts, thus challenging the cultural pathologization of lesbian sexuality. The intricate, curlicued forms of Wilson's *Wig/Cunt* (1990) ink drawings, juxtaposed with printed illustrations of old-fashioned men's and women's wigs, bear a striking resemblance to the elaborate hairdos. Based on drawings of clitorises made in 1948 by a male physician who claimed he could "reveal homosexuality" through the observation of women's genitals, they make the medicalization of lesbianism look as quaintly absurd as the wigs (cf. fig. 48, Wilson's 1994 *Daytona Death Angel*).

Opie's photographs of gay and lesbian members of the S&M subculture exploit the conventions of heroic Renaissance portraiture. As Opie explains,

I didn't like the way the leather culture was being represented in the mainstream culture . . . We have had a bad rap [and] I was also facing my own internalized homophobia . . . I wanted to do a series of portraits of this community that were incredibly noble.[10]

Two self-portraits, close-ups of the artist's bare chest and back, combine beauty and violence. In *Pervert* (1995), delicate cursive letters spell out the word "pervert" gouged into Opie's flesh with a knife, while *Cutting Number One* (1995) shows a child-like stick-figure image of two girls holding hands, executed in the same manner. The photographs, like the cuttings, incisively embody the violence inflicted by stereotyped representations of social outsiders, as well as Opie's desire to violate those stereotypes.

Other artists satirized the feminist concept of female imagery, as well as the historical notion of male artistic genius. Rachel Lachowitz, for example, cast reproductions of sculptures by famous male artists in brilliant red lipstick, introducing a note of irreverence into the high-stakes commercial and critical art establishment.

Not all artists approached their subject matter with irony in the 1980s. Ann Hamilton's installation for the 1988 *Home Show* in Santa Barbara, which lyrically displayed "the labor of tending," is nearly impossible to categorize. The repetitive, gestural work involved in creating the installation, with its walls of wax-encrusted leaves and its 800 ironed and folded men's shirts, bears comparison with Jay DeFeo's obsessive process, as well as the endless repetitive work of keeping

house. In the same spirit as DeFeo, Hamilton offers a model of human subjectivity based not on definitive action, but on indeterminacy and patient effort.

Between Past and Future: The Revisionist 1990s

In the final decade of the twentieth century, European American women artists in California drew on a multiplicity of artistic strategies developed over the last fifty years, synthesizing the lessons of the past as they look toward the future. The 1990s saw renewed interest in the feminist art movement of the 1970s, along with "feminine" media and imagery. More striking still was the revived interest in abstraction and notions of

formal beauty. Artists of the 1990s have infused representational and abstract painting with new life, creating images of lushness and beauty, as well as trenchant social and psychological commentary. An awareness of the cultural and political implications of art remains, however, although these meanings may appear more open-ended now than before.

Kim Dingle's "Priss" and "Wild Girl" paintings intervene in the patriarchal, imperialist myths of the American West, turning loose dozens of girls in frilly dresses to tumble, wrestle, and chase one another through the landscape. Dingle's western scenes buzz with the erotic, violent desire to touch, discover, and move, while her lushly painted surfaces convey a similar history of movement and struggle in their making. Squeak Carnworth, a Bay Area-based artist, buries fragments of text and personal narrative in determinate fields of brushed color on layered translucent surfaces. Recent abstract painters such as Monique Prieto and Ingrid Calame eschew the metaphysical ambitions of modernism, imbuing their potentially impersonal forms (Prieto's are computer-generated) with a quirky anthropomorphism. Deborah Oropollo tempers the disciplined formalism of her compositions—built up from repeated silk-screen images of model railroad tracks joined and severed, or floating clock faces without hands—by scrubbing, wiping, and painting over their surfaces, in a manner that

29

Kim Dingle, *Crazy's Pig*, 1997.
Oil on wood panels, 60 × 96 in.
Photo: Tony Cuña. Los Angeles
County Museum of Art, pur-
chased with funds provided by
the Pasadena Art Alliance and
the Modern and Contemporary
Art Acquisition Fund.

compounds her symbolism of spatial and temporal disorientation. Anne Appleby's monochrome
encaustic paintings, on the other hand, are lyrical
abstractions referencing the cyclical seasonal
change of the natural world nurtured during a
fifteen-year apprenticeship with an Ojibwa elder
in Montana. (Appleby herself is part Ojibwa.)

Sculptors are taking renewed pleasure in the
medium's capacity to confound perceptual expectations and delight the imagination. The cultural
meanings and gender associations implicit in
materials remain a given, however, at the same

time their formal limitations are extended in new
directions. Liz Larner's "heavy metal" steel-
frame sculpture, *2 as 3 and Some Too* (1997–98),
reads like a quavery line drawing of two interlocking cubes, an amateur's attempt to create the
illusion of three-dimensional space, in what is
actually a deft undermining of our expectations
of idealized geometry. Known for her playful
élan with industrial materials, Larner recently
received a commission to create a footbridge for a
new Disney building designed by architect Aldo
Rossi. Conversely, in *Mattresses and Cakes* (1993),

30

Liz Larner, *2 as 3 and Some Too*, 1997–98. Mulberry paper, steel and watercolor, two elements, 5 × 5 × 5 ft. each. Photo: Joshua White. The Museum of Contemporary Art, Los Angeles, purchased in memory of Stuart Regen with funds provided by Ethan and Thea Westreich, Pam and Dick Kramlich, Norman and Nora Stone, and Chara Schreyer.

the case of a mechanical, "truth-telling" apparatus like the camera. Sharon Lockhart's glossy Cibachrome prints, mounted behind reflective Plexiglas, implicate the viewer visually, as well as conceptually, in their indeterminate narratives. Catherine Wagner uses medical imaging devices to home in on biological systems—the brain, the heart, the carotid artery, and the rapidly multiplying cells of the human embryo—that form the basis of human life, yet are not recognizably human.

Since the 1990s women artists have played an increasingly prominent role in shaping public spaces. Public monuments and installations by Johanna Poethig, Anna Valentina Murch, Susan Schwartzenberg, and Ann Chamberlain nurture the imagination within the urban environment, emphasizing the intersections of social and psychological space. Johanna Poethig is an artist and teacher from the Bay Area who focuses her efforts on collaborative installations for public schools and neighborhood arts projects and centers. Anna Valentina Murch, as part of a team of artists commissioned to help design the St. Louis Metro, recycled 160,000 pounds of rejected colored glass to create a shifting, ephemeral light show, *Light Passageway* (1993–99), in the Stygian darkness of the tunnel leading from the last urban metro stop. Transforming viewers' physical journey into a psychological one, Murch strives, in all her work, to connect people with

Nancy Rubins molds the feminine domestic raw materials into a threatening, bulging sculpture suspended some twenty feet high. Her use of beds and cakes suggests both the self-indulgence of sugar, sex, and slovenliness, and the storage (and threatened release) of terrific amounts of energy, which is a theme that runs throughout Rubins's work.

Recent photography emphasizes the open-endedness of interpretation that inheres even in

32

Anna Valentina Murch, *Light Passageway*, St. Louis Metro, 1993–99. St. Louis, Mo., Washington University Medical Center Tunnel Area located immediately west of the Central West End Station and eliminated in 1999 for the Medical Center expansion. In collaboration with Austin Tao Associates, Landscape Architects, and Bob Banaskeck, Electrical Engineer. Mixed media, crushed art glass, stainless steel screen, lights, native plants, 150 × 750 ft. Courtesy of the Bi State Development, Arts in Transit, St. Louis, Mo.

their sensations and perceptions, thus nurturing a sense of self in an often alienating urban environment. Working in diverse media, including books, installations, and memorials, Susan Schwartzenberg introduces social narratives into the built environment. For a 1992 installation on Market Street in downtown San Francisco, *Market Street Economics*, for example, she recorded a diverse group of respondents' views on the economic recession, and posted photos and text on advertising kiosks to create a virtual public forum.

Ann Chamberlain's public installations are designed to commemorate shared experience and foster a sense of community. The *Mt. Zion Story Garden* (1996–98) at the cancer center of the University of California, San Francisco, is flanked by a seventy-foot wall of ceramic tablets, each recording the story of a patient, friend, or family member who has dealt with illness. San Jose's Mexican Heritage Plaza (1998), designed by Chamberlain in collaboration with Mexican American artist Victor Mario Zaballa, symbolically refers to the indigenous Mesoamerican notion of *cemanahuac*, or the location of the individual within the community and the cosmos.

Since World War II, women artists have played a leading role in shifting the paradigms of contemporary art. Doubly distanced from the mainstream, by virtue of both sex and geography, women artists in California claimed their freedom to challenge modernist art institutions and practices. Along with other artists working in California, European American artists form an integral part of the dynamic cultural whole. At the start of the twenty-first century, with historical racial divisions giving way to increasing exchange, and cultural norms growing more flexible, we can look to California women to explore previously untapped subject matter, to pioneer new, more inclusive modes of address and production, and to redefine the function of art in the environment and the community.

Notes

1 Herschel B. Chipp, "Art News from San Francisco," *ARTnews* 55, no. 2 (April 1956): 20.

2 At the time, critic Dore Ashton noted female sexual symbolism in Remington's paintings, citing their symmetry and their ovoid shapes. See Dore Ashton, "New York Reviews: Deborah Remington at Bykert," *Studio International* 173, no. 890 (June 1967): 317.

3 See Helen Alameda Lewis and Josine Ianco Starrels, *Generation of Mentors* (Los Angeles: California Council of the California Committee of the National Museum of Women in the Arts, 1994).

4 Nancy Marmer, "Pop Art in California," in *Pop Art*, ed. Lucy Lippard (New York: Praeger Publishers, 1966), p. 158.

5 Clement Greenberg, "Modernist Painting" (1965), in *The New Art: A Critical Anthology*, ed. Gregory Battcock (New York: Dutton, 1966), p. 74.

6 Faith Wilding, "The Feminist Art Programs at Fresno and CalArts, 1970–75," in *The Power of Feminist Art*, ed. Norma Broude and Mary D. Garrard (New York: Harry N. Abrams, 1994), p. 35.

7 Thalia Gouma-Peterson, "Miriam Schapiro: An Art of Becoming," *American Art* 11, no. 1 (Spring 1997): 32.

8 Steven Durland, cited by Jan Breslauer, "Woman's Building Lost to a Hitch in 'Herstory,'" *Los Angeles Times*, January 7, 1992.

9 Eleanor Antin, quoted in *Eleanor Antin*, ed. Howard N. Fox (Los Angeles: Los Angeles County Museum of Art, 1999), p. 88.

10 Catherine Opie, cited in Suzanne Muchnic, "L.A. Story," *ARTnews* 97, no. 8 (September 1998): 151.

Education lifts man's sorrows to a higher plane of regard.
A man's whole life can be a metaphor. **Robert Frost**

TO WE WHO WERE
SAVED BY THE STARS

Lorna Dee Cervantes

Nothing has to be ugly. Luck of the dumb
is a casual thing. It gathers its beauty in plain
regard. Animus, not inspiration, lets us go
among the flocks and crows crowded around
the railroad ties. Interchanges of far away
places, tokens of our deep faux pas, our interface
of neither/nor, when we mutter moist goodbye and ice
among the silent stars, it frosts our hearts on
the skids and corners, piles the dust upon our grids
as grimaces pardon us, our indecision, our monuments
to presidents, dead, or drafted boys who might have
married us, Mexican poor, or worse. Our lives could be
a casual thing, a reed among the charlatan drones,
a rooted blade, a compass that wields a clubfoot
round and round, drawing fairy circles in clumps
of sand. Irritate a simple sky and stars fill up
the hemispheres. One by one, the procession
of their birth is a surer song than change
jingling in a rich man's pocket. So knit, you
lint-faced mothers, tat your black holes
into paradise. Gag the grin that forms
along the nap. Pull hard, row slow, a white
boat to your destiny. A man's whole life
may be a metaphor—but a woman's lot
is symbol.

AMALIA MESA-BAINS

CALAFIA/CALIFAS
A Brief History of Chicana California

Calafia, the dark-skinned Amazon, was the mythical ruler of an island paradise, a legendary site of verdant promise sometimes associated with our own California. This is, perhaps, the origin of "Califas," the slang term for California among Chicanos. These two names seem to be the metaphoric intersection of the cultural and gendered geography so pertinent to a history of Chicana/Latina artists.[1]

The period we focus on in this book begins after World War II, but for Chicanas/Latinas the history begins much earlier, for it is important to recall the prehistory of Spanish occupation and Anglo settlement to fully situate the artwork of contemporary Chicanas/Latinas. This unique relationship to California ancestry calls for a deeper understanding of feminist examinations of gender, race, class, and geography. It is, of course, impossible to do more than capture the texture of this past within the limits of this essay.

Looking at the history of California as the context in which to understand Chicana and Latina artists requires us to examine the intersection of social, political, economic, and labor history that has taken place within the human geography of this state. The visual and cultural production of these artists is an unfolding genealogy of shared histories often best understood from the moments of struggle in the fields, in the workplace, and in the home. Chicana/Latina history is filled with the vestiges of colonialism, the *mestizaje* of mixed-race ancestry and their representations and stereotypes in American popular culture. The Latina are women who have been portrayed in stereotypic images from the American greaser films of the 1930s and 1940s, to the contemporary exotic Other of multiculturalism. The 1960s, in the aftermath of civil rights victories, brought a cultural reclamation led by a new generation. These young women wanted to free the memories of their mothers from the silence of the past and saw themselves tied to earlier labor struggles for social justice and cultural rights. I want to tell this history not solely by simple chronologies of events but also by the memorable moments of family tales—*corridos*—from the voices of women that embody our everyday lives.

Prehistory, or when Ramona lost her way and Josefa met her end

I want to locate this ancestral prehistory in the figures of two women, one fictional, the other infamous. In some sense they represent the polarities of all women, innocent and debased. At the same time, they particularly reflect our indigenous and mestiza heritage, the extremities of the Spanish mission period and the turmoil of Anglo intervention. The two figures are Ramona, the romantic character of an Anglo novel of the Californio period, and Josefa, the first woman to be hanged in California.

In the years following the Mexican-American War of 1846–1848, the United States annexed more than half of Mexico's northern territory, leaving the Mexican population of California an internal colony that suffered land loss, language loss, and cultural upheaval despite the proclaimed protection of the Treaty of Guadalupe Hidalgo. Leading Californio families and working-class *cholos* of the region found themselves at the bottom of the society. Years of discrimination and violence followed, and as a result many women found themselves at the mercy of Anglo society, which did not accord them the same rights and protections as the white women for whom they labored.

In Hemet, California, local residents continue to celebrate the Ramona Pageant, derived from the pastoral recreations of *Ramona*, a romantic novel by Helen Hunt Jackson published in 1884. Part of the mythmaking of the Mexican Californio era, the novel's oversimplification of the rancho and mission periods added to the pastoral Spanish fantasy heritage that was later to influence the tourist industry that sprang up throughout California. Seeking to bring attention to the plight of the Indians of Southern California, it focuses on Ramona, the mestiza heroine, and her Indian suitor. Ramona's struggle to avoid Anglo intermarriage and to remain true to her Indian betrothed expresses the theme of racial and sexual domination experienced by Mexican women.

The Land Act of 1851 helped to create desperate

conditions for Mexican landowners, with escalating land taxes, uncertainty about ownership papers, and eventual loss of their property to Anglos. In an attempt to hold onto their lands and to garner status in the rapidly Anglicized early California, many Mexican Californios were forced to barter their daughters in intermarriage to Anglo settlers. For the Anglo, intermarriage was a means of acquiring land. Consequently, the image of the wild señorita had to be refashioned into the purity of a marriageable "Spanish" woman, which was fostered through the novels and songs of the era. Much of this racialized gentility remains to this day an ideal in many parts of the state, where lineage is connected to economic and social power. The reality, however, is that Californio women became part of the exchange in the Anglo occupation and control of Mexican land titles. Our contemporary roles and struggles in part spring from the sexually racialized relations of power established in this period of land transformation.

The story of Josefa offers another revealing glimpse into the perception and treatment of Mexican women after the annexation and in the midst of the California Gold Rush. Josefa was a Mexican woman accused of killing an Anglo man who had abused her. Following a trial of dubious impartiality, she was condemned to die on the gallows. In what is the first documented case in the history of California of a woman who was hanged, Josefa was executed on July 5, 1851, in the town of Downieville.[2] The historic representations of the Mexican woman in California have been created through film, theater, and image as personifications of mestiza, mulatta, and indigenous characters. But the real history is a story of enslavement within a dominant mission system and a greedy Anglo society. Josefa and Ramona represent the polar constructions of transgression and innocence, objects of desire, commerce, violence, and fear.

The wave of immigration that followed the Mexican Revolution was the next juncture of change for the fortunes of Mexican women. Between 1900 and 1930 the Mexican population in the United States grew from 100,000 to 1.5 million. In the aftermath of the revolution, many displaced Mexicans were attracted by the immigrant worker programs sponsored by the United States from 1917 to 1920. It was then that my grandmother Mariana Escobedo entered the United States, bringing my father, his brother, and their uncles first to Pueblo, Colorado, and eventually to California. My grandmother, like so many Mexican women of the time, looked to labor in the fields, packing plants, and in the homes of white families as a necessity to support their family. In the eyes of Anglo society, women like her were the key to acculturating the Mexican to Anglo values. The rationale of an Americanization program aimed at Mexican women was stated baldly: "The children of these foreigners are the advantages to America, not these naturalized foreigners. These are never 100 percent Americans, but the second generation may be. Go after the women and you may save the second generation for America."[3]

Americanization programs tried to inculcate what were viewed by the dominant Anglo society as superior norms of health, diet, cleanliness and, of course, birth control. Ironically, the Americanization movement sought to have Mexican women care for Anglo children as domestics but ignored the child-care strains that labor outside their homes created for them and their own children. The attempts to change the cultural patterns of child-rearing, language, and values were not successful except in drawing more Mexican women into the labor force to serve the needs of the larger Anglo society, particularly in the Southwest's clothing manufacturing, laundry, domestic services, and food service industries. Within the domestic and vernacular life of these communities, the handcrafts that marked the daily life of women prevailed. The maintenance of home altars and yard shrines attested to the ongoing spiritual traditions of the family in which women had a central role, in counterpoint to the patriarchy of the Church. Despite the richness of the cultural practices within the Mexican communities, the perception persisted of Mexican women as indo-

lent, uncivilized, and unfit for American life save as laborers. Many of these stereotypes continue to this day.

This was also the period when the urbanization of California made Los Angeles into the second largest Spanish-speaking metropolis in the world, after Mexico City. To Latinos and Mexicans alike, Los Angeles would become a mecca for employment. The long-standing history of the Mexican founding of Los Angeles would reassert itself in prolonged battles for land and space, as Los Angeles redevelopment would become Mexican relocation. From the bulldozing of Sonoratown in downtown Los Angeles to the struggle over the razing of Chavez Ravine and its replacement by Dodger Stadium and as well the loss of the Bunker Hill community for the Music Center, Mexicans would pay the price for progress and wealth in the real estate fervor and urban renewal of Southern California.

Labor and Leadership

While the feminist lineage for white women stretches from Susan B. Anthony to Betty Friedan, for Chicanas the labor organizers of the 1930s and 1940s mark their feminist ancestry. Inspiration from activism and the values of social justice does not stem from the Mexican revolutionaries Emiliano Zapata and Pancho Villa, but the legendary and charismatic labor leaders who heroically faced growers and labor bosses, like

Luisa Moreno of the United Cannery, Agricultural, Packing and Allied Workers of America (UCAPAWA). Moreno, from a wealthy Guatemalan family and educated in the United States, who gave up her inheritance and rose to leadership in the Los Angeles-based Congreso de los Pueblos de Habla Español, is renowned for her famous 1940 speech, "The Caravan of Sorrow," in which she reminded the country that Mexicans had lived the "grapes of wrath" in silence and obscurity.[4] Women organized in the garment, hotel, and agricultural industries. The stories of the moments of hardship and violence in the strikes of the Depression era are part of an oral history that has been passed on from woman to woman through family narratives. The cotton strikes of the San Joaquin Valley in 1933 are memorable examples. These strikes brought 18,000 pickers out of the field. Women made up over half of the 3,500 strikers, walking the picket lines, cooking, caring for the children and, with unprecedented courage, facing down the strikebreakers. The lives of these women were changed by their unity and collective spirit and even the perceptions of the men of their families were changed by the women's role in the strikes.

Larger issues affected women when the repatriation movement of the Depression era sought the deportation of over a half a million Mexicans, many of whom were American citizens, as a solution to unemployment. Against the background of an unprecedented number of labor strikes, the fear of deportation was used as a scare tactic that set the stage for "voluntary" repatriation. Repatriation, which indeed began voluntarily as a U.S.-Mexican project, swiftly became a tool for the forced division of families, hitting labor activists and their families hardest. By 1933, almost half of the Mexicans in the United States had returned to Mexico. Often described as "birds of passage," Mexican men and women were portrayed as "temporary Americans" ready to return to their native land. During the scarcity fears of the Depression, the movement of repatriation succeeded in scapegoating Mexican laborers and setting the stage for the wholesale displacement of workers. The removal of Mexicans changed the racial face of farm labor in the 1930s, as they were replaced with white workers leaving the dust bowl states.[5] Thus, while the U.S. government spearheaded the deportation of Mexicans, it addressed the welfare of white farmworkers through New Deal programs.

In the wake of World War II, during the misnamed "zoot suit riots" (which were violent attacks on Mexican, blacks, and Filipinos in the streets), Mexicans were brought back into the country as braceros (temporary workers) through government-sanctioned programs. But the Bracero Program was followed by Operation Wetback when, in the 1950s, the Immigration and Naturalization Service conducted large-scale sweeps

33

Yolanda M. Lopez, *"Who's the Illegal Alien, Pilgrim?"* 1978. Pen and ink on paper, 22 × 30 in. First published for the Committee on Chicano Rights, Herman Baca, Director, San Diego, Calif. Photo: Bob Hsiang. Collection of the artist.

to hunt down and deport undocumented workers the government had encouraged to enter the United States in the first place. A climate of fear gripped Mexican communities across the Southwest. Moreover, the 1950 McCarran Act had expanded the focus to include naturalized citizens, thereby creating a second-class citizenship. Even heroic labor leaders like Luisa Moreno fell victim to deportation during McCarthyism. These moments of rupture often left women as single heads of household, as they were separated from their husbands and made to fend for themselves. Amidst this turmoil, Latina and Mexican women sought to stabilize their families and earn a living.

Historic issues of class and race discrimination as well as economic struggle were, therefore, insistent elements in the coming of age of Chicanas in the political movement for social justice and cultural rights of the 1960s. One of the most important transitional figures between this history of labor activism and the contemporary Chicano national movement is Dolores Huerta, who worked side by side with Cesar Chavez in the lettuce and grape *huelgas* of the United Farm Workers. She has remained a force in securing union contracts and demanding fair labor conditions for men and women.

The human geography of Latina California has been a terrain marked by sites of struggle and resiliency from the farming communities of Blythe to Pixley, from Corcoran to Delano, and in the streets of Los Angeles and San Francisco. Latinas have organized, demonstrated, and sacrificed to demand fair wages and working conditions and ultimately to support and protect their families and their communities. The role models of the Mexican labor movements were significant for Chicana artists, particularly in California. The labor activists of the Mexican and Latina communities of California helped shape the contemporary discourse on feminism and the engagement with art insofar as the narratives of these civil rights actions were often the inspiration for artists and writers of the 1960s and 1970s to voice their own realities and to reclaim their history in public forms. For the Chicano movement of the 1960s, critical Marxist theories on labor production were linked to the understanding of cultural production in profound ways. Artists who gained consciousness in this context described themselves as cultural workers. Art was viewed as an integral part of everyday life and functioned as a means of emancipation and liberation.

Chicana or Chicano

The contemporary framework within which to understand the artists discussed here begins in the Chicano movement of the 1960s. For many artists, both male and female, the Chicano movement was fundamental to their coming of age and self-definition. At its deepest level, it was a move-ment of social justice and cultural identity, where the right to land, language, education, and working wages was marked by an overriding theme of cultural reclamation. The critical issues included the *huelgas*, land and water rights in the Southwest, bilingual education, and support for community institutions. Chicano/a identity was influenced by nutrient experiences, including labor struggles, everyday barrio events, familial histories, regional terrain, shared ceremonies and celebrations, folk practices, spiritual worldview, urban and rural enclaves, and even the mythic past. Within this context, the arts served as a vehicle for expressing a cultural history founded in class, race, and gender.

Artists developed their role within the intersection of their individual life history and the historical moment of their group. For women artists, the experience of struggle was a double battle for rights in the society and within the patriarchy of the Mexican family and community. These artists and advocates provide an even greater understanding of cultural reclamation and redefinition because in their communities it is the women who often uphold the intimate family structures in which language, oral histories, and cultural practices are maintained. In this sense, Chicana artists and activists are engaged in creating a cultural narrative that is committed to the community. But, like the women of the fields and factories before them,

Chicana and Latina artists are laborers in the field of cultural production and as such they also continue the tradition of struggle for justice and rights. As artists, they were engaged in the making of meaning that consists of both a personal and collective expression of liberation.

In the early years of the movement the conflict between feminist independence and the collective integration of women's issues was critical. The often-contradictory aspects of race, class, and gender within a family-centered cultural model, place Chicana activists in a unique position. The tension between issues of ethnic solidarity and feminism that rose to the surface in the early gatherings of youth was pivotal for the first Chicana generation, particularly for the artists. It produced differences in the very content of art making which led to the formation of groups like Las Mujeres Muralistas in San Francisco and the Social Public Art Resources Center (SPARC) by Judith F. Baca, Christine Schlesinger, and Donna Deitch in Los Angeles.

The Mujeres Muralistas were a Latina/Chicana collective which included Patricia Rodriguez, Consuelo Mendez, Irene Perez, Graciela Carrillo, and often Ester Hernandez; their murals introduced themes of family life, the role of women, and pan-Latino heritage into the genre. Baca and her colleagues sought to insert a feminist critique of patriarchal aspects of Chicano culture through their support for diverse histories and women in the mural production. SPARC's focus on public artworks brought the issues of Chicanas and women of color out from the private domestic setting of the home and family into the public and social space of the community. To have women on the scaffolding handling physically challenging "men's" mural-making work, previously associated with Diego Rivera, José Clemente Orozco, and David Alfaro Siqueiros—the grand triumvirate of Mexican muralists—was revolutionary.

The Chicanas of the early movement were caught between a hegemonic cultural nationalism and an irrelevant and unresponsive white, middle-class women's movement. Legendary figures emerged who served as role models and supports for an emerging Chicana generation, including the prolific writer and Chicana cultural worker Elizabeth Martinez; labor organizer and activist Maria Varela; Dorinda Moreno and Maruja Cid, leaders of cultural institutions and collectives in the San Francisco Bay Area; and the actress Margo and activists Graciela Pick and Lola de la Riva in Southern California. Recent scholarship by groups like the Mujeres Activas en Letras y Cambios Socials (MALCS) mounted a deeper critique of the early dilemma between feminism and cultural nationalism. To be sure, understanding the context of this foundational period is a critical aspect of our own development as cultural workers, critical thinkers, and social activists. The need is great, for the language and terminology of the white women's movement has been ill-suited to capture the unique character of the struggle for emancipation, justice, and cultural rights inherent to the particular Chicana/Latina condition. The tensions of women as workers and mothers, artists and lesbians, scholars and comrades are the rich material of Chicana and Latina feminism.

Images and Ideologies

Contemporary artists of the Chicana/Latina community have developed critical content for their work from the retrieval of personal histories, urban experiences, rural memories, and domestic tensions. The ability to construct identities that can be reproduced and disseminated through visual material is the real power of art making. To this effect, artists have participated in the interpretation of a community spirit through the construction of images recalling the everyday world. The details of home altars, domestic work, celebrations, ceremonies, and labor are potent signs in the work of many of the artists discussed here. In the San Francisco Bay Area, artist and teacher Yolanda Garfias Woo was widely influential in providing knowledge and support for the reassertion of folk traditions, particularly the Día de los Muertos (the Day of the Dead), the ancient Mesoamerican practice of honoring the dead. As a member of an Oaxacan family still tied to the traditions of Mexico, Garfias Woo played a semi-

nal role in cultural reclamation. Her early childhood experiences of discrimination in South Texas and her dedication to the vernacular spurred Carmen Lomas Garza to retrieve the skills of *papel picado* and other craft related to the celebration. Like many artists of her generation inspired by the indigenous past, Carmen Lomas Garza has studied *danza* (Aztec) and has portrayed the women deities significant to Chicanas. Many of the Chicana artists have elaborated their feminism through the readaptation of spiritual icons such as the Virgin of Guadalupe/Tonantzin, Coatlique (the Aztec Mother goddess) and Coyolxualqui (the warrior sister). For example, Yolanda M. Lopez's classic series of Guadalupe/Tonantzin images exemplifies the conditions of labor, equity, and family. Lopez situates the family images within the context of the Virgin. She depicts her mother sewing the Virgin Mary's cape, her grandmother skinning a serpent, and her own image as a runner amidst the rays and the crown of the Virgin.

The representation of the Virgin as an active figure is a feminist icon reproduced around the world. A new generation of artists is working in photography, film, and performance, as well as more traditional art media, in ways that are expanding the images and critiques of the Latina experience. While it would be impossible in this brief essay to recognize all the artists whose work has contributed to the history of Latina/Chicana work, the following artists are those whose works are most familiar to me.

There have been several prominent exhibitions that have helped to distribute these works to a wider audience and to counter the dominant view of Chicano artists. They include the 1971 exhibition at the Galeria de la Raza, *Third World Women's Show*; the 1976 Los Angeles group show *Las Venas de la Mujer*; and, in 1985, the Chicana roundtable "The Mexican Museum Voices and Visions" at SPARC and the exhibition *Women by Women* at the Galeria de la Raza. The representation of women was a serious issue in Chicano institutions and cultural centers throughout the 1970s, but began to be resolved by the assertive action of Chicanas organizing for their right to be included in the decision making processes and in the exhibitions by the mid-1980s.

Ester Hernandez

The visual representation of the battles in the fields and of Chicana labor history in general was most eloquently captured in the work of Ester Hernandez. Her early years in the San Joaquin Valley, laboring with her family and living close to the land, have brought a sincere insight to her work. Starting from but also going beyond the personal, she has crystallized the intense indignation about her own experience into a wider view of the symbolic and the social. Her screen print *Sun Mad* (1982) (see fig. 62) was inspired by

the artist's discovery that the water table of her region was poisoned with pesticides. It occupies that rare position of an enduring work of art that is understood in the popular culture and also commands critical acclaim in the art world. The skeletal figure it portrays brings stark attention to the pesticides and acute labor conditions of underpaid Mexican, Central American, and Filipino farmworkers. In a 1989 installation, *Ofrenda for My Father*, the same image becomes the basis for commemoration on the occasion of her father's death. The artist placed inside a circle of stones an offering of the farmworker's hat and scarf, poignant reminders of a life of toil and dignity in one of America's most shamefully exploitative industries.

Carmen Lomas Garza

Carmen Lomas Garza is a key figure in understanding the visual representations of Chicano culture. Her "monitos," or little people paintings are an important body of work which have served as an alternative chronicle of communal, familial, historical, and cultural practices. The specific geographic siting of many of her pieces within the natural landscape heightens the work's rural aspect and its evocation of memory. In her detailed depictions of family events, the artist has drawn us a cultural map marked by the deposits of memory. The *loteria* game, the *cumpleaños* (birthday) party, the cakewalk gathering,

34

Carmen Lomas Garza,
*Cumpleaños de Lala y Tudi
(Lala and Tudi's Birthday)*,
1989. Oil on canvas,
36 × 48 in. Photo: Wolfgang
Dietze. Collection of Paula
Maciel Benecke and Norbert
Benecke, Aptos, Calif.

and the faith healing of the *curandera* accumulate in her chronicling to create a mapping of Chicano cultural values and identity. Within this mapping Lomas Garza, like all storytellers, provides us with characters, locations, time, and moments of importance. She is a textural weaver who incorporates both the sinister and the familiar. Scholars Tomas Barra-Frausto and Victor Zamudio Taylor have both remarked on the edge of the uncanny, the disquieting aspects of wonderment and mystery found in Lomas Garza's paintings. Although the artist has remained true to the historiography of her life and her community, the tales she depicts have larger allegorical references to death, aging, innocence, and faith. The flattened figures and embellishment of dense and precise detail are reminiscent of the pre-Columbian codices where moral lessons and the recording of significant personages and events were scrupulously noted with the same use of doll-like figures. It is noteworthy that Lomas Garza's paintings have come to serve her community much as the pre-Columbian codices functioned in an earlier time. Her chronicling of the community is at the same time a personal feminine record. Filled with the domestic dialogue of women, Lomas Garza's paintings capture a feminine lineage with their depictions of healing and spirituality. Archival details of home altars, icons, dress, and conviviality lie before us. Her characters include *la abuelita*, the grandmother; *la tía*, the aunt; *la curandera*, the healer; and *la chola*, the homegirl—all personas of a female world that people Lomas Garza's chronicles in an intimate domestic dialogue that transforms everyday women into central figures of action and strength.

Judith F. Baca

Large-scale public mural-making has been an area in which women have struggled to make a place for themselves. There are many artists who could be considered, including Juana Alicia of the San Francisco Bay Area and Barbara Carrasco and Judith Hernandez of Los Angeles. But it is Judith F. Baca who has manifested the most consistent dedication to muralism and caused the greatest innovation to the tradition. I hope to articulate through her work aspects of mural image-making across a number of dimensions. Baca has been able to maintain a focus on murals through a variety of collaborative and individual practices. As a result of this work and similarly that of others, murals have come to function as a visual history for communities whose past has been largely invisible.

Baca began her work within the context of barrio turf, gang warfare, inner city poverty, and limited resources. In this conflicted public space the need for reconciliation and reparation was great. Baca's early work in mural development assisted gang youth to maintain their much-needed urban space, while learning to respect the space of other neighborhoods.

The artist developed her model for social activism and artistic image-making in her *Great Wall* project in Los Angeles, begun in 1976 by a racially and ethnically mixed group of ten artists and eighty teenagers under the direction of Baca. Situated in a flood-control channel, it reflects the history of minorities in California, offering an alternative chronicle and bringing to consciousness the international aspect of the culturally diverse society that is the United States. By 1983, the project had become national, incorporating over forty scholars, four assisting artists, over a hundred support staff, and 450 multiracial youth around the country, with each site creating its own mural. The model developed in the *Great Wall of Los Angeles* project established many of

DIVISION OF THE BARRIOS & CHAVEZ RAVINE

35

Judith F. Baca, *Division of the Barrios and Chavez Ravine*, section of the half-mile mural *Great Wall of Los Angeles*, 1976–83. Tujunga Wash Drainage Channel, San Fernando Valley, Calif. Acrylic on cement block. Courtesy of Social Public Art Resource (SPARC), Los Angeles.

the salient tropes for the telling of stories through images used today. Baca's work captures some of the stories of women as leaders described in this essay. Similarly, the running narrative of the *Great Wall* is a groundbreaking exercise as dust bowl immigrants, displaced Chicanos, incarcerated Japanese, and civil rights activists are depicted in the historic moments of massive national and world politics.

In her *World Wall* project, begun in 1987 and ongoing, Baca has developed the technique of portable murals to illuminate the issue of global peace so important today. Her ongoing project has brought together teams of Russian, Finnish, Israeli, and Palestinian artists at various sites around the globe. But the vision of the *World Wall* project is just one of her innovative applications of mural making. Baca currently leads the way in the application of technology to digital mural-making.

Patssi Valdez

At age seventeen, Patssi Valdez walked out of Garfield High School in the Chicano blowouts of

1969 and, two years later, became a founding member of the legendary performance art collective ASCO (nausea). Valdez has been both an icon and an icon maker through photographs, performance, installation, and painting. Her work marks a transformation from the use of images as persona to self-portraiture, from narratives of domestic ruin to visions of regeneration. What began as individual self-examination has come to signify a collective urban tale of Chicana life. In ASCO, Valdez was both an object of beauty and a collaborative participant in costume, pose, and performance. For over twenty-five years she has produced art that embodies a struggle for self-representation that questions the condition of women. Making her way through a turbulent life in Los Angeles, Valdez has created a visual autobiography filled with domestic tension and miraculous hope.

Valdez's focus on racialized beauty has made an important contribution to the discourse on race, class, and gender. Her images of dark Madonnas are one of the connective threads through-out her work. In an era when most representa-tions of beauty were white, the artist produced her own discourse on desire through paintings and installations depicting virgins and queens. Whether constructing full installations dedicated to the Black Virgin or paintings of deities called queens, Valdez persists in the racialization of feminine icons. Often the icon will appear in the smallest details of domestic interiors as a statue, holy card, candle, or memento.[6]

Her installation work is different from the forms of installation of the 1980s and 1990s, which responded to the precariousness of the museum object. Rather, it is an expression of Chicano popular culture practices such as home shrines, commercial store display, and home decoration from a working-class perspective. Valdez's work is in the tradition of *rasquachismo*, which has been described as the gesture and style of those who must make the most from the least. Chicana artists have adopted the tradition of *rasquachismo* to express an aesthetic practice based on their own distinct experiences as women. "Domesticana," or Chicana *rasqua-chismo*, combines techniques of subversion with traditional imagery and cultural materials.

Within this body of work we can begin to apply critical viewpoints of feminist theory. It is important to recognize that the domestic sphere, with all its social roles and practices, remains fixed in patriarchy unless representations of that world call such practices into question and thereby contribute to its change. Through *ras-quachismo*, women treat the domestic experience with humor and satire. The domestic tension between the cherished aspects of home and fam-ily and the desire for independence and self-determination is in a sense acted out through the domesticana aesthetic, which contrasts the mate-rials of the private and the representations of the public.[7]

In her paintings, Patssi Valdez has focused on interior spaces. They depict rooms and furnish-ings that are askew. Enclosed rooms have multi-ple windows and doors are slightly ajar. Walls curve and undulate with motion in the paint stroke. Carpets spiral and bleed, punctured by pointed table legs, dancing umbrellas, and falling knives or thorns. There are signs of inhabitation and we are left to wonder what the future holds for the inhabitants of these mystical rooms.

The concerns of the artists who have used photog-raphy, film, and performance have contributed to the narrative of the body as well. For instance, Christina Fernandez has contributed to the excava-tion of the body using her own representations to examine its spirit. Her photography links the his-tory and geography of the feminine body to the corpus of culture. Both Fernandez and photogra-pher Laura Aguilar compose images that question

39

Nao Bustamante, *America, the beautiful*, 1995. Performance piece at Xteresa, Mexico City, Mexico. Photo: Monica Naranjo. Collection of the artist.

desire, representation, beauty, power, and size. The metaphors of nature and healing are also thus articulated through these images. The performances of Guadalupe Garcia and Nao Bustamante pursue the contemporary concerns with transgression and the body to critique relations of power. The intersection between photography, performance, and film brings to the surface issues of image and representation and an examination of visual language. The contemporary use of media in the hands of many of these artists has helped us to subvert the disfiguring identity constructions that are so much a part of popular consumption.

From the earliest, filmmakers such as Sylvia Morales, Frances Salomé España, Lourdes Portillo, Renee Tajima-Peña, and Esperanza Vásquez battled to gain access to a field dominated by Chicano filmmakers and to support an increasingly expensive art form. Yet these women have envisioned some of our most powerful memories and histories through their woman-centered vision of the Chicana life and struggle.[8]

The works of the artists highlighted in this essay are but instances of the larger tropes and themes of their communities. They have expressed the urban and rural, the private and public, the corporeal and the mythic, the personal and the societal, in ways that reflect on many other artists who have addressed the Chicana and Latina condition. Their stories are our histories, too, a history composed of the fluid boundaries of gender, sexuality, class, and race and an unfolding record of our lives and our bodies.

From the Chicanas who wielded their bodies in the labor strikes, to those who wield to create, to paint, to photograph, and to document the extremities of our lives, artists have been historians, activists, lovers, caretakers, healers, and dreamers. We are all these things in our lives as image makers linked to the history and geography of Califas.

Notes

1 Although this essay deals mainly with Chicana early history, many concerns regarding cultural representation are relevant to the Latina experience of California as well.

2 Rodolfo Anaya, *Occupied America: A History of Chicanos* (New York: Harper & Row, 1988), p. 118; Elizabeth Martinez, *500 Years of Chicano History in Pictures* (Albuquerque, N.M.: Southwest Organizing Project, 1991), p. 23.

3 Alfred White cited by George J. Sanchez, "Go After the Women: Americanization and the Mexican Immigrant Woman, 1915–1929," in Ellen Carol DuBois and Vicki L. Ruiz, eds., *Unequal Sisters: A Multicultural Reader in U.S. Women's History* (New York: Routledge, 1990), p. 250.

4 Anaya, *Occupied America*, p. 238.

5 Devre Anne Weber, "Mexican Women on Strike: Memory, History and Oral Narratives," in Adelaid R. Del Castillo, ed., *Between Borders: Essays on Mexican/Chicana History* (Encino, Calif.: Floricanto Press, 1990), p. 175.

6 Amalia Mesa-Bains, "Patssi Valdez: Glamour, Ruin and Regeneration," in *Patssi Valdez: A Precarious Comfort* (exhibition catalogue) (San Francisco: The Mexican Museum, 1998).

7 Amalia Mesa-Bains, "Domesticana: Chicana Rasquachismo," in *Distant Relations* (exhibition catalogue) (Dublin, Ireland: Museum of Modern Art, 1996).

8 Rosa Linda Fregoso, "Chicana Film Practices: Confronting the Many Headed Demon of Oppression," in Maria Herrera-Sobek and Helen Maria Viramontes, eds., *Chicana (W)rites on Word and Film* (Berkeley: Third Woman Press, 1995), p. 259.

REVOLUTIONARY LETTER #21
Diane di Prima

Can you
own land, can you
own house, own rights
to other's labor, (stocks, or factories
or money, loaned at interest)
what about
the yield of same, crops, autos
airplanes dropping bombs, can you
own real estate, so others
pay you rent? To whom
does the water belong, to whom
will the air belong, as it gets rarer?
the american indians say that a man
can own no more than he can carry away
on his horse.

JOLENE RICKARD

UNCOVERING/RECOVERING

Indigenous Artists in California

This essay is about the artistic arrival of Native artists and those Native artists influenced by Indigenous nations in California, in particular, northern California. My position, as a Tuscarora artist/art historian based on the East Coast looking in from the outside and as an academic, informs my view. As an Iroquoian art historian, I map my identity based on a legal, cultural, spiritual, and political platform of sovereignty. Therefore, when I contemplate Indian America, I see hundreds of Native nations with discrete political, cultural, and spiritual borders. As an academic, a similar process occurs when I consciously reject the universalizing, hegemonic, theoretical constructs that are used to frame Indigenous art.

There already exists an ongoing discussion concerning how Native art functions outside of Indigenous experience within the art world and museum discourse. Instead, I am interested in looking at the way art functions from within our communities. The art historical tendency to "universalize" this work compromises the opportunity to understand how "Native art" actually serves our communities. I am interested in the way expressive acts by Native artists function in our Indigenous nations and urban spaces. What is the dialectic between the Native artist and the Native community? How does this art contribute to traditional systems of knowledge? What impact does art have on retraditionalization attempts? How does one articulate the relationship between art and sovereignty in Native nation-building?

143

ALCATRAZ

The 1969 occupation of Alcatraz was actually the third and most successful attempt by Indian people to reclaim the island prison. Two earlier attempts were short-lived and not as representative of the general Indian population of the Bay Area. Alcatraz Island was the first permanent military prison in the United States. During its history many Native people who resisted colonial oppression were incarcerated there. Unlike other sites of Indian resistance, Alcatraz was both highly visible and inconvenient to get to. Its symbolic importance could not be ignored. In November of 1969 a group of Native people, including members of the Mohawk, Seminole, Seneca, Pit River, and Round Valley peoples, sailed to Alcatraz Island and took up residence there. The presence of both Native California peoples and Indians from other places reinforced the national presence of Indigenous politics in the Bay Area. Even though the occupation is often considered unsuccessful, it brought general focus to Native political concerns. The occupation of Alcatraz is also considered the catalyst for the founding of D-Q University, an Indian university established on land allotted near Davis, California, while Alcatraz was being occupied. The island remains symbolic for Native people today and is the site for "Unthanksgiving" celebrations every year.[1]

I have decided to look closely at several artists working within an "urban" (and arguably diasporic) space, and at one artist working within the geographic and cultural space of her Indigenous nation. The artists to be discussed include Tsalagi (Cherokee)/Euro-American Kim Shuck; Seminole/Creek/Dine Hulleah Tsinhnahjinnie; Seneca Sylvia Lark; and Paiute/Pit River Jean LaMarr. My view has been accentuated by knowing Janeen Antoine, Theresa Harlan, Jean LaMarr, George Longfish, and Hulleah Tsinhnahjinnie since the early 1980s. My awareness of more recent art has been stimulated by Sara Bates, Ed Burnham, and Frank LaPena. This essay is also greatly enriched by discussions and e-mail correspondence with the California-raised artist Kim Shuck, whose insight allowed me to draw some parallels between the national discourse on Native arts and what is happening at the grassroots level in California.

During the last twenty-five years the national spotlight on Indigenous activity in California was focused mainly on an urban intra-tribal experience based on the people's occupation and resistance at Alcatraz in 1969. Parallel to the way Indian country responded to news about Wounded Knee in 1973, the activity at Alcatraz and around the San Francisco Bay Area made a bleep on our radar screen of contemporary resistance. Along with urban-based grassroots movements like the American Indian Movement and Women of All Red Nations, the events at Alcatraz spoke to a generation of Indians searching for decolonizing opportunities. But, I do not believe that we thought much about the Indigenous people of California per se at the time, since most of these movements were powered by Indians from all over the country. The historical legacy of Indigenous peoples of California was not at the forefront of any Indian imaginary.

Moreover, any attention paid by Native Studies programs nationally or by the art world to the cultural and political conditions of Indigenous people in California, was very limited. Indeed, to this day, the intensity of the colonization trauma experienced by Natives of California, a combination of Spanish conquistadors and missionaries from the south, Russians from the north, and westward expansion fueled by the Gold Rush, has yet to be uncovered and understood. Certainly, the resistance at Alcatraz could be contextualized as part of a centuries-old resistance to extermination by Indigenous peoples in California. Similarly, the art of Native artists working within the geopolitical space of California needs to be contextualized within a colonial and resistance narrative. All too often, the real history of Native peoples is swept aside and the focus is placed only on exclusively "traditional" cultural expressions. But even the most "traditional" form, like basket weaving, is actually a demonstration of Indigenous renewal, survival, and political and environmental awareness. In this sense, the notion of retraditionalization is tied to resistance.

THE IMPACT OF COLONIZATION

Inspired by the rumors of a rich northern Indian civilization, including tales of the Seven Cities of Cibola or the "Northern Mystery," the Spanish conquerors Francisco Vásquez de Coronado, Hernando do Alarcon, and Melchor Diaz led expeditions in 1540; the Portuguese Juan Rodriguez Cabrillo followed with an expedition in 1542. The English sent Sir Francis Drake in 1579. Spanish authorities in Mexico sent Sebastian Rodriguez Cermeno in 1595. The merchant Sebastian Vizcaino made another exploration in 1602. The founding of the first of twenty-one missions in California was on July 16, 1769.

Three major epidemics occurred during Spanish occupation, decreasing Native population by 45 percent: the common cold in 1777, pneumonia in 1802, and measles in 1806. Colonization is divided into three periods: the Mexican period beginning in 1821 and ending with the Treaty of Guadalupe Hidalgo of 1848; the American period, which saw massive Anglo land grabs from the Yuki, Cahto, Yurok, and Tolowa throughout the nineteenth century; and the termination period, whose landmark is Public Law 280, passed in 1953.

Gold mining operations adversely affected salmon fishing and destroyed fish dams, interrupting the food supply. The impact of the Gold Rush led to a 65 percent loss of life due to disease, institutional kidnapping of Indian children, and termination legislation like the Dawes Act of 1887. In 1851, California governor John McDougall outlined the state's genocidal aim, calling it "Jacksonian logic": "That a war of extermination will continue to be waged between the races until the Indian race becomes extinct, must be expected . . . the inevitable destiny of the race is beyond the power of wisdom of man to avert" (California Legislature Senate and Assembly, 1851:1).

The twentieth century witnessed termination strategies through land allotment, boarding schools, and Public Law 280, which unilaterally terminated the trust responsibilities of the United States to Indians in California. After stripping them of most of their lands and rendering traditional lifestyles impossible, the government cut them loose to fend for themselves. The Rancheria Act of 1958 authorized Indians to vote to terminate themselves. After considerable pressure, thirty-six rancherias voted to terminate themselves for financial reasons, resulting in their losing 5,000 acres of trust property.[2]

The "arrival" of Indigenous peoples of California at several national Native arts conferences in the 1990s signaled the reemergence of these cultures. They brought their songs, dances, foods, and spiritual strength to these events and reminded us that we were in their homeland. As Pomo basket makers lined the entryway to the main ballroom, Wintu/Nomtipan Frank LaPena opened the AltAtl Conference in 1996 in his own language with a dance and song.[3] Perhaps one

could argue that this is a form of authentication but it should also be understood as a statement of strength.

The retraditionalization process in which artists from California are immersed, blurs the colonial boundaries of the "state," thus kindling a renewed sense of what it means to be Indian on the furthest western point of Turtle Island. As part of the construction of Indigenous sovereignty, it is important to challenge the colonial implications of identifying the artistic experience of "Indigenous people in California," or rather, to challenge the idea that these artists are "from" California. The artists provide the opportunity to recognize that California is within the homelands of Wintu, Pomo, Coast Miwok, Maidu, Yurok, Chumash, Luiseno, Tolowa, and many more Native "nations." Precisely because of the formation of the state of California, hundreds of thousands of Indigenous people were dispossessed from their homeland and relocated and systematically punished for being Indian. In Public Law 280, further aggression against the Indians of California was expressed by Californians in 1953. It was a unilateral termination of the so-called "trust" relationship between Natives in California and the U.S. government. This failed attempt at erasure of Indigenous "presence" in California underscores the incredible survival strength these Native communities demonstrate to this day.[4]

There would be no need to "retraditionalize" if these communities had not undergone some form of trauma. In this sense, the role that the artist plays in recovering cultural practice contributes to an overall movement toward self-definition and self-determination. These ideas and expressions take a cultural, spiritual, political, and legal form identified as "sovereignty."

Art became a way in which the colonizing of the Americas has been challenged by Indigenous artists nationally. This methodology for looking at the Americas implies a critique of the impact of contact and nineteenth- and twentieth-century relocation policies, viewed as part of an overall governmental strategy to dismantle Native nations, which is articulated as genocide. Thus, the complex intra-tribal urban space of Indigenous America must be a part of this assessment or projection of "sovereignty," not the least of which is the case of Indigenous art. Would you discuss Inuit art without acknowledging the impact of the April 1, 1999, redrawing of the Canadian map to include Nunavut territory? However, let me hasten to add that I am hesitant to use this example because it risks collapsing the complexity of the sovereignty issue into a narrow political interpretation. Rather, I recognize in this art a much broader call for self-determination, decolonization, and retraditionalization, which serves the larger goal of sovereignty.

SOVEREIGNTY

Sovereignty for Indian people in California is a legal, political, cultural, and spiritual issue. Indians were not "granted" citizenship in the United States until 1924. It should be noted that many Native peoples do not consider themselves to be citizens of the United States but members of their own Native nations. The Haudenosaunee (also known as the Iroquois) base our ideas of sovereignty on the knowledge that our societal structure of governance and spirituality predate contact. We have never let go of our worldview or sociopolitical organization of "the Great Law." At contact, our ancestors negotiated our separate, not subjugate, relationships: first to the European invaders and then to the emergent United States government. The most significant markers of this agreement are the wampum belt, known as the "Two Row," and the Treaty of Canadaigua of 1794.[5]

When I began questioning the role of the artist in California I found a complex mix of experiences in this region. California, or more appropriately, "Indigenous" California, was in our (national) consciousness because of artists such as Tuscarora/Seneca George Longfish, Seneca Sylvia Lark, Nisenan/Maidu Harry Fonseca, Yuki/Wailaki Frank Tuttle, Karuk Brian Tripp, Wintu/Nomtipan Frank LaPena, and Paiute/Pit River Jean LaMarr. As Indian artists we were aware that Longfish and Lark had moved out to California

40

Pamela Shields, *Motoki in Soho*, 1993. Digital iris print, 14 x 16 in. Collection of the artist.

In contrast, Fonseca, Tuttle, Tripp, LaPena, and LaMarr are artists making work in their own homeland. The relationship between artists working from within their own communities to those working from without yet connected to "new" Native communities, both urban and rural, is very compelling. Longfish and Lark both identify as Iroquoian but draw from a wide band of influences for their work. Longfish's work is identifiable as having Native-directed themes. Lark's work does not function overtly as "Indigenous." Although one could argue that the lyrical quality of Lark's work echoes a notion of unity described in Iroquoian teachings, I do not know how important the Iroquoian influence really was for Lark. It remains to be clarified what place Lark's work will occupy in the historic discourse on contemporary Native American art as it functions within the communities. But, she was an influential teacher and generally a strong and generous advocate for Native arts. Longfish continues to contribute as an artist and an educator. The work of younger photographers, such as Blackfoot Pamela Shields and Seminole/Creek/Dine Hulleah Tsinhnahjinnie, is consistent with

from Iroquois territories back East. Therefore, it is not possible for me to think about California-based Native artists without their inclusion. Today, one might argue that Longfish and Lark are part of an Iroquoian diaspora that has strong political ties to California.

Longfish's process in that they also actively contribute to the shifting artistic dialogue both regionally and nationally.

Tsalagi (Cherokee)/Euro-American Kim Shuck (Shuck's maternal family has been in California for generations, her paternal family is in Oklahoma), who is an accomplished weaver, further problemitizes an easy mapping of Indigenous cultural space. Since her work is directly influenced by the traditions of Indigenous peoples of California and her own heritage, Shuck is redefining notions of essential "traditionalism."

I put forth that art by artists working in relation to adopted communities functions in a slightly different way than that by artists who are practicing directly within their own communities. I am not suggesting that one is better, I am merely calling for a further clarification of the important roles that artists play in relation to the physical and conceptual location of their communities. California in the 1940s and 1950s became an end point for the U.S. government policy of relocation. How is it that after 503 years of punishing contact, Indians remain fixed on maintaining "Indian" spaces? The work of Native women artists in California provides insight into the motivation of defending and maturing a place called "Indigenous America," as we discuss below, thus further revealing the complex journey of Indigenous experience.

One might ask, what are the futures of Indi-

SYLVIA LARK

When artists use specific images from their own culture they take on, consciously or unconsciously, the symbolic baggage of those images. Sylvia Lark's work, as abstraction, crossed these borders. Lark became very well respected in the art world. Her paintings use color and line to convey emotion, rather than a language of tight symbolism. Layer upon layer of pigment is laid down to create light effects. In some work layers are removed to reveal underlying colors. The paintings are heavily emotional. In her *Jokhang* series (see fig. 89), layers of colors are painted over with a sooty black that leaves the viewer with a sense of half-seen activity. Lark stated clearly that these paintings were in emotional response to her visit to the Jokhang Temple in Lhasa, Tibet. One interviewer asked if she went to "exotic places . . . to get away from civilization" or to "make contact with primitive societies." Lark responded the she was seeking "a spiritual feeling . . . a feeling that is gone from much of Western civilization . . . (they) are closer to the earth and that affects me."

Lark's work predates the contemporary sense of connection between Indigenous peoples of the world. Her study of Tibet is most interesting because the people of Tibet have been as fetishized by the West as have Native American people. The cherished image of these very sacred people off in nearly impenetrable mountains recalls the stories of the seven cities of gold in the American Southwest. The similarities are striking. Lark's response to the realities of her experience in

Tibet—the smoke, the chanting, the movement of the people—is a great strength in her work. It presents a sense of the ritual without the fantasy.

A concept of the sacred is something that humans have in common; this idea is a connection between us, if you will. The objects we invest with this notion of sacredness may differ, but the idea that there is something that we can connect with, something that inspires wonder—this is what Sylvia Lark painted. This sense of spirit, when removed from specific cultural identifiers, can touch people from many backgrounds. The repeated gestures evident in Lark's paintings suggest that she not only responds emotionally to rituals that she witnessed, but also engages in her own ritual in the painting. This feeling of immediacy combined with her personal mysticism made Lark's work accessible to many people and insured her a position in the accepted art world.[6]

genous Americans? And can art be read as any kind of indicator? First, if we agree with Lakota scholar Vine Deloria's notion that we are "nations within nations," I would suggest that Native "communities" across the Americas are moving toward multiple expressions of a legal, political, and spiritual sovereignty. Secondly, if we agree that art provides insight into society's desire, then we can reflect upon art as a way into what people in Indigenous communities "aspire to."

The work artists are doing in our "nation," our homelands and extended diaspora, is critical within this sovereignty/aspiration rubric as a projection. Artists are the people that are helping us to imagine the terms of our decolonization. If one probes the landscape of Indigenous America, each nation/community is at a different stage of reemergence/establishment, which depends upon a number of factors. In California these include: (1) the recent contact (mid to late 1800s); (2) restrictive and punishing laws prohibiting cultural expressions; (3) the contemporary condition that the land in California remains in high demand due to boomtown economics. The pressure that these conditions have placed on the Indigenous nations of northern California is only now beginning to be counteracted.

It is difficult to address only Native Californian women's art because the framing it implies is contradictory to the way art functions in these communities. For instance, Kim Shuck, who has an insider's view about the way the arts have changed in California, says that she couldn't think about Native California art without recognizing the cultural advocacy of any number of people. As an example, Shuck points to Tolowa/Karuk Loren Bommelyn, who has helped to reenergize northern Californian traditions by building dance houses and by teaching the Tolowa language. The dance houses call for the use of the

Tolowa language in song and in the making of dance objects by the artists. The actual "art" in a Western sense would be located predominately in either the woven hats, dance aprons, and baskets, or perhaps the dance or song. But it is the entire statement that constitutes an expressive creative and spiritual act for the people. Therefore, the role of each of these individual "makers" becomes intricately interdependent to the culmination of the full expression or the "ceremony." Thus, the role of the artist in contemporary California is intricately connected to the recovery of ceremony in these communities. Since it is impossible to secularize many of these expressions, there is a necessary awareness that the purpose for these events is "spiritual." In this sense, the artist has a direct role in maintaining the ongoing physical and psychological well-being of the community. This does not undermine the significance the actual object has in maintaining a sense of community. Weaving requires not only considerable skill but also environmental advocacy. Indeed, the continuance of traditional cultural ceremony has been greatly impacted by the dumping of toxins, by logging, and by the threat of fire in California. This extends the duties of the artist to that of being a guardian to the natural resources essential to creative expression.

Within the field of art history new methodologies and framing must emerge in order to discuss

THE PROTECTION OF PLANTS

The most common misconception about traditions of basket weaving is the assumption that plants suitable for weaving are found randomly lying about in nature. On the contrary, plants that produce weaving materials often need to be carefully maintained from year to year in order for them to produce high-quality material. These plants are not farmed, in the general meaning of the word, but they are tended diligently. Most Indian weavers do not own large pieces of land on which to grow willow, redbud, bear grass, or any of the other weaving plants. They must, therefore, gather plants in "wild" areas or in state parks. It is now possible to get permission to gather in such areas, but weavers can be impacted by the use of herbicides and pesticides. Many weavers have become sick, and even died, as the result of state policies in these areas. The relationship of a weaver to the plants she uses can provide valuable information about those plants. There has been more cooperation between state park personnel recently, but more needs to be done in the area of communication.[7]

these practices responsibly. Scholars in this field must meet the challenge for "deconstructing" the artificial hierarchies between fine art and craft or folk art, realizing that those categories are a form of ongoing colonization. If, as I have suggested, the "ambition" of Indigenous people is to realize the full potential of our sovereignty, then coming to terms with the multiple valences of coloniality still present in our lives must be addressed.

In *Woman, Native, Other* (1989), Vietnamese filmmaker Trinh T. Minh-ha identifies this relationship of "women of color" to the West as a "triple bind." Trinh recognizes that with a growing ethnic-feminist consciousness, women of color are forced to place their loyalties. In her case, she must ask herself: Writer of color, woman writer, or woman of color? For her, language is a focal point of cultural consciousness and social change. She states: "writing weaves into language the complex relations of a subject caught between the problems of race and gender and the practice of literature as the very place where social alienation is thwarted differently according to each specific context."[8] Importantly, Trinh clearly rejects the further subjugation of locating herself on the "fringe" and goes on to note that "like any common living thing, I fear and reprove classification and the death it entails, and I will not allow its clutches to lock down on me, although I realize I can never lure myself into simply escaping it."[9] Fundamentally, Trinh rejects the ability of the dissecting, classifying, synthesizing tendency of the "West" to pin her to the butterfly board.[10] But how do women of color or as Pueblo scholar Annette Jaimes, author of *The State of Native America* (1992) prefers, "people of culture," articulate their "standpoint" to the ideological West?[11]

The emergence of ceremony for Indigenous nations in California is a profound marker of this consciousness. The role of the "artist" is integral to this process and must be acknowledged. The artificial hierarchy in our own communities, which exists between traditional, abstract, and conceptual art, needs to be reexamined in this context. An artist like Jean LaMarr serves her community as both an internationally recognized artist and as a hands-on educator within her community through her print workshop. Both of these activities help to define a "community" of northern Californian Indigenous artists. Her work lends insight into the complex space of traditional knowledge under continuous assault by colonizing acts. That fine border zone between us and them has been artfully honed by LaMarr. LaMarr's way of making the connection between the Native woman's body and the land is a counter-hegemonic statement. She focuses on the necessary recovery of the representation of our bodies as well as on the requirement of an analysis of race, colonization, and class in order for the body to be singularly mediated by individual women.

Euro-American critic Lucy R. Lippard acknowledges in *The Pink Glass Swan: Selected Essays on Feminist Art* (1990) that establishing the intersection between the feminist historical and theoretical discussion and the visual space gives import to the importance of new theories emerg(ent) from media analysis, especially film criticism. She sees these ideas as being part of the so-called post-feminism of the early 1980s to the present, citing the influence of European scholars—Sigmund Freud, Jacques Lacan, Hélène Cixous, Julia Kristeva—who echo the main focus of the British feminist left, from the mid 1970s.[12] Lippard identifies that the analysis of the socially imposed and debilitating image of women—and its effect on our lives and sexuality—has been a bulwark of feminist art since 1970. But, she constructs this argument with an air of disdain, acknowledging that "to reject all aspects of woman's experience as dangerous stereotypes often meant simultaneous rejection of some of the more valuable aspects of our female identities."[13] Lippard is sensitive to how the disappearance of female identification with the earth, with nurturance, with peace (and more problematically, with motherhood) would serve the dominant culture all too well. Another equally important position about the subjectivity of the gendered body was established by Laura Mulvey, the British critic and filmmaker, who says that the "image of woman as (passive) raw material for the (active) gaze of men [takes] the argument a step further into the structure of representation, adding a further layer demanded by the ideology of the patriarchal order as it is worked out in its favorite cinematic form—illusionistic narrative film."[14]

Therefore, how do we approach LaMarr's figures, which are always an integral part of the environment? It is rare to see a Native woman's body, yet in LaMarr's case the body is central to the environment. It is the focal point of the work even though the scale of the body is small. By offering up the Native woman's body for observation LaMarr risks romanticizing the already burdened image. The patterns surrounding the images form a cohesive sacred ground wherein Indian women, in languid posture, occupy a landscape of contact. Her work suggests that women are central in our environments, not by force or might but through balance. Her works are always tactile delights, offering many layers of texture and detail to fill out the context of a world in which LaMarr visualizes "woman as center." In a sense, the figure is surrounded by the West yet it maintains its own stronghold, thus acting as a metaphor for the role of women in Native society, which, as LaMarr indicates in all of her work, is also a condition of all of society.

Jean LaMarr's photo-etched prints made in the 1990s range in topics. For instance, she intermixes MX missiles and nuclear bombs pointed toward the Nevada border (close to LaMarr herself) with the Statue of Liberty, evoking a sardonic wit. Cowboys and turbo jets, barbed wire and the red-tailed hawk all cross LaMarr's landscapes. The surfaces of her pieces are scarred with glass, glitter, lace, and scratch marks, ren-

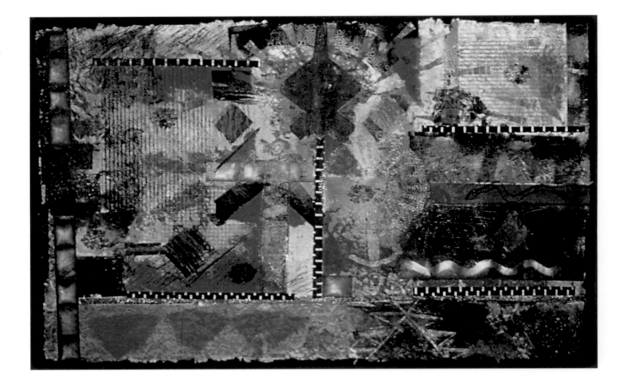

dering an eerie archeological feel of uncovering layers of the past. Here, LaMarr's patience is evident in every detail. Her women are static, stationary figures, watching as the constructions of the "west" pass through the land. The patterns in her collages are more than just repeated decorations, they are evidence that life is a cycle and this phase will pass.

The 1994 work of Seminole/Creek/Dine Hulleah Tsinhnahjinnie entitled *Photographic Memoirs of An Aboriginal Savant: Page 73 (Living on Occupied Land)* may serve as a logical point of departure for this discussion. Tsinhnahjinnie's fifteen-part series acts as a counterweight to the multiple colonized constructions of Native people in popular media and the academic canon. The notion of an "Aboriginal Savant," a sage or scholar in occupied land, twists the perception of where "Indians" are situated. Each image simultaneously constructs a view of Tsinhnahjinnie's experience as a Native woman while unraveling 500 years of highly reduced notions of Indianness.

Although Tsinhnahjinnie grew up in Dine territory, she has made California her second home for decades. Tsinhnahjinnie's work acts in opposition to the stereotypical construct aptly named by Cherokee/Jewish scholar Rayna Green in her influential 1975 article as the "Pocahontas Perplex"; in her article, titled "The Pocahontas Perplex: The Image of the Indian Woman in American Culture," Green outlines the cultural icon of the "Indian Princess" which has constrained the image/meaning of Native women within white, American culture:

> as a model for the national understanding of Indian women, [Pocahontas's] significance is undeniable. With her darker, negative viewed sister, the Squaw—or anti-Pocahontas . . . —the Princess intrudes on the national consciousness and potential culture waits to be resurrected when our anxieties about who we are make us recall her from her woodland retreat.[15]

Activist Debbie Wise Harris reinforces this position in her 1991 article, "Colonizing Mohawk Women: Representations of Women in the Mainstream Media." Harris asserts that Green is specific about the rules of the Pocahontas Perplex. This framework identifies that "Indian women have to be exotic, wild, collaborationist, crazy, or 'white' to qualify for white attention."[16]

Therefore, the very form that Tsinhnahjinnie's work takes—an advertisement style book page—

42
Hulleah J. Tsinhnahjinnie,
Photographic Memoirs of An Aboriginal Savant: Page 73 (Living on Occupied Land), 1994. Digital image, 14 × 11 in. © 1995 Hulleah J. Tsinhnahjinnie. Collection of the artist.

along with her personal memoirs which she incorporates, creates a potent fusion for the "Aboriginal Savant" to act as another counter-contact/hegemonic narrative of the Pocahontas stereotype. Tsinhnahjinnie reinforces or reveals the fact that we do live in the souped-up formula car called "Indian"—a powerful elixir of real memories and forced stereotypes. She merely provides the visual keys with titles like *Chinle High*, *Don't Leave the Rez Without It*, and *Geronimo in Florida* as a strategy to direct the trajectory of the journey.

But what remains consistent between the work of Jean LaMarr and Hulleah Tsinhnahjinnie is that both artists are attempting to reclaim and articulate the authority of the presence of the Indigenous woman's body against a legacy of colonization. In LaMarr's case, it is a body repositioned with a colonial yet Indigenous geographic landscape. In Tsinhnahjinnie's case, the body is used to reinscribe American consciousness and counter-hegemonic Indigenous positions.

This terrain is further complicated by the work of Tsalagi (Cherokee)/Euro-American weaver Kim Shuck. Her work is consistent with the Indigenous artists in northern California because it is deeply invested in the "teachings" or knowledge systems of their individual nations. But at the same instance it is an expression of how these ideas are commingled with the experience of contact. The art under examination is not "ceremonial" in the traditional sense, though it does offer an opportunity to reflect on the significance of traditional knowledge at the close of the machine age. One aspect of this is the understanding that "traditional knowledge" has been undermined by the triumph of quantifiable "facts." But now, as "science" reconsiders its platform of "facts" due to the recent changes in the field, it's time for cultural critics to reconsider the value of "other ways of knowing."

Shuck is part of a large Cherokee diaspora in northern California. She acknowledges the influences on her basket making from her grandmother Etta Mae Rowe and from the established traditions of basket making in California. She describes her baskets as a form of teaching vessel. But I believe it is difficult for most to access the deep knowledge invested in this art form because of our historic bias toward the basket. I argue that it is largely trapped in an unproductive "folk" binary of high/low or anthropologically seen as "utilitarian." This narrow view of the basket is additionally reinforced by a century of "authenticating" photography as visual anthropology.

Just as Trinh questions theoretical categorization and associates it with colonization, and Tsinhnahjinnie's "Aboriginal Savant" is seen in the context of the complex issues condensed in Pocahontas, Indigenous arts like basket making

43
Kimberly Shuck, *Net #2*, 1998.
Woven paper, yarn, and hickory
bark, 3 × 2 × 2 ft. Photo: Brian
Dang. Collection of the artist.

need to be understood in terms of the anthropological photograph. Allow me the following example to illustrate my point.

Photographic representations of Indigenous women and basket making are congruous with a set of anticipated tropes representing the colonized "Other" in the nineteenth century. In particular, a fairly common image is that of the bare-breasted woman and her "craft," underscoring an anthropological framing. The desire to "measure" the body occurs repeatedly along with bodily activities, like breastfeeding, basket making, hide scraping, and other "cultural" activities. The woman's gaze is invariably averted, but the exposure of her skin confirms Native "primitivism" to the Western mind. If one understands the process of basket making and can overcome personal bias about brown naked breasts, there is a great deal of information here. The notion of progress or technological advancement remains a tenet of Western thought. Therefore, the desire to locate the state of technological development of a people was often an unacknowledged goal of many photographers. An indirect yet equally effective way to establish the technological acumen of Native people was to document their production or "level of technology." The basket is handmade from the materials of the earth, relegating it to a "low" in contrast to "high" mechanistic form of technology.

Ironically, the basket is a significant innovation and invention of human ingenuity. The basket actually had multiple roles. Native people over millennia had developed an intimate knowledge of their relationship to their environment. Across the Americas a philosophical approach to sheltering this knowledge was to develop a world-view where everything was understood as being "alive." All living things, including rocks, the soil, plants, trees, animals, and insects, were recognized as having what some refer to as a "spirit." Another way to understand the wisdom of this perspective without categorizing Native people as "animists" is to consider the resulting creation of sustainable communities. The basket in this case

is just a hint at the complex web of ideas in play in Indigenous culture. The basket is the end result of thousands of years of "field" research. The basket is evidence of the generational passage of knowledge. It is confirmation of a community of people living cooperatively. The basket also had medicinal or healing functions. Weavers knew which fibers could hold water, had strength, and could sustain the weather. This intimate knowledge of every blade of grass is magnified by knowing which plant had what particular properties. The way Native people remembered this breadth of knowledge was to "characterize" it by its effect on the human body. In a sense, an energy measurement was assessed on everything in their environment and named accordingly.[17]

Specifically, Kim Shuck talks about basket making as a form of mathematics. Simultaneously appropriating from Indigenous cultures and Western science, Shuck is challenging the established hierarchy of fine and folk art. Working with materials from both Oklahoma and northern California, she twists these fibers into three-dimensional conceptual expressions. The moment that the fibers move from being flat to a three-dimensional shape is an intellectual and highly abstract thrill for her. Yet, the tactile quality of working with bloodroot, river cane, and acorns continuously teaches her about the interconnectedness of all of creation. Essentially, Shuck's understanding of the basket bridges inherited knowledge of the earth with a very modern notion of time and space as "abstract."

These artists are not just looking at that which exists in Indian communities, they are looking to find a way to continue as Native people. The political language used to identify this attitude is expressed as "self-determination." "Self-determination" in the minds of Indigenous artists is like a thin blade that cuts the borders of neocolonial representation. The position of "self-determination" is articulated in Point 5 of the Beijing Declaration of Indigenous Women at the 1995 United Nations Fourth Conference on Women held in Huairou, China: "We, the women of the original peoples of the world have struggled actively to defend our rights to self-determination and to our territories which have been invaded and colonized by powerful nations and interests . . . this has been shown in our tenacity and capacity to withstand and survive the colonization happening in our lands in the last 500 years."

Against the tyranny of missionization, disease, the Gold Rush, and termination, LaMarr, Tsinhnahjinnie, Lark, and Shuck all state "we are here." Each in her own distinct way reclaims and reconnects to the land. Land ownership and occupation are why all the blood was shed. LaMarr's Indian women physically occupy the land. Tsinhnahjinnie appropriates the colonizers' tools and reimagines them as statements of empowerment, a conceptual occupation. Lark makes a spiritual connection to the land. Shuck uses fibers and conceptual forms to reconfirm the importance of traditional knowledge as central and dynamic. These artists are living in a state known today as California, but hopefully moving toward a state of Indigenous consciousness.

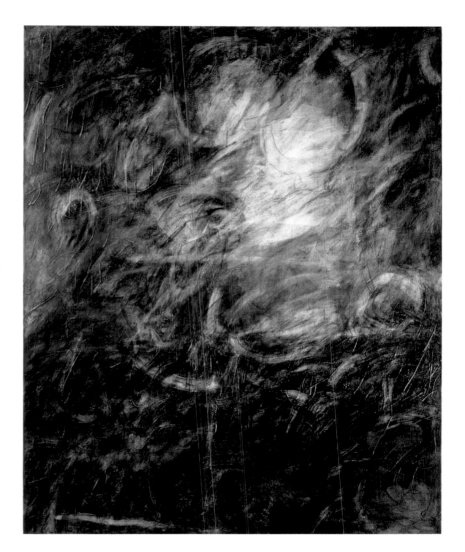

Notes

1 Information gathered from the Alcatraz Web site: *www.nps.gov/alcatraz*.

2 Summary of colonization taken from Edward D. Castillo, "History of Indian–White Relations," in William C. Sturtevant, ed., *Handbook of North American Indian*, vol. 8, edited by Robert F. Heizer (Washington, D.C.: Smithsonian Institution, 1978).

3 See essay by Jolene Rickard on the AtlAtl Conference in San Francisco in *Afterimage: The Journal of Median Arts and Cultural Criticism* 27, no. 2 (1998).

4 The sidebar on the impact of colonization describes Public Law 280. To add to the complexity, we need to distinguish between California Indians and Indians in California. Urban California boomed after World War II, and some Indian veterans from various parts of the United States moved to the San Francisco Bay Area and the greater Los Angeles area. Soon thereafter the U.S. government began a policy of relocating people to these urban areas from their home reservations. Cherokee people from Oklahoma and Lakota people from the Dakotas were among those relocated to California. Some Indian people were familiar with California from boarding school. Sherman Indian School in Riverside, California, was founded in the early part of the 1900s and has been a major destination, voluntary and involuntary, for Indian children from many states. Throughout the war in Vietnam, many Native people after their discharge from the military came to live in urban California. Today many Native people come to California for educational and work opportunities. All of this contributes to the complex nature of the Indian population in the state.

5 See John C. Mohawk and Oren R. Lyons, eds., *Exiled in the Land of the Free: Democracy, Indian Nations, and the U.S. Constitution* (Santa Fe, N.M.: Clear Light Publishers, 1992).

6 Conversation with Kim Shuck, January 2000. The critique of Sylvia Lark's work was written by Kim Shuck.

7 Conversation with Kim Shuck, January 2000.

8 Trinh T. Minh-ha, *Woman, Native, Other: Writing Postcoloniality and Feminism* (Indianapolis: Indiana University Press, 1989), p. 6

9 Ibid., p. 48.

10 Ibid.

11 M. Annette Jaimes, ed., *The State of Native America: Genocide, Colonization, and Resistance* (Boston: South End Press, 1992).

12 Lucy R. Lippard, *The Pink Glass Swan: Selected Essays on Feminist Art* (New York: New Press, 1995), p. 271.

13 Ibid., p. 270.

14 Laura Mulvey, "Visual Pleasure and Narrative Cinema," in *Art After Modernism: Rethinking Representation*, ed. Brian Wallis and Marcia Tucker (New York: The New Museum of Contemporary Art, 1984), p. 372.

15 Rayna Green, "The Pocahontas Perplex: The Image of the Indian Woman in American Culture," *Massachusetts Review* 16, no. 4 (1975): 689–714.

16 Debbie Wise Harris, "Colonizing Mohawk Women: Representations of Women in the Mainstream Media," *Resources for Feminist Research/Documentation sur la Recherche Feministe* 20, nos. 1–2 (Spring/Summer 1991): 17.

17 See F. David Peat, *Lighting the Seventh Fire: The Spiritual Ways, Healing and Science of the Native American* (Secaucus, N.J.: Carol Pub. Group, Birch Lane Press, 1994).

INTERSECTIONS

LEY LINES

DANIELA SALVIONI AND
DIANA BURGESS FULLER

BURNING DOWN THE HOUSE: FEMINIST ART IN CALIFORNIA

An Interview with Amelia Jones

DANIELA SALVIONI: How would you define feminist art?

AMELIA JONES: I don't know that I would try to define it in a singular way. I think it depends on the context and what period you are talking about. For the early 1970s it is easy to come up with a whole rubric to talk about it because people were so actively defining it. But, to come up with a global definition that crosses the last three decades I think is really impossible.

DS: In your book, *Sexual Politics*, you write: "feminist artists are artists who in some way attempt to re-value women as creative subjects or to critique aspects of patriarchy in their work." Does that mean that an artist's intentions are crucial to the definition of feminist art?

AJ: Intentionality is one of the most important methodological issues. That quote notwithstanding, for me it is very important to focus on the reception of the work, rather than on what the artist thought she was doing. That is an issue especially with the earlier artists such as Lee Bontecou, many of whom adamantly refused to be labeled feminist. In spite of what Bontecou says, her work had a definite feminist impact. More precisely, I would say that it is feminist within a certain context. For

163

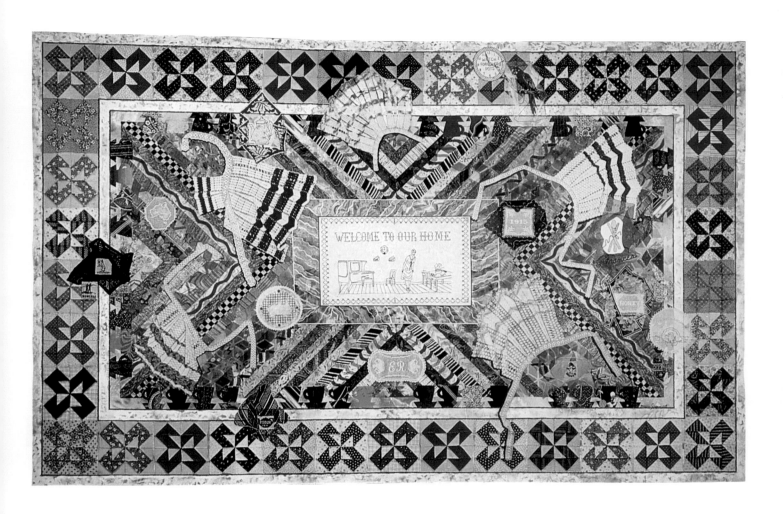

45

Miriam Schapiro, *Wonderland*,
1983. Acrylic and fabric on
canvas, 90 × 144 in. Collection
of The National Museum of
American Art, Smithsonian
Institution, Gift of an anonymous
donor. Courtesy of Steinbaum
Krauss Gallery, Palm Beach, Fla.

example, in the famous article "Female Imagery,"
written by Judy Chicago and Miriam Schapiro in
1973, the Bontecou piece illustrated becomes a
feminist icon.

DIANA FULLER: Yet, there seems to be a difference between when an artist incorporates the
stereotypical domestic paraphernalia associated

with women's things—the highest exaggeration
being doilies and lace—like Miriam Schapiro,
and when an artist makes abstract paintings
with mere echoes of feminist attributes, like
Bontecou.

AJ: I would still focus strongly on reception.
Helen Frankenthaler's work was dismissed

because it appeared "feminine" (because it looked like menstrual blood stain, or what have you) by people who obviously had no interest in feminism. I would have trouble if someone started calling Frankenthaler's work feminist because she was opposed to any suggestion of her gender or to feminism being an issue. This is different from an artist like Joan Brown who, while not a self-professed feminist, understood that there was a battle. Of course, you can say that Frankenthaler's work feminizes abstraction, but that doesn't get you very far; in fact, it confuses what we know about her. In saying this I do dip into intentionality, in the sense that I am concerned about historical record and wish not just to take someone out of context and place them in a wholly other context. Yet, I would not take Frankenthaler's words as a transparent revelation of what she intended to do either.

The big change in women's art came in the 1970s when there was an intense political urge to specify and to make overtly political what otherwise could be oblique. Judy Chicago could not resist writing some long descriptive text on her most abstract pieces, in an attempt to make their meaning more explicit. Bontecou's work remains oblique unless you put it in the context of cunt art, in which case it takes on a specific meaning.

DS: When does the feminist art movement start?

AJ: The feminist art movement really started around 1968. But, there were artists like Carolee Schneemann doing work before 1968, before she becomes explicitly feminist, that is proto-feminist, in which she was already putting her experience on the surface of the work.

I tend to think that New York in the 1960s was more activist-oriented. The women in the Art Workers Coalition got pissed off about how badly they were being treated and became feminists as a result of that experience. However, they were still closely connected to the male-dominated art world; for instance, a lot of them were married to male artists. The feminist art movement in California got under way in 1970, when Judy Chicago founded the Feminist Art Program at California State University, Fresno. In California the women artists were much more separatist and they established alternative institutions much more aggressively than in New York.

DS: Would you say that putting personal, or internal, experience on the surface of the work is what most distinguishes 1970s feminist art?

AJ: Yes, perhaps this is one strong characteristic. But, let's not forget artists like Vito Acconci, who were doing the same thing.

DF: Terry Fox is another male parallel; he externalized his internal malfunctions in his work.

AJ: But, having put forth that we don't want to look just at women on this subject, I would hasten to add that for a woman to turn herself inside out, as Carolee Schneemann does in *Interior Scroll* (1975), has a radically different effect from that of

Acconci's self-exposure. Formal and narrative similarities exist between this type of work done by men and women but, because of the differences we assign to femininity versus masculinity, they mean something totally different. For a woman to turn herself inside out becomes about vaginal sexuality, which Schneemann played on in *Interior Scroll.*

Another example would be to compare Acconci's whining self-disclosure in a piece such as *Line Up* (1973), where he complains about his ex-girlfriend, to Hannah Wilke's *Intercourse with . . .* (1977), where she plays her answering machine tapes and comments on all the people with whom she had a relationship. They are completely different, partly because of the way in which they are presented, but partly because of the different ways in which we perceive men versus women. For Wilke to comment on her relationships had a very charged meaning, especially in the mid-1970s when "the personal is political" was the major feminist clarion call. Whereas for a man to talk about his relationships, and especially in the way in which Acconci does, it is totally narcissistic. His work is rather about being in his own head and dealing with sexual difference through the male desire for power.

Recall, however, that it was Wilke who was repeatedly trashed for being narcissistic. The perception was that for Acconci to be narcissistic was radical because he was ugly and had a pimply back,

while for beautiful Wilke who, the argument went, "really just wanted us to look at her," the effect was of a shallow "feminine" narcissism.

DF: At what point does feminist art shift its focus to the body as site, and why, when so many women artists were exploring formalist elements of abstraction up to that moment?

AJ: I discuss the shift toward the body, particularly toward the ways in which the inside is expressed or enacted by the body in *Body Art/ Performing the Subject.* To explain it, I think you have to go back to Dada and, in the post–World War II period, to Jackson Pollock, especially to the way in which Pollock's paintings became known through the photographs of his body performing the act of painting. In the late '50s this galvanized younger artists who were frustrated with abstract expressionism and who thus developed Fluxus and "happenings," which involved working with aspects of the body.

But, Pollock was not the only source. I don't think you can ever abstract what is going on with artists from the larger social context. I think that political activism and the Civil Rights movement were really important to developing the sense that the body is political. Feminism learned a lot from the way the Civil Rights movement and the New Left movement put political activism on the surface, and this influenced feminist art practices—the idea that you could make a difference by participating physically in a social movement. For example, Martin Luther King and the freedom marches and Rosa Parks's action were crucial. Not that no one had ever protested before, but in the '50s and '60s in the U.S. it took a really dramatic form. The social movements of the time undercut the bogus abstract notion of the individual which was promoted by the American culture and made the individual concrete, specific, and, in the case of the Civil Rights movement, black. This completely exploded the so-called universal idea of the individual, and opened up possibilities for the body as a new focus. The protest actions had the meaning they had because of the particular identity perceived to be lodged in the particular body of the participant.

DS: Do you think that performance art is a privileged artistic form for feminist art because of the centrality of the body?

AJ: I do. I willfully read it as a radicalization of subjectivity because of the way that it so dramatically enacts the feminist notion of the personal is political. You could say that of cunt art, you could say that of a lot of feminist art, but body art makes it incontrovertible. Moreover, historically, a very raw kind of performance was absolutely key to the Feminist Art Program from the beginning. It was, perhaps, the most powerful vehicle for self-transformation, public intervention, and community building developed at the Woman's Building in Los Angeles (1973–1991).

The visual arts have an obvious relationship to expressing the personal is political: they can be quite explicit. In the early '70s it was assumed that if you put yourself out there and expressed hitherto forbidden feelings (at the time it was inadmissible to talk about things like menstruation or rape) that was itself a political act. I would say that this idea was implicit in what all feminist artists did, but it was not necessarily as consciously worked through or as fully theorized as positions would be later.

Mierle Ukeles, whose work is about labor and the politics of labor, was one of the most successful artists to integrate fully an overtly political critique with performance. Another is Suzanne Lacy.

DS: Provocative performance has a strong legacy in San Francisco, as well. Linda Montano sutured art and life through the construction of various personas (e.g., a nun, a blues singer). Later she and Annie Sprinkle mentored each other and linked the issue of sexuality to class via the sex worker, on the one hand, and to New Age spirituality, on the other. Karen Finley combined performance with a punk attitude. More recently, Nao Bustamante explores sexuality and relations of power. Does their work exemplify what you have called body art performance?

AJ: I define body art in the broadest sense possible, as being art in which the artist uses his or her body. In some ways it is broader than performance art, but in some ways it is narrower, because I am interested in a specific bodily enactment that is not so much narrative-, or theater-oriented, but more specifically about the body, about the body as an enactment of the self. It is closer to installation art: the particular place of the body and how it is being enacted is so crucial to the meaning of the piece. Karen Finley's work, for instance, is not like that. Her work is narrative: she gets up for an hour and a half and tells us all sorts of stories about all sorts of issues, and language is very important, but her main thrust is not her body as an enactment of subjectivity, though this is a component of her work.

The heyday of body art, as I define it, was the late '60s and early '70s. Then the emphasis starts to shift to artists who use their bodies in photographic performance like Cindy Sherman, and later to installations by younger generations of feminist artists who use objects signifying body fragments or parts, like Millie Wilson and Lauren Lesko.

I think that early Janine Antoni performances consisting of reduced actions, like the piece in which she washes the floor with her hair, are very close to some of the Feminist Art Program performances in which they turned women's work into a conceptual practice, such as Sandra Orgel's *Ironing* (1972), in which she irons in real time. But, for the most part, by the 1980s and '90s performance art becomes almost a separate genre, more connected to theater. Laurie Anderson is an obvious example of this shift to narrative and theatrical performance art.

DS: In the 1970s, much art done in San Francisco aimed to fuse art so totally with daily existence that some performances lasted for years and had very public profiles. For example, Bonnie Sherk's Crossroads Community project, "The Farm" (1974); Lynn Hershman Leeson's "Roberta Breitmore" character in the 1970s; Linda Montano's "Chicken Woman" series (1972). In this context, the city street became a prime arena for art. Was this also the case in L.A.?

AJ: There was street performance in L.A. too. Senga Nengudi and David Hammons, along with other black performers in the early 1970s, were doing performances under the freeways. The Chicano group ASCO, which included Patssi Valdez, was doing incredible street performances. Interestingly, that was in East L.A. where there is much more street life, so it had a different resonance there. Non-white, non-middle-class artists were doing all sorts of art in the streets of L.A. I wouldn't say the women in those groups, like Senga Nengudi and Patssi Valdez, were explicitly feminist; they were working in a coalition formed on the basis, rather, of race and class. White women were also doing public interventions. Suzanne Lacy's modus operandi, for instance, was to intervene in the public sphere. It was the white male artists who generally were not doing work in the streets.

46

Lynn Hershman Leeson,
*Roberta's Continuing
Constructions, Suggested
Alterations*, 1975. C print,
30 × 40 in. Collection of
the artist.

DS: Is it fair to associate cunt art with Los Angeles?

AJ: Yes. I do think it was an explicit ideology that was developed here. Not that no one else was doing it, but I think as far as calling it female imagery or cunt art, yes, it is fair.

Artists such as Judy Chicago and Miriam Schapiro saw the cunt as the site of their feelings of disempowerment. They argued for a feminist strategy of zooming in on the site of their feminine lack, to the site of their subordination to men even in just the most obvious sexual way of being penetrated by men, to the site for which they were always made to feel inferior. Taking that which is devalued and valuing it is a powerful strategy. One of my favorite examples is

Chicago's 1975 *The Female Rejection Drawing*, consisting of a visceral image that looks like flesh being torn away and a long, handwritten biographical text about her feelings of violation and rejection by the art world. Another example is Tee Corinne, in Northern California, who does photographs of women's genitalia which she reconfigures into trippy, psychedelic collages. Her point of view is very much indexed to lesbian sexuality, but you wouldn't know it just by looking at her abstract images because they are quite formalist. Or, take Ann Severson's film *Near the Big Chakra* (1972), which is a fabulous film, fifteen minutes long, of one cunt after another. That is all the film is. After a while the genitalia start to look incredibly abstract and weird. I found a lot of the cunt art that started coming out in the 1980s very appealing aesthetically but also somewhat distressing because it seemed to be reinventing the wheel. Judie Bamber's brilliant, meticulously realist cunts from 1994 are perhaps the best-known examples.

DS: The radical concreteness of body art performance and the essentializing illusionism of cunt art seem to imply opposing theoretical outlooks.

AJ: Both can be viewed as "concrete" as well as "essentializing." There is a tendency to view '70s feminism dichotomously, but I think at the time there was much less separation. At the Feminist Art Program artists would create performances out of psychodynamic situations (ones drawn from consciousness-raising sessions) which would finally also find their way into the visual imagery.

I also have a problem with the dichotomy made between conceptual work and feminist work, whereby the former is thought of as obviously theorized and the latter as intuitive, naïve, and overly sincere. Take Faith Wilding's *Waiting* (1971). Of course, there is a clear desire to express inner feelings directly, but I think you could also argue a piece like that is very much about femininity as mediated and socially contingent: your experience of being a woman is also about waiting for things to happen to you.

DS: Post-structuralist feminist discourse, which inspired much art of the 1980s and 1990s, investigates visual pleasure, the gaze, and mediated experience. From this perspective, Judy Chicago's *The Dinner Party* (1979), which for many epitomizes '70s American feminist art, is problematic. You, instead, chose to revive Chicago's work in your 1992 exhibition *Sexual Politics*. How do you see the terms of this debate?

AJ: I wanted to re-place *The Dinner Party* within the history of feminist art, from which it had always been isolated out—either completely ignored by art critics and historians, or presented as the one feminist monument in Gardner's *History of Art*.

The Dinner Party's kitsch populism makes us cringe because we are in the art world and we are

cynical. But, Griselda Pollock, in arguing that *The Dinner Party* is not effective feminist art, ends up saying exactly the same thing as Hilton Kramer about *The Dinner Party*, albeit from the opposite end. She is legislating quality, just as he did. She says that feminist art should be political in a Brechtian way: that it should distance the viewer and not absorb her or impart any visual pleasure. If it does, then it is bad art, kitsch, etc. Kramer said that art should not be about politics, but he also said that it should not be kitsch. Pollock's argument had incredible explanatory force in the 1980s, but it is limited.

Pollock's critique of Chicago is elitist because it denies the fact that the vast majority of people who have seen the piece and who have participated in it adore it and, in their own words, have been deeply affected by it. Its popular appeal is good enough reason to consider its importance. One doesn't have to like it, but for me it is deeply problematic to suppress it because it violates one's idea about what art—or feminist art—should be. At the other extreme there is Mary Kelly's work, which is so esoteric, arcane, and specific to the universe of Freudian thought that, frankly, most people in the art world don't understand it, let alone the person in the street. It doesn't transform the world. It might affect people in increments, as they come to understand it gradually, and I would never deny its crucial role in galvanizing feminist discourse. But that is a very different dynamic from Chicago's populism, which appeals to so many people outside the art world. Kelly is very important, but her work enacts a totally different kind of melding of the political and the individual.

For me the real political issue is how history gets told, because I am an art historian, and one thing that really bothers me is to see a whole group, a very large group, a very vital group of feminist thinkers completely shut down. When *October* published their roundtable on feminism, twenty-five years after the fact, they made the most bizarre choice of women to include and, of course, there was not even one of the historical figures of American feminist art among them. In spite of the increased visibility of feminism in art discourse, we are still viewed as kind of marginal. For example, I wrote an essay on Faith Wilding

that I cannot get published. To me she is a major artist who has never been really written about. But the kind of responses I got was very interesting. Of course, no one would say, "She is a woman, she is not important, we are not going to publish anything on her." Rather, they say things like "This essay covers an artist whose work isn't well enough known yet." Well, what a catch 22!

In my opinion the perceived division between Mary Kelly and Judy Chicago—smart British social constructivist, psychoanalytic, Brechtian feminist versus dumb essentializing American '70s feminist—has been the most damaging division in feminism since the early 1980s.

DS: Are you saying that we should appreciate feminist artists for raising hell, reaching a wider audience, but not necessarily for the actual works of art they produce?

AJ: I don't see the two as separable: they are really the same thing. I think that art is an activist gesture. That is clearer in some cases than others. This is really obvious in Suzanne Lacy's work, while in the case of Harmony Hammond it is less so. But, I believe that we should express appreciation and acknowledge what these women did. Whether we like Harmony Hammond's work or not, we should still admire her for setting the stage for younger women artists to be taken seriously.

What I personally enjoy is distinct from what I think is worth writing about. I don't have any idea how to legislate quality and I don't really want to. Annie Sprinkle's work is on my walls and I love it, but I am not there to judge whether or not someone else should like it. For me it is easier to justify what I think is important historically, and that I can argue very comfortably. Of course by so arguing I am, to a certain extent, making it so (writing the work into history).

DS: You have said that the difference between work produced by feminists in the '70s and today is one of attitude and emphasis. Would you elaborate on this?

AJ: The role of the activist artist is no longer just to recuperate and present positive images of women, of black people, and so on. That was the shift in the '80s, against recuperation and toward critique. Then, in the early 1990s queer politics in many complicated ways came to dominate feminist art. Right now I feel like there is very little political point of view. Most often '90s art doesn't even explicitly critique. It is about different issues. With the reemergence of installation, there is a lot of work about the body in space and the public versus private. These are much more complex, less unilaterally-based positions. That causes a lot of consternation on the part of older generations because there is such a huge stake in believing that you can and should reduce identity to a singular category. But, there are a lot of similarities in the strategies and the materials used between the early work and 1990s art by women, and the focus on the body and some of the messages end up being similar. But, what I see now is mostly a diffusion and a turning away from feminism, unfortunately.

DS: What do you mean by a diffusion of feminism?

AJ: Feminism becomes implicit in everything and not explicit in anything. It is perfectly okay to talk about women artists up to a point, as long as you don't politicize it, as long as you don't talk about feminism.

It has to do with the art market and the way in which race, ethnicity, sexual orientation, and gender became marketable in the late '80s. The upside was that artists who were not being recognized before have been made much more visible. But only up to a point. There was tons of feminist art throughout the '80s and into the early 1990s which never got a big museum show. For instance, it is fashionable to include a photograph by Laura Aguilar in a show about self-portraiture, but she doesn't have gallery representation—she can't make a living off her work. Things have changed a lot, and yet in some crucial economic and institutional ways they haven't at all.

The diffusion of feminism is also caused by feminism increasingly acknowledging ethnic and class differences and really deeply thinking them through to rectify its past myopia. In some ways this is good because, how long can you maintain a separate politics for something that is based only on the idea of being a woman? With everything else subordinate to it? Maybe now gender is just not the major factor of difference that is guiding our experience—it is certainly not viewed as such by most people. And, once you complicate sexual difference, it isn't so easy to just be direct and expressive. That is why we question the early '70s work. Because it seems too simplistic.

But, while I often find myself feeling that feminism, per se, may not be the single most important polemic today, then I will be hit in the face with some incredibly egregious example of sexism. There are these weird, disconcerting ways in which we are constantly being told that feminism is just an interest group, or that we are being ideological.

The diffusion of feminism can be very dangerous. Feminism is so built into the way younger women see themselves, and yet they have no idea that feminism is why they are able to see themselves that way. On the one hand, this makes them more liberated, but on the other hand they are not at all because they have no historical consciousness about what it means to wear a pointy bra and throw yourself around like Madonna does.

DS: Lorraine O'Grady has written about how a black woman is not going to walk around naked in a performance because it is very highly charged for her to expose herself that way. A cunt is not just a cunt. Do you see the problematization of the

body reflected in the work of artists today?

AJ: Absolutely. In art school and outside there is a lot of discussion about the psychic and cultural structure of experience. I would say that most artists under the age of forty put that in their work. For example, the late '80s artists doing the body part work, like Judie Bamber and Millie Wilson, or Connie Hatch's text-image work.

Diana Thater is an interesting case because there is nothing remotely literal about her work; it doesn't have anything directly to do with feminism or identity politics, but I think that the work has everything to do with questioning the kind of bias that accrues to a normative point of view. The normative cinematic or video viewer is completely disoriented by her installations.

Jennifer Steinkamp's work is a lot about gender differences, but you would never know by just looking at it without inside knowledge. Susan Silton makes her recent distorted self-portraits by pulling her face across a computer scanner. You wouldn't know looking at it that she is a queer artist. But if you know, the distorted faces suddenly seem to be metaphors of queer subjectivity.

I worked on a project with other art historians, artists, architects, and activists to design a virtual space on the Web called WomEnhouse (*http/www.cmp.ucr.edu/womenhouse/*). We decided that the '90s version of the 1972 feminist art project *Womanhouse* (a collaborative project consisting of feminist art installations in a derelict building the artists renovated themselves) was to teach women Web or computer skills to build a virtual house with grouped clusters of women doing sites together. For example, Alessandra Monteczuma is an artist and activist who designed the front yard, which in Latino communities is an extension of the house. These kinds of interventions are, I think, rendering more complex the notion of feminism, forcing it to be about all kinds of other identities.

DS: How would you summarize the impact '70s feminist art has had on subsequent generations of artists?

AJ: The impact is really broad and it happened on a lot of different levels, but it is also in most instances very subtle. The Woman's Building set the stage for empowering women artists. However conscious or unconscious the younger feminists are, they owe a huge debt to those women for establishing a feminist pedagogy and establishing the idea that women had a right to be artists.

I think feminism had a deep structural effect on the broader public's appreciation of women artists. The broader feminist movement's message was that what we do is not just of no significance, not just "private"; rather, it made the point that what we experience privately is of public importance. The feminist art movement put that into play in really visible ways. As a result, I

48
Millie Wilson, *Daytona Death Angel,* 1994. Synthetic hair, steel, wood, 66 × 36 × 24 in. Collection of the artist.

think the sensibility of younger feminist artists is much more open-minded than that of the older generation. There is an ease to being a woman artist in the '90s, which is a privilege that women in the '70s didn't have. I think that this is because of what the older generation put in place.

DS: Is the feminist art strategy of exteriorizing the personal something that has carried over into today?

AJ: Absolutely. I think the whole so-called abject art trend is very much an extension of that. You wonder how much of this exteriorization is consciously done out of knowledge of that earlier work, since '70s artists had already done so much work like that.

Generally, the feminist art strategies of the 1970s—which included political activism, autobi-ography, the transformation of the self through multiple personae, and the appropriation and critique of mainstream culture—clearly shaped the art concerns of the '80s and '90s.

DS: What landmark artworks did feminist art produce and what is their particular significance?

AJ: The obvious two pieces are Judy Chicago's *Dinner Party* and Mary Kelly's *Post Partum Document*. Those are probably the best known. Aside from that, I would think more in terms of artists, rather than major pieces. I would think of Judy Baca, Miriam Schapiro, Adrian Piper, Nancy Spero and, interestingly, some of the artists we think of as '80s feminist artists, but who were actually making pieces in the '70s, such as Barbara Kruger, Maureen Connor, and Harmony Hammond.

TEREZITA ROMO

A COLLECTIVE HISTORY

Las Mujeres Muralistas

Our intent as artists is to put art close to where it needs to be. Close to the children; close to the old people; close to everyone who has to walk or ride the buses to get places.

Las Mujeres Muralistas[1]

During the 1970s, the San Francisco Bay Area became one of the greatest centers for mural production in the United States. In this period of intense idealism, civil rights activism, and cultural nationalism, many artists left individual careers to pursue collective artistic projects in service to their community. Murals painted on neighborhood walls became the public art preferred by many community artists. Though produced by artists from all racial groups and painted throughout various neighborhoods and cities in the Bay Area, it was the murals of San Francisco's heavily Latino Mission District that came to the forefront of media attention.

As was true of other art forms, at first mural production was almost entirely the province of male artists. This was reflected in their murals' thematics: "At that time, a lot of the images were of men. All the heroes were men and it seemed like historical events only happened to men, not to families or communities."[2] Las Mujeres Muralistas would change this. Formed in direct reaction to the historical male exclusivity, the San Francisco-based collective was begun by Patricia Rodriguez and Graciela Carrillo with their first joint mural in 1973 and expanded later that year to include Consuelo Mendez and Irene Perez. Although the group remained together for only six years, its impact both on mural making and on other Chicana and Latina artists was significant.

The revival of muralism in the United States in the mid-1960s was markedly different from its social realist forerunner in Mexico and the United States some forty years earlier. Rather than being government-sponsored and painted on government buildings, the contemporary mural movement in the United States sprang from the people themselves and continues to thrive today, with murals appearing on community and campus-building walls. Perhaps the biggest difference, however, was the process. In the Mexico of the early twentieth century, murals resulted from the vision of individual artists. In today's barrios and ghettos in the United States, murals are produced by artists working with local residents on design and creation. "This element of community participation, the placement of murals on exterior walls in the community itself, and the philosophy of community input, that is, the right of a community to decide on what kind of art it wants, characterized the new muralism."[3]

Community engagement was characteristic of the Chicano art movement as a whole, for Chicano art evolved from the same foundations as the Chicano civil rights movement of the mid-1960s. Both were a direct response to the needs of Mexican American people living in the United States, their fight for the right to adequate education, political empowerment, decent working conditions, and a call to end social discrimination. Artists joined other cultural workers in making political statements and played a key role in taking these statements to the public. Noted scholar Tomás Ybarra-Frausto writes that "Artists functioned as visual educators, with the important task of refining and transmitting through plastic expression the ideology of a community striving for self-determination."[4]

Chicano activist-artists developed collectives and established *centro culturales* that functioned as the propaganda arm of the Chicano sociopolitical movement. "Integrally related to the human concerns of their local neighborhoods, artists pursued the vital tasks of creating art forms that strengthened the will, fortified the cultural identity, and clarified the consciousness of the community."[5] However, while the movement's leaders called for ethnic and racial equality, the need for gender parity in the areas of leadership and decision making was often overlooked. Consequently, Las Mujeres Muralistas not only had to dedicate themselves to reclaiming an artistic legacy, but also to creating within the Chicano movement a new organizational structure along gender lines and a uniquely Latina aesthetic.

The Women

Patricia Rodriguez and Graciela Carrillo first met in 1969 at University of California, Berkeley's

Third World Student strike. A native of south Texas, Rodriguez came to the Bay Area in 1966 to become an artist. Through her instructor at Merritt College in Oakland, the muralist and poster artist Malaquias Montoya, she was introduced to the Mexican American Liberation Art Front (MALA-F) and the Chicano movement. "There were a lot of things going on, lots of demonstrations, a lot of exciting moments . . . It was the ideal of trying to be liberated and trying to be feminist, of trying to work for something you could never achieve otherwise because society wouldn't let you."[6] In 1970, she was admitted to the San Francisco Art Institute's painting program on a fee-waiver scholarship.

Graciela Carrillo was born in Los Angeles and attended California State University in San Jose. In 1969, she moved to San Francisco to pursue an art career and soon enrolled at the San Francisco Art Institute, also on scholarship. Carrillo and Rodriguez became roommates, renting an apartment on Balmy Alley in San Francisco's Mission District, which would become a focal point of the mural movement.

Consuelo Mendez, whom they met in 1972, was born in Caracas, Venezuela. Through her father, himself a painter as well as a doctor, she met Cesar Rengifo, an artist interested in the Mexican mural movement and its leftist politics, who would be a great influence on her. Initially a medical student at Rice University, in 1972

Mendez enrolled in the San Francisco Art Institute's printmaking program.[7]

The youngest of the muralists, Irene Perez came from a migrant farmworker family that had settled in East Oakland. She first studied commercial art, and then, through Michael Rios, an accomplished muralist, she met Rene Yañez, who facilitated her acceptance to the San Francisco Art Institute under the fee-waiver program. Unfortunately, the fee-waiver program was terminated before she could finish her degree.

The Beginning at Balmy Alley

The Bay Area was an important epicenter for the various student movements of the late 1960s and early 1970s, including the Free Speech, anti–Vietnam War, and Third World Student movements. But, for the three Chicanas and the Venezuelan it was a very frustrating time. As the only Latinas at the Art Institute, they lacked a support structure and role models. Moreover, the splendid Diego Rivera mural that graces the school notwithstanding, the painting department showed a strong preference for abstraction. "I was having a bad time with trying to be more formal," recalled Rodriguez, "trying to express myself in the code of colors which didn't represent the real me, the emotional and spiritual aspects."[8] Thus, the four began to meet to talk about art and its role in their lives and in the Chicano movement. Perez recalls that Mendez was adamant about her support for Latino, versus only Chicano, issues. This perspective became one of the defining elements of the Mujeres' artistic philosophy and aesthetics.

Through their association with the artists Yañez and Rios, the four women were aware of the burgeoning mural movement in San Francisco, but they were not invited to participate in the exclusively male projects. Meanwhile, murals began to appear on their home street, Balmy Alley. The first one was painted in 1972 by Mia Galivez with children from the neighborhood community childcare center. Soon, other artists began to paint murals on all available walls, garage doors, and fences. In 1973, Rodriguez and Carrillo initiated their own project on a garage across from their apartment. According to Rodriguez,

> It was a total learning process. We had to experiment with what we had, since we were art students with no money. So we got the scaffolding from the Arts Commission. The outdoor paint was donated by the neighbors who gave us a lot of half-filled cans. We didn't even know what the wall grid process was; we just eye-balled it.[9]

While the public's response was overwhelmingly positive, there were men, including Yañez, who urged them to quit, saying, "It's too much for you."[10] But they persevered.

That same year, Perez created her own mural, also on Balmy Alley. Situated over a garage door, it consists of two figures sitting with their backs to each other playing flutes. Drawing on her personal experience, she wanted to make a statement against the overtly political imagery characteristic of the majority of the murals in the Mission District. "I felt a lot of murals were very political, disclosing injustices, which to me were very violent. True, it is part of our experience. But what about the other parts—the quiet, positive images of our experience?"[11] This belief in an expanded definition of "political art" that included aspects of nature, culture, and the family, came to characterize the work of Las Mujeres Muralistas. Although a point of contention with their male counterparts, their commitment to this philosophy was such that it altered the history of mural practice. It is exemplified in the collective's first collaborative project, *Latinoamérica* (1973).

Latinoamérica

Our people and culture are our images. Full of color, of life, and the strength to continue the struggle. **Consuelo Mendez**[12]

In 1973, Rodriguez was commissioned to create a mural on two interior walls for the Jamestown Community Center on Fair Oaks Street in the Mission District. She approached Mendez to help her. In order to accommodate the participation of other artists, the artists created a tree motif as a unifying structure for the whole. "It was after this, when the project was rolling that I contacted Rene [Yañez]. He brought in Rios and all the other artists."[13] For her section, Mendez chose bright yellows, reds, oranges, and blues to create a pre-Conquest death god awaiting the death of a heroin addict. In its reference to a recognizable cultural image, Mendez claimed the Jamestown Center as a Latino space, and its central antidrug message addressed a serious concern of the community.

Also in 1973, Mendez was commissioned to make a mural for the Mission Model Cities building on Mission Street near 25th. The 20 x 75 foot wall was much larger than her previous project, so she enlisted Rodriguez, Carrillo, and Perez to participate. They decided to work collectively and to approach the planning, designing, and painting collaboratively. For the first time they had a small budget but, more importantly, Perez notes "we were going really big and outdoors."[14]

They agreed that the mural should be colorful and send a positive message about Latino culture, with a special focus on their individual histories, families, and culture. Mendez explored imagery from Venezuela and chose to focus on the family. Rodriguez incorporated traditional images from Bolivia and Peru. Carrillo researched the Aztec heritage of Chicanos and reworked its imagery in an innovative way so as not to repeat the prevalent pre-Conquest imagery of other murals. Perez's images of magueys and cornstalks were emblematic of her parent's birthplace in Mexico.

The group was also concerned with sharing the space effectively. They chose the images through consensus, utilizing Perez's graphic art skills to cut and paste them into a unified whole. In what is an astounding procedure, the colors to be used were not chosen in the design stage. Rather, beginning with only a line drawing, they inserted color as they painted. According to Rodriguez, "Our greatest strength was our instinctive sense of color that we all shared."[15]

The mural was a stunning tribute to the cultural traditions, peoples, and landscapes of Latin America. Described as an "ode to life," it merged the natural, human, and spiritual dimensions of each culture. Referencing the countries of Bolivia, Peru, Venezuela, Guatemala, and Mexico, the motifs were chosen for their uniqueness and their special relationship to the residents of the Mission District. Images of banana palms, cornstalks, and magueys form the foundation of the mural in direct reference to their key sustenance role for Latin American peoples. Other natural resources, such as the reed and alpaca from Peru, were also depicted. There was also a commitment to portraying everyday people, especially women and children. In fact, women in beautiful traditional costumes flank both sides of the mural. Acknowledging its significance within Latino culture, the central image is a family

49

Las Mujeres Muralistas (Graciela Carrillo, Consuelo Mendez, Irene Perez, and Patricia Rodriguez), *Latinoamérica,* 1974. Mission Model Cities Building, Mission and 25th Streets, San Francisco. Paint on concrete, 20 × 75 ft. Photo by Ralph Maradiaga and Patricia Rodriguez. Courtesy of the artists.

encircled within a sun. Located on both sides of the central motif are the Venezuelan and Bolivian devil figures representing the spiritual and ceremonial aspects of culture, while at the same time symbolizing the merger of indigenous spirituality with the Catholic religion. There was also a conscious attempt to represent the indigenous concept of duality with different symbols, such as the sun and the moon, day and night, and male and female. At the far right is a scene depicting the people of the Mission. Rendered in black and white to evoke newsreel footage, it includes Latinos, blacks, and Asians from different generations. Thus, even though the mural was a celebration of the Latino presence, it also recognized the reality of the Mission's present and future ethnic evolution.

Latinoamérica reflected sophisticated technique as well as aesthetics. Through the unorthodox process of assigning color at the site, the Mujeres achieved a distinctive palette. They were very creative in their approach to architectural challenges. For instance, Rodriguez incorporated an already existing gas pump into the mural design by painting a Bolivian devil emerging from it, thus making a statement on gas rationing then in force. The group was just as innovative in reworking Chicano images that were becoming cliché. For example, they included a pyramid leading up to the image of the family, but it is subtle and well hidden. "At that moment it was a breakthrough. It was no longer the same repetitive symbols borrowed from Siqueiros or Rivera, but an experiment done in the community for Latinos by Latinas."[16]

Other women assisted them, four of whom remained throughout the project: Ester Hernandez, Xochilt Nevel, Miriam Olivo, and Tuty

Rodriguez. The Mujeres sought to have the apprentices contribute in a meaningful manner to the project and learn mural painting techniques in the process. According to Rodriguez, "we wanted to create a camaraderie not only within ourselves, but with our sisters so that we could open the door to other women interested in murals."[17]

Even before it was completed, *Latinoamérica* received major community and media attention. People from the neighborhood not only came by to look, but many also provided the artists meals in appreciation. Everyone was shocked to learn that the muralists were women. "We received a lot of publicity and became well known. It helped us in our own community because, as women in the Chicano community, we were not taken seriously."[18] With the heightened media attention, the group felt the pressure to be identified collectively. According to Perez, Ralph Maradiaga, codirector of the Galeria de la Raza, called them Las Mujeres Muralistas, and the name stuck.[19]

With *Latinoamérica* the group gained prominence, a name, and more members, but ironically it would be the first and last time that the core members Carrillo, Mendez, Perez, and Rodriguez would work together on a mural. Subsequent murals painted under the name of Las Mujeres Muralistas were designed and directed by only one or two of these artists. Their other obligations—particularly the need to support themselves financially and their own individual artistic pursuits—meant they had less time to devote to mural projects. But the group's greatest challenge was the maintenance of their collective structure in the face of requests from other women to join. They settled on a structure in which whomever from the original core was available would spearhead the mural project, with assistance from the other artists.[20]

Para el Mercado

My community, the people on this block, they may never leave the Mission. So whatever you can do around here is going to be the most effective. **Graciela Carrillo**[21]

In 1974, Mendez and Carrillo painted the mural *Para el Mercado* (To the market), with the help of Susan Cervantes and Miriam Olivo.[22] It was commissioned by a taqueria owner in response to the opening of a McDonald's down the street. Continuing the Latin American theme, *Mercado* was a vibrant montage of people and animals set against landscapes that ranged from lush tropics through clear streams to arid ground. The vibrant colors of the natural world were accentuated by those of parrots, fish, and women's traditional woven garments. There were scenes of men and women preparing food, fishing, harvesting, and kneading dough. Interspersed were people from ancient through modern times at the market, buying and selling food items. The people in *Mercado* reflected the various racial groups of

50

Las Mujeres Muralistas, detail
from *Para el Mercado,* 1974.
Paco's Taco Fence, South Van
Ness and 24th Streets,
San Francisco. Politec and
Cal-Western acrylics on wood.
Courtesy of the artists.

Latin America, including the Natives, mestizos, and Afro-mestizos. Though some community members thought the people portrayed were "too dark," the media response was laudatory. The neighborhood paper, *El Tecolote,* proclaimed that "The ideas and images of the cultures they blend are bold achievements in the move toward unity. South America and the barrios of Aztlan have taken a stand and we stand together."[23] However, male muralists continued to criticize their lack of overtly political imagery. About this, Rodriguez says, "There are other things that one can say, especially as an artist . . . I never believed that you had to be so dogmatic, in fact, I resented it."[24] At this point, Mendez, who had always grappled with the issue, decided the murals were no longer sufficiently political and left the group.[25] In 1976, she returned to Venezuela where she pursued her political graphic art.

Various configurations of the original core (minus Mendez), assisted by other artists, continued to paint murals as Las Mujeres Muralistas. By 1979 their individual artistic pursuits and the frustrations stemming from the collective ideal being stretched too far brought the Mujeres as a group to an end. In 1979, Rodriguez took a teaching position at the University of California at Berkeley and turned to creating box assemblages.

Carrillo married and moved to Arizona. Perez took a job at a community clinic and returned to printmaking.

The Legacy

The beauty and pride we all feel for our culture is expressed through artists who act as our hands to make the praises of our culture visible and tangible.[26]

Las Mujeres Muralistas hold a very unique and significant place in Chicano art history. They developed a reputation for their distinct artistic style and collective techniques. Their unique iconography, with its emphasis on Latin American cultural traditions and landscapes, formed a new vocabulary of images that extended and redefined the political nature of muralism. As the first all-woman collective, they shattered the long tradition of male muralists and encouraged other Chicana artists. Other groups followed in their footsteps: Celia Rodriguez, Rosalinda Palacios, and Antonia Mendoza in Sacramento painted a mural celebrating women on a pillar in San Diego's Chicano Park in 1975; Yolanda Lopez and a team of young women from San Diego also painted a pillar at Chicano Park; and Las Mujeres Muralistas del Valle, a group of fifteen women who created murals in the mid-1970s in their hometown of Fresno.[27] Women continued to make murals throughout the 1980s and 1990s, culminating in the San Francisco Women's Building murals completed in 1994. The legacy of Las Mujeres Muralistas had come full circle.

Notes

1 Victoria Quintero, "A Mural is a Painting on a Wall Done by Human Hands," *El Tecolote* 5, no. 1 (September 13, 1974): 6.

2 Ibid.

3 Eva Cockcroft and Holly Barnet-Sanchez, eds. *Signs From the Heart: California Chicano Murals* (Venice: Social and Public Resource Center, 1990), pp. 9–10.

4 Tomás Ybarra-Frausto, "The Chicano Movement/The Movement of Chicano Art," in *Exhibiting Cultures: The Poetics and Politics of Museum Display*, ed. Ivan Karp and Steven D. Lavine (Washington, D.C.: Smithsonian Institution Press, 1991), p. 140.

5 Cockcroft and Barnet-Sanchez, *Signs From the Heart*, p. 67.

6 Taped interview with Patricia Rodriguez, October 30, 1982, Califas Conference at University of California, Santa Cruz, transcript p. 4.

7 Shifra M. Goldman, "Querida Consuelo," *La Opinion* (n.d.), pp. 8–9.

8 Interview with Patricia Rodriguez, December 11, 1999.

9 Ibid.

10 Taped interview with Patricia Rodriguez, October 30, 1982, p. 5.

11 Interview with Irene Perez, December 11, 1999.

12 Goldman, "Querida Consuelo," pp. 8–9.

13 Interview with Patricia Rodriguez, December 11, 1999.

14 Interview with Irene Perez, December 11, 1999.

15 Interview with Patricia Rodriguez, December 11, 1999.

16 Taped interview with Patricia Rodriguez, October 30, 1982, p. 9.

17 Interview with Patricia Rodriguez, December 11, 1999.

18 Theresa Harlan, "My Indigena Self: A Talk with Irene

Perez," in *Irene Perez: Cruzando la Linea* (exhibition brochure) (Sacramento: La Raza/Galeria Posada, 1996), n.p.

19 Interview with Irene Perez, December 11, 1999.

20 Ibid.

21 Interview for WKQX-TV5, produced by Huascar Castillo, San Francisco, 1975.

22 Timothy W. Drescher, *San Francisco Murals: Community Creates Its Muse, 1914–1994* (San Francisco: Pogo Press, 1994), p. 23.

23 Quintero, "A Mural is a Painting on a Wall," pp. 6–7.

24 Cockcroft and Barnet-Sanchez, *Signs From the Heart*, p. 75.

25 Ibid., p. 138.

26 Quintero, "A Mural is a Painting on a Wall," pp. 6–7.

27 Shifra M. Goldman, *Dimensions of the Americas: Art and Social Change in Latin America and the United States* (Chicago: The University of Chicago Press, 1994), p. 214.

THERESA HARLAN

INDIGENOUS VISIONARIES
Native Women Artists in California

The Chumash were flogged and tortured,
the Maidu stolen for slaves,
and later marched at gunpoint
to a distant reservation.

We glance at one another,
fall silent.
Americans do not know these things
nor do they want to know.

But each of us knows stories
we have never even whispered.

Janice Gould, from
"Blood Sisters" [1]

In 1950, Navajo/Wyandotte/Cherokee artist Leatrice Angel, then fourteen, went with her mother to visit friend and artist Clara Barney, a Karuk living in San Francisco's Mission District. In her studio, Angel saw Barney's large oil painting depicting an encounter between a white frontiersman and a Native man. For Angel, this was new; she had never seen an art studio, especially not one belonging to a Native woman. The kinship between the two Native women artists was established there, when they discovered a mutual love of art, a need for Native companionship, and a shared experience of the complexity of racial and cultural differences in a white-dominant society.

Barney and Angel's meeting was an indirect result of the U.S. Bureau of Indian Affair's (BIA) relocation program. Relocation was part of the government's continuing effort to "civilize" the Native. From the 1940s to the 1960s under this program, Native people migrated to San Francisco, Los Angeles, Denver, Minneapolis, Chicago, and New York to find technical and clerical work. Barney, originally from Happy Camp, four hundred miles north of San Francisco, was among them, only she was more ambitious—she wanted to be a professional artist. She died in 1952 without ever finding a gallerist or curator interested in her heroic, representational art of the Native peoples.

Both European and European American racial ideology and colonization drove indigenous peoples to the fringes of white society, leaving them disenfranchised and locked in a "primitive" paradigm. However, this state of disempowerment had not always existed. According to cultural historian Brian Bibby, the land now known as California at one time was home to "some 500 autonomous (indigenous) communities speaking as many as 80 mutually unintelligible languages."[2] The Spanish and Mexican occupations and the rise of the state of California would decimate the indigenous population, reducing their numbers from an estimated high of 350,000 to a dangerously low 30,000. Indigenous men, women, and children were removed from their ancestral homelands, enslaved by Franciscan missionaries, economically exploited and demonized by a white Christian society, and confined to jail and government boarding schools in order to make room for frontier fantasies of a paradise of gold. Sociologist Luana Ross recounts, "Historically, Native people formed free, sovereign nations . . . Today, Native people are not free; they are a colonized people seeking to decolonize themselves."[3] Native artists seek to set a Native world free through their visions, voices, and actions.

The Eurocentric biases that Barney encountered would continue to be felt by later artists, such as Vivien Hailstone, Jean LaMarr, Hulleah Tsinhnahjinnie, L. Frank Manriquez, Pamela Shields, Debora Iyall, Judith Lowry, Kathleen Smith, and Linda Santiago Peterson, who are discussed in this essay. While known in their own communities, their work receives but a cursory look from the larger, non-Native art circles. Only a few have gained national recognition, and all exhibit predominantly in the few Native-operated exhibition spaces that exist and/or in Native-specific group exhibitions held at non-Native spaces.

The reason for the small number of Native women artists recognized outside of Native communities is more complex than the statistics of a "minority" population and fails to represent the number and diversity of Native women artists living and creating in California. The fact that Native women artists are confined to art spaces "designated" as Native and that their work is perceived to speak only to multicultural issues of identity is itself a form of racial and cultural censorship. But, to restrict our discussion within the parameters of exclusionism is also to confine Native women to a margin of victimization. Native women artists are not victims; instead, they work on multiple fronts centered within their Native communities. Many were activists in the various movements for self-determination of the 1960s and 1970s, and they all see their work as being grounded in and strengthening a continuing Native existence. For instance, Tsinhnahjinnie describes her work as "a message carrier, a survival method, the next step, the continuances of Native thought from petroglyphs, pictographs to photographs."[4]

Eighty-five-year-old basket weaver and cultural educator Vivien Risling Hailstone was always an advocate for Native people in California. Born in 1913 in Moreck, where the Klamath and Trinity rivers meet in northwestern California, Hailstone was from a family of women basket weavers. As a child she followed her mentors on their trips to gather materials for baskets and listened to their stories and songs. At the age of ten her family moved to the Hoopa Reservation to start a sawmill. Once enrolled as a member of the Hupa Tribe, she and her siblings were forced to leave

1969

Native people from all over California occupy Alcatraz Island to establish an educational and cultural center. Both the University of California at Berkeley and UC Davis establish Native American Studies programs in response to community protest.

1973

The Native American studies program at UC Davis establishes the Carl Gorman Museum in honor of founding Native American Studies instructor and Navajo artist Carl Gorman. D-Q University, a two-year college for Native American and Chicano students, is established on military surplus land outside Davis.

1975

Governor Jerry Brown sponsors "I Am These People," a group exhibition of 72 Native artists, 23 of whom are women; the exhibition is displayed in the Governor's office.

her family's home and attend the Indian boarding school. In a 1991 interview, Hailstone remembers children being punished for speaking Native languages and their nighttime cries for their parents: "We were never told anything to make us feel happy or glad about Indian people . . . The children began to feel bad about being Indian."[5] By the time Hailstone graduated from the eighth grade, her father, David Risling, Sr., was elected to the school board where he successfully argued for converting the boarding school into a day school.

In the early 1960s, Hailstone approached the College of the Redwoods in Humboldt County to offer California Indian basket weaving classes, but without success. The administrators rejected her offer and laughed at her. "At the time, being Indian wasn't that popular. It hurt. I thought we were doing beautiful things."[6] Undaunted, she followed her father's example and eventually become chair of the college outreach program. Soon afterward, the College of the Redwoods offered basket weaving, regalia making, and language classes for college credit. Hailstone taught basket weaving classes for over forty years.[7]

Hailstone's own medium of art is jewelry woven from basket making materials with abalone and dentalium shells. She describes her art as "based on traditional values and methods (like the people I came from); it has evolved into a modern form . . . Indian art is like Indian people, it grows, changes, and is never stationary."[8] Academic folk craft specialists discount her work as not traditional enough, while for curators it is too imbedded in craft. Hailstone's work carries symbolism and meaning of the Karuk, Yurok, and Hupa peoples' relationship with the natural world, expressed through a medium as powerful as the earth itself.

Hailstone's ideas about an evolving and continuing Native existence through art encouraged contemporary Native artists such as Jean LaMarr, a Paiute/Pit River from Susanville. LaMarr came to the Bay Area through the BIA's relocation program. At the University of California at Berkeley in the 1960s, LaMarr saw her work rejected by her art instructors, who favored abstraction over the representational art that she felt reflected her contemporary experiences as a Native woman. In response, LaMarr devised a two-step approach to making art that would satisfy her professors and herself: she submitted abstract work in the classroom and later at home added Native figures and symbolism, which she refers to as "the real stuff." She also formed an alliance with her Chicano/Chicana classmates Ray Patlan, Ester Hernandez, and Patricia Rodriguez and with Chicano Studies professor Malaquias Montoya to reject the elitism and Eurocentrism of Western art. They proceeded to cut their own path toward cultural, social, and political empowerment through community-based murals and silk-screen prints.

Jean LaMarr took her artistic skills back to her home in Susanville, where she produced Bear Dance posters and historical murals. The Bear Dance renews the relationship that exists between the people, the bear, and the rattlesnake and reminds the bear and rattlesnake not to fear or harm people when they gather basket making

51

Jean LaMarr, *Cover Girl #3*,
1987. Monoprint on handmade
paper. Collection of the artist,
courtesy of the American Indian
Contemporary Arts.

materials or berries. LaMarr sees her murals of
local Paiute and Pit River heroes as physically
marking and reclaiming indigenous ownership
of the land, calling attention to the accomplishments of Native people in their struggle to survive
a conflicted western frontier.

While at Berkeley, LaMarr found a photograph
of her Aunt Lena as a young woman in a photo
collection meant to document the physical appearance of northern Californian Native people.
She appropriated the image into a silk-screen
work entitled *Aunt Lena, Then and Now* (1984),

and combined it with a family photograph of Lena
as an elderly woman, framing the diptych with
roses intertwined with basket designs colored in
soft hues of lavender, pink, and red. This work
removes Aunt Lena from being a "specimen" and
places her back within the protection of her family and culture.

Although romantic colors dominate LaMarr's
work, the feminizing style hardly indicates a soft
or naïve approach to the representation of Native
women. In *Intimate Frontiers: Sex, Gender and
Culture in California*, historian Albert Hurtado

details the dehumanizing and deathly impact of white male sexual deviance against Native women, which is still an open wound. LaMarr's work directly addresses this exploitation and sexual commodification of Native women in frontier California.

In the *Cover Girl* series (1987), LaMarr appropriates and undermines nineteenth-century Army photographer Will Soule's debasing photographs. Soule depicted imprisoned young Native women at Fort Sill, Oklahoma, in the mid-1860s, bare-breasted and posed on props simulating fainting couches. They are clothed only in army blankets tied at the waist, wearing long necklaces that fall between their breasts. LaMarr silk-screened tops and additional shell necklaces onto the photographs of the women to conceal their nudity. She placed baskets around them. On the lower border she mixed lace pieces and patterns, as well as designs of the diamondback rattlesnake. In LaMarr's work the women are no longer erotic curiosities; rather, they become basket weavers possessing spiritual and cultural knowledge that roots them to the earth. But, LaMarr's intent is not to erase all traces of a colonized existence, as can be gleaned from the title and the image of a jet that she has inserted above the women, in the act of bombing.

Of the fourteen Native students that enrolled in California College of Arts and Crafts (CCAC) in 1978, only Hulleah Tsinhnahjinnie would graduate with a degree. The daughter of Navajo painter Andrew Tsinajinnie,[9] Tsinhnahjinnie was raised amid her father's artistic environment in Phoenix, Arizona. She moved to California to study art. As with LaMarr, Eurocentric art professors rejected Tsinhnahjinnie's stylized use of color and of Native figures, ignored her Native art heroes, and instructed her to emulate the European masters. Only the printmaker Malaquias Montoya encouraged her to create art centered within the contemporary Native existence and layered with Native history and culture. Tsinhnahjinnie's response was to abandon painting entirely and to turn to photography as the tool with which to create affirming Native imagery.

After graduating from CCAC, Tsinhnahjinnie helped found a Native contemporary art gallery and has documented Bay Area Native urban existence for over twenty years. The first works to attract real attention were Tsihnajinnie's seminal photographs in her *Metropolitan Indian Series* (1984) (see fig. 5), in which she acknowledges the persistent presence of Native people in urban cities and attests to the communities that they built. This piece provided one of the first occasions for the Bay Area Native community to see itself positively represented as a group of contemporary people living beyond the stereotyped existence of the celluloid "Indians" portrayed in westerns on television and in the movies.

Metropolitan Indian Series juxtaposes Native people dressed in ceremonial regalia against urban scenes. In one of Tsinhnahjinnie's portraits, Janeen Antoine, a Brule Lakota, stands in front of a Harley Davidson parked on San Francisco's Valencia Street, wearing a white buckskin dress and holding a long-fringed shawl. The fringe shimmers against the polished chrome of the motorcycle as dashes of light speed cross the sky and form a crown around her uplifted head. Tsinhnahjinnie creates urban hagiographic portraits of Native women, timeless images conjuring the spirits of Native people who still occupy the land and walk ancient paths through metropolitan cities in a celebration of continuing Native existence in a postmodern world.

Tsinhnahjinnie's 1994 *Photographic Memoirs of An Aboriginal Savant: Page 73 (Living on Occupied Land)* (see fig. 42) is a complex, multipart piece that is inspired by the tragic story of Ishi, a Yani man who was considered to be the "Last Wild Indian" in the first decades of the twentieth century. Anthropologist Alfred Kroeber, under the auspices of the Smithsonian Institution, turned Ishi into a living specimen, despite Kroeber's paternalistic good intentions. When Ishi died, Kroeber donated his brain to the Smithsonian Institution.

Memoirs includes a fictional conversation with Alfred Kroeber in which Tsinhnahjinnie takes him to task about the role of anthropology in sub-

1983

Ken Banks and Janeen Antoine co-found American Indian Contemporary Arts, a nonprofit art gallery solely dedicated to the promotion of contemporary Native American art.

jugating Native peoples. She says, for instance, "The absence of an anthropologist makes it easier to exist." Tsinhnahjinnie assumes the role of Ishi in a photograph in which she wears a suit much like the one he was made to wear for a portrait. Text wraps around her head stating, "A moment of reflection from the aboriginal savant. 'Don't Fuck with Me!' " The mirror-image text of the digitized photograph reads, "Thought for the day from the Aboriginal Savant, 'Beware of Native Bureaucrats who are satisfied.' " She dons a "suit of assimilation" to underscore Ishi's fate at the mercy of paternalistic "good" intentions within the context of the very institution that supported Kroeber's study.

L. Frank Manriquez was born in 1952 in Santa Monica, California, and grew up knowing she was Indian, but it was only as an adult that she learned of her Gabrielano Native ancestry. She has subsequently chosen to employ only the original names of her tribes, Tongva (Gabrielano) and Ajachmem (Juanino). Manriquez makes clever

52

L. Frank Manriquez, *Be Afraid*,
1993. Line drawing, pen
and ink, 5 × 7 in. Collection
of the artist.

use of Southern California stereotypes to describe her process of cultural recovery: "I think
the more southern your tribe is in California, the
harder it is to get a grip on your cultural heritage. But we've got fax machines and e-mail, and
we can get on the freeway and hunt people down
who can explain things for us."[10] It was when
she met Maidu basket weavers Dorothy Stanley
and her daughter, Jennifer Bates, that Manriquez sought to recover her ancestral and cultural knowledge. Subsequently, Manriquez
extended her recovery efforts to assist others
by becoming a founding member of the Advocates for Indigenous California Language
Survival. Manriquez is also a board member of
the California Indian Basketweavers Association
(CIBA), a support group that meets annually to

develop environmental policies and promote the
appreciation of contemporary basket weaving.

Manriquez is most widely known for her line
drawings in which Coyote and Rabbit explore the
world, traveling back and forth through time. Her
sardonic captions are presented backwards, forcing the viewer to pay especially close attention.
She resurrects Tongva and Ajachmem out from
the darkness of an identity imposed on the eigh-
teenth-century Catholic neophytes. Her line
drawing *Be Afraid* (1993) depicts a farmer Coyote
dressing a scarecrow in a Franciscan robe accompanied by the words, "Be afraid. Be very afraid."
Manriquez's missionary scarecrow carries a double meaning. It can be read as a warning against
missionaries (agents of colonialization) or as
heralding the reemergence and revitalization of
the Tongva and Ajachmem people.

Judith Lowry, part Mountain Maidu/Hamawi
Pit River and part Australian, was born in
Washington, D.C. in 1948. She received her master's in art from California State University Chico
and became concerned with shifts in power and
representations of spiritualism. Lowry paints
large acrylic canvases depicting mythic worlds
and family stories. Lowry's proscenium paintings are beautiful and disquieting, mixing
European Renaissance styles with Mountain
Maidu references and Hollywood's post—World
War II glamour. They reflect her childhood
experiences as the daughter of a lieutenant

53
Judith Lowry, *Shopping*, 1996.
Acrylic on canvas, 82 × 68 in.
Photo: Lee Fatheree. Collection
of the artist.

colonel in the United States Army, an Australian mother, and their peripatetic life throughout the world. She uses the incongruity of her personal history to tell stories of colonial encounters and convergences.

Shopping (1996) portrays the rise of Christian beliefs and the repression of indigenous deities.

We see a pre-Columbian Mayan goddess mother and daughter in a dress shop with an "Eve Arden"–type saleswoman who is showing them the latest in goddess fashions, a red and green cape. The young goddess fingers the fabric, testing the weave. She is unsure about this strange cape (which we recognize as the cloak of the

Virgin of Guadalupe). Lowry's representation of the Mayan goddesses is memorable. Their faces are drawn in the fashion of Mayan renderings, their bodies strong and voluptuous, adorned in gold and turquoise jewelry and their blue-black hair styled in topknots. This encounter between pre-Columbian female deities and the Christian Church's mother of Christ, revisits the issue of whether the Virgin of Guadalupe is an appropriated Mayan goddess with ancient indigenous roots and powers, or an assimilated Christian substitute disengaged from any indigenous origin. Lowry pictorially renders the complex history of convergence and conflict.

In *Marine Phoenix* (1999), Lowry borrows from Botticelli's fifteenth-century *The Birth of Venus* to tell the story of her own origins. The painting depicts the arrival of her Australian-born mother, June Shirley Harrison, in the United States to marry Leonard Lowry, a Mountain Maidu/Hamawi Pit River/Euro-American man. Lowry casts her mother as the Venus, but unlike Botticelli's modest version, Harrison appears as a blond Hollywood diva. Lowry's Venus rises from a moonlit San Francisco Bay self-powered instead of propelled by the breath of Zephyrus. The figure stares coolly. The man sits on a rock by the Golden Gate Bridge, awestruck by the vision of her. He wears a satin boxing robe over his Army uniform, a boxing glove on his right hand and a feathered war bonnet in his left. Lowry has cast her parents as two lovers caught in a Hollywood romance of miscegenation. The union of a Native man and white woman was forbidden by early California law, but Lowry's portrait reconfigures stereotypical perceptions of Native people by depicting her own complex interracial and international origin.

Pamela Shields, a Kanai, born in Salt Lake City in 1956, grew up in Calgary, Canada, and settled in San Francisco, where she found less racial resentment. Over the years she has experimented with printing photographs on organic materials such as hide, leather, and handmade paper. Now, she uses digital technology to create multilayered images of early twentieth-century Native people and contemporary urban scenes representing cultural and social fractures. In her diptych *Bird Woman* (1997), from the series *Nitssapani, My Blood,* Shields adopts a similar strategy to that of Jean LaMarr in her work *Aunt Lena, Then and Now.* Shields is a Native woman artist who "repatriates" an original photograph depicting a Native woman and labeled "Blood Woman" by the European Americans who catalogued the archives of the National Museum of the American Indian (now in New York; originally assembled by the Smithsonian Institution). Unlike LaMarr's Aunt Lena, the figure in the found photograph was not known to Shields. But her act of repatriation—in which she returns "Blood Woman" to a Native domain through appropriating the image into

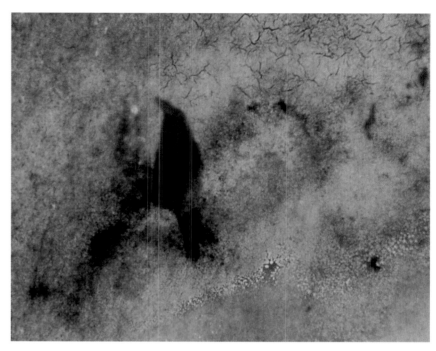

her artwork—is a similar act of resistance, a reclamation of sovereignty. Moreover, this Kanai woman—small, alone, standing bare-chested and wearing a beaded leather skirt—becomes a repository for Shields's own experiences of the harsh government boarding school that isolated her from her family. In the left panel, the woman stands off-center in a barren brick courtyard reminiscent of a grim institutional setting, and a close-up of the woman's face floats below. The illusion of the woman's shifting presence, enhanced by the drifting red, green, and gold colors, creates an ephemeral atmosphere. The same barren ground of the brick courtyard is repeated in the right panel, empty except for a bird pecking at the ground. In *Bird Woman*, Shields reclaims shared Native experiences that span generations.

In her current work, Shields embarks on an erotic journey of womanly sensuality and sexuality. For her *Pocahontas Erotica* series (1999), Shields inserted photographs of herself, semi-nude, striking seductive poses in water-filled glass globes aswirl with glitter and feathers. Another artist whose work focuses on her own sexuality is Debora Iyall. Iyall makes linoleum cuts depicting herself actively engaged in sex, which she describes as "female positive, active

54
Pamela Shields, *Bird Woman*, 1997. Digital iris print, diptych, 14 x 16 in. each. Collection of the artist.

Native Women Artists

with an element of mischievous sacredness."[11]
Both artists' erotic works are distinct from earlier
exploitative representations of Native women;
here there is no pretense of "scientific" investigation of primitive people, or racially driven
justification for their sexual exploitation. Rather,
both artists celebrate their self-confidence as
sensual women.

Iyall, Yakima/Cowlitz, was born in Spokane,
Washington, in 1954 and moved with her mother
to Fresno, California, as a toddler. In 1969, at
fourteen, she sought to find a Native community
by joining the occupation of Alcatraz Island. But
she only stayed on the island six days, feeling
alone and out of place with the reservation and the
urban Native activists. She studied performance at
the San Francisco Art Institute in the late 1970s
and formed a band, Romeo Void, which lasted six
years. She returned to art making in 1990, and in
1995 she started InkClan, a community-based
printmaking studio at the South of Market Art
Center in San Francisco which provides Native
people access to the arts and printmaking.

Kathleen Smith studied filmmaking at the San
Francisco Art Institute in the late 1950s. There
she met Frank LaPena, Hopi artist Linda Loma-
haftewa, and Pomo poet Gloria Armstrong (who
herself emerged as a visual artist in the 1980s).
Smith, a Olemitcha Miwok/Mihilakawna Pomo
artist and basket weaver, was born in 1939 in
Santa Rosa and grew up in Healdsburg, California. Her work reflects upon the connection to
nature and indigenous creativity. Smith's 1997
watercolor *Fresh Fruits* depicts the annual Strawberry Dance, in which women adorn their hair
with flowers and celebrate Spring by presenting
the first fruits of the year. Smith speaks of trying
to recreate California Native life and movement
in her paintings. Her figures are full and soft,
evincing a deep understanding of the movement
of water and pigment across paper. In *Miwuk
Dancer with Magpie Headdress* (1997) we see the
full magpie headdress with feathers and plumes
and the feathered cape worn by a young male

dancer. He follows the tradition by entering the dance circle backwards and then swirls his body around, the feather cape following his movements. The dancer sways and moves in circles, as if to manipulate the space around him. Smith's paintings are more than depictions of Native people dressed in ceremonial regalia; they are testimonies to Natives who continue ancestral belief systems despite more than two hundred years of Christian "missionization." Ceremonial practitioners gather to renew their spiritual relationship with the earth, with themselves and on behalf of every living thing, including non-Natives. Smith also writes about Pomo ways of preparing food and basket making and contributes frequently to *News from Native California*.

Many Native women artists sacrifice their own artistic career to work with their community. Linda Santiago Peterson, for instance, works with the youth in her Yowlumne Yokut community of the Tule River Reservation in southern Central California, teaching Yokut history and culture. Peterson's 1999 painting *Bird, I Want Your Children*, depicts the Snake Ceremony that is no longer held. According to Peterson, the Yokuts held the annual Snake Ceremony to keep evil and rattlesnakes away. She portrays the snake doctor wearing a feathered skirt and headdress and holding the basket for snakes, while a magpie sits in a tree watching a rattlesnake reach for her nest. Blue hues fill the background and a dark

1993

Jean LaMarr establishes the Native American Women's Graphic Workshop. Basket weavers, artists, and teachers gathered at her studio on the Susanville Rancheria to live, celebrate, and work together. Lowry remarked, "It was like the way the young girls in the old days would learn to make baskets, in a circle with the older women, learning by seeing, by doing, by talking, and by sharing."[12]

1999

The American Indian Contemporary Arts gallery in San Francisco closes its doors after sixteen years of exhibiting California and national contemporary Native artists.

blue band runs across the lower part of the painting carrying a string of Yokut words.

The connections, collaborations, and friendships that Native women artists have made with each other, including connections made to Native people of the past, are all part of a moving resistance to colonization and assimilation. Native people have continued to gather to pray, to sing, to dance and to create, following the ways of their ancestors. The U.S. government's relocation program was meant to weaken Native people's embrace of their traditional beliefs and practices. Instead, Native people have taken their beliefs and practices with them to the cities. They have established connections across diverse Native nations and tribal affiliations, and stimulated a flow of information from their home communities to urban areas and back. The work and art of Native women artists contains ideological, historical, and cultural information that is transmitted through these connections.

As the state of California commemorates the 150-year anniversary of the Gold Rush, Native American women artists in California continue to create art enacting the cultural recovery of their ancestors and to plant the seeds for cultural autonomy.

Barney's act of identifying herself as an artist and a painter of Native heroes was in itself a heroic act. She refused to settle for Western mis-

representations of Native people. She understood and felt her own power to create and wanted to share her visions of Native people with others. Unfortunately, the world did not see her for who she was, a Native artist and survivor, except for young Leatrice Angel. Tsinhnahjinnie speaks to the condition of all Native artists when she says, "[It was] a beautiful day when I decided that I would take responsibility to reinterpret images of Native peoples. My mind was ready, primed with stories of resistance and resilience, stories of survival. My view of these images is aboriginally based, an indigenous perspective, not a scientific Godly order, but philosophically Native." I would add, "and free."[13]

This essay is dedicated to the memory of my mother, Elizabeth Campigli Harlan, Coast Miwok (1925–1998); my friend Vivien Hailstone, Yurok, Karuk and enrolled Hupa (1913–2000); and Clara Barney.

Notes

1 Janice Gould, "Poetry by Janice Gould," *News from Native California* (Fall 1996): 35. See also Gould's *Earthquake Weather* (Tucson: University of Arizona Press, 1996.)

2 Brian Bibby, *The Fine Art of California Indian Basketry* (Sacramento and Berkeley: Crocker Art Museum with Heyday Books, 1996), p. 1.

3 Luana Ross, *Inventing the Savage: The Social Construction of Native American Criminality* (Austin: University of Texas, 1998), p. 3.

4 1994 artist statement.

5 Vivien Hailstone quoted in Betty Lease, "Vivien Hailstone: Proud of Indian Ancestry," *Redding Record Searchlight*, October 13, 1991.

6 Ibid.

7 Vivien Hailstone was the co-founder of one statewide organization, two regional organizations, and also set

policy for California State parks.

8 Vivien Hailstone quoted in Theresa Harlan, *Watchful Eyes: Native American Women Artists* (Phoenix: The Heard Museum, 1994), p. 22.

9 Father and daughter spell the last name differently.

10 L. Frank Manriquez, *Acorn Soup: Drawings and Commentary by L. Frank* (Berkeley: Heyday Books, 1999), p. 9.

11 Conversation with the artist, 1999.

12 Judith Lowry quoted in Ray Moisa, "Weaving Contemporary Ceremony: Native Women Weave their Lives and Artwork Together," *News from Native California* (Winter 1994/95): 9.

13 Hulleah Tsinhnahjinnie, "When is a Photograph Worth a Thousand Words?" in *Native Nations: Journey in American Photography* (exhibition catalogue) (London: Barbican Art Gallery, Barbican Center, 1998), p. 42.

JUDITH WILSON

HOW THE INVISIBLE WOMAN GOT HERSELF ON THE CULTURAL MAP

Black Women Artists in California

When I consider the history of African American women's activity in the visual arts in California since 1950, I am struck by three things: (1) the amazing proliferation of talent in the past three decades; (2) the seeming improbability of this sudden efflorescence; and (3) the extent to which chroniclers of all but the most recent phases of California cultural history take what I call "the Swiss bankers' approach" to inconvenient inquiries, as in the following responses:

"Black women artists? There weren't any."

"If there were, we no longer have any record of them."

"What records we have suggest they were insignificant . . . "

A combination punch, this strategy of denying and discounting California black women's visual heritage aims to both discourage aspiring artists and delegitimize those who succeed in defying what Mark Twain would have called the "greatly exaggerated" rumors of their nonexistence.[1] Minimizing or erasing their predecessors' footprints positions each new wave of Afro-California women artists outside the gates of a cultural enclave that remains firmly barricaded against collective black and/or female incursions. Because it also provides a rationale for inequities in arts funding, public programming, media coverage, and the forms of cultural indoctrination known as "education," this ethnic- and gender-cleansing of California's art history affects us all.

56

Edmonia Lewis, *The Marriage of Hiawatha*, 1868. White marble, 29 × 11¹/₂ × 12 in. Photo: Hunter Clarkson (Alt-Lee, Inc.). Collection of Walter O. Evans, Mich.

Miss Edmonia Lewis' statuary exhibition at the rooms of the Art Association is receiving a fair share of patronage, over a hundred persons having visited it on Monday and as many yesterday. As there are only five small pieces of sculpture on view, . . . only lovers of art who desire to see the creations of a lady of color, whose education as a *figuriste* in marble was obtained in Italy, are likely to derive any pleasure from inspecting her works.　**San Francisco Chronicle, September 3, 1873**[2]

The subject of this sketch was born in the city of Oakland, county of Alameda, June 27, 1872. . . . She was educated in the public schools of Oakland. . . . Miss Powell had several paintings on exhibition at the Mechanic's Institute fair in 1890 . . . They were the first paintings ever before exhibited by a colored artist in this State at any of the art exhibitions.

Noted Negro Women (1893)[3]

I was born in 1952 in Oakland, also my mother's birthplace in 1920. Poking around my grandmother's attic one day at about age eleven or twelve, I discovered a dust-coated artist's portfolio beneath a pile of magazines and books. It was full of expertly rendered, pen-and-ink-and-wash drawings of women in 1930s garb. How, I wondered, had they landed in my grandmother's attic?

"Oh, those? They're your mother's. She did them in high school. She could have been a fashion illustrator. But you know your mother . . . She never had any ambition."

If I was startled by my grandmother's explanation, my mother's was even more disturbing:

"Why didn't you continue?" I asked.

"Well," she sighed, "around graduation time our guidance counselor asked each of us what we wanted to do when we got out of school. I told him I wanted to study fashion illustration and he said, 'Colored girls can't do things like that, Elaine.' So I went to work at a dress pattern maker's until your father and I got married."

My mom graduated from Roosevelt High School in Oakland in 1938. A few grades behind her was the future U.S. representative to the 1997 Venice Biennale, Robert Colescott (born 1925). If Roosevelt's conversion to a junior high hadn't forced him to eventually transfer to another high school, might someone as gifted as Colescott been counseled out of the annals of American art history? Probably not. Although he'd always been an avid draftsman, Colescott didn't consider art as a career option until he enrolled at the University of California at Berkeley after an army stint during the war. On completing his undergraduate degree in 1949, the young painter took advantage of the GI Bill to spend a year in Paris studying with Fernand Léger. And the rest, as they say, is history . . . [4]

There was no postwar Rosie-the-Riveter bill of rights to help American women fulfill *their* career goals. And it is doubtful that would-be artists who were black and female in postwar California had any more knowledge than their prewar predecessors about the existence of Edmonia Lewis, a part–African American, part Native, member of the American expatriate women artists community in Rome, who had visited the state three-quarters of a century earlier and demonstrated what colored girls could do.[5] Nevertheless, the 1940s were a better time than the 1930s had been for artistically inclined black Californians of both sexes. The catalogue for the Harmon Foundation's 1933 national exhibition of Negro art, for example, states there was only one "recognized artist" at work in California, Bay Area sculptor Sargent Johnson (1888–1967).[6] In the 1940s, he was joined by painters Harlan Jackson (1918–1993) and Thelma Johnson Street (1912–1959).

Apparently the first black woman to operate professionally as an artist while residing in California, Street was a native of Washington State who had studied at the Portland Museum Art School (now Pacific Northwest College of Art) and the University of Oregon during the mid-1930s.[7] During the mid- to late 1930s, she spent time in New York, Chicago, and San Francisco, settling in the latter city around 1940.[8] In San Francisco, Street worked on the Works Progress Administration's Federal Art Project (WPA-FAP), and got to know Sargent Johnson and his protégé Lester Mathews (born 1912), the only other black artists on the project in the Bay Area.[9] In 1941, she exhibited at San Francisco's M. H. de Young Memorial Museum.[10] The following year, she had a solo show at a gallery in New York, from which

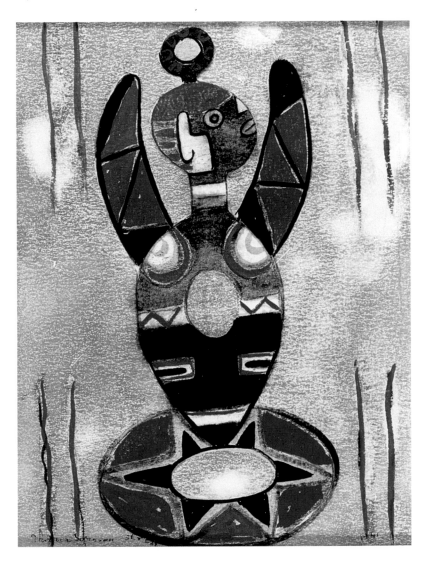

Alfred H. Barr purchased a painting for the Museum of Modern Art.[11] Streat's admirers also included Diego Rivera, whose mural she worked on at the Golden Gate International Exposition in San Francisco in 1939.[12] In a 1945 article, Rivera, who owned a self-portrait by Streat, extolled her art as "one of the most interesting manifestations in [the U.S.] at present" and labeled it "sophisticated enough to reconquer the grace and purity of African and American art" without being "an imitation."[13]

After 1945, although she continued painting, Streat turned increasingly to dance, touring Europe, North America, and the Pacific Islands to perform "rhythmic interpretations" based on her research in Haiti, Mexico, Hawaii, and the Pacific Northwest.[14] She also engaged in textile design and—in a kind of multiculturalism *avant la lettre*—collaborated with her husband, a white playwright and storyteller known as "John Edgar" (Edgar Kline), to promote racial tolerance through art education.[15] Previously, she had experimented with children's book illustration, which makes Streat a precursor to printmaker Margo Humphrey and painter/sculptor Faith Ringgold, who have both excelled as illustrator-authors of children's books.[16] Streat's double life as a dancer and visual artist prefigures Senga Nengudi's and Maren Hassinger's dual allegiances to dance and sculpture in the 1970s, as well as Suzanne Jackson's involvement in dance and painting during the same period. Unlike them, however, the relative brevity of Streat's career as a primarily visual artist and a California resident marks her as a transitional figure.[17]

Prior to Streat's emergence in the early 1940s, the history of African American women artists in California is largely a record of dilettantes and gifted amateurs. The earliest of these, Pauline Powell-Burns (1872–1907), a landscape and still-life painter, became the first African American to contribute paintings to an art exhibition in the state when she participated in an 1890 fair.[18] Although her offerings are said to have won "great praise" from both the fair's award committee and the public, most of the two-page entry on Powell in an 1893 text focuses on her accomplishments as a classical pianist. Indeed, in a 1919 history of African Americans in California she is mentioned only as a now-deceased piano instructor.[19]

The latter source devotes one entire chapter to Afro-California musicians and another to writers, but names only one visual artist—sometime Oakland resident Patricia Garland (1882–?). Garland, we are told, "contributed Spanish drawn-thread work, embroidery, crochet-work and many pieces of hand-painted china" to a 1908 exhibition sponsored by the National Federation of Colored Women's Clubs and subsequently studied at the California College of Arts and Crafts. Tantalizingly, the author claimed Garland was one of "many colored ladies in California who are great artists in both oil and also the art of china-painting."[20]

Foregrounded here, and a continuing thread throughout the history of black women's visual art activities in California, is a relatively fluid relationship between their practice of so-called fine and applied arts. Only two of the eight or nine African American women I have been able identify who were active in the visual arts in California prior to the 1930s—painters Pauline Powell-Burns and Katherine Patton (active 1914–1937)—seem to have worked exclusively as fine artists. Patton, whose watercolor of the English coast was favorably mentioned in a review of a 1914 show at the Pennsylvania Academy, would take first prize in an exhibition of black Los Angeles artists two decades later.[21]

That women have traditionally flourished as decorative artists in Western culture while fine art remained an overwhelmingly male bastion, is a familiar maxim of feminist art history. Afro-California art history deviates from this "rule," however, in that the applied arts have often been more hospitable to *both* men and women of African descent than nonfunctional brands of visual art. For example, the first African American known to have been active in the visual arts in California, Grafton T. Brown (1841–1918), made his living as a commercial lithographer for over two decades and only turned to painting landscapes in California and the Pacific Northwest in the 1880s.[22] The most prominent black California artist of the first half of the twentieth century, Sargent Johnson, regularly shuttled back and forth across fine and applied art boundaries, creating objects ranging from ceramic teapots to architectural murals, as well as sculpting heads and figures that frequently employed media and modalities traditionally associated with the decorative arts.[23] And, it is striking that the most successful African American in the visual arts in California *ever*, Paul R. Williams (1894–1980), was an architect—that is to say, a practitioner of the one fine art in which function conventionally outweighs form.[24]

The 1933 Harmon Foundation catalogue that dubs Sargent Johnson California's only "recognized" black artist mentions two other Afro-Californians: Los Angeles painter Julian C. Robinson (?–1938) and Oakland sculptor and ceramist Eleanor E. Paul (active 1930s). Both produced fine art but depended on applied or commercial art skills to support themselves. In Robinson's case, this meant "ornamental modeling and casting for the building trades," while for Paul, it was a matter of creating "posters and magazine illustrations."[25] Perhaps the most clear-cut evidence of the shared inability of black male and female Californians to focus exclusively on fine art pursuits comes from a 1948 article in which Prix de Rome-winning sculptor Lester Mathews's shift to furniture making is explained:

"A San Francisco draftsman during the war, Mathews brought his postwar hopes to Los Angeles, placing his hand-wrought pieces of stone, clay and wood in Hollywood art galleries on the theory that the well-paid movie colony would give patronage to fine art. But a bitter year of no sales and no commissions followed. . . ." After a couple of weeks spent working as a ditch digger, Mathews was hired to sand and paint furniture for an interior decorator; recognizing a lucrative alternative, he decided to apply his sculptural skills to the design of modern free-form custom furniture. In his first year in business, he earned over $8,000—a healthy income by 1948 standards.[26]

While carpentry and the building trades sustained artistically gifted black males, black women seem to have gravitated toward needlework and apparel design, on one hand, and domestic craftwork, on the other. The 1919 history that claims "many" black women painted in oil and on china, also discusses a San Francisco embroiderer, two Los Angeles dressmakers, and a Bakersfield milliner.[27] The Harmon Foundation's 1928 exhibition included a textile by Pasadena artist Geraldine Charles (active 1920s–1930s).[28] And, in her production of textiles, wall decorations, woven rugs, and handmade tableware during the 1940s, Thelma Johnson Streat also fits this category.[29] The fact that Streat drew inspiration from the arts of non-Western cultures and conducted ethnographic research in the Pacific Northwest, Mexico, Haiti, and the Pacific Islands, however, points to a completely different set of impulses from the combination of genteel social mores and economic necessity that seems to have constrained her predecessors.

Like Sargent Johnson, with whom she shared an understanding of African American identity as congruent with a Pacific Rim multicultural outlook, Streat's apparent indifference to high/low aesthetic hierarchies deviates from traditional Western values.[30] By the mid-twentieth century, of course, countless white Western modernists had already embraced popular art forms and humble materials and versed themselves in non-Western artistic traditions.[31] Unlike their white counterparts, however, African American multicultural modernists like Johnson, Streat, and the East Coast's Hale Woodruff were not in retreat from *their* assumed racial heritage, but engaged in projects of ethnocultural redemption and retrieval.[32] Black Pacific Rim postmodernists like Noah Jemison, Betye Saar, John Outterbridge, Mildred Howard, and David Hammons, who emerged in the 1960s and 1970s, have preserved this critical difference. Although they developed new formal strategies, their underlying aesthetic and cultural projects remain remarkably similar to Johnson's and Streat's.[33]

The career of Los Angeles-based sculptor Beulah Ecton Woodard (1895–1955) overlaps Streat's and exhibits both significant parallels and pronounced differences. Like Streat, Woodard is a relatively obscure figure about whom we currently have an extremely fragmentary, but nonetheless intriguing, record. Like Streat, too, Woodard received major mainstream institutional recognition in the form of a museum show early in her career. But, while Streat's multiple artistic identities and peripatetic lifestyle seem to have pushed her off art historians' radar screens until recently, Woodard was demoted from professional status as a fine artist to provincial "hobbyist" and producer of "primarily educational" objects.[34]

Born in rural Ohio, Beulah Ecton was raised in Los Angeles, studied architectural drawing at Los Angeles Polytechnic High School, and subsequently worked as a maid. In her early thirties, she began to "mess around in clay" in her spare time. When an admirer of one of her early efforts urged her to study in Europe, she was discouraged from this scheme by parental objections, became despondent and, eventually, severely ill. Marriage in 1928, however, freed her to exploit her artistic gifts, and she began studying privately with maverick ceramist Glenn Lukens and others, and taking classes at Otis Art Institute, the Los Angeles Art School, and the University of Southern California.[35] In February 1935, Woodard had her first show—in the storefront window of the *California News*, a Los Angeles African American weekly

postwar backlash against women-as-workers-
outside-the-home thwart her ambition? Does the
language used to describe Woodard and her activities in the 1950 articles simply echo the gender
biases of the time? Or, did she ultimately find
the art world so inhospitable that she came to
prefer working on its sidelines as an amateur,
a hobbyist, slighted professionally but also
shielded from art establishment rebuffs? Without
more biographical information, it is impossible
to decide.

At present, even the artist's stylistic development is uncertain. Photographs of four circa
1935–37 heads by Woodard show African, African
American, and European American subjects,
depicted in a style that blends careful scrutiny of
individual features with expressive treatment of
surfaces to recall the "psychological portraiture"
of Auguste Rodin.[38] Indeed, her contributions to
a 1937 show were praised for exhibiting a "knack
[for] catching a flash of movement" and for
eschewing abstraction in favor of "emotion."[39]
By the mid-1940s, however, she seems to have
taken a different tack. Descriptions of her "real-
istic African masks" from this period suggest she
had traded individual psychology for ethnographic detail and ethnological representative-
ness. Intentionally didactic, these works were
meant to inspire African American pride and
promote greater knowledge of African cultures.[40]

The two 1950 magazines in which Woodard is

newspaper that also ran a feature on the artist.
That fall, a one-woman show at the Los Angeles
County Museum made her the first African American to exhibit there.[36] Yet, by 1950 Woodard
was being described in two of the nation's leading
black journals as a "Los Angeles housewife" who
made sculpture as a "hobby."[37] What went wrong?

Did she suffer another physical and/or psychological decline? Did the terms of her marriage eventually impede her career? Did the

labeled a "Los Angeles housewife who makes masks of African aborigines for a hobby" include photographs of this work.[41] The masks' appearance is consistent with assertions by art historian Lizzetta LeFalle-Collins that Woodard's sculpture involved "no experiments with abstraction" and evinced no concern with "truth to materials and their inherent properties" that might detract from the work's pedagogical function. But neither the 1930s heads nor an undated wood sculpture entitled *Creation* (in which a human face is partially visible emerging from the organic contours of part of a forked tree branch) fit this description.[42] Until Woodard's art is more thoroughly documented and the full sequence of her stylistic development can be established, it seems rash to assume the work that gained her the most publicity exhausts her stylistic range.[43]

The little we know about Woodard's art and life strongly suggests she was what would have been called in her day "a race woman"—meaning a black woman preoccupied with the political, social, and cultural status of African Americans. A childhood encounter with an African visitor is said to have "sparked her life-long interest in the people and customs of that continent" and led to her extensive self-study of African history and anthropology.[44] In discussing her ethnological masks with the author of a 1944 article, the artist explained she was attempting "to preserve the details of various Negroid types for future study" and asserted that traditional African culture contained "much of which Negroes today should be proud."[45] As LeFalle-Collins has pointed out, Woodard's interest "in visually referencing an African heritage for African Americans" was shared by her East Coast contemporary Richmond Barthé, probably the most commercially successful African American sculptor of the 1930s and 1940s.[46] Similarly, Woodard's belief that accurate depiction of African costume and features could enhance African American pride resembles Sargent Johnson's recruitment of African sculptural traditions in his project of redeeming the African American visage from a history of anti-black stereotypes.[47] Woodard departs from both her male colleagues, however, in pursuing her culturally self-assertive agenda in the institutional arena, as well as in her art.

In December 1937, the *California Eagle* reported that "[o]ver 2,500 persons have visited the Negro Art Exhibit held at the Stendahl Art Galleries, 3006 Wilshire Blvd., from November 14 to 21."[48] The exhibition was organized by the Los Angeles Negro Art Association, a group Woodard was instrumental in founding.[49] Despite the show's impressive attendance, the event was not repeated and, perhaps stymied by the hardships of the Depression, the organization disbanded. But Beulah Woodard would try again, serving as the director of an artists' cooperative gallery, 11

Associated, which opened its doors on South Hill Street in Los Angeles in 1950.[50]

A decade later, when retired postal worker and art aficionado Ruth G. Waddy founded Art West Associated in Los Angeles in 1962 and artist and art administrator Evangeline Montgomery launched Art West Associated–North in the Bay Area five years later, they were attacking a linked set of problems that Woodard and other members of 11 Associated had faced but failed to over-come: the lack of a collective identity *as* black California artists and a corresponding dearth of institutional support (in the form of exhibition and sales venues, sustained critical attention, historical documentation, and preservation).[51] In the course of the 1960s and 1970s, thanks to an unprecedented series of historical conjunctions, on one hand, and to the vision, resourcefulness, and stubborn perseverance of Waddy, Mont-gomery, and artist/art historian Samella Lewis, on the other, significant change would finally come.

In a pattern replicated to varying degrees throughout the country, the growth of the Civil Rights movement and the frustration produced by continued resistance to integrationist demands, eventually triggered an urban cataclysm, the 1965 Watts rebellion. Watts, in turn, propelled an increasing shift from cultural assimilation to cul-tural autonomy that spawned a host of black-owned and black-operated galleries and commu-nity art centers in Los Angeles. At the same time, the period's heightened social tensions led some of the city's dominant cultural institutions to make token gestures of inclusion toward local black artists in an effort to defuse the situation. And, by the early 1970s, the emergence of a vocal feminist art movement in Southern California was fostering the visibility of African American women artists to an unprecedented degree.

Thus, when Betye Saar was catapulted to national attention by a 1975 solo show at New York's Whitney Museum of American Art and her subsequent inclusion in the groundbreaking 1978 PBS television series "The Originals/Women in Art," a history of collective activity among Los Angeles black artists had paved the way for her ascent and fostered her development of a unique sensibility closely tied to Saar's black Angeleno roots. Saar's art, in turn, has been tremendously influential for a younger generation of California black women artists. Bay Area mixed-media and installation artist Mildred Howard, for example, has called her "my mentor."[52] What Howard obviously shares with Saar is a canny use of found materials in a surreal blend of autobio-graphical reference and cultural history. That history includes the rich spiritual traditions of the African diaspora, as well as the "make do" inventiveness that is a hallmark of black vernac-ular expression.

Working in photographic media, both Carrie

Mae Weems and Pat Ward Williams have combined admiration of black vernacular culture with a sociopolitical acuity that recalls their medium's documentary heritage. Both women have cited the example of the distinguished African American photographer Roy De Carava, who majestically bridged the "art photography"/"street photography" chasm with his 1955 book of Harlem scenes, *The Sweet Flypaper of Life*.[53] But it is notable that Weems's recurring engagement with African American folkways is shared by black California women artists as markedly different from Weems as Howard and both Betye and Alison Saar. The "documentary" side of Weems's and Williams's work is a reminder that among the few black women photographers to enjoy commercial success prior to the 1960s were two Californians: Ruth Washington, who operated a Los Angeles portrait studio from 1940 to 1948, and Vera Jackson, a staff photographer for the *California Eagle* throughout the 1940s.[54]

Since the 1960s, "storytelling" has been an especially prominent feature of a number of black California women's art. Narrative is often evoked in the richly allusive imagery and titles of Betye Saar's work and has been a key element in Faith Ringgold's story quilts, as well as in the image-text suites by Carrie Mae Weems. Abstract painter Mary Lovelace O'Neal's elliptical titles make viewers complicit in the production of would-be scenarios for her big, bold, operati-

cally sensuous canvases. The stories told by Camille Billops, a ceramic sculptor, graphic artist, and filmmaker, however, tend to be scandalous. A Los Angeles native who has lived in New York for the past three decades, Billops lifts the rug to reveal family secrets in her films *Suzanne Suzanne* (1983), *Older Women in Love* (1987), and *Finding Christa* (1991). In the process, women viewers are invited to join the artist and her female kin in shedding various socially imposed psychological constraints. *Finding Christa* violates the ultimate taboo by showing us a black woman (Billops herself) who has traded motherhood for life as a globe-trotting artist with no regrets about the decision. "I just unshackled myself," she once informed a reporter.[55]

Although their creative styles and artistic visions differed widely, in the 1990s African American women artists in California could no longer be viewed as scarce or insignificant. With Billops and her partner Jim Hatch taking the 1992 Grand Jury Prize at Sundance for *Finding Christa*, Saar and fellow Los Angeles black artist John Outterbridge serving as U.S. representatives to the 1995 São Paulo Biennale, work by Weems gracing the cover of a recent issue of *Art in America*, and O'Neal becoming Art Department chair at University of California, Berkeley, black women artists working in California have clearly gotten themselves on the cultural map. And today, several waves of younger black women seem poised to claim an even wider swath of artistic territory.

Notes

1 See Mark Twain's 1897 cablegram: "The reports of my death are greatly exaggerated."

2 "The Colored Sculptress," *San Francisco Chronicle*, Wednesday, September 3, 1873.

3 Monroe A. Majors, M.D., *Noted Negro Women: Their Triumphs and Activities* (Freeport, N.Y.: Books for Libraries Press, 1971; orig. published, Chicago: Donohue & Henneberry, 1893), pp. 217–218.

4 Colescott in telephone interview with Judith Wilson, February 8, 1981.

5 While in California, Lewis sold all five of the statues discussed so dismissively by the *San Francisco Chronicle*. Her week-long San Francisco exhibit drew about a hundred viewers a day and her subsequent display at the San Jose fair seems to have attracted "over sixteen hundred visitors in a week's time." *San Francisco Chronicle*, September 3, 1873. *Daily Evening Bulletin* (San Francisco), Monday, September 8, 1873. *The Elevator* (San Francisco), Saturday, October 4, 1873. Philip M. Montesano, "The Mystery of the San Jose Statues," *Urban West* (March–April 1968): 26, 27.

For more biographical information on Lewis, see Tritobia Hayes Benjamin, "Triumphant Determination: The Legacy of African American Women Artists," and Judith Wilson, "Hagar's Daughters: Social History, Cultural Heritage, and Afro-U.S. Women's Art," in *Bearing Witness: Contemporary Works by African American Women Artists*, ed. Jontyle Theresa Robinson (New York: Rizzoli, 1996), pp. 52–54, 96–103.

6 Delilah L. Beasley quoted in "News Happenings in the Field of Negro Art," *Exhibition of Productions by Negro Artists* (exhibition catalogue), The Art Center, New York, February 20–March 4, 1933, p. 17.

7 Theresa Dickason Cederholm, "Streat, Thelma Johnson," *Afro-American Artists: A Bio-bibliographic Directory* (Boston: Trustees of the Boston Public Library, 1973), p. 270. For the correct name of the museum school Streat attended, see the Portland Art Museum's online history for the period from 1909 at *www.pam.org*.

8 Ann Gibson, *Abstract Expressionism: Other Politics* (New Haven: Yale University Press, 1997), p. 187. Edan Milton Hughes, "Streat, Thelma Johnson," *Artists in California, 1786–1940* (San Francisco: Hughes Publishing, 1989), p. 540.

9 Ann Gibson, "Two Worlds: African-American Abstraction in New York at Mid-Century," *The Search for Freedom:*

African American Abstract Painting 1945–1975 (exhibition catalogue), Kenkeleba Gallery, New York, May 19–July 14, 1991, p. 20.

10 Cederholm, "Streat," p. 270.

11 Ibid. "Library Inventory List, Part IV (S-Z)" (unpublished), Museum of Modern Art, New York, February 21, 1984, p. 318.

12 Lena M. Wysinger, "News of Activities of Negroes," *The Oakland Tribune*, September 15, 1940.

13 In referring to the art of the indigenous peoples of the Americas as "American art," Rivera pointedly refuses Euro-Americans' appropriation of "American" identity. While it is unclear to what extent Streat shared his sophisticated understanding of the art world's ethno-cultural politics, Ann Gibson has mounted an intriguing argument that her practice embodied a parallel resistance to dominant cultural assumptions. Rivera quoted in Catherine Jones, "Thelma Streat Comes Home," *The (Portland) Oregonian*, Sunday, June 17, 1945, sec. 3, p. 5. Gibson, *Abstract Expressionism*, pp. 157–162.

14 "Dance Program," *The Oakland Tribune*, April 7, 1946. Bill Rose, "Brilliant Negro Artist Is Here to Study Indian Lore," *The Vancouver Sun*, Friday, August 16, 1946. May Ebbitt, "Hypnosis Aids Artist In Work," *The (Montreal) Standard*, August 18, 1951, p. 3.

15 "Artist-Dancer Will Appear," *Honolulu Advertiser*, Sunday, February 8, 1948. "Illustrations Textile Designs," *Honolulu Advertiser*, Sunday, February 15, 1948.

16 Lizzetta LeFalle-Collins mentions that her 1942 painting *Robot* "was an illustration for a children's book." LeFalle-Collins, "Streat, Thelma Johnson," in *St. James Guide to Black Artists* (Detroit: St. James Press, 1997), p. 513. See Humphrey's *The River That Gave Gifts* (1987) and Ringgold's several children's books, beginning with the award-winning *Tar Beach* (1991).

17 Streat seems to have spent a substantial amount of time in the Bay Area during the first half of the 1940s, but even then she was fairly peripatetic. While Portland newspapers reported she had recently returned "home for a short stay" after "ten years in San Francisco, Los Angeles, New York and Chicago" in June 1945, she seems to have resided in the Bay Area, at least sporadically, as late as the summer of 1946. But after signing up with the National Artists Concert Bureau that year, her time was spent increasingly on the road, giving concerts, exhibiting her paintings and textile designs, and conducting "ethnographic" research. Plans to launch a center for documentary children's films, first in Mexico in 1948, then in Santa Barbara in 1953, were never realized by Streat and her manager-husband. Instead, sometime between 1948 and 1950, Honolulu became the couple's "home" during breaks from their frequent travels. Elinor Pillsbury, "Portland Artist Wins Praise With Negro Labor Paintings," *Oregon Journal*, Sunday, June 17, 1945, p. 12D. Jones, "Thelma Streat Comes Home." "Dance Program," *The Oakland Tribune*, April 7, 1946. Bill Rose, "Brilliant Negro Artist Is Here to Study Indian Lore," *The Vancouver Sun*, Friday, August 16, 1946. "Artist-Dancer Will Appear," *Honolulu Advertiser*, February 8, 1949. "Noted Dancer-Painter to Show In First Local Performance Today," *Honolulu Advertiser*, Saturday, February 14, 1948. "Dancer Appears at Recital At Exhibition of Paintings," *The (Portland) Oregonian*, Saturday, October 14, 1950. Charles McHarry, "Paints to Live, Yet Calls Art Too Costly," *[Honolulu?] Sunday News*, December 31, 1950, p. 14. "Negro Dancer of Portland Weds Caucasian Manager," *The (Portland) Oregonian*, Tuesday, December 14, 1948, p. 1. " 'Children's City' Plan of Artist-Author Pair," *Santa Barbara News-Press*, Sunday morning, May 31, 1953.

18 Lizzetta LeFalle-Collins, "Working from the Pacific Rim: Beulah Woodard and Elizabeth Catlett," in *Three Generations of African American Women Sculptors: A Study in Paradox*, curated by Leslie King-Hammond and Tritobia Hayes Benjamin (exhibition catalogue), The Afro-American Historical and Cultural Museum, Philadelphia, March–September 1996, p. 38. Majors, *Noted Negro Women*, p. 218.

19 Majors, *Noted Negro Women*, pp. 217–219. Delilah L. Beasley, *The Negro Trail Blazers of California* (1919; San Francisco: R & E Research Associates, 1968), p. 216.

20 These nameless others were left undocumented, however, because Garland alone managed to supply autobiographical information in time for the writer's deadline. Beasley, *Negro Trail Blazers*, p. 234.

21 Eugene Castello, "The Annual Exhibition of the Fellowship, P.A.F.A.," *Art and Progress* 5 (July 1914): 333. "Katherine Patton Receives First Prize in Negro Art Exhibit," *California Eagle*, Thursday, December 2, 1937, p. 5A.

22 Lizzetta LeFalle-Collins, "Grafton Tyler Brown: Selling the Promise of the West," *International Review of African American Art* 12, no. 1 (1995): 27–31, 34, 37, 40.

23 See my discussion of this aspect of Johnson's work in Judith Wilson, "Sargent Johnson: Afro-California Modernist," in Lizzetta LeFalle-Collins and Judith Wilson, *Sargent Johnson, African-American Modernist* (exhibition catalogue), San Francisco Museum of Modern Art, March 13–July 7, 1998, p. 30.

24 During his six-decade-long career, Williams designed some 3,000 projects, ranging from movie star mansions to the Los Angeles General Hospital. Having served on Los Angeles's first City Planning Commission from 1920 to 1928, he was one of two black architects chosen in 1936 to design the nation's first federally funded public housing project. In 1957, Williams became the first African American elected to the American Institute of Architects (AIA) College of Fellows. His futuristic theme building from the 1960s welcomes travelers to Los Angeles International Airport. David Gebhard, "Paul R. Williams and the Los Angeles Scene"; "Selected Listing of Projects Designed by Paul R. Williams"; and "Biographical Chronology," all in Karen E. Hudson, *Paul R. Williams, Architect: A Legacy of Style* (New York: Rizzoli, 1993), pp. 19–29, 228, 230–235.

25 Beasley paraphrased in "News Happenings," p. 17. Robinson's paintings are discussed in an unsigned report on his only solo exhibition, which opened a few weeks after the artist's death by drowning. "Posthumous Art Exhibit Thrills L.A.," *California Eagle*, Thursday, June 30, 1938, p. 3A. Lynn Moody Igoe, *250 Years of Afro-American Art: An Annotated Bibliography* (New York: R. R. Bowker, 1981), p. 1001.

26 "Modern Furniture," *Ebony* 4, no. 1 (November 1948): 27–30.

27 Beasley, *Negro Trail Blazers*, pp. 232, 233, 242, 243.

28 *Harmon Foundation Exhibit of Fine Arts* (New York, 1928), p. 11.

29 An undated announcement for a Streat exhibition at the "Artist and Craftsman Shop" of the City of Paris, a San Francisco department store, lists "[w]all decorations in tempera, watercolors, woven rugs and tableware" by the artist. In 1948, the *Honolulu Advertiser* reports that "several" of Streat's textile designs "have recently been secured by Koret of California for use on their spring textiles." A solo show at the Honolulu Academy of Arts that February featured many of these designs, along with examples of her children's book illustrations. The designs are described as "delightful drawings of strange and amusing little animals" in which "Negro and Indian motifs are employed in an unusually creative manner." Beatrice Judd Ryan [signed exhibition announcement, ca. 1940–41], City of Paris Galleries, City of Paris. "Artist-Dancer Will Appear," *Honolulu Advocate*, Sunday, February 8, 1948. "Illustrations/ Textile Designs," *Honolulu Advocate*, Sunday, February 15, 1948.

30 LeFalle-Collins, "Working from the Pacific Rim," p. 38. Wilson, "Sargent Johnson," pp. 29–31.

31 For ample, if inadequately contextualized, documentation of these white modernist preoccupations, see *"Primitivism" in 20th Century Art: Affinity of the Tribal and the Modern*, vols. 1 & 2, ed. William Rubin (New York: The Museum of Modern Art, 1984), and Kirk Varnedoe and Adam Gopnik, *High & Low: Modern Art and Popular Culture* (New York: The Museum of Modern Art, 1990).

32 For Johnson and Woodruff in this regard, see Lizzetta LeFalle-Collins, "Sargent Johnson and Modernism: An Investigation of Context, Representation, and Identity," in LeFalle-Collins and Wilson, *Sargent Johnson*, p. 18; Wilson, "Sargent Johnson: Afro-California Modernist," in ibid., p. 35; and Judith Wilson, " 'Go Back and Retrieve It': Hale Woodruff, Afro-American Modernist," in *Selected Essays: Art and Artists from the Harlem Renaissance to the 1980's*, ed. Crystal A. Britton (exhibition catalogue), National Black Arts Festival, Atlanta, July 30–August 7, 1988, pp. 41–49.

33 For an especially insightful discussion of the new strategies developed by black California artists in the 1960s and 1970s, see Kellie Jones, "Flying and Touching Down: Abstraction, Metaphor, and Social Concern—The Use of Conceptual Forms Among Mexican and African American Artists, 1968–1983" (Ph.D. dissertation, Yale University, December 1999), pp. 13–14.

34 There has been a recent upsurge of interest in Streat, however, by her inclusion in Kenkeleba Gallery's 1991 survey of African American abstract painting. In addition to her writing on the artist for that exhibition catalogue, Ann Gibson has included Streat in a 1995 article on abstract expressionist-era women artists and the 1997 book in which she provides a major revision of accounts of abstract expression. The 1997 *St. James Guide to Black Artists* contains a brief, but insightful, essay on Streat by Lizzetta LeFalle-Collins, the premier historian of California African American art. Gibson, "Two Worlds," p. 20; Gibson, "Universality and Difference in Women's Abstract Painting: Krasner, Ryan, Sekula, Piper, and Streat," *The Yale Journal of Criticism* 8, no. 1 (Spring 1995): 103–132; Gibson, *Abstract Expressionism*, pp. 157–162; *St. James Guide to Black Artists*, pp. 512–513.

35 Woodard quoted in Verna Arvey, "By Her Own Bootstraps," *Opportunity* 22, no. 1 (Winter 1944): 17; see also pp. 17, 42. LeFalle-Collins, "Working from the Pacific Rim," p. 39.

One of the founding fathers of the studio ceramics movement, Lukens brought California ceramists to national attention when he won first prize at the National Ceramic Exhibition in Syracuse in 1936. A proponent of "elementally simple forms, bold . . . solid color, and naturalness," his innovations included being "the first to partially glaze a vessel, leaving some of the clay body exposed." The resulting " 'Organic' look" became dominant in postwar ceramic circles. Nancy Dustin Wall Moure, *California Art: 450 Years of Painting and Other Media* (Los Angeles: Dustin Publications, 1998), pp. 220, 331.

36 Cederholm, "Woodard, Beulah," *Afro-American Artists*, p. 316. LeFalle-Collins, "Working from the Pacific Rim," p. 40.

37 Both journals use the terms "housewife" and "hobby" in their descriptions of Woodard and her activity. "Speaking of People," *Ebony* 5, no. 6 (April 1950): 5. "Mask Making Hobby," *The Crisis* 57, no. 5 (May 1950): 282.

38 The Woodard heads I have in mind are her *Fulah Kunda/African Man* (ca. 1935), plaster with faux bronze pigment, height 10¼ in.; *Bad Boy* (ca. 1936), bronze, height 6¾ in.; *The Philosopher* (ca. 1937), fired clay, height 16 in.; *Maudelle* (ca. 1937), bronze, height 12¼ in., all reproduced in King-Hammond and Benjamin, *Three Generations of African American Women Sculptors*, pp. 42–43.

For a discussion of Rodin's mastery of the psychological portrait (with his 1892 *Portrait of Baudelaire* illustrated as an example), see Albert E. Elsen, *Origins of Modern Sculpture: Pioneers and Premises* (New York: George Braziller, 1974), pp. 42 and 43, fig. 57.

39 From a review by the art critic for the Hollywood *Citizen-News* of the December 1937 Negro Art Association show in which Woodard took third prize, quoted in Arvey, "By Her Own Bootstraps," p. 42.

40 Ibid., p. 42. Jessie P. Guzman, "The Social Contributions of the Negro Woman Since 1940," *The Negro History Bulletin* 11, no. 4 (January 1948): 88.

41 "Mask Making Hobby," *The Crisis*, p. 282. The *Ebony* article contains remarkably similar language.

42 If, as I suspect, *Creation* is a late work or one produced at the same time as the ethnological masks, it belies the claim that an exclusive "focus . . . on educating through her art . . . prevented her from creative exploration of materials and expanding her themes." Similarly, Woodard's subtle use of opaque polychrome glazes to accentuate the ear and hair ornaments in another undated work, the glazed terracotta *African Woman*, raises questions about the impact of her study with ceramist Glenn Lukens, as well as the extent to which her style may have varied with her medium.

Lizzetta LeFalle-Collins, "Woodard, Beulah (Ecton)," *St. James Guide to Black Artists*, p. 585. *Creation* is reproduced in Francine R. Carter, "The Golden State Mutual Afro-American Art Collection," *Black Art: An International Quarterly* 1, no. 2 (Winter 1976): 20.

43 The tendency of black journalists in her lifetime and a black scholar writing posthumously to focus on Woodard's African masks to the exclusion of other aspects of her oeuvre parallels the fallacy for which Kymberly N. Pinder has acutely criticized white authors of art history survey texts—i.e., the assumption that "the authenticity of African American art is inextricably bound to its racial content." Pinder, "Black Representation and Western Survey Textbooks," *Art Bulletin* 81, no. 3 (September 1999): 533.

44 LeFalle-Collins, "Working from the Pacific Rim," p. 39.

45 Arvey and Woodard quoted in Arvey, "By Her Own Bootstraps," p. 42.

46 LeFalle-Collins, "Woodard," *St. James Guide to Black Artists*, p. 585.

47 LeFalle-Collins, "Working from the Pacific Rim," p. 39.

48 "Art Exhibit Draws Huge Attendance," *California Eagle*, Thursday, December 2, 1937, p. 5-B.

49 LeFalle-Collins, "Working from the Pacific Rim," p. 40.

50 Arthur Millier, "Los Angeles Events and Exhibitions," *Art Digest* 14 (August 1, 1950): 29.

51 As a result of her efforts to organize and promote the work of Los Angeles's black artists, Waddy eventually became an artist (specifically, a printmaker) herself. "African-American Artists of Los Angeles: Ruth G. Waddy," unpublished transcript of interview by Karen Anne Mason (Oral History Program, University of California, Los Angeles, 1993), pp. vi–vii (biographical summary). Richard J. Powell, "The Visual Arts and Afro-America, 1940–1980" (unpublished paper), August 1986, p. 27.

52 Howard quoted in "Talking With Mildred Howard," by Meredith Tromble (exhibition brochure), San Jose Museum of Art, San Jose, May 1994.

53 Andrea Kirsh, "Carrie Mae Weems: Issues in Black, White and Color," *Carrie Mae Weems* (exhibition catalogue), The National Museum of Women in the Arts, Washington, D.C., January 7–March 21, 1993, p. 10. Paul Von Blum, "Pat Ward Williams," in *Other Visions, Other Voices: Women Political Artists in Greater Los Angeles* (Lanham, Md.: University Press of America, 1994), p. 180.

54 "Black Leadership in Los Angeles: Ruth Washington," unpublished transcript of interview by Ranford B. Hopkins (Oral History Program, University of California, Los Angeles, 1991), p. v (biographical summary). Jeanne Moutoussamy-Ashe, *Viewfinders: Black Women Photographers* (New York: Dodd, Mead, 1986), pp. 87–88, 180.

55 Billops quoted in Patricia A. Smith, "Mother-and-Child Reunion: On PBS, An Adoption Story Told Without Regrets," *The Boston Globe*, Monday, June 29, 1992, p. 38.

INTERSECTIONS

THEMES AND PRACTICES

JENNIFER GONZALEZ

LANDING IN CALIFORNIA

California, like all human geography, is a territory and a concept, a real space and an imaginary site. Established in the sixteenth century by Spanish colonialism, maintained by Mexican nationalism, overtaken by U.S. expansion, transformed by waves of immigration from the eastern United States as well as Europe, Asia, and Central and South America, California exists as much in myths of popular culture and the minds of its inhabitants, as in its urban streets, windy deserts, high mountains, rough coastline, and cultivated fields. To categorize art on the basis of a geographical boundary is to presume a nontrivial, historical coherence or correspondence between different works of art produced within that boundary. Similarly, to categorize art on the basis of gender presumes some quality or condition shared by a group of artists *because* of their gender. To think broadly about women artists working in California is to look for correspondences or intersections between their works that might perhaps reveal a new conceptual and historical terrain.

Such is the goal of this essay, to examine metaphoric and metonymic references to land (as a concrete medium and as an ideological construct) and the state (as a social system, a political territory, and an economic condition) in the work of women artists working in California. By assessing geographical and, to a lesser extent, gender-specific references in the work, it is possible to chart some of the historical and present relations that exist between women and the state, represented by three conceptual frameworks: land as metonym, land as the condition of labor, and land as environment.

Land as Metonym

Metonymy is a linguistic term describing a rhetorical expression of substitution by association; for example, when a sail is used to denote a ship. The part-object or associated object stands in for the actual referent. The semantic structure of metonymic phrases also occurs in nonlinguistic form, in museum displays or collections, for example, where an object stands in for the person who owned it, or where a painting represents a particular art movement or historical era. The object represents both itself and a larger concept to which it refers and with which it is materially linked.

In the second half of the twentieth century, land itself has frequently been used as a metonym in works of art—particularly in sculpture, conceptual art, and installation art. Fragments of earth (literally dirt, sand, and rocks) have been brought into exhibition spaces as a way of gesturing to a larger geography or territory beyond or outside gallery walls. Although the focus of this essay is the recent work of women artists working in California, I begin with a brief look at works by Walter de Maria and Robert Smithson from the 1960s. This comparison, which may seem out of place in a book about women artists, allows

important distinctions to emerge concerning the use and the conception of land as a medium and as social space.

Dirt in the House: Walter de Maria and Robert Smithson

In 1968, Walter de Maria exhibited his first *Earth Room*, a gallery space filled with earth piled 56 centimeters high. That same year Robert Smithson produced his first *Non-Site*, a sculptural work that included a set of containers holding rocks, soil, and other organic material. Both artists established an oscillation between inside (gallery) and outside (rural location) that relied upon the metonymic quality of the earth as evidence of its own origins.

A relatively radical gesture at the time, the work contributed to new conceptions of land use, yet certain ideas remained unchanged. Land was represented in these works primarily as a formal resource or as an elemental substance without history. The artists addressed qualities in the land that were more physical than cultural. Mediated through this instrumental lens, the earth became purified of both use and exchange value. With an emphasis on thresholds and reflections, the artists emphasized the perceptual habits of an undefined human body and human gaze in the completion of the work, intentionally or unintentionally repressing signs of social specificity, and biography.

Intersections: Themes and Practices

Intimate Geology: Vija Celmins

A similar kind of anonymity marks the work of Vija Celmins, who lived in California between 1963 and 1981, and is perhaps best known for her meticulous photo-realistic graphite drawings of the cresting surface of the Pacific Ocean. In these finely crafted small-scale images, the sculptural surface of the sea merges seamlessly with the surface of the paper, creating a vertiginous illusion of surface and depth. Neither the traditions of landscape painting nor those of scientific illustration comfortably account for the precision and focus of Celmins's *Untitled* ocean drawings (begun in 1969). If anything, the closely cropped views of the water have the quality of a portrait of a particular moment in time. Yet, their subject is so vast that the drawings always appear as a mere fragment of that which they truly represent. The same is the case with her star field paintings, where limited views of the night sky evoke an expanse far beyond the frame of paper or canvas. In these two-dimensional works, Celmins situates the audience within her own floating imaginary grid that divides the visible world into discreet but unique rectilinear units. The sections of ocean she draws appear literally lifted from the surface on which they once rested—a metonym for the unseen whole of the sea.

Like Smithson and de Maria, Celmins experiments with the viewer's phenomenological relationship to land and nature through a formal, almost abstract vocabulary. Yet, her works evoke the conceptual logic of a microscopic rather than macroscopic domain. Instead of creating sculptural works that compete with the scale of hills, valleys or lakes, she takes the viewer into an intimate, but no less monumental, reading of the skin of the earth. Perhaps her most powerful work, and one that explicitly uses land as a metonym, is the five-year project *To Fix the Image in Memory* (1977–1982). For this work the artist cast unique desert rocks in bronze and carefully painted these copies to exactly mimic the surface and color of the originals. Every vein, every crevice, every crack and mottled surface of the rocks is rendered with remarkable precision. The work is nevertheless *not* about the skill of the artist, but rather about the very act of being attentive: attentive to detail, attentive to form, and attentive to nature more generally. The moment of sublime shock when the viewer realizes that the rocks in Celmins's display are originals paired with reproductions is followed by a secondary recognition of the inherent humor in the work. *To Fix the Image in Memory*, the artist herself has suggested, may take up where Jasper Johns left off, with his painted bronze beer can and light bulb of the 1960s.[1] Yet, unlike Johns's Pop aesthetic which consciously references mass-produced and man-made objects, Celmins's work is a circular statement, a formal and visual tautology about nature and culture, about production and reproduction. The earth becomes a value deserving or even requiring exceptional attention, but it is the attentiveness itself, the "fixing of the image," which becomes the final focus of the work. Although Celmins would no doubt deny an underlying ecological motivation in her work, her close attention to the land, the sea, and the sky necessarily brings to the attention of her audience the larger whole of which these elements are a part.

Border Topography: Amalia Mesa-Bains

Like the work of de Maria and Smithson, the work of artist Amalia Mesa-Bains addresses the formal relations of inside and outside, thresholds, topography, and mirrored reflections in the space of the gallery. Yet her installations, dated some twenty years later, are an important break from these earlier conceptual and minimalist experiments. For Mesa-Bains history, biography, and culture become central organizing features in her use of land as metonym. She brings earth into the gallery to reflect upon the relations between immigration and identity, memory and death, which are intimately tied to her experience as a Mexican American woman born in California of immigrant parents. While formal elements of Mesa-Bains's work parallel and indirectly rely upon works such as Smithson's *Non-Site* series, they are equally indebted to a vernacular tradition of altar and shrine building in the Chicano/Chicana community in Northern California.

In the *Ofrenda for Dolores del Rio* (1984), Mesa-Bains pays homage to a secular icon of Hollywood cinema through an ornamental canonization that takes the form of an altar. Flounces of pink cascading satins and lace frame the space of the altar and glorify the figure pictured within. To formulate a visual argument about the role of del Rio as a central figure in Chicana history and in her own imaginary, Mesa-Bains develops a topographical map of cultural and institutional affiliations grounded in symbolically charged artifacts. Lace fans, lipstick, and glamorous Hollywood photographs are placed opposite childhood playthings, teacups, and a Mexican national flag. Two sides of del Rio's life—Mexican and American—come together in a mirrored shrine surrounded by a carpet of crushed rose petals, earth, and bright glitter. The work encapsulates the existential condition of existing across borders: living in the state of California and, at the same time, living a deracinated life. The paradoxical condition of the immigrant who is not rooted precisely because she has more than one home, and yet is always defined by her relation to place, is here represented by the land she inhabits as well as by the topography of artifacts by which she is identified.

Mesa-Bains addresses the experience of immigration more explicitly through her installation

60

Amalia Mesa-Bains,
An Ofrenda for Dolores del Rio,
1984; reconstructed 1990.
Mixed-media altar installation,
96 × 72 × 48 in. Photo
courtesy: UCLA at the Armand
Hammer Museum of Art and
Cultural Center, Los Angeles,
Calif. Collection of the artist.

entitled *Borders* (1990). Staged as a domestic tableau, the work includes a large chest of drawers atop which is erected a small private altar and beside which lies a suitcase packed with letters. Rich, dark earth overflows the dresser drawers and covers the floor around its base, as if spilling from a fountain within. The unlikely presence of earth folded into the crevices of domestic furniture invokes both a burial and remembrance of land and life left behind. It also signals the burial of those who have disappeared in the transition across borders. On the wall is inscribed a story told by a young boy: "The coyote [the hired guide who helps others cross the border] put me in a sack in the back of a truck with potatoes and told me to be totally quiet until he came. It was so hot I couldn't breathe. I cried with no sounds. After hours he came to get me. We had gotten across, but where was my mother? She had given me an address, but I didn't know how to get there and was afraid to ask for help." A child's individual memory is a poignant reminder of familial ties broken by economic hardship. Land becomes a metonym not only of that which has been left behind, but also of the great distances covered in the process of migration, and the unfamiliar territory newly encountered.

Land as the Condition of Labor

After the Mexican-American War, all native Mexicans were excluded from participation in the California State Senate and in 1851 the California Land Law was passed depriving all Mexican residents of their property. Over 200 Mexican landowners were forced to give up more than 14 million acres of land.[2] In 1862, once the Gold Rush had transformed the state into a destination for immigrants from around the world, the California legislature passed a law entitled "An Act to Protect Free White Labor against Competition with Chinese Coolie Labor."[3] In 1877 the California legislature addressed an argument against further Chinese immigration to the U.S. Congress, asserting that "the white laborer cannot compete with the Chinaman, who needs neither a civilized abode, nor decent clothing, nor education for his children." Admitting that the state supported the illegal removal of Chinese miners from their land claims, the legislature goes on to complain of their subsequent success, once displaced, as laborers in the city. It becomes clear from the document submitted to the U.S. Congress that Chinese laborers were both more skilled and more industrious than their European American counterparts and yet were considered an inferior race that should be barred from entrance into the country, precisely because of their competitive advantage. Such fear of competition eventually led to the Chinese Exclusion Act of 1902.

Despite these explicitly racist laws, both Asian and Asian American labor were considered vital to the growth of California. Chinese labor was instrumental in building the Central Pacific railroad and Japanese labor was necessary for agriculture.[4] Cheap and subservient labor by Asian Americans and other ethnic minorities was accepted, but land ownership and competitive business practices were not. In 1920, citizens of California voted 3 to 1 for a law forbidding land acquisition by "aliens ineligible for citizenship" at a time when eligibility for citizenship was limited to "free white persons."[5] Alien land laws remained on the books in California until 1956.

In 1942, as a result of the labor shortage created by World War II, agricultural growers and the federal government established the Bracero Program with Mexico, welcoming large numbers of workers into the United States. In the more competitive postwar job environment, the U.S. government undertook Operation Wetback to stem illegal immigration and eject visiting workers who were no longer needed. In the process, both Mexicans and Mexican Americans were sometimes indiscriminately rounded up, arrested, detained, and deported to Mexico, often in violation of their civil rights. Such opportunistic programs have characterized California's labor policies in the past and continue in the present day under different guises. Given this history, it is not surprising that artists whose work takes labor in California as its focus choose to examine the topic critically.

Underground: May Sun

May Sun's *L.A./River/China/Town* (1988) is one such critical work addressing the complex history of Chinese immigrants in California, particularly in the city of Los Angeles. In collaboration with stage director Peter Brosius and composer Tom Recchion, May Sun's large-scale installation consisted of a staged scene that told a history of Chinese immigration and labor through metaphors of transition and translation. Viewers entered the installation by crossing a wooden bridge that led them to a sandy courtyard. There viewers were led by directional lighting past a sequence of four white tents, reminiscent of those in which Chinese railroad laborers slept. Images of people and places, both historical and contemporary, were projected onto the tent walls that served as slide screens, allowing several specific histories to emerge: the 1849 flood in China and the consequent wave of immigration to the United States; the life of the Chinese railroad workers who lived along the Los Angeles River in the 1870s; the 1871 Chinatown massacre that took place in downtown Los Angeles; an allegory about the flooding of the Los Angeles River; and the story of Homer Lea, a European American resident of Santa Monica who trained troops for the Chinese revolution.[6] In the center of the installation a hanging sculpture of Chinese gongs played by falling grains of rice provided a subtle accom-

61
May Sun, *L.A./River/China/Town*, 1988. In collaboration with Peter Brosius and Tom Recchion. Multi-media installation, 10 × 14 × 10 ft. (each tent). Santa Monica Museum of Art, Santa Monica, Calif. Photo: David Familian. Collection of the artist.

paniment to a recorded musical score that included sounds of nature, speech fragments, and a narrative of historical events. Jan Breslauer suggests that the work addresses the need to research and understand suppressed history, commenting, "Forgotten for more than a hundred years, the laborers who built the railroads were given back their own images, their place in the making of today."[7]

May Sun's *Underground* (1991) addresses the history of agricultural workers, particularly in the orange groves of Southern California. Archival photographs of both Chinese and

Chinese American men working in the fields, picking fruit from the trees under the surveillance of European American employers, become an artistic resource for conceiving and representing interracial labor practices and hierarchy. What is often unacknowledged or unexplored about the history of California labor is how precisely ethnic difference was affected by class solidarity. Although Mexican American, Japanese American, Filipino American, and Chinese American laborers worked side by side and suffered similar forms of racial discrimination, low wages, and hard working conditions, workers' associations and strikes regularly were organized by ethnic affiliation and were sometimes necessarily competitive and clandestine. As in the case of the railroad laborers, the history of agricultural labor is hidden beneath the topsoil of the present. The last fifty years in Southern California have seen a dramatic shift from a largely citrus-based agricultural landscape to a residential sprawl of urban and suburban housing, shopping malls, and freeways. The history of agricultural labor in the southern valleys of the state has been literally paved over by asphalt and cement. Existing "underground," it must be unearthed by artists such as Sun in order to be seen by the public at large.

In the Heat of the Sun: Ester Hernandez

If the labor history of Southern California is buried in the dust, that of more recent labor struggles in Central and Northern California is the driving force behind the work of many California Chicana and Chicano artists. It is impossible, in fact, to tell the story of Chicano/Chicana art in California without reference to the labor movement started by Dolores Huerta and Cesar Chavez, around which the Chicano civil rights movement revolved. Art was considered an integral part of a larger project of social activism and grassroots mobilization to improve the lives of Mexican Americans in the United States. As a result, the years from 1968 to about 1975 wit-

62
Ester Hernandez,
Sun Mad—The Installation,
1989. Mixed-media installation
(dimensions variable). *Sun Mad*
© 1989 Ester Hernandez.
Collection of the artist.

nessed an emphasis on public art that could reach a large audience, such as murals, posters, and filmmaking. The work of activist artist Ester Hernandez often took the form of prints or silkscreens that could be easily reproduced for distribution. Much of her work, including later paintings and installations, addresses the state of laboring classes in California or establishes symbols for women's struggles. From her stoic portrait of a young girl seated near a bag of flour, *California Special* (1987), to the abstract painting entitled *San Francisco Police Beating Dolores Huerta* (1988), the artist never flinches from representing the daily and heroic struggle of workers, particularly women, who face opposition and discrimination.

One of Hernandez's best-known works, *Sun Mad* (1981), has been reproduced on postcards and sold at art venues and museum bookstores throughout the country. A parody of the Sun Maid brand of raisins, the image shows a skeleton dressed in a red bonnet with curling dark locks, holding a basket of grapes labeled "unnaturally grown with insecticides, miticides, herbicides and fungicides." Reversing the notion of a naturally grown product, the work draws our attention to the real conditions of large-scale agriculture business. In 1989 the artist produced a room-sized installation, bearing the same title as her earlier *Sun Mad* screen-print, that makes the working conditions of field laborers more explicit. In the installation, a tall hanging screen made of vertical panels painted on two sides hovers above an earthen altar. One side of the panels shows an agricultural worker who is picking grapes, wearing a hat, gloves, and bandana for protection against poisonous residues left on the fruit. On the other side is the image of the *Sun Mad* skeleton. Below lies a circle of sand and rocks within which are placed family mementos, including a laborer's hat, a bandana, harvesting implements, and photographs. Candles lit on four sides of the circle create the aura of a sanctuary or memorial. Given the health risks agricultural workers face due to exposure to poisonous residues, the altar also serves as a monument to those who have died as a result of their labor. Just as in the work of May Sun and Amalia Mesa-Bains, the sand and stones in Hernandez's installation function as a metonym for the land upon which so many Californians have labored.

In the work discussed in this section, geographical regions of California provide the context for the exploration of labor history and the relation of women to that history. Even in the case of May Sun's work, which focuses largely on the labor of Chinese men, the women who supported this labor are not invisible. They form a delicate web of references in archival images and text throughout. The work of all three artists also arises in a context of second wave and third wave feminism (1970–1990), a period when women's labor contributions have been increasingly championed by activists and the mainstream. Unlike middle-class feminists who fought to leave the confines of a domestic life in search of gainful employment, however, women of the poorer classes labored outside the home by necessity. This difference of class, which in California is often correlated to ethnic difference, produced distinct forms of feminist art practice. May Sun and Ester Hernandez address the largely invisible history of both men and women who work the land, transforming the economy and shape of California.

Land as Environment

Since the late 1960s, with the rise of environmental activism and the inauguration of Earth Day in 1970, California as a state has paradoxically been at the forefront of environmental reform *and* home to a record number of environmental abuses. Artists have responded by joining protest movements as the producers and designers of agitprop, by affectionately painting disappearing forests, deserts, or coastline, by reducing their own uses of hazardous materials, and, in some cases, by taking the project of remediation of the environment into their own hands. Artists have also responded by drawing our attention to the relation of humans to specific sites, constructed environments, and the "development" of the land.

Saving the Earth: Betty Beaumont, Bonnie Sherk, Helen Harrison, Reiko Goto

Annually, Los Angeles and Long Beach harbors alone move more than 9 billion gallons of petroleum products on 1,000 tankers, and experience roughly 500 spills of between 1,000 and 10,000 gallons each.[8] The technique used for cleaning the spills—with steam ejected from high pressure hoses—is known to cause considerable ecological damage itself. In response to the 1969 Santa Barbara oil spill—one of the worst in U.S. history—artist Betty Beaumont documented the devastation in a series of photographs. *Steam Cleaning Santa Barbara Shore* (1969) offers one of the first visual accounts of a major ecological disaster by an environmental artist in California. Her photographs depict a small figure dressed in protective clothing carefully cleaning individual stones, surrounded by a wasteland of oil-blackened shoreline, suggesting both the futility and the necessity of human response to such catastrophes. Although most of her artistic interventions in coastal ecosystems have taken place outside of California since her student days, she is an important figure in the early environmentalist approach to art practice along the coast.

In 1974, artist Bonnie Sherk took the notion of environmental cleanup and transformation even further with her groundbreaking Crossroads Community project in San Francisco (also known as The Farm). One of the first community-based

63

Betty Beaumont, *Steam Cleaning Santa Barbara Shore*, 1969. Santa Barbara, Calif. Black-and-white photograph, 11 × 13 in. Collection of the artist.

integrative artist projects to be directed by a woman, Crossroads Community shared the experimental and pedagogical methods of other conceptual and activist art of the time. Located below a set of intersecting highways, The Farm was set in a row of abandoned buildings transformed by Sherk into an experimental environment for the growth of plants, animals, and ideas. There were a series of gathering spaces: a farmhouse, a theater, a school without walls, a library, a darkroom, and a healing center. According to the artist, The Farm drew public attention to the availability of a five-acre tract of open land that was subsequently purchased by the city of San Francisco for use as a neighborhood park.[9] As a result, where there was once a barren lot, there now grows a lush green garden, with lawns and trees. Conceived as a microcosm of human encounters with the natural environment, local economics, city planning, politics, and reclamation, the project developed from Sherk's notion of "Life Frames," a conceptual term for what the artist calls "life-scale environmental performance sculpture" designed to heighten the experience or awareness of life itself. In 1985, the artist developed an ongoing project called "The

Living Library" that consists of an international electronically linked network of indoor/outdoor "culture-ecology" parks with accompanying curricular materials for ecological and cross-cultural education. In conjunction with this project, Sherk has created a traveling installation called *A Garden of Knowledge*, which has been displayed in New York and Houston. By emphasizing the diversity of plant, animal, and cultural life around the globe, the exhibition invites viewers to be more attentive to their own local flora and fauna, and to consider the intersections between humans and the built environment. Taking a holistic approach, Sherk is a model for other artists who wish to integrate community and environmental activism in an experimental form.

Developing a visual vocabulary for the assessment and critique of land use has been the central focus of artist Helen Harrison who, in collaboration with her husband, Newton Harrison, has studied environmental conditions and environmental policies in California and worldwide.

The Farm is a social art work and incorporates the divergent fields of all the arts and literature, education, appropriate technology, community service, public health, the environment, economics, city planning, politics, and real estate. It is a vehicle for connecting life scale elements of physical form, spirituality (feeling states), and ideas, all of which are interconnected. The whole Farm is a metaphor for civilization. It is a microcosm. The Raw Egg Animal Theatre (TREAT) at The Farm is a microcosm of The Farm, and so on. And because The Farm is really small and framed, you can see a myriad of different relationships—struggles, differences, similarities, and coincidings. You can see large swelling forms and very flat shapes—technological and non-mechanized. The Farm is a painting and a theatre piece. It's a play, a sculpture, and a sociological model. There are also elements of plumbing. The Farm has to do with finding a way to survive and making it wonderful.

Based at the University of California, San Diego, the team has focused their attention on the ecological and political impact of humans on specific sites or natural systems. *Meditations on the Sacramento River, the Delta and the Bays at San Francisco* (1977) examined how agricultural lands of California's Central Valley will eventually erode and be reduced to a dust bowl as a result of excessive dam building and water diversion. The artists explicitly criticize government and taxpayer subsidies that perpetuate inefficient, intensive irrigation practices which, at the time, accounted for 85 percent of water usage in the Central Valley.[10] The Harrisons have also used radio, posters, and billboards in the city of San Francisco to inform the public about environmental degradation. As with all of their projects, *Sacramento Meditations* sought to link the natural ecosystem with the human ecosystems including wasteful uses of resources, flawed state legislation, aggressive consumption practices, and mass media advertising.

The Harrisons' largest, most comprehensive project to date is *Lagoon Cycle*, a study focusing on food production and watersheds; begun in 1972, it continued to grow in complexity and size until 1982, culminating in a 350-foot-long mural that focuses on seven different sites. *The Sixth Lagoon* (1979) is a study of the Colorado River watershed from the Gulf of California to the Continental Divide. Aerial photographs of mighty, multimil-lion-dollar structures that reshape the natural environment are accompanied by an almost poetic text describing how the system of dams and human-made waterways is not only damaging to the previously thriving ecosystems in this area, but is the result of a self-justifying system of belief resting on a general misguided notion of progress.

While the Harrisons' work is largely analytic, some of their more recent projects have included concrete proposals for the reclamation or transformation of specific sites. *The Arroyo Seco Release: A Serpentine for Pasadena* and *Devil's Gate: A Refuge for Pasadena* (both 1984–87) included a plan to release the water of the Arroyo Seco River from its artificial course and to restore its native woodland ecosystem. In 1985, after public debate and media exposure, the city of Pasadena included the *Devil's Gate* project in their master plan.[11] The transformation of public policy through artistic practice is precisely the outcome Helen and Newton Harrison desire for their land-based research projects.

Reiko Goto and her husband, Tim Collins, were both led to environmental art practice, at least in part, through an encounter with the social and ecological philosophy of Bonnie Sherk's Crossroads Community project. Goto, who visited The Farm, became fascinated by the life of the swallowtail butterfly and went on to study the unique habitats and diets of various species found in the

65
Helen Harrison, *The first
proposal to restore the river
from the mountains to its
outfall into the LA River*,
1985–91. In collaboration with
Newton Harrison. Aerial photo
and drawing, 54 × 96 in.
(photo includes Devils Gate,
Rose Bowl, Lower Arroyo
Seco, Calif.). Courtesy of the
artist and Newton Harrison.

Bay Area. Her interest developed largely from a powerful memory of butterflies from her childhood in Japan and led her to create several installations that served as gardens for the support of the butterfly life cycle. For her landscape installation in downtown San Francisco's Yerba Buena Gardens, *Butterfly Garden* (1991), Goto created, in the artist's own words, an "urban garden for butterflies."[12] The project drew attention to the fact that many of the plants that support the butterfly life cycle are considered weeds in traditional gardens. Goto devised a maintenance plan which included only organic techniques. Above all the artist hoped to contribute to a larger ecological

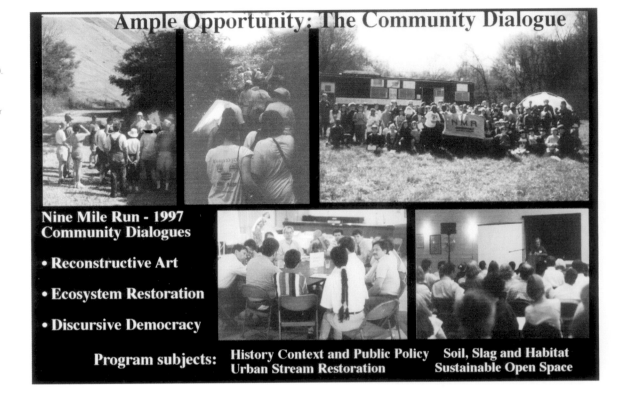

project that might include the development of a wildlife corridor through the city and the state.

Reiko Goto has continued to work on the analysis of local habitats and ecosystems. In collaboration with Collins she has completed a number of projects that include analyses of waterways, such as the Brooklyn waterfront and a project for the Three Rivers Art Festival in Pittsburgh, Pennsylvania. Her work explores the relationships between human development and plant and animal life, bringing that which has been pushed to the margins by human expansion to public attention.

The *Nine Mile Run Greenway Project* (1997–99), involving Goto, her husband, and two other collaborators, focused on the polluted flood plain area in and around Pittsburgh. An experiment in public discourse, the project provides the opportunity for community members to consider the meaning, function, and ecology of postindustrial space. As Goto states, "we must define what nature means within the context of our urban community . . . we need to work within the community to identify a socially acceptable solution that is economic, aesthetically rich and ecologically sound."

On the Road: Catherine Opie and Susan Schwartzenberg

If anything has changed the look of the California landscape in a dramatic way in the last fifty years, it has been the growth of the highway system that, like so many veins and arteries, winds through the hearts of cities and branches across the body of the state. This network of open road—promisingly named a "freeway"—became an expansive metaphor for escape from the fetters of a traditional, geographically rooted life.

Between 1994 and 1997, photographer Catherine Opie produced a series of platinum prints of freeways. Better known for her color-saturated and richly detailed portraits, Opie in this series turns to a black-and-white landscape format, using a large (7 x 17 in.) horizontal negative printed at an intimate 2¼ x 6¾ in. Despite their small size, Opie's stark and majestic images of the freeways' concrete arches and curves evoke monumental scale. The beauty of their form recalls August Sander's industrial photography of the early century, as well as the emptiness in the work of Eugène Atget. Whether fascinated with electrical turbines or the streets of Paris, the documentary impulse of these photographers, which Opie shares, locates their images within a precise historical moment. When industrial and architectural landscapes are pictured as uninhabited spaces, an uncanny quality emerges, a simultaneous timelessness and anticipation that allow the image to overflow its documentary limits. Opie and these earlier photographers use time—in the form of an evacuated moment—as if it were *itself* a formal element of the image. By eliminating the most obvious traffic and, in some cases, all cars and people from her images of freeways, Opie has created an eerie, almost post-apocalyptic vision of Los Angeles. She comments, "In traveling the freeways, I started to think of them as the structures that would be left behind, that they are Los Angeles's monuments." Devoid of most architectural references, the work satisfies a commuter's (rather than a traveler's) fantasy of the open, empty road, and simultaneously maps the intersections between nature and relentless human construction where frail trees, dry grasses, and shrub-covered hillsides are dwarfed by the smooth surfaces, mechanical forms, and sweeping lines of asphalt. Cranes and steel beams litter the barren earth beneath overpasses, and floodlights brighten the armature of new bridges and ramps at night. Appearing from nowhere and going nowhere in particular, the freeways extend the earth into the air, and descend again into the land. As a documentary photographer, Opie captures a California phenomenon, not because highway construction of this scale is unique to

Catherine Opie, *Untitled #1*, from *Freeway Series*, 1994. Platinum print, 2¼ × 6¾ in. (edition of 5). Collection of the artist, courtesy Regen Projects, Los Angeles.

236

the state, but rather because it is emblematic of it. By developing and printing the photographs in such a way as to reference an earlier era of industrial development, Opie claims a monumental as well as memorial status for her subject. Whether envisioning the freeway as already antiquated, or implying that it will be so in the future, Opie's simultaneously majestic and miniaturized views place this dominant network of roads in critical perspective: the fantasy of the open road is reframed as a fantasy of the empty road and, perhaps in the future, the road abandoned.

On a more pedestrian scale, Susan Schwartzenberg examines relations between individual biographies and cityscapes, particularly urban streets and plazas. Her *Cento: Market Street Journal* (1996), published by the San Francisco Arts Commission, examines the life history of a single boulevard at the heart of the city. Sifting through a sediment of historical texts and archival images that record the life of this busy thoroughfare, the artist juxtaposes stories from the past with those she gathers in the present, creating an experimental guidebook or map for Market Street. Combining archeology with documentary, Schwartzenberg interweaves narratives of everyday life with key historical events. Interviews became a central component of the work. The artist states that she "took to the streets with a camera and tape recorder talking with anyone who was in the mood to talk." She interviewed "important" and "not so important" people including city planners, police officers, architects, historians, and homeless people as well as archivists, archeologists, Muni drivers, office workers, and sales clerks.[13] The book's remarkable variety of sources and its diversity of voices are enhanced by the voices of Michel de Certeau, Karl Marx, Italo Calvino, Charles Baudelaire, and other writers who have reflected on city life. Such references transform the local focus of the book into a model for reading any boulevard in any metropolis. Using the linear order of Market Street as its guide, the book begins at one end of the boulevard (near the pier where many immigrants arrived in search of gold in the nineteenth century) and follows personal stories and key cultural sites toward the far end. The Office, The Plaza, The Underground, The Department Store, The Hotel, The Archive, and The Frontier serve as a conceptual and spatial taxonomy for ordering the artist's progress block by block, chapter by chapter. From a corporate businessman who claims he has been inside every high-rise building in the city, to a lunchtime conversation between women at the Emporium, to an archivist who dreams the history of the city at night, to Harvey Milk's call for the rebuilding of neighborhoods, the stories that appear in the book are stories about living in a particular place and being defined by a unique locale. The power of the project is that it illuminates how any city street might be mined for an equally intricate network of human encounters. Whether the narratives included are about belonging or alienation, development or decay, Schwartzenberg's project reveals the interdependence between biography and geography, subjectivity and environment.

New/Old Ecologies: Natalie Jerimijenko

If there is indeed something that can be called "ecological" art, the artworks addressed here remind us that the concept of ecologies must never be limited to the idea of "nature" naively conceived. Ecologies are always heterogeneous, interconnected systems involving a variety of human and nonhuman actors. Natalie Jerimijenko has explored such social, economic, and material ecologies for several years as an independent artist and as an "engineering officer" at the Bureau of Inverse Technology (BIT), "an information agency servicing the Information Age." The projects undertaken by the BIT are presented on the Internet as numbered "products," and generally take the form of what might be called social surveillance. The 1996 *Suicide Box*, a motion detection system, was installed on the Golden Gate Bridge to capture on camera any vertical motion in the vicinity of the bridge. In 100 days the camera recorded 17 "bridge events," thus supplying the public with "frame-accurate data of a social phenomenon not previously accurately quantified."[14] By correlating the *Suicide Box* data with the rising and falling index of the Dow Jones Industrial for each bridge occurrence, the artist also constructs a "despondency index," implying a direct link between the financial success of Silicon Valley and local suicide rates. "Landing" in the context of this work is a somber prospect. After all, falling bodies do land, as do falling stock prices. But the ecology registered in the work, whatever its morbid implications, is not merely an ecology of death but is rather a cultural mapping of otherwise invisible social relations. Why is it, the work implicitly asks, that we measure some drops—some "vertical motions"—and not others? While the work clearly asks us to consider the relation between capital accumulation, financial security, and the rate of despondency in San Francisco, it is also, and perhaps more radically, signaling the wide range of significant human activity that remains "unquantified." In 1997 the BIT launched their *BIT Plane* aerial reconnaissance project over Silicon Valley. During the height of the economic boom there, secrecy and privacy ruled the manicured campuses of Santa Clara and Palo Alto. Not unlike a police state, Silicon Valley was a maze of off-limit territories, security checks, and office intrigue. By attaching a tiny video camera to a radio-controlled airplane, the BIT was able to survey the territory from the air. Shooting grainy black-and-white images that bear a strong resemblance to images taken during early Cold War reconnaissance missions, the camera captures the curve of the horizon, the geometric grid of streets, and the airplane's own shadow, as well as the innocuous banality of the orderly gardens,

the industrial architecture, and the parking lots below. Access to land or property is contingent here upon membership, wealth, and specialized knowledge. Into a well-established ecology of surveillance, the Bureau of Inverse Technology introduces a new hybrid species, a new invasive device. *BIT Plane* demonstrates the canny wit of its producers while inviting viewers to examine the rhetoric of "information access" that pervades high tech industry.

In addition to her work with the Bureau of Inverse Technology, Jerimijenko has developed a series of investigations into the domain of bio-engineering. Her *OneTree* project evolved from recent debates over the question of genetic determinism. One thousand clones of a single biological sample micro-propagated in culture (aptly named "Paradox" trees) were displayed at the Yerba Buena Center for the Arts in San Francisco for the *Ecotopias* exhibition in 1999. Each clone is to be planted throughout the city of San Francisco, involving the general public in a collaborative, collective husbandry. "Because the trees are biologically identical," the artist writes, "in subsequent years they will render the social and environmental differences to which they are exposed."[15] The trees will respond to the microclimates of the city in unique ways, developing over the years in what Jerimijenko calls a "long, quiet and persisting spectacle of the Bay Area's diverse environment." *OneTree*'s experiment with "artificial" life also includes an algorithmic model of the "Paradox" trees online. The growth rate of these idealized simulations, stimulated by a carbon dioxide sensor at the serial port of computer terminals, offers a parallel spectacle to the complex growth phenomena occurring throughout the city. Jerimijenko's new ecology of artificial life effectively transforms the environmental health of the region while demonstrating to the public how the urban landscape is in fact a large-scale social, political, and biological laboratory.

Landing in California

Like most of the state's residents, many of the artists discussed here came from elsewhere. Each has responded to the material conditions of the land or environment discovered during her stay. Formally their work is wide-ranging: from tradi-

tional photography and sculpture to temporary installations and public art. Some have engaged the idea of land as an abstraction; others have changed the way the history of the state is viewed through the critical assessment of labor conditions or the environmental impact of development; and still others have explored the ties between territory and biography. Common to them all is an exploration of human relationships to the land and their transformation over time. In my introduction, I suggested that the work examined here might reveal a new conceptual and historical terrain. What the artists have unearthed is the state of California itself—its fragments of earth, its immigration history, its populations, its biographies, its ecological habitats. The new terrain is really an old terrain rediscovered and reconceived.

Notes

1 Vija Celmins, Chuck Close, and William S. Bartman, *Vija Celmins* (New York: A.R.T. Press, 1992).

2 Richard A. Garcia, *The Chicanos in America 1540–1974* (New York: Oceana Publications, 1977), p. 2.

3 Angelo N. Ancheta, *Race, Rights and the Asian American Experience* (New Brunswick, N.J.: Rutgers University Press, 1998), p. 28.

4 David L. Bender, *Asian Americans: Opposing Viewpoints* (San Diego: Greenhaven Press, 1997), p. 19

5 Ibid., p. 102.

6 Jan Breslauer, "May Sun: L.A./China/Left/Right," in *Mapping Histories: Third Newport Biennial* (exhibition catalogue) (Newport Beach, Calif.: Newport Harbor Art Museum, 1992), p. 68.

7 Ibid., p. 68.

8 Chris Calwell, "California Energy and Global Warming," in *California's Threatened Environment,* ed. Tim Palmer (Washington, D.C.: Island Press, 1993), p. 53.

9 Bonnie Sherk, "Crossroads Community (The Farm)," Center for Critical Inquiry position paper, 1st Inter-

national Symposium, San Francisco Art Institute, 1977.

10 Barbara C. Matilsky, *Fragile Ecologies* (New York: Rizzoli, 1992), p. 67.

11 Ibid., p. 72.

12 Ibid.

13 Susan Schwartzenberg (artist's statement), *Cento: A Market Street Journal* (San Francisco: San Francisco Art Commission, 1996), n.p.

14 See Natalie Jerimijenko, *www.bureauit.org*.

15 See Natalie Jerimijenko, *www.nyu.edu/natalie/OneTree/OneTreeDescription.html*.

SANDRA S. PHILLIPS

WOMEN ARTISTS IN CALIFORNIA AND THEIR ENGAGEMENT WITH PHOTOGRAPHY

California has been rich territory for women who have used photography either as their primary aesthetic medium, or for those who chose to incorporate photographs into a larger artistic schema, such as the production of collage or installation work. Upon reflection, this emphasis on the mechanically reproduced image is hardly surprising: with the film industry located in Los Angeles, the critical understanding of, and aesthetic responses to, its culture of artifice are taught at the neighboring art schools and universities, California Institute of the Arts and the University of California campuses at both San Diego and Los Angeles. San Francisco, on the other hand, was the historical center for a much different tradition, the dedicated application of photography as a form of fine art since the 1930s. The photographers of the "f/64 Group" were inspired by the aesthetics of cubism, a purist approach to the medium and a desire to make beautiful photographic prints. Through Ansel Adams's long-standing presence—not only as a creative personality, but also as a teacher and active practitioner—so-called "straight photography" still remains a force to be reckoned with. (Adams and Minor White started the photography department at the California School of Fine Arts, now the San Francisco Art Institute, and Adams was an important early activist at the San Francisco Museum of Art, now the San Francisco Museum of Modern Art.) Although she received little acknowledgment or credit from her male colleagues until late in life, Imogen Cunningham was also a member of this group. She is recognized today for the precisionist images created in the late 1920s and the influence of her emphatic and penetrating portraits.

Even with the important development of a true Northern California fraternity of conceptual artists in the 1970s,[1] photographic activity in the Bay Area, in general, has been less defined by conceptualism than it has in Southern California. Much San Francisco-based photographic work still adheres to modernist purity, though it is now often inflected by conceptual concerns.

Perhaps because of this very tradition of modernist truth to media, one of the more experimental and original approaches to photography in California was by Bay Area painter Jay DeFeo. We are only recently coming to understand DeFeo's abiding interest in this medium, which would seem at odds with someone so invested in pure gestural abstract painting, but photography seems to have had some visceral or perhaps even talismanic role in her art. In creating the obsessive painting *The Rose* (1958–65), DeFeo was careful to have its many stages of production documented, usually by professional photographers or friends. There are many pictures of the painting, not only as a solitary object but also as a presence in the studio, seen in the morning light at some distance, or as a backdrop to her own portraits, or to those of her friends. Through the many years that this painting evolved, its photographic record-keeping must have been an acknowledgment of its continuing presence in her life, an obsession as well as a burden. Her record of its many and various changes and permutations was probably a demonstration of, or the hope for, a kind of progress.

When she was finally forced to abandon the studio she occupied during the time she worked on the painting, the side of the building had to be cut away to remove it. In Bruce Conner's film of the event, she is seen as a vulnerable figure who almost drops out of the hole in the wall to join the painting as it is carted away. Her friend, the artist Wallace Berman, must have understood how she identified with *The Rose*, and how her need to have pictures of it was an almost physical one, some kind of necessary link to it. He photographed her in front of *The Rose* and in front of her drawing *The Eyes* (1958), made after a photograph of her own eyes and related to the painting. Her photo-collage *Blossom* (1956), which she finished before she began the painting, and her collage *Applaud the Black Fact* (1958) both depict exploding female bodies, vertiginous but also radiant like *The Rose* itself. After the forced termination of her work on *The Rose*, she stopped making art. When she resumed, she worked extensively in photo-collage, again with very concrete bodily references. Her 1972–73 photographic self-portraits amalgamate all kinds of curious objects (light bulbs, cacti, pictures of her jewelry, or teeth), which refer to herself or her environment specifically, or to bodies generally. For DeFeo, photography appears to have been a tactile reminder of the passage of time and the physical experience of an external, actual world in dialogue with her abstract impulses.

Like artistic expression in other forms, women photographers or women artists who used photography were affected by and often participated directly in the larger political and social activism of the 1960s and 1970s. One of the most important women to explore photography in a conceptual way was Eleanor Antin. When her husband, the writer David Antin, took a position at the University of California, San Diego, in 1968 (where she has also been on the faculty), she moved to Southern California. There she has continued to produce work that emanated from the rich cultural activity that she had known in New York. Antin's artistic production in California reflects her origins in theater and her awareness of the activities of art and poetry on the East Coast, especially her ties to the Fluxus artists, as well as her relationship with early feminism. Fluxus, that loose admixture of high-spirited, creative people most interested in crossing the divide between art and life experience, between serious art and play, and between the accepted disciplines of art production, explored the radical democratic principle of sending art through the mail and holding early

68

Jay DeFeo, *Applaud the Black Fact,* 1958. Collage on paper mounted on painted canvas, 50 7/16 × 36 1/8 in. © 2001 Estate of Jay DeFeo/Artists Rights Society (ARS), New York. Photograph © 1999: Whitney Museum of American Art. Collection of Whitney Museum of American Art. Purchased with funds from the Photography Committee and the Drawing Committee.

"manifestations" or performances. Although now the Fluxus movement is best known through the modest but curious and provocative objects its members sent to each other—the boxes with absurd instructions, the games that are deliberately impossible to follow or play, the odd assortments of industrial effluvia in paper wrappers—they are the props or excuses, the offhand and charming mementos of a larger spirit of art making as a freeing life experience, not something done for "artistic expression" or high moral purpose, much less for remuneration. But even as Antin was constructing such objects as *Blood of a Poet Box* (1965–68), which is very closely related to the cachements of oddities the Fluxus artists were fond of concocting, she was also making photo-collages, or collages that interwove different realities in a startling and seamless new context. In these collages Antin usually conflates art (from reproductions) and fashion (from magazines) with her own blend of a kind of magical surrealism, probably created with an acknowledgment of Joseph Cornell. The fusion of fun and art, and the stagy, campy attitudes from the fashion magazines placed into some unstated but amusing narrative context would be persistent motifs in her fully mature work, and these qualities certainly inform her most well known and much admired conceptual piece, the series *100 Boots* (1971–73).

100 Boots "documents" the funny exploits of an assortment of old rubber boots, literal stand-ins for human adventures. Photographed "visiting" the desert, or at an open-air drive-in movie theater (where they assemble patiently), or in the field of humanoid oil pumps, or on the way to the amusement park, the boots explore the pleasures and banalities of Southern California life. But, like their author, the boots also "stage" events in New York. Antin photographed them standing attentively on the Staten Island ferry and, marking the closure of this tall tale, she created an installation which took the form of a group appearance at New York's Museum of Modern Art, along with the pictures. Antin's wonderfully oddball photographs of these clusters of boots on their parade through a duck farm, or their odd and particular groupings in and around eucalyptus trees, always marching onward, always exploring, were not only conceived as pseudo-documentary photographic records of non-events, but also as mail art. By sending these handmade postcards through the mail, Antin effectively subverted the commercial, exclusionary gallery marketing system and made the communication system offered by the post office a democratic, alternative way to reach her audience.

The seriousness of humor and whimsy in making art was not just the exclusive purview of the Fluxus artists, or of Antin in Southern California. Indeed, the artists who lived and worked there and had ties especially with the universities, often evoked a deadpan, old-fashioned klutzy humor. William Wegman, John Baldessari, Ed Ruscha, and Robert Cumming were all engaged in the serious use of humor and specifically the use of the photograph for scientific or objective description of a pseudo-scientific experiment as proof of some ridiculous, outrageously irrelevant proposition. Why was photography's essential "nature" as an objective, scientific measuring medium spoofed at this historical moment?[2] And why did the most serious wisecracking take place in Southern California? Certainly the overwhelming message of the film and television industries, based as they are on selling fantasy, must have generated a reaction. How otherwise can we begin to explain the articulate, Marxist posture of much of the art making in Southern California in the late 1960s and the 1970s? The media culture generated there seems to almost demand deconstruction, a rational critical investigation devoted to unraveling hype and artifice and to revealing the sources of political power and cultural control. The earlier photographs by Baldessari, Wegman, Ruscha, and Cumming are, however, not political, at least not overtly so, except in their certain disdain for objective proof and scientific distance. They subvert the certitude of the photograph as a tool of objective, scientific evidence and reveal its potent artificial possibilities. Perhaps another explanation for the importance of conceptualism in the art of California has to do with the relative paucity of collections of important original art, especially modern art, in the state at the time.

Such multi-referenced art, or the push toward trespassing the boundaries between art and life, was also reflected in the assemblages made by Wallace Berman and Edward Kienholz, constructed as an approach to understanding the complex, unnerving, and historic events of the time. It also coincided with the renewed interest, particularly in Los Angeles (but also in the East), of experimental printmaking at the Gemini GEL, Tamarind, and Cirrus Editions workshops. This humorous task-taking of photography might also be explained as a kind of antidote to the contemporary high-minded seriousness of minimalism, as well as to the increasing desperation of such political events as the Vietnam War. Certainly Robert Heinecken's outrageous juxtapositions

using imagery found in the public media were open arguments with conservative society's attitudes toward sexual, social, and racial injustice. (Heinecken was an important teacher at UCLA, as well as a practicing artist with a vivid reputation.) By the early 1990s, as the arts were ever more challenged by conservative political forces which increasingly weakened the public support for art institutions, socially conscious art became an accepted form of social critique and, again, much activity was based in the universities where many of these artists were employed as teachers.

Although the work of the first generation of conceptualists was made in a moment of great social upheaval, it alluded to social concerns without being overtly political. Many works, for instance, questioned the authority of the museum, which was seen as a patriarchal institution, or examined the "appropriateness" of certain forms of art, or of the hierarchies in art and of the genius of the (usually male) artist. Much art of the mid-1960s through the early 1970s was made to circumvent the traditional art market: it was deliberately unsalable, sometimes boring or anti-attractive as an object, located in inaccessible places (the Nevada desert, for instance), or made available to the public at a modest price. The "artist's books" of Ed Ruscha, informed by an American style of deadpan humor, certainly relate to the absurd picaresque of Antin's boots, for instance. In an interview with John Coplans,

Intersections: Themes and Practices

Ruscha said, "I think photography is dead as a fine art, its only place is in the commercial world, for technical or information purposes."[3]

All this changed in the next decade. The humorous work of art, the gesture of inaccessibility, the appearance of scientific argument or investigation, the guise of boredom that characterizes much art of the 1960s and 1970s disappeared, or was radically transformed. In great part this was the result of political and social critique, especially feminist criticism. Martha Rosler's examination of the premises of documentary photography as well as her work in video and still photography have been very influential. The ingenious fictional "Roberta Breitmore" project assembled by Lynn Hershman Leeson was itself inspired as much by feminism as by Marcel Duchamp. Both Rosler and Leeson engage us in a kind of sly politicized humor.

Surely no one figure has been more important in the depth and variety of her investigation of the photographic medium, in her assured innovation, or so eloquent in her resonant and highly political content as the slightly younger Carrie Mae Weems. This important artist, more than any other of her generation, has created art of great originality and intelligence. Weems's work embraces her African American heritage, displays deep knowledge of the tradition of documentary photography as well as an awareness of the emergent, politically conscious work produced and encouraged by her teacher, Fred Lonidier, in San Diego. The result is a diverse art that relies on the ambiguous resonance and power of photographs and that has proved to be the best of its kind.

Preferring the term "image maker" to that of photographer or artist, Weems aligns herself with those that question the traditional hierarchies of painting and photography, and seriously investigates the popular arts and folk culture. Carrie Mae Weems came to study art after extensive experience at working-class jobs and an increasing awareness of the political shift in feminism in the late 1970s. From the beginning, she was taught to question the presumed objectivity of classic documentary work, not only of the photographers working in the 1930s who advocated social awareness and change (Dorothea Lange and Ben Shahn are the obvious examples from those working under the auspices of the federal Farm Security Administration), but also of the street work assumed to be without political inflection, such as the photographs of Garry Winogrand and Bruce Davidson, two prominent figures in the 1970s and 1980s. Weems looked to Roy De Carava, the black photographer of his native Harlem, and found his affectionate and unsentimental pictures rewarding territory for her. In a series, *Family Pictures and Stories*, an installation really, she conjoined snapshots, family records, personal commentary on tape, and written com-

70
Carrie Mae Weems, *Untitled (Man Smoking)*, from *Kitchen Table Series*, 1990. Silver print, 28¼ × 28¼ in. (edition of 5). Collection of the artist, courtesy of Pilkington-Olsoff Fine Arts, Inc. (PPOW), New York.

mentary into a rich admixture of elements that was both new and entirely personal. De Carava taught her that her work had to acknowledge its political as well as personal content—in the phrase of the day, "the personal is political." Soon she discarded the informal snapshot aesthetic, so tied to the documentary form, and began to create more deliberate, posed pictures with a larger-format camera, continuing to examine the resonant interrelationship of word to image. Some of these were explicit investigations of racism—for example, the *Ain't Jokin'* series (1987–88); others pursue narration and show her connection to literature (especially the work of African American women authors Zora Neale Hurston and Toni Morrison) and the special language of black folklore. Her *Kitchen Table* series (1987–90) is truly innovative on several levels: it challenges the perception of the woman as the focus of the male gaze by empowering her with her own vision and voice, and by the exquisite relationship of language to carefully made, simple, and beautiful photographs of domestic interiors. In the *Sea Island* series (1991–92), Weems extends her interests further by incorporating folkloric language, eccentrically stacked and organized panels of text, arranged in an installation, which often include plates with printed text. The photographs, by their simplicity and beauty, invest the folkloric practices they depict with majesty and magic.

Weems's *Sea Island* series was followed by her *Africa* series (1993–94), a further investigation of text and photographs mainly of the ancient mud-walled architecture of Ojenne in Mali. Her quest for origins, for an understanding of an Edenic preslavery state of grace was balanced by a series of copy photographs commissioned by the Getty Museum and inspired by an exhibition held there of nineteenth-century photographic portraits of African Americans. For Weems, this collection of pictures provoked a larger critique of photographic representations of black Americans, including nineteenth- and twentieth-century pictures. She reproduced all kinds of photographs, including the anthropological daguerreotypes of the Southerner J. T. Zealy, which were made for Swiss-born scientist Louis Agassiz probably to demonstrate a great physical divide between whites and blacks. She also considered representations of Africans in contemporary American culture by Garry Winogrand, Robert Frank, and Robert Mapplethorpe. These enlarged copies are printed in blood red and over them are reactive phrases etched in the protective glass. Weems has stated her aims with bold eloquence: "I want to make things that are beautiful, seductive, formally challenging, and culturally meaningful. I'm also committed to radical social change."[4]

Several other women working in California have been committed to using their art to effect social awareness and provoke change, some with direct formal links to the kind of work Weems has produced. Pat Ward Williams utilizes the interrelationship of photographic image and text to highlight the photograph as the cultural signifier of a kind of truth. Williams's work is engaged in the social world, and she seeks to engender change through her art. Unlike Weems, the work tends to be more straightforwardly political but less ambiguously beautiful and less formally adventurous.

An artist based in Northern California whose work also reflects social awareness is Ann Chamberlain. Among her many accomplishments, Chamberlain created *The Glass House* (1994), an installation with stacked water-filled jars, each containing photographs from a single family album, preserved, so to speak, for future examination, while remaining ambiguous, potent objects that represent a precarious and changeable structure of identity—a form of mutability especially resonant for women artists.

Chamberlain says of her motivations: "Perhaps the greatest difficulty in art is to make active the process of looking, to enable the viewing of work to become an act of participation, a witnessing. How can we, as makers of photographic images, easily disposed to voyeuristic consumption create a situation in which the act of viewing does not distance and objectify but actively engages and provokes our imagination?"[5]

Chamberlain's use of the enlarged reproduction of earlier photographs as a kind of document exposing a potent ambiguity—about the past, about the use of the medium as a mark of authenticity—is also found in the work of Connie Hatch. In her series *Some Americans: Forced to Disappear* (1990–91), the very simple means of mounting a photographic transparency on acrylic, attaching it to the wall, and throwing a light which casts a gentle reflection enhances these simple portraits with disturbing connotations. Since the pictures are mainly copied from publicly available sources such as magazines and represent people who have died under mysterious circumstances, the re-photograph and its shadow carry metaphorical implications as well as embodying a kind of tangible nostalgia. Many of the "disappeared" are women—from Marilyn Monroe to a female Argentinean political prisoner (this information supplied by Hatch's accompanying "briefing sheets")—and thus the work also performs a feminist critique. Mention must also be made of Mildred Howard, whose work often uses photography for its associational meaning. The historic fragments of photographs, documenting past lives and events, often creased and torn, elicit a memory of historic oppressions intimately tied to events both public and personal.

72
Ann Chamberlain, *The Glass House*, 1994. Photo emulsion on glass jars, 5½ × 6 × 10 ft. Photo: Sibilla Savage. Collection of Lorrie and Richard Greene.

73
Judy Dater, *Chinese Woman*,
1997. Gelatin silver print, 24 ×
20 in. © Judy Dater, 1997.
Collection of the artist.

There are other photographers who have worked within a more documentary tradition, shaping it to fit their aesthetic needs and growth. In Judy Dater's photographs of women, the subjects are allowed to reveal their complexity and psychological depth; they are not idealized, but somehow rendered heroic. Dater's invention of personalities, a catalogue of the San Francisco hippie culture of the late 1960s and early 1970s, is appreciative of this historic theater and narcissism. She advances the tradition of empathetic photography employed by her good friend and

74

Catherine Wagner, *Arch Construction #4, George Moscone Convention Center Site*, 1981. Gelatin silver print, 20 × 24 in. Collection of the artist, courtesy Jack Shainman Gallery, New York.

mentor Imogen Cunningham, but her images reveal a very personal insight. Catherine Wagner began her career by recording the enormous, biblically proportioned excavations for the vast convention center that was constructed in the South of Market area in San Francisco. More recently, her examination of the artifacts by which people define themselves, most often realized in triptych format, constitute a kind of deconstruction of personal habitats that incorporates her interest in documentary objectivity, her respect for the purity of the medium, and her

75

Laura Aguilar, *Clothed,
Unclothed Series, #12*, 1991.
Gelatin silver print, diptych,
20 × 32 in. each. Collection
of the artist.

Intersections: Themes and Practices

awareness of, and creative reaction to, contemporary theoretical concerns and formal innovations.

This survey of women's role in the contemporary photographic practice of California would not be complete without the recognition of artists who have used their art to express lesbian identity, among other examinations of self. Laura Aguilar, a Southern California Chicana photographer, has made a series entitled *Clothed/Unclothed* (1990–94) in which her friends pose in front of a neutral backdrop in formal Polaroid studio portraits, dressed and nude. These diptychs show

their subjects to be comfortable with their bodies and with the presence of the photographer, displaying openness, vulnerability, or cocky self-confidence. It is important to Aguilar that the project describes a range of personalities, ethnicities, and sexual orientations, which she feels is truer to the experiences of many Americans than is commonly appreciated.[6] This series is also a kind of riff on anthropological photography of the nineteenth century, and as well a typological relative of standard police identification photography. The comparison between a portrait of the same person clothed and unclothed is provocative because it reveals nothing except what we expect to see: the mystery unveiled is actually no mystery at all, and the real ambiguity lies in the profound reticence of the photographs themselves. Catherine Opie also works in different styles and formats, but her most important pictures are the highly colored documents of the gay, lesbian, transgender, and transsexual figures, many of them her acquaintances and friends, seen with dispassionate clarity. Her depictions of people involved in S&M practices and body scarification are relentlessly unsentimental and vivid, and include her own person.

Photography has been an important medium for women artists working in California in the last forty years. Earlier, the dividing line between media was memorably broadened by Jay DeFeo in her very personal and expressive conjoining of abstract impulses in painting with the talismanic use of photography. In the late 1960s and early 1970s, an ironic and amusing conceptualism, such as practiced by Eleanor Antin, incorporated photography in a lighthearted but also egalitarian way. Later artists, most notably the important work of Carrie Mae Weems, have used photography's record-keeping qualities to question social assumptions and conventions. While this does not exhaust the many innovative ways in which artists have used photography in California (others are discussed elsewhere in this book), it is the

case that photography in general has gone from being used as an expression of the personal to something cooler, more analytical and detached. Photography-based work that plays on the notion of the photograph as document is a prime example of this development. The trend toward the cool is no doubt an acknowledgment of the major role played by the mass media.

Notes

1 See San Francisco Museum of Modern Art, *Space Time, Sound: Conceptual Art in the San Francisco Bay Area: The 1970's* (exhibition catalogue), ed. Suzanne Foley (San Francisco, 1980; distributed by University of Washington Press).

2 See *Eleanor Antin* (exhibition catalogue), ed. Howard N. Fox (Los Angeles: Los Angeles County Museum of Art, 1999), p. 46.

3 John Coplans, "Concerning Various Small Fires: Edward Ruscha Discusses his Perplexing Publications," *Artforum* 3, no. 5 (February 1965): 25.

4 From Weems's wall text at the Everson Museum exhibition, 1998–99, quoted by Ernest Larson in "Between Worlds," *Art in America* (May 1999): 124.

5 *Artweek* 25, no. 7 (April 7, 1994): 18.

6 See Diana Emery Hulick, "Laura Aguilar," in *Latin American Art* 5, no. 3 (1993): 52–54.

ROSA LINDA FREGOSO

CALIFORNIA FILMING

Re-Imagining the Nation

In the short film *Illusions* (1982), Julie Dash undermines the image of the nation created by the Hollywood industry, exposing its submerged racial narrative. Set in a Hollywood studio during World War II, the film features two African American women, Mignon Dupree, passing for "white" as a studio executive, and Esther Jeeter, a singer hired on a regular basis to dub over the singing voices of white film stars. It is during the dubbing or post-synchronization scene that the film portrays the occulted presence of African Americans in the movie industry most effectively. As Mignon intently watches over the recording session, Esther lip-syncs into the microphone, standing beside the screen-size image of a very blonde and white movie star who pretends to sing. By juxtaposing these two female images on the screen—the black singer whose disembodied voice services the body of a white movie star who was projected onto 1940s movie screens in the fictional universe of *Illusions*—the filmmaker pays tribute to the unacknowledged labor of black female workers in Hollywood. In resurrecting the absent presence of black female bodies in history and, by extension, exposing the historical invisibility of people of color, Dash earnestly re-imagines the nation in the California imaginary.

The images of the nation shot through the lenses of women artists like Dash are not the prevailing imagery I grew up with. No, the California of my childhood was the world embodied in the glamorous movie star—never-ending sunshine, beaches, back-

yard swimming pools, bikinis, vast and expansive freeways, palm trees, health fads, exotic homes and glamorous lifestyles, upward mobility, endless consumption—a make-believe world in a California dream invented by the filmmakers and scriptwriters of the Hollywood machine. In the period following World War II, California became the model for the nation and Hollywood played a major role in marketing its "American dream." Promoters sold California not just "as promise, but as the embodiment of the American future—the dream made flesh."[1] In the business of selling dreams and fantasies, their image of California was far removed from its realities. For while the state has been the gateway to non-European, non-white, and women immigrants since the nineteenth century, one would not know it from

watching mainstream movies and television. For the past fifty years, the overwhelmingly male and white movie industry has projected its own image as the basis for the nation's identity, systematically ignoring or perhaps even disavowing the racial, gender, and class dynamics as well as cultural heterogeneity of the state.

Fortunately women artists working on the fringes of the commercial mainstream have been telling a different kind of story, re-visioning an alternative image of the nation. If California is indeed the "nation's bellwether for the future," then prevailing notions of national identity are outdated. And it has been the state's women filmmakers whose images have contributed to new understandings of the nation and to radical transformations in the meaning of national identity. "When I was growing up," explains film-maker Renee Tajima-Peña, "identity was always framed in terms of assimilation, 'How do people become American?' Today the question is more aptly, 'How has America become its people?'"[2]

The women filmmakers examined in this essay have been shaped by the intellectual currents and cultural complexities of the past fifty years. They have had their eyes, ears, and hearts tuned to the everyday realities of California, to its darker side—its history of conquest, exploitations, and development; they are bearing witness to the configurations of social, cultural, and historical forces that have made California the first multira-cial and multicultural state of the nation. The films I will be discussing have contributed to a new vision of the nation, to its re-vision and re-imagination. If Hollywood has generally ignored the complex heterogeneity and diversity of the nation's cultural field, these women filmmakers provide testimony regarding the contradictory historical circumstances and intersecting reali-ties shaping not only their own personal visions, but also the nation-building project.

Even in the early days of silent cinema, women like Lois Weber, Beatrice Michelena, Ruth Anne Baldwin, and Dorothy Arzner worked in the film production industry. Arzner was one of the few women directors to make the crossover into sound production, continuing to work in the industry throughout the 1930s and 1940s. Those

women who were shut out of the film industry altogether "found an arena of expression within its parallel artisanal universe, the avant garde."[3] A key figure in the post–World War II revival of the avant-garde was the Russian immigrant Maya Deren, whose film *Meshes of the Afternoon* is con-sidered a foundational text in the West Coast explosion of the experimental film movement during the 1940s.

Deren made *Meshes of the Afternoon* in Los Angeles in 1943 with her husband, Alexander Hammid, and they both starred in the film. The film is a pathbreaking exploration into the sub-conscious realm of the psyche. Its major pro-taonist (played by Deren) is caught in a surreal, repetitive dream, and the film hauntingly ren-ders female subjectivity through the fantasies of desire, seduction, and death. Unlike the sim-plified notions of womanhood prevalent in the nation's cultural imaginary of the period, *Meshes* features a complex woman with emotional am-bivalence and whose relationship to her lover is less a source of comfort than an occasion for dreadful fear. Based on Deren's poetic rumina-tions, her pioneering *Meshes of the Afternoon* anticipates many of the concerns of women filmmakers of the next generation.

One of the early practitioners of poetic experi-mental filmmaking in the 1960s was San Francisco-based filmmaker Gunvor Nelson who, along with Dorothy Wiley, made *Fog Pumas*, a sur-

78

Gunvor Nelson, *My Name Is Oona,* 1969. Still from 16 mm film. Muir Beach, Calif. Collection of the artist.

real abstract short, in 1967. Around the same period, Chick Strand produced several films reflecting the experimental tradition of nonnarrative abstraction, including *Eric and the Monsters* (1963), *Angel Blue Sweet Wings* (1966), *Anselmo* (1968), and *Waterfall* (1968).

Many of Gunvor Nelson's poetic personal films deal with themes related to female identity and subjectivity. *My Name Is Oona* (1969), for instance, is a well-crafted exploration of gender identity, imaginatively recreating a young girl's journey toward self-awareness and self-realization. In a related vein, *Moon's Pool* (1973) portrays a woman's transformative journey, using an innovative style which includes images shot under water, symbolic of the realm of the unconscious, while its portrayal of the nude female body (played by Nelson) makes reference to a woman's vulnerability in searching for her own identity. As a metaphor for the inner workings of the psyche, the water in *Moon's Pool* also symbolizes the womb and its metaphoric role in the female subject's desire for imaginary unity and wholeness. Foreseeing the concerns which would occupy feminist filmmakers in the next decade, Nelson and Wiley made *Schmeerguntz* in 1966. A classic film dealing with female stereotypes, *Schmeerguntz* juxtaposes media images of glamorized femininity with "real" images of women in their everyday domestic context. In *Kirsa Nicholina* (1969), Nelson takes up another

important theme of the women's movement. One of the first films to deal honestly with the subject of reproduction, *Kirsa Nicholina* portrays a home-birth in a sensitive and lyrical fashion. A celebration of the wonders of the birthing process, the film also pays genuine tribute to the strength and power of women's resistance.

Challenges from women and racial minorities to the masculine and ethnocentric definition of citizenship and national identity first occurred on a broader scale during the 1960s. Indeed, the major transformations in the postwar nation-building project came as the Civil Rights movement of the previous decade inspired the formation of various new social movements—the antiwar movement, the New Left, black and Chicano nationalisms, and the student movement—and joined to undermine the dominant definitions of national identity. And while women in mainstream political organizations had been advocating, since the mid-1960s, for media reform in the hiring practices of the advertising, television, and film industries as well as for the elimination of sexist imagery, it was out of the new social movements that the new generation of feminist filmmakers would emerge.

The development of portable, hand-held cameras during the 1960s made equipment and training both affordable and available to political activists, many of whom were women. Learning technical skills while filming antiwar demonstrations and protests, filmmakers directly involved in the Women's Liberation movement and its consciousness-raising groups began to produce works designed to combat the oppression of women under patriarchy. As the decade came to a close, a substantial number of works by women became available, mostly through film festival venues. Even though not all films by women provided a feminist analysis of women's condition under patriarchy, they nonetheless documented aspects important to women's lives. Some films focused on the private domestic sphere of women's lives—the family, reproduction, and sexuality—while others validated women's culture and contributions; many documented the lives and struggles of women; others contributed personal, autobiographical, and biographical portraits of women. And while the documentary prevailed as the favorite genre for women filmmakers during the 1970s, the stylistic range of

documentaries was enormous (from verité, realist techniques to experimental ones; from the personal to the distanced approach; from the poetic and meditative to the ironic and humorous; from a subversive to an informative approximation). Often two or more stylistic approaches were combined in a film.

One of the first filmmakers to deploy avant-garde techniques in portrayals of sexuality from a lesbian perspective is Barbara Hammer. In 1974 she made the lesbian erotic film *Dyketactics*, as part of her concerted effort to render the "invisible visible" and "to bring the hidden and taboo subjects of female sexuality onto the screen."[4] Its experimental, nonnarrative style features intercutting of sensual imagery and sounds from nature and familiar domestic objects with erotic sequences of lovemaking. Drawing from her own sexual experiences as a lesbian, Hammer first explored the experiential quality of cinema in *Dyketactics*, highlighting the relation between touch and sight. During the 1970s she would continue to examine the connection between touch, sight, and female sexuality in *Women I Love* (1976), *Multiple Orgasms* (1978), and in her poetic testimony to lesbian love, *Double Strength* (1978). Hammer also combined humor with formal experimentation to celebrate women's experiences in *Meses* (1974), a satire about menstruation, and *Superdyke* (1975), a silent feminist fantasy film about "super" women taking over city institutions.

During the same period several filmmakers gave voice to women's experiences through documentary portraits that deployed a more personal, autobiographical, and biographical tone. In *Trollstenen* (1973–76), a personal documentary of her family life in Sweden, Gunvor Nelson sensually recreates the events of her family's past through her haunting memories and dream sequences. Esperanza Vásquez made *Agueda Martinez* (1977), an eloquently crafted film depicting the everyday life and struggle of an elderly Chicana. Vásquez's film exemplifies the thematic and formal strategies of women filmmakers of the period and their efforts to recover female predecessors through portrayals of positive qualities, strengths, and independence.

A pioneer in blending avant-garde techniques with documentary, Chick Strand deliberately reworked the conventions of ethnographic filmmaking thirty years ago, nearly two decades before the theoretical debates in the field of anthropology interrogated the scientific claims of the discipline. In 1969, Strand made *Mosori Monika*, an expressive documentary about the colonial encounter in Venezuela. The film is told from the point of view of three women, an elderly Warao Indian, a Franciscan nun, and the filmmaker. Introducing various techniques of experimental cinema, including rapid camera movement and editing, fragments of movements and objects, as well as close-ups, Strand deconstructs the scientific claims to truth, objectivity, and detachment inherent in the ethnographic film tradition. *Mosori Monika* strategically counterpoints modernist, casual, linear time (embodied in the Franciscan nun) with premodern, circular time (represented by Carmelita, the Warao Indian). Unlike traditional anthropologists, the filmmaker in this case does not remain detached but takes a critical stance against the Franciscans' colonialist perspective and affirms the organic worldview of the Warao, a way of being which has been disrupted by the colonization process. Strand's expressionistic, experimental style continued to inform her other films on Latin America, including *Cosas de Mi Vida* (1976), a poetic ethnographic documentary about the life and struggle of a Mexican Indian; *Guacamole* (1976), a lyrical experimental depiction of a child's loss of innocence and search for identity; and *Mujer de Mil Fuegos* (1976), a sensuous tribute to women, focusing on a Latin American woman who, in the midst of the daily, repetitive monotony in her life, undergoes a psychic breakdown that eventually leads to her transformation. In each case, Strand's innovative experimental aesthetics hints at the impossibility of capturing the "truth" of an individual or a culture through the cinematic gaze.

Critiques of the West's colonial gaze evident in the works of white filmmakers like Strand were in

79

Chick Strand, *Mosori Monika*, 1969. Still from 16 mm color film. Orinoco River Delta, Venezuela. Collection of the artist.

large part inspired by the emergence of Third World liberation movements during the post-colonial era. As solidarity with anticolonialist struggles spread, Third World filmmakers in the United States, including women, turned their attention to the racial structures of domination within the nation-state, further puncturing the monolithic view of national identity. Together, their films express the experiences of racism and discrimination, contest the racist images used to legitimate the oppression of various racial and ethnic communities, and give voice to the process of coming into consciousness. Locating their stories at the intersection of gender, nation, culture, race, sexual, and class borders, films by women of color affirm the multiplicity of cul-

tures, and in so doing, re-fashion the nation in terms of its racial and cultural differences.

Some of the early films by women of color demonstrate that the project of historical recovery is a necessary step in the formation of ethnic identity and consciousness. For example, Loni Ding's documentary *How We Got Here*, made in 1976, recounts the history of Chinese immigration to California. Using classic interview techniques, graphic illustrations, and voice-over narration, the filmmaker traces the history back five generations to a reenactment of a recruitment letter in Hong Kong, and details the hardships endured by Chinese immigrants working in the agriculture and fishing industries, as well as in the construction of railroads. Her Emmy Award-winning film, *Nisei Soldier* (1984), recuperates the untold history of Japanese soldiers of the 442nd battalion—the most decorated unit during World War II. Similarly, *The Color of Honor* (1987) deals with Japanese American experience, this time focusing on the Nisei translators during the war. Deploying a female voice to tell the painful memories of Japanese history, Ding ingeniously blends documentary footage with reenactments of the removal of thousands of California's Japanese Americans into concentration camps as a result of President Roosevelt's Executive Order 9066.

Two films by Pat Ferrero, *Quilts in Women's Lives* (1981) and *Hearts and Hands* (1987), trace the connection between history, politics, and creative self-expression in the lives of women quilt-makers from various racial groups. Interweaving diaries, photographs, and quilts, *Hearts and Hands* tells the tale of women's struggle and resistance through the craft of making quilts, and unveils the role quilts play in women's coming to voice. As Ferrero's films illustrate, there is more to quilts than elaborate designs and creative patterns. Quilts also embody women's social history, including stories of racial and class differences, tales of women workers in the textile mills of New England, migration experiences, as well as the history of women's political involvement. As concrete manifestations of the connection between history and female identity, quilts express a gendered form of social protest, especially evident during the Abolitionist movement when the geometric patterns of quilts made for the Underground Railroad tracked the pathways of runaway slaves.

The links between historical recollection and identity formation were first examined for Chicanas by Sylvia Morales. Her short film *Chicana* (1979) inscribes a feminist consciousness within the context of 500 years of Chicana history in the Americas. Making extensive use of stills, photographs, music, and poetry, as well as on-camera interviews, Morales recuperates a female historical lineage of struggle against racism, conquest, and domination. The film stages a strong critique of patriarchal nationalism, portraying the multiple forces, internal and external, affecting the lives of women. And while *Chicana* stresses Chicano nationalism's concerns with equality, social justice, and freedom, through its ongoing engagement of male privilege, the film goes beyond the nationalist agenda.

Undoubtedly, films by women of color pluralized the notion of gender by locating their critiques of the nation at the intersection of multiple social identities, and like Morales, several other filmmakers of color tackled variable forms of oppression and social conditions affecting the lives of women in their communities. In the late 1970s Lourdes Portillo made her first film, *Despues del Terremoto (After the Earthquake)*, co-directed with Nina Serrano. A delicate and earnest portrait of a domestic worker who migrated from Nicaragua to California, *Despues del Terremoto* also deals with the conflicts a Latina immigrant faces as she struggles to define her own autonomy and independence within Latino patriarchy. The film actively pushes the boundaries of political film with its syncretic style—the blend of neorealism and *telenovela* aesthetics—but it was also ahead of its time, telling the story of the Nicaraguan diaspora in dramatic form, at a time when most political films used documentary formats. Portillo's commitment to the plight of Third World women's struggle against patriarchy informed her next film, about the mothers of the disappeared in Argentina: *Las Madres: The Mothers of the Plaza de Mayo* (1986, co-directed with Susana Muñoz). With cinematic intensity, the film depicts the toll of the Argentinean military regime's "dirty war" on the nation's inhabitants, showing the brutality of a dictatorship that was responsible for the disappearance of 11,000 Argentineans, and focuses on a group of mothers who defied the brutal military junta. Blending realist strategies of interviews with news footage and voice-over narration, *Las Madres* tells the riveting tale of women's struggle against a violent, repressive regime and gives voice to a female mode of resistance which emerges out of the historically social role assigned to women: motherhood.

One of the first filmmakers of color to interrogate the family "as a site at which black women and children suffer the varied and conjoined effects of racist and patriarchal exploitation"[5] is Camille Billops. Her film *Suzanne Suzanne* (1983), co-directed with James V. Hatch, examines the issue of domestic violence within a black family. The documentary tells the story of Billops's niece, Suzanne, a recovering addict who, in the course of giving her testimony, reveals details of physical abuse by her father. The filmmaker effectively juxtaposes photo-stills and home movies with documentary footage and relies on a counterpoint strategy, undermining the picture-perfect family captured in the home movies of Suzanne's nuclear family with on-camera revelations about an abusive father and husband. Billops's second film, *Older Women in Love* (1987), celebrates women's sexuality and independence. However, it is her third film that is even more intimate for the filmmaker. In the personal documentary, *Finding Christa* (1991), Billops stages an emotional encounter between herself and Christa, a daughter the filmmaker gave up for adoption in the 1950s. The story begins with Christa contacting Billops in 1981, after obtaining her name from an adoption agency. As *Finding Christa* unfolds, viewers learn of the choices which Billops confronted in making her decision to give Christa up for adoption, including the consequences of raising a child alone in the 1950s (Billops was abandoned by Christa's father), the perceptions of Billops's decision by family members, and the filmmaker's ultimate choice to pursue a lover as well as her career as a visual artist rather than face the grim fate of an unwed mother.

An alternative image of the family is poignantly rendered in cinematographer/filmmaker Emiko Omori's *Hot Summer Wind* (1991). A drama inspired by Hisaye Yamamoto's two short stories, the film spotlights a family's life on a farm in Salinas, California during the Depression. The events are told from the perspective of a young girl who witnesses her mother's passion for writing and her father's failure to understand the mother's need for creative self-expression. In

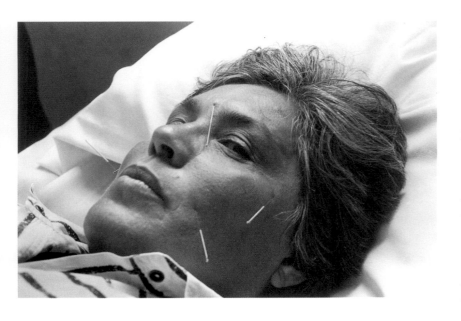

mystery-detective theme of the film serves as a ruse for a more probing glimpse into politics and secrets, not just of the domestic private family (represented by Portillo's) but also of the public, national family embodied in Mexico's ruling party, the PRI.

Arlene Bowman takes up the theme of the interplay between the self and the communal in *Navaho Talking Pictures* (1986). A chronicle of the filmmaker's search for her Navaho identity, the film exposes the contradictions often inherent in the return to the homeland. *Navaho Talking Pictures* mines the ambivalences of the process through the ongoing conflicts portrayed between Bowman and her Navaho grandmother. Yet the filmmaker's greatest obstacle is her grandmother's refusal to be documented—a refusal based on the Navaho taboo against picture taking. From the grandmother's perspective, Bowman's insistence on filming represents a violation of cultural tradition, but the filmmaker's transgression serves as the basis for her exploration into the interplay between various social and cultural processes, including tradition and modernity, acculturation and cultural retention, oral culture and visual representation. Bowman expands the search for cultural identity in her next film, *Song Journey* (1994). In this personal documentary Bowman deals with the "powwow," a gendered indigenous ritual in which women rarely sing and drum. Following the

the end, the narrative threads of marital discord are resolved for the better. Nonetheless, the film provides a sensitive glimpse into the dynamics of Japanese patriarchy and domestic violence.

Lourdes Portillo's *The Devil Never Sleeps* (1994) shifts the discussion of the family to a new level. A film that tells the story of the filmmaker's investigation into the death of her beloved uncle Oscar, who died under mysterious circumstances in Mexico, *The Devil Never Sleeps* also sketches the permeable boundaries between nations, genres, and political/familial identities. Portillo crosses the border to lead a probe into the unresolved death of her uncle, utilizing his life to weave the strands of her inquiry. However, the murder-

powwow circuit throughout the United States and Canada during its spring and summer sessions, Bowman's road trip charts her ongoing search for female drummers. In many ways *Song Journey* is a way to define what it means to be a woman within Native American societies, a way of bringing Bowman closer to her people and back to her tradition. By learning to dance the Rain Dance and to speak Navaho, Bowman's journey is a remarkable testimonial to the evolving interplay between a woman and her community.

The conscious search for the meaning of political and cultural identities is eloquently captured for Asian Americans in Renee Tajima-Peña's *My America*. As in Bowman's film, Tajima-Peña deploys the metaphor of the "road" to render Asian American experience and grapple with what it means to be Asian American in the late twentieth century. Tajima-Peña is similarly at the center of this story, utilizing her personal memories and childhood history of travel to weave the strands of her narrative. As a third-generation Japanese American whose cultural nationalist politics led her to filmmaking, Tajima-Peña brings her multicultural formation as a political activist to bear on *My America*. Complicating the usual narrative of Asian migration, *My America* threads a fluctuating web of Asian American immigration to the Americas, dating back to the Spanish colonial period. As in her earlier film, *Yellow Tale Blues* (1990, co-directed with

Christine Choy)—and as in Loni Ding's *Four Women* (1982)—Tajima-Peña refuses to constitute a singular notion of "Asian" identity, portraying instead the plurality of Asian American ethnicities. In many ways, *My America* mines the territory between the personal and the communal, reflecting the filmmaker's own trajectory across the emotional, political, and cultural landscapes of social history.

Although exorcising the evils of racism in their communities figures prominently as a major aim among filmmakers of color, in some of their films, the issue of racial justice assumes precedence over other thematic concerns. Such is the case in Christine Choy and Renee Tajima-Peña's *Who Killed Vincent Chin* (1988). They started shooting the film in 1983, shortly after the brutal murder of Chinese American Vincent Chin in Detroit, during the height of xenophobic resentment against the rising tide of Japanese auto imports. The film tells a carefully textured story, influenced by a Rashomonian aesthetic style, with a fractured story-telling structure and metaphoric associations. Its narrative orchestrates various story lines, including the racially motivated killing of Chin by two autoworkers after a barroom scuffle; the trial of the two perpetrators, Roger Ebens and his stepson, Michael Nitz; the crisis and unemployment in the auto industry, set against the cultural backdrop of Motown; the politicization of Chin's mother, Lilly

81

Renee Tajima-Peña and
Christine Choy, *Who Killed
Vincent Chin*, 1988. Detroit,
Mich. Still from 16 mm film,
1983. Photo: Nancy Tong.
Collection of the artists.

Chin; and the rise of Asian American political mobilization. The filmmakers rely on multiple points of view, along with the noticeable absence of voice-over narration, to convey the complexity of race relations. While Tajima-Peña and Choy ultimately adhere to the side demanding racial justice, the film nonetheless is commendable for cultivating the "gray areas" of race relations in the post–civil rights era.

Sylvia Morales centers her concerns for racial justice across the borders of national, gender, and racial subjectivities. Her transborder film, *Esperanza* (1985), dramatizes the plight of undocumented immigrants living in California. *Esperanza* tells the compelling story of a girl's

coming of age as she struggles to survive on the streets of Los Angeles with her younger brother, after immigration officials have deported their mother. Made ten years prior to the passage of Proposition 187 in California, *Esperanza* also anticipates the effects of anti-immigrant racism on the lives of undocumented children. Loni Ding's *Island of Secret Memories* (1987) similarly traces the plight of immigrants through the eyes of a child. Utilizing magic realist aesthetics, the film tells of the injustices suffered by Chinese immigrants who were held captive at the processing center on Angel Island in San Francisco Bay. During a school field trip to the island, a young Chinese boy's grandfather is resurrected and serves as the boy's special tour guide. The film is a lyrical testimonial to the past, to the "secret memories" of old-timers, the voices trapped in the walls of abandoned buildings and in the poetic writings of Chinese immigrants.

The relationship between memory and history is the subject of Emiko Omori's *Rabbit in the Moon* (1999). Omori's personal memoir details the psychological and social effects of Japanese incarceration during World War II on the lives of Omori and her older sister, Chizu, as well as on the lives of other Japanese Americans. Interlacing the history of racism behind the mass removal of 120,000 Japanese from the West Coast in 1942 with archival footage, photographs, and newly available home movies, the film is a heart-moving meditation on the Omori's family past, beginning with the silences surrounding their mother's death at age 34, one year after the family's release from Poston internment camp in Arizona. Omori makes eloquent use of metaphors ("the rabbit in the moon" is how Japanese culture describes the face of the moon; the lost urn of Omori's mother's ashes symbolizes the secret memories of camp living) to tease out the complexities of the Japanese racial experience. As in Ding's *Color of Honor*, Omori recounts the history of resistance and protests by many detainees in the camps. However, *Rabbit in the Moon* goes one step further, carefully attending to the divisiveness created by the loyalty-oath questionnaire administered in the camps, and shedding new light on the internal fissures within the Japanese community, especially those between the Issei and Nisei generations.

Beginning in the 1970s and continuing on through the following two decades, women of color worked mainly in documentary formats even as narrative "assumed precedence over documentary as the favored medium among filmmakers."[6] While the turn to feature-length films begins early, it is clearly established by the 1990s. In her *Chick Flicks*, B. Ruby Rich cites several reasons for this shift, including the econom-

82

Emiko Omori, *Rabbit in the Moon*, 1998. Still from video. Photo: Bob Hsiang. Collection of the artist.

83

Barbara Hammer, *Nitrate Kisses*, 1992. Models: Frances Lorraine and Sally Binford. Still from 16 mm black-and-white film. Distributed by Frameline, San Francisco. Photo: Barbara Hammer. Collection of the artist.

ics of funding, specifically cuts in public sector financing for documentaries; the fact that fiction allows women more leeway in terms of individual self-expression; and the prestige afforded by feature-length films. Yet some white filmmakers continued to work in shorts. Gunvor Nelson, for instance, released the final short in her collage series, *Natural Features*, and a short experimental film about her mother, *Time Being*, in the early 1990s. Barbara Hammer's groundbreaking film on lesbian and gay history and sexualities, *Nitrate Kisses* (1992), is to a great extent considered a feature, but its theme is not necessarily rendered in fictional narrative form. Hammer's

film is rather a highly theoretical meditation on the gaps and silences in lesbian and gay social experience; despite its unconventional, experimental narrative style, the film is less staged than most fictional features. And some, like Trinh T. Minh-ha, refused to abide by any of the generic categories.

Indeed, the writer, poet, and filmmaker Trinh T. Minh-ha is considered one of the key figures in the theoretical turn of independent cinema, and her remarkable films have consistently worked to alter viewers' consciousness. Rather than define her work in terms of usual categories or genres, Trinh T. Minh-ha prefers to speak of "different degrees of stages or unstaged material." Her unconventional and uncompromising style works simultaneously at various levels, on the borders of documentary and fiction, experimental and narrative, across the axes of gender, nation, and culture. The refusal of what she terms "transparent descriptions or immediate experiences of Reality"[7] came early on, in her first film, *Reassemblage* (1982). Shot in Senegal, *Reassemblage* confronts our ethnographic expectations with the impossibility of ever knowing the "truth" or the "absolute reality" of a culture. In this case, as in her later films, Trinh T. Minh-ha destabilizes the Western gaze of ethnographic film, its claims to render the objective reality or "authenticity" of Third World subjects. Her second film, *Naked Spaces: Living Is Round* (1985), is also shot in Senegal. Here too the filmmaker relies on visual gaps and cracks as a means of disrupting anthropological discourse. The film's cinematic intensity ensues from its continual interruption of the flow of unmediated reality through repetitive imagery and nonsynchronized sound.

Shoot for the Contents (1991), Trinh Minh-ha's film about the Tiananmen Square uprising, tackles nonfiction documentary's claims to represent reality in factual and truthful terms. Its critique of rational, transparent communication is rendered through the film's indirect narration, its refusal to translate languages, and its use of overlapping narration. Two films in particular deal with Vietnamese women's position on the border between nation and gender. *Surname Viet Given Nam* (1989) rewrites Vietnam from a feminist perspective, giving voice to the position of women in pre- and post-revolutionary Vietnam. The film renders the fictions of documentary through its extensive use of stories, proverbs, folk songs juxtaposed against archival footage, photographic stills, historical commentary, and interviews, but also against the filmmaker's skillful manipulation of visual images, in particular unstable framing, camera angles, and highly styled costuming. Trinh Minh-ha's feature film *A Tale of Love* (1995), co-directed by Jean-Paul Bourdier, tells the story of Kieu, a Vietnamese immigrant living in the United States, who is investigating the "Tale of Kieu," an epic poem about Vietnam's mythic heroine, whose tragic love life is a metaphor for Vietnam's destiny. In the course of unraveling the significance of "Kieu's" heritage, the young woman discovers the meaning of love, the bonds between women, the links between her own past memories and present-day realities, but also the meanings of her nation's collective past and present.

Another important filmmaker who has made it a project to expand viewers' notions of reality is Nina Menkes, whose extraordinary skills in experimentation succeed in conveying women's interiority in visual form. Since the early 1980s, Menkes has consciously translated into cinematic language the innermost dimensions of the female psyche, in particular the sense of isolation and alienation which women experience in patriarchal society. Her short *The Great Sadness of*

84

Trinh T. Minh-ha, *A Tale of Love*, 1995. Still from 35 mm color film. Courtesy of Moongift Films.

Zohara (1983) portrays the spiritual journey of a woman (played by Nina's sister, Tinka Menkes) through Jerusalem and Morocco. Her first feature, *Magdalena Viara* (1986), also focuses on a woman, Ida (played by Tinka), as its main character, in this case a prostitute who is falsely accused of murder. In each of her films, Menkes meticulously deploys color and framing to convey the female character's relation to her environment. The filmmaker's extensive use of heavily stylized framing and settings, surreal lighting, and vibrant color more than compensates for the minimalist plot-structure of her films. In *Queen of Diamonds* (1991), a story of the blackjack dealer Firdaus, Menkes follows a similar trajectory, making methodical uses of extreme long-takes and one-shots, often lasting for an entire scene. The narrative's repetitive structure brilliantly underscores its female protagonist's isolation in a desert gambling town. And while Menkes keeps her camera stationary and at a distance from the film's subject, the emphasis in this as well as her previous films is on expanding our perceptions of reality.

Even though other women filmmakers resorted to more conventional narrative styles, their thematic and formal concerns similarly undermined the monolithic images of the nation projected by the classic realist aesthetics of mainstream cinema. Allison Anders is one of a handful of independents who has managed to produce a body of work within the Hollywood industry without compromising her independent vision and approach to making films. Her first film, the underground punk rock feature *Border Radio* (1982), co-directed by Dean Lent, was made while Anders studied at UCLA's film school. Her next two films feature the type of women rarely encountered with dignity in commercial cinema. *Gas, Food, Lodging* (1992) brings to the screen the life of a working-class single mom, living in a trailer park, working as a waitress as she struggles to raise two teenage daughters in New Mexico. Made during the height of the Christian Right's "family values" campaign which demonized single motherhood, *Gas, Food, Lodging* humanizes the lives of working poor women while broaching the difficult themes of sexual violence and trauma, unwanted pregnancy and dead-end jobs. The everyday hardships faced by single mothers coping with and without men is once again treated in her next film, *Mi Vida Loca* (1994), the first Hollywood film to portray the lives of Chicana homegirls sympathetically. Following the neorealist tradition, Anders mixes "real" gang members into the film's cast. Set in the Echo Park barrio of Los Angeles, the film is a sisterhood saga, featuring three interlocking stories of young Chicana homegirls whose lives are marked by violent conflicts which turn into camaraderie, affection, struggle, and survival. Shot in a style Anders calls "romantic realism," where camera

Intersections: Themes and Practices

movement follows character's emotion, *Mi Vida Loca* enables a space for collective female identities neglected in other films about gangs.

The topic of camaraderie between women in an urban setting informs Cauleen Smith's first feature film, *Drylongso* (1998). Set in the milieu of inner-city life (in this case Oakland) under siege by a serial killer targeting young African Americans in the face of police indifference, *Drylongso* centers on the life of Pika, a young college art student who spends her evening hanging flyers alerting residents about the "Westside slasher." This inspirational story tells of Pika's efforts to create a photographic tribute to the "endangered species" of the young African American men in her community. Amidst a chaotic home life, Pika bears witness to many of the concerns faced by young inner-city women, including random violence, abusive lovers, and dysfunctional families, and yet she goes on to establish an intimate bond with another young woman. In Smith's unflinching glimpse into the life of an African American woman, not every aspect of inner-city life is destructive, for in the end, Pika's photographic exhibit manages to bring the best out in her family and neighbors, blazing a trail to community healing.

Kayo Hatta's *Picture Bride* (1995) is a beautifully crafted melding of personal and historical themes. The story is set in 1918 in Hawaii, as a Japanese woman enters into an arranged marriage with a plantation worker she knows only through a photograph. Like so many other Japanese women who became picture brides, the main character, Riyo, is destined for a life of hardship working in the sugarcane fields of Hawaii. Though she is initially disgusted by the much older man, a love affair later blossoms between Riyo and Matsuji. Seamlessly weaving various levels into a complex, organic whole, *Picture Bride* is brimming with wonderful insights into the strategies of resistance of women workers who, because they were forbidden by plantation managers to vent their anger, imaginatively created "hole hole bushi" (work songs) which European bosses couldn't understand. A film produced, directed, and written entirely by women, *Picture Bride* is a haunting visual testimonial to the camaraderie among women who have been forced into a form of domestic slavery.

One of the most spectacular instances of a mytho-poetic renaissance in independent cinema is Julie Dash's feature *Daughters of the Dust* (1992). Set among the Sea Island Gullahs, who live off the coast of North Carolina and Florida, the story focuses on four generations of women and on the Ibo landing myth that sustains the African American tradition of resistance to slavery. *Daughters of the Dust* is resplendent with luscious metaphors, and its imaginative cinematography conveys a broad range of female subjectivities—the power and beauty of African

American women defined less in terms of romance or stereotypes than by their affective bonds, strengths, and independence as women. The film is as much about the retention of West African cultural traditions in the New World as it is about women's histories of struggle. It inventively resists the narrative conventions of Hollywood cinema, weaving multiple intersecting points of view and a nonlinear narrative structure to excavate the imminent links between the past and the future, spirituality and culture, personal memory and collective history. Carefully deploying various techniques—dissolves for transitions, wide angles and deep focus, sensuous camera zooms—*Daughters of the Dust* achieves epic scope while still reverberating on the intimate realm of women's vernacular experiences.

As we enter the twenty-first century, films by California's women will undoubtedly continue to shape new understandings, new ways of seeing, and new ways of being in the world. As we have seen, their cinematic lenses are cultivating the spaces in-between genres, aesthetic traditions, social identities, and national boundaries, and they incessantly bear witness to California's complex histories—its racial, cultural, and national configuration—to the evolving interplay of social identities and realities. Following in the tradition of California as trendsetter, films by women artists are setting a precedent for re-imagining the nation. In bearing witness, women filmmakers have situated themselves at the crossroads of the major transformations of our era, as agents of social change. For, as in the Latin American tradition of the *testimonio* (testimonial), the cinematic observations of California women filmmakers alert us "to the role of witnessing in our time as a key form of approaching and transforming reality."[8]

Notes

My special thanks to Kim Owyoung, whose research assistance made this article possible.

1 Peter Schrag, *Paradise Lost: California's Experience, America's Future* (New York: The New Press, 1998).

2 Renee Tajima-Peña, unpublished essay.

3 B. Ruby Rich, *Chick Flicks* (Durham, N.C.: Duke University Press, 1998), p.181.

4 Cited in Bonnie Marraca and Guatam Dasgupa, eds., "Ages of the Avant-Garde," *Performing Arts Journal* 16, no. 1 (January 1994): 9–57, 48.

5 Valerie Smith, "Telling Family Secrets: Narrative and Ideology in *Suzanne Suzanne*, by Camille Billops and James V. Hatch," in *Multiple Voices in Feminist Film Criticism*, ed. Diane Carson et al. (Minneapolis: University of Minnesota Press, 1994), p. 380.

6 Rich, *Chick Flicks*, p. 82.

7 Trinh T. Minh-ha, "All-Owning Spectatorship," *Quarterly Review of Film and Video* 13, nos. 1–2 (January 1991): 189–204, 97.

8 Ruth Behar, *The Vulnerable Observer* (Boston: Beacon Press, 1996), p. 27.

PAMELA LEE

CONSTRUCTION SITES

*Women Artists in California
and the Production of Space-Time*

Reflecting on a childhood spent in Los Angeles, it is hard to square the memories of one's past with the received wisdom on its built environment. Clichés surrounding the space of the metropolis wreak havoc with personal history. How does the image of the city as an endless, grid-like tract, veiled in penumbral smog and lacking in both inter- est or incident, reflect the reality of everyday life, with all its material complexity, social engagements, and intimate gestures? In what ways do its labyrinthine freeways, the architecture of road rage and "sig alerts," speak to personal history? Where, in other words, is the space of individual dwelling in this picture? The City of Quartz of cultural mythos—a city of both masculinist proportions and presumptions—is not the topography of my own city.[1]

The images of this city, oft-repeated, monolithic and grim in their capitulation to the dictates of urban planning, tend to repress or marginalize alternative visions of space produced by its female inhabitants conventionally left out of the official narra- tives of the city's history. How might women represent their *own* relation to space, one that exceeds the notion of a geographically fixed and determined place alienated by the strictures of cartography, real estate, and property rights? Space is not to be understood here as an absolute, immutable, and neutral category, something which one occupies passively. Rather, to follow Henri Lefebvre on the subject, it is as much a product of its subjects' daily habitus as it produces them in turn.[2]

In this essay, I wish to consider the ways in which women artists working in California deal broadly with the terms of what I will call constructed space. This notion of space is as diverse as its artists' respective aims are distinct, ranging from architectural and domestic space, to sites of cultural memory and exile, to spaces of spiritual and meditative retreat. Where one works, where one plays, where one reflects, what space one is allowed access to or alternately barred from: all of these concerns are implicitly addressed by these artists. The spaces that they construct, however, are not simply physical in nature, for to speak of artistic construction is to appeal to the self-fashioning of women and the production of artistic subjectivity itself.

The Promise of Space

The feminist philosopher and theorist Elizabeth Grosz reminds us that female subjectivity is also an embodied subjectivity, and that the terms of that embodiment, however socially constructed, are necessarily sexed terms. She speaks crucially to the corporeal stakes of that subject in space and the importance of rethinking its terms. As she writes in *Space, Time and Perversion*, "If bodies are to be reconceived, not only must their matter and form be rethought, but so too must their environment and spatio-temporal location."[3] Female subjectivity might be understood dialectically as a process that acknowledges both the

history of the space occupied and the relative autonomy of its inhabitants over it.[4]

It is hardly incidental that one of the canonical texts of nineteenth-century feminist literature, Charlotte Perkins Gilman's short story "The Yellow Wall-paper," is devoted to a woman's lack of control over her external surround.[5] The fictionalized, diaristic account witnesses its narrator forcibly restricted to an upstairs bedroom, where she progressively suffers hallucinations about the confines of the room. Gilman's text is a brilliant early assault on patriarchy and domesticity, on a woman's restricted social and political autonomy reflected in her limited freedom within architectural space. But as Sandra M. Gilbert and Susan Gubar point out, it is also a story of creativity blocked and censored.[6] The protagonist's husband sternly forbade her to write and accordingly limits her spatial mobility. The question or possibility of art making for Gilman's protagonist is thus analogized to the promise of space, with the narrator's domestic scene understood as a prison and the act of writing seen as model for negotiating the symbolic order. As such, Gilman's famous narrative of architectural space represents not only the historically repressive conditions of lived space by women but also, importantly, serves as an allegory for women's potential liberation and productivity as artists through space.

Gilman's text historically anticipates (and implicitly theorizes) the chiasmatic relationship between women's space and the processes of art making: how space affects—but can also be affected by—its female occupants. But it also suggests that works of art have their own instrumental value and can themselves shape spatio-temporal experience. In conflating the terms of space with the art object, women's art-making assumes a formative (not merely reflective) logic all its own.

Home Work

At roughly the same time that women were staking a claim for themselves as artists in the late 1960s and 1970s, other feminists were discovering the rewards of building as architects, construction workers, and contractors—of producing space in ways both metaphorical and literal. Tirza Latimer, a doctoral candidate in the Department of Art and Art History at Stanford University, recalls the struggles, politics, and ultimately, pleasures of being a woman construction worker in the 1970s. As a member of a women's carpentry collective formed in Berkeley called the Seven Sisters, she remembers the "centering" experience of constructing, of defying roles conventionally assigned to men, and of finding satisfaction in contributing to "certain stereotypes of lesbianism: [being] physically and mentally tough, competent and aggressive."[7] Among the collective's priorities were "to establish and defend a feminine position in the trades, to train

85

Tirza Latimer, *Tirza Latimer, a construction worker with the Seven Sisters Carpentry Collective, Berkeley,* early 1970s. Black-and-white photo. Courtesy of Tirza Latimer.

women in construction, and to make it possible for women (including ourselves) to own/build/remodel houses/businesses."[8]

Latimer's recollections point to the historical necessity for women to construct their own space, as well as an implicit critique of their relative inaccessibility to the means for producing (and thereby controlling) the spaces that preceded theirs historically. Women artists in the 1970s took on these issues in other ways. For many, it was the space of the domestic that served as a critical focus point, soliciting a range of artistic responses. Some artists thought through and parodied its structural codes (as in Martha Rosler's at once biting and hilarious 1975 video *Semiotics of the Kitchen*); others performed and thereby re-situated its activities as critique (Mierle Ukeles's 1974 series *Maintenance Art*); while still others reclaimed the debased arts of the home through the notion of a feminized (if not wholly feminine) aesthetic (the pattern and decoration movement). There is no doubt, however, that the challenge to and reclamation of domestic space by women artists in California found its principal locus in the collaborative 1972 project *Womanhouse*.

Located in Hollywood, *Womanhouse* was constructed over a period of six weeks by twenty-one students of the Feminist Art Program at the California Institute of the Arts in conjunction with their teachers Judy Chicago and Miriam Schapiro, and their teaching assistant, Faith Wilding. Granted use of the abandoned house by the city of Los Angeles, the students worked on the site for (at least) eight hours a day in endless dialogue and collaboration with one another, transforming the building's seventeen rooms into environmental works of art. While each room partook of a relatively distinct aesthetic, all of them suggested the tasks and cultural roles assigned to women in their homes.

The process-oriented component of the work

revealed a certain transformation of labor within the domestic sphere. As Arlene Raven writes:

Abandoned and condemned, the house on Mariposa Avenue was still architecturally imposing but also in need of extensive reconstruction . . . for the Feminist Art Program workers, skills such as carpentry and window glazing became part of the creative process. Before picking up a paint brush, etching plate, sculpting tool or video camera, each young artist had already used electric saws, drills and sanders.[9]

Thus the collaborative efforts of female art students implied a new model of pedagogy—a creative and intellectual exploration of the cultural imago of the house. Raven's remarks also speak to women literally reshaping their metier through the acquisition of new production skills. Finally, the work recuperates from the mandates of alienated space the most vexatious cultural site for feminists.

By contrast, Ann Hamilton's approach to domestic space assumes a more personal, and perhaps more ambiguous, cast. In her performative and installation-based work, the small, repetitive, and intimate gestures at the heart of domestic life are endowed with a gravity that approaches ritual. The "labor of hands" is a pervasive interest for Hamilton, who has taught at the University

86

Ann Hamilton, *Still Life*, 1988.
Installation (dimensions variable).

of California, Santa Barbara, and has produced important site works throughout California. These projects involve the collaboration of numerous co-workers obsessively engaged in tasks which seem to monumentalize the banality of everyday life and its materials.[10] However, Hamilton suggests a more equivocal relation to these jobs than what they might initially seem. Photographs of her installation entitled *Still Life* (1988), produced for the group exhibition *Home Show: 10 Artists' Installations in 10 Santa Barbara Homes*, present the artist sitting at a dining table piled high with a mass of white men's shirts. When the work is seen in profile, however, the shirts are barely recognizable. Ironed, folded, starched and flattened, they appear as brittle sheets of paper, with none of the sheen or texture associated with fabric. The "labor of tending" to the shirts was matched only by Hamilton's treatment of the room's walls, which she covered in a sheer scrim of wax. In a painstaking and equally tedious process, the artist then pressed eucalyptus leaves into its surface, producing a delicate, shadowy pattern on the walls.

Hamilton's treatment of the shirts invokes the gestures of women's domestic labor critiqued in *Womanhouse*. Acknowledging the drudgery involved in producing such work and its larger associations with the space of the home, she writes, "The home is often a sanctuary, a refuge, a place where one is tended, but tending can get claustrophobic. It can strangle and destroy the very thing it's trying to create. [The shirts] . . . were so tended they were rendered dysfunctional."[11] At the same time, the place of touch in Hamilton's work—the sensuality of a gesture such as preserving a leaf in wax, for instance—endows her installations with a sense of intimacy. The notion of rendering something "dysfunctional," literally "workless," under the auspices of house *work* underscores the paradoxical streak in Hamilton's art. Asked whether or not *Still Life* was a "critique of needless labor," the artist spoke to a more personal reading of the piece.

The day the piece was completed, the home-owner told me about the death of her first husband. Although the house wasn't built at the time, they had lived on the same property, and her husband had been an opera singer. . . . Anyway, they used to sit around the dining room table and sing opera. There was an opera playing in my piece. And then she said that when he died she had continued to wash and iron his shirts and that it wasn't until a friend came and took them away and made a quilt for her that she started to live again. And there I was, bringing all these shirts back in and placing them on a dining room table.[12]

However unintentional, Hamilton's piece recalled a different kind of work for the homeowner: the work of mourning. The loss of her husband was acknowledged in an activity with seemingly mundane implications. But also at stake in the washing and folding of his shirts was the homeowner's attempt to connect metonymically with a loved one who had recently died, as if the repetition involved in treating shirts was an act of remembrance and recollection. Hamilton had no recourse to this biographical information as she constructed *Still Life*, but its reception attests to the dual meanings of work in the domestic sphere. As much as it can be read as claustrophobic and "dysfunctional," it might also reflect a more personal history of the woman who tends to the home, who transforms the acts of everyday labor by investing it with the dignity of her touch.

The Work Room and the Museum Space: Maria Nordman

Maria Nordman engages phenomenological and architectural space that resists being narrated or described in any easy or coherent fashion. And yet what this difficulty suggests for the reception of her work is at the crux of her practice. Just as it rejects being fixed through language, particularly the language of the visual arts, so too does the experience of the work deny the stable grounding of space. Indeed, the relationship between the uses of language and the image of her art is a central concern of the artist. Of her early *Saddleback*

Mountain project, she has remarked that "The information is not coming in only visually . . . I am interested in a range of experience that happens with one's whole body sensing and conversing over a period of time."[13] Paradoxically, because the temporal dimensions of architecture and space are deeply internalized in her work, Nordman's articulation of space-time is a dislocated one.

Born in 1943 in Goerlitz, Silesia, Nordman now lives in Los Angeles and abroad. At UCLA, where she studied film and sculpture, she encountered the work of the filmmaker Josef von Sternberg, and her work is deeply informed by a cinematic as well as photographic logic. Its consideration of temporality and its effects on the status of the "image"—in this case, the self-imaging of its viewer's experience within her environments—is not far removed from the phenomenology of film, with its shifting modes of address to the spectator. The effect is further reinforced by Nordman's use of light within her work, which is always bound to its material or urban context. The viewer becomes "self-inscribed" or "self-imaged" in her art with the passage of light through the day, much as the development of a photograph depends on the quality of light bestowed upon it. Nordman clears the space for the emergence of such an image, with her work serving as the "screen" onto which her observers are projected.

The artist's particular engagement with light and the spatial dynamics of interior and exterior space stems further from her research on coherent light models. Having investigated these issues in her studies and early work, her interest in the material quality of light was subsequently reinforced by the architecture of Richard Neutra, with whom she worked as an editorial assistant. Accordingly, Nordman's sculpture (the term she prefers over "installation") highlights the confluence and contact of various registers of space, challenging the divide between interior and exterior, public and private, often by reversing the conventional roles each term plays within architecture. As one critic observed of her practice, "the human body cannot be distinguished from its context. The environment is not the product of a demi-urge, projected a priori, but an individual's contingent construction, situated in concrete space."[14]

Nordman's project *Workroom*, begun in 1969 and inactivated by the city of Santa Monica in 1999, eloquently demonstrates these principles. Located on Pico Boulevard in Santa Monica, *Workroom* was installed in an empty storefront reshaped by Nordman's subtle investigations of space. Ann Goldstein has observed of this space:

The room is entered through a door directly from the sidewalk. Three steps lead up to a wooden seating platform, which is at the base of a large window glazed with a two-way mirror filter. The fixtures of electrical illumination have been removed. From the outside, in the daytime, the window reflects the passerby in the mirrored surface. From the inside, the window frames the images and sounds of the street. A passerby would see an image of the room, and the person inside would see him- or herself reflected in the window.[15]

Nordman enabled the viewer inside to watch the activities of the street without being seen (due to the coating on the window) in the daytime. Interior or "private" space was granted access to the outside, without itself being made a spectacle. As Nordman wrote of the work, "Street sound and twenty percent of the light enters to the person inside and the rest of the light is reflected back out as an image of the street during the daytime."[16] The reversal of interior and exterior space—their mutual projection and introjection into each other—was underscored by her use of light.

Nordman continued to explore the concrete potential of light, reflecting upon the meeting ground between architecture and art in *Negative Light Extensions* (1973; also called *There are no Ocean Streets*), created on the occasion of a group show at the Newport Harbor Art Museum. It consisted of a concave wedge that opened onto an alley that had the effect of "subtracting" space from the museum itself.[17] As Nordman wrote:

Tangents of the sun light at 12:39 February 28,
determine shape construction that projects
into building through existing opening in alley.
On that time and day sun light completely fills
the white construction. Removal by addition.
Viewer walks from street into alley ½ block from
ocean.[18]

Again, the internalization of time within architectural space generated the construction of
Nordman's sculpture. But the terms of this space
were also coordinated around the dictates of the
museum, in which the public viewing of art is
expressed through the works' visual accessibility
within public space. Just who has access to
museum space—regarded as both neutral and
open—is implicitly addressed and criticized by
Nordman's work. As *Negative Light Extensions* literally subtracts from the space of the museum, it
is hardly "readable" as a work of art to the casual
passerby. At the same time, the work's quietude
and subtlety belied its physical openness.
Removed from the spatial hierarchies of the
museum's architecture, its portal remained accessible through the passage of light.

Nordman works in contexts that are nonsepa-
ratist. Her use of space is not gender-specific
insofar as she treats the structural boundaries of
spectatorship itself. Playing with internal and
external, public and private, museological and
work space, one may extrapolate to other binary

oppositions conventionally assigned to those
spatial registers, particularly the feminine and
masculine. Nordman's emphasis on the temporal
specificity of the viewer's encounter with her
works underscores the performativity of its
observers—the sense in which the formation of
spectatorship itself, insofar as it is socialized, is
processed in time. And because this formation
is a process for Nordman—and not a mandate—
she grants some spatial latitude to those entering
into her work. As she writes of her practice, "I
propose to give the unknown speaker the first
word."[19]

Dislocations: Sites of Cultural Memory and Spaces of Difference

Accepting the terms of Nordman's art is to recognize the inadequacy and rejection of absolutist
models of space. Her installational "conditions"
give rise to a more fluid sensibility of constructed
space, one that is not tethered to the immediately pressing conditions of architecture and
urbanism.

For women artists who are considered doubly
"Other"—because female and of non-European
descent—the possibility of producing such space
takes on particular cultural meaning. What constitutes the space of everyday life in California
might be construed as a different matter for
artists of color, many of whom have produced
work that underscores the specificity of their dif-

Yong Soon Min, *Dwelling*, 1994.
Mixed-media installations, 6 × 5
× 3 ft. Photo: Eric Landsberg.
Executed for the Asia Society,
New York. Collection of the
artist.

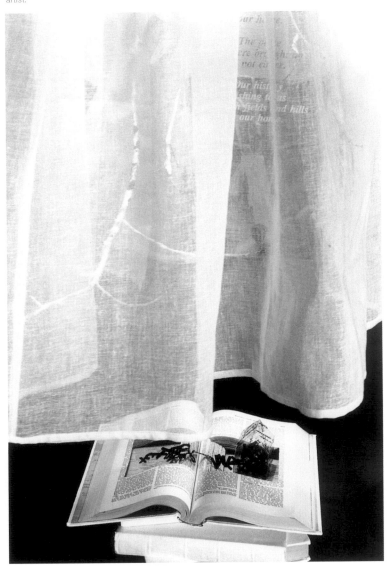

ference, the particularities of their habitus, and the importance of reclaiming sites of cultural memory.

The work of Yong Soon Min points to the heterogeneity and the decidedly nonmonolithic character of these sites, recuperated from the official cartographies of American culture. A Korean-born artist who lives in Los Angeles, Min articulates a sense of cultural liminality throughout her work, which includes photography, installation, and sculpture. In *Dwelling* (1994), the artist has constructed a place of contemplation in the present and a recollection of more distant topographies from her past.[20] A mixed-media installation, the work is organized around the form of a *hanbok* (a traditional Korean dress constructed from gauzy material), which is suspended above a display of items with telling personal attributes. A set of open books and a model of a Western-style house placed beneath the dress attest to the question of personal domain in a transcultural upbringing. Yet as delicate as *Dwelling* at first appears, the installation has a sculptural presence that suggests that this traditional costume represents a space of inhabitation nonetheless. And as a feminine attribute, the *hanbok* locates the politics of spatial identity along gendered terms.

Issues of cultural and spatial dislocation are explicitly referenced in the work. Min cites the words of the Korean American poet Ko Won to reflect upon this condition: "To us . . . a birth-place is no longer our home. The place where we were brought up is not either."[21] Such words articulate a condition which is not the province of Korean American women artists alone. If Min points to the phenomena of dislocation that is at the crux of transcultural experience, she also resituates the thematics of dwelling on her own terms in this work.

The Imaging of Spiritual Retreat

While my account has focused on the externaliza-tion of space and its social and phenomenological implications, other variants of constructed space are spiritual in nature. The attempt of women artists to give such space physical and visual form suggests that it is not wholly transcendent and immaterial. In fact, the imaging of spiritual retreat for women artists working in California bears markedly feminist implications.

Part of this may be a function of California's religious and spiritual pluralism, itself attribut-able to deeply material phenomenon: its geo-graphical proximity to Latin American countries and its Pacific Rim orientation; the diversity of its native and immigrant populations; and its widely held cultural status as a progressive state. Indeed, none of the artists discussed in this grouping take institutional religion at face value, often chal-lenging its restrictive and patriarchal conven-tions by producing a more personal or private

spiritual vocabulary. Since the late 1970s, for example, the photographer Linda Connor has made spiritual questing central to her artistic project, but her iconographic references are het-erogeneous, finding the sacred in a diversity of multicultural sources ranging from Nepal to Peru to Ireland to Egypt to Thailand.

Connor is frequently described as a land-scape photographer, but the designation seems strangely limited, as if the subject of her work is little more than a topographical phenomenon. Instead, her richly shadowed black-and-white images illuminate the geography and architec-ture of sacred places, as well as the almost spiri-tual resonance of objects. Images of ancient cere-monial caves in Hawaii or dolmen formations in France evoke premodern ritual, while photo-graphs of crumbling monasteries, still in use, convey the continuity of religious traditions in the present. Connor's representation of these spaces is understood in feminist terms. Writing on the artist's work, Rebecca Solnit suggests that "her reverence for the earth, like that of many contemporary feminists and ecologists, has affi-nities to the earth-worship of earlier cultures, and the ties between respect for the earth and matriarchal cultures, as discussed by Lucy Lippard. . . ."[22] But Connor's practice, while turning its focus on earlier cultures, has marked implications for the contemporary status of women. As Solnit reminds us, "both the identity

Linda Connor, *Kapokohe,*
Lele, Ancient Ceremonial Cave
for Pele, Goddess of Volcanos,
1986. Toned photograph,
contact print, 8 × 10 in. Puna,
Hawaii. Collection of the artist.

of the sacred and the role of women are fundamentally different in cultures where the earth is
sacred."[23]

The painting and print work of Sylvia Lark
(1947–1990) follows similar principles. A Seneca
born in Manhattan, she was a highly respected
teacher at the University of California at Berkeley. Lark painted in an abstract idiom throughout her career, but while her art bears some
resemblance to abstract expressionist work, her
practice was not dictated by the formalist criteria
of high modernism. Her work was a far more personal treatment of abstract space that attempted
to link her contemporary search for spiritual

meaning with her Native American heritage and its system of beliefs.

Like Connor, Lark traveled extensively in order to chart the religious activities of diverse non-Western cultures. Her work attempts to close the space between such religious practices and her own. Visits to Africa and Tibet, for instance, pro-vided inspiration for a series of paintings dating from the early 1980s. In Lhasa, the Jokhang Temple in particular became a source for her *Jokhang* paintings (1983), shadowy, lyrical works which in their translucent layering of color and form evoked the dim light admitted into the space of the monastery. In later paintings, the addition

Mineko Grimmer, *Seeking for the Philosopher's Stone*, 1985. Mixed-media installation, 96 × 96 × 24 in. Los Angeles Municipal Art Gallery, Hollywood, Calif. Photo: Grey Crawford. Collection of the artist, courtesy of Koplin Gallery, Los Angeles.

of fragmentary objects to her abstract tableaus is suggestive of the collection of relics and amulets. The paintings' shifting tonalities and arrangement of simple materials produce an intimate and reflective space.

If Lark uses color, gesture, and relics to such ends, the minimal, architectonic installations of Mineko Grimmer employ silence and sound to produce a space of resonant contemplation for her audience. Born in northern Japan, Grimmer moved to Los Angeles in the 1980s. Her work bridges references from both Eastern and Western sources, including the architecture of Shinto shrines recalled from her youth, minimalist aesthetics absorbed in art history classes, Zen gardens, and notions of time common to both contemporary American art and Shinto philosophy.

In 1980, Grimmer began making work that incorporated ice, and she noticed that it took on a sonorous character as the melting process began. Inspired by the work of John Cage, Grimmer arrived at the idea of producing art that incorporated chance in the making of sound. While Grimmer is hardly alone in this practice—indeed, she is part of a long tradition of artists interested in chance procedures—she directs it to specifically meditative ends. The basic elements and structure of Grimmer's work would remain constant, including, as Mary Davis MacNaughton writes, "an open wooden box, holding a shallow pool of water, into which pebbles [drop] from an inverted pyramid of ice, suspended by a rope."[24] When the ice pyramid begins to melt, "the solitary note of the first pebble [dropping] from the ice pyramid . . . slowly builds with a staccato of falling stones, and finally reaches a crescendo of cascading pebbles before ending in serene stillness."[25]

Grimmer's art internalizes the experience of duration for the viewer, who must wait patiently for each installation to produce its unorthodox music. While her work is kinetic, the quality of its movement is dramatically slow, demanding a degree of endurance on the part of her audience extremely rare in the consumption of contemporary art. As a result, stillness takes on an almost palpable quality in her work and silence reverberates as loudly as the occasional sound of a pebble breaking the surface of water. In the quietude and slowness of these installations, the spectator herself shifts focus. Attending to the subtlest changes in time and environment, she is rewarded not only by the music of the object, but the meditative space which it opens up.

Space Studies: Vija Celmins's Perspectivism

The virtual stilling of space that is crucial to Grimmer's sculpture brings us full circle to the question of constructed space that began this essay. In closing, I'd like to consider an artist who, in telescoping distance in her images, conjures for the viewer the strange paradox of the intimacy of space while reflecting on the nature of perspective itself.

Vija Celmins was born in Latvia in 1939 and emigrated with her family to the United States ten years later; in the early 1960s, she studied art at UCLA.[26] She is perhaps best known for a remarkable series of untitled drawings (begun in 1968) of views of the Pacific that simultaneously evoke both the awesomeness and closeness of natural space through a dramatic compression of scale. Composed of graphite on paper that has been covered with an acrylic ground, the drawings are slowly wrought horizontal images, painstaking in their articulation of each crest and swell. Yet, if Celmins's drawings are derived from photographs taken from the Venice Pier, her emphasis on visual detail is not photorealistic.[27] The absence

of a horizon line renders the process of scaling the scenes extremely difficult, paradoxically conveying the effects of both nearsightedness and magnitude. Oceanic breadth is thus telescoped into intimate focus, and determinations of perspective become a decidedly subjective matter.

Her drawings of the lunar surface (also begun in 1968) reiterate the strangely equivocal character of her space. Inspired by a photograph of the moon from a Russian space mission, they represent scenes taken at an enormous distance from the artist—literally studies of space in space. Yet Celmins makes each feel proximate, intimate, as if her eye were little more than a few inches from the moon's surface. The effect is such that the perspective reads as miniaturized or compressed, even though the distance between viewer and object depicted is great.

The oscillation of distance and proximity in Celmins's work provides the ultimate object lesson for the notion of construction sites. Space is rendered deeply intimate and subjective for Celmins; it is the ground of both lived experience as well as an evocation of sublime distance rendered close through the artist's hand. To claim transcendence for this space, however, is to miss the point. On the contrary, Celmins's work underscores its subject's perspectivism, conveyed through her art's own radical attenuation of perspective.

What this suggests for the "fate" of space for California women artists is salutary, offering a parallel to other developments in the larger culture. There is no doubt that conventional notions of space have undergone a dramatic transformation since mid-century. Developments in digital technologies—the rise of the Web and the Internet in particular—signal the progressive collapse of traditional conceptions of distance and space. If women artists working in California sought to intervene into or reject totalizing spatial forms, perhaps the virtual worlds of new media offer another means of expanding their spatial semantics. It is a promise of space long understood by the artists treated in this essay, for whom the act of construction both registers and exceeds the dictates of conventional site.

Notes

1 By "masculinist space" I am referring to recent urban-studies discussions of the city, which universalize the experience of urban life as necessarily male. For an important critique of such accounts, see Rosalyn Deutsche, "Boys Town" and "Men in Space," both in her *Evictions: Art and Spatial Politics* (Cambridge: MIT Press, 1996).

A "sig alert" is a familiar term to Los Angeles and Southland residents and commuters who use the freeway on a daily basis. "Sig alerts" are regular radio announcements that detail traffic jams, general congestion, and automobile accidents. They have come to symbolize the frustration Southland drivers experience on the highways.

2 Henri Lefebvre, *The Production of Space*, trans. Donald Nicholson-Smith (Oxford: Blackwell, 1991).

3 Elizabeth Grosz, *Space, Time and Perversion* (London: Routledge, 1995), p. 104.

4 See, for instance, Deutsche, *Evictions*; Gillian Rose, *Feminism and Geography: The Limits of Geographical Knowledge* (Minneapolis: University of Minnesota Press, 1993); and Beatriz Colomina, ed., *Sexuality and Space* (Princeton: Princeton Papers on Architecture, 1992). For literature on the domestic and its relationship to art history, see *Not at Home: The Suppression of the Domestic in Modern Art and Architecture*, ed. Christopher Reed (London: Thames and Hudson, 1996); *Dirt and Domesticity* (exhibition catalogue), Whitney Independent Study Program (New York: Whitney Museum of American Art, 1992); also see Helen Molesworth's analysis of the Duchampian readymade and its repressed ties to the domestic (PhD. diss., Cornell University, 1997).

5 Charlotte Perkins Gilman, "The Yellow Wall-paper," in *"The Yellow Wall-paper" and Selected Stories of Charlotte Perkins Gilman*, ed. Denise D. Knight (Newark: University of Delaware Press, 1994).

6 Sandra M. Gilbert and Susan Gubar, *The Madwoman in the Attic: The Woman Writer and the Nineteenth-Century Literary Imagination* (New Haven: Yale University Press, 1979).

7 Tirza Latimer, e-mail communication with the author, July 17, 1999, p. 3. For a recent history of women in construction work, see Susan Eisenberg, *We'll Call You If We Need You: Experiences of Women Working Construction* (Ithaca, N.Y.: Cornell University Press, 1998).

8 Latimer, e-mail communication, July 17, 1999.

9 Arlene Raven, "Womanhouse," in *The Power of Feminist Art*, ed. Norma Broude and Mary D. Garrard (New York: Harry N. Abrams, 1994), p. 50.

10 Lynda Forsha, "Introduction and Acknowledgments," in *Ann Hamilton: Between Taxonomy and Communion* (exhibition catalogue) (San Diego, Calif.: San Diego Museum of Contemporary Art, 1990).

11 Ibid., p. 67

12 Ibid.

13 Maria Nordman, *Saddleback Mountain* (exhibition catalogue) (Irvine: University of California at Irvine, 1973), n.p.

14 Germano Celant, "The Work of Maria Nordman," in Mark

Rosenthal, *Andre, Buren, Irwin, Nordman: Space as Support* (Berkeley: University of California Press and the University Art Museum, 1979), p. 19.

15 Ann Goldstein, "Maria Nordman," in her *Reconsidering the Object of Art* (exhibition catalogue) (Los Angeles and Cambridge: The Museum of Contemporary Art and MIT Press), p. 184.

16 Nordman, quoted in Celant, "The Work of Maria Nordman," p. 19.

17 Other works by Nordman that subscribe to these principles include the series *DE SCULPTURA: Works in the City* (1986, Munich); *New Conjunct City: Proposals DE MUSICA* (1993, Lucerne); and *DE SCULPTURA 11* (1997, Stuttgart).

18 Nordman, quoted in *Saddleback Mountain*.

19 Nordman, "Notations on a Work," in Rosenthal, *Andre, Buren, Irwin, Nordman: Space as Support*, n.p.

20 Margo Machida, "Out of Asia: Negotiating Asian Identities in America," in *Asia/America: Identities in Asian-American Art* (New York: The Asia Society and The New Press, 1994), p. 94.

21 Ibid.

22 Rebecca Solnit, "The Seventh Direction," in *Linda Connor: Spiral Journey, Photographs 1967–1990* (Chicago: The Museum of Contemporary Photography, Columbia College, 1990), p. 15.

23 Ibid.

24 Mary Davis MacNaughton, "Sound and Silence: The Sculpture of Mineko Grimmer," *Arts* 5, no. 62 (November 1987): 54–58.

25 Ibid., p. 55.

26 Biographical information on Celmins is derived from Susan K. Larsen, *Vija Celmins: A Survey Exhibition* (exhibition catalogue) (Newport, Calif.: Newport Harbor Art Museum, 1979), p. 9.

27 Ibid., p. 26.

MOIRA ROTH AND SUZANNE LACY

EXCHANGES

I wonder if future art historians will be able to conjure up vividly enough the central place… friendships have in our lives as well as in our art and writing—and the conversations in which we generate ideas collectively.

Moira Roth, "Two Women:
The Collaborations of Pauline
Cummins and Louise Walsh," 1992

Suzanne Lacy, an artist-writer, born in Wasco, California, has resided for a good part of her life in California. Moira Roth, a historian-critic, born in London, England, has lived in California since 1960. Lacy and Roth live a mile or so apart from one another in the Bay Area. This exchange—one in which they explore the notion of relational history and its relevance to California women artists—is a continuation of their twenty-five-year-long conversations in public and private about feminist art.

The 1960s

MOIRA ROTH: In the spring of 1960, I moved from the East Coast to California, and a few years later entered the art history graduate program at the University of California, Berkeley. Thus, my experiences of the 1960s, including my encounters with early performance art (in which I participated), began here in the context of radical politics, student demonstrations, and the counterculture of the Bay Area. Civil rights and antiwar demonstrations were part of the daily scene on the UC campus, colliding with timid retreats, on my part and those of other graduates, into the library to read singularly formalist versions of art history.

From the start I saw Northern California performance art as something totally distinct from regular art history (e.g., European Dada theater) and the East Coast music and dance experiments in the Cage-Cunningham-Rauschenberg circles. For me these early events, often romantically staged in streets, on mountaintops and in studios, were vivid echoes—visual representations—of the epoch's moods and beliefs. I didn't then experience them as art, but rather as aspects of our turbulent contemporary life.

SUZANNE LACY: Although I studied art in college, my degree was in zoology, with emphases on premedical studies and philosophy. When I joined VISTA [Volunteers in Service to America] in Washington, D.C. after college, my opinions about oppression were dramatically politicized. As a child, I had been outraged by the distinct racial barriers I saw around me. But, in VISTA I learned from Saul Alinsky's writings on community organizing and I worked for patient rights in a black community in Richmond, Virginia, which left me with a deeper and more radical understanding of poverty, racism, and power.

Among my teachers in VISTA were exciting and charismatic men versed in the radical Left social movements. Ironically, in admiring, learning from, and being ultimately misunderstood by these men, the ground was set to understand my own situation as a woman. Soon after leaving VISTA, I was introduced to feminism by East Coast refugees from the gender struggles in leftist circles. Inchoate feelings, rages, and depressions became clearer when seen through this lens. My sight was inverted, returned to its original state; I felt like this was a reality that had always laid just below consciousness. At the end of the decade, I naively thought that we of the same gender had a bond that cut across class and culture. I probably still do, but the cords of class and culture are thicker than I had thought, and harder to negotiate than I could have ever known at that time.

The 1970s

MOIRA ROTH: In the fall of 1970, age 38, I moved down from Berkeley to Los Angeles and it was here that I first encountered feminism.

I immediately plunged headlong into the Southern Californian feminist art world (and, to a lesser extent, into the New York one), meeting at Joyce Kozloff's house and breakfasting at June Wayne's to strategize the L.A. women's art movement. Angered by the all-white, all-male *Art and Technology* show at the L.A. County Museum of Art, we analyzed the museum's permanent collection (virtually all male) and, after extensive negotiations, the museum committed itself to produce a major historical survey of women artists, *Women Artists 1550–1950*, which opened in 1976. I visited the Woman's Building and Judy Chicago's studio while she was creating *The Dinner Party*, participated in a consciousness-raising group with artists, read feminist literature as well as early feminist art history, followed feminist events around the country and abroad, and wrestled with my own art history training. At first in an awkwardly piecemeal fashion, I began to make

93

Jerri Allyn, Anne Gauldin,
Denise Yarfitz, Leslie Belt,
Jamie Wildman, Patti Nicklaus
(The Waitresses), *Ready to
Order?* 1978. Seven-day,
site-specific conceptual art
event in Los Angeles, Calif.
restaurants—Performance
vignettes over mealtimes in
various restaurants; evening
panels about issues raised
(work, food, money,
stereotypes of women,
sexual harassment).
Photo: Maria Karras.

space for women artists in modernism, and later took on underlying questions about the construction of museums, collections, and art history itself. All the while I was dazzled by the passion and frenetic pace of feminist art, especially performance.

I taught at the University of California at San Diego, with Eleanor Antin, Helen Harrison, and Patricia Patterson, and also with many visiting performance artists, you among them—indeed, that is where we first met. At UC San Diego, I ran the Mandeville Art Gallery for a couple of years, putting on one-person exhibitions of Jo Hanson, Miriam Schapiro, and Barbara Smith. There were many other key figures in the San Diego area at the time—Martha Rosler, Kathy Acker, Norma Jean Deak, Mary Fish, Joyce Cutler Shaw, Pauline Oliveros, and Linda Montano. For years, I regularly drove into Los Angeles to see performances by, among others, Jerri Allyn, Nancy Angelo, Nancy Buchanan, Cheri Gaulke, Leslie Labowitz, Rachel Rosenthal, Barbara Smith, and the col-

Linda M. Montano, *The
Chicken Piece*, 1967–75.
From performance:
*Chicken Woman/Live Saint
Series*. Photo: Mitchell Payne.
Courtesy of the artist.

despair, hope, wit, desire, the urge to reveal painful past injuries, and by utopian visions for restructuring society. Fictional characters appeared (Antin's King of Solano Beach and Lynn Hershman's Roberta Breitmore) and autobiographical recountings were presented (Nancy Buchanan's analysis of the life and politics of her physicist father and Rachel Rosenthal's reconstruction of her Parisian childhood). Frequently performer and audience member had experienced similar emotions, and the performances were cathartic for many. One of the key memories for me is the collective nature of the realities portrayed in these early feminist performances.

If during the 1960s performance art had been a refuge for me from my academic art history studies, in the 1970s it became a focus for my own contributions to contemporary art history and criticism. I was deeply convinced that performance could play a major role in inspiring and sustaining feminist activism and visually and verbally capturing feminist issues. Engaging with feminism gave me a different sense of what could be done in history and criticism. I responded with documenting, mapping, interviewing, curating, writing, accumulating archives, and speculating endlessly with others. It was a giddy period—one which I was later to name *The Amazing Decade* in my book by the same title on women's performance art of the 1970s—with its endless gatherings and conversations, celebra-

lectives the Feminist Art Workers, the Sisters of Survival, and the Waitresses. I attended events at the Woman's Building. One of the most memorable was "The Oral Herstory of Lesbianism," directed by Terry Wolverton, in which we watched a shifting array of poignant and hilarious vignettes, including "Stalking the Great Orgasm," accompanied by prowling figures and climactic music.

Performances during this period in Southern California were inspired varyingly by anger,

95
Rachel Rosenthal, *Charm*, 1977.
Performance featuring members
of Rosenthal's "Instant Theatre"
Company. Photo: Cindy Up-
church. Courtesy of the artist.

tions and mourning rites, feuds and rivalries, and evolutions of lifelong friendships and alliances (both in California and elsewhere) between feminist artists, historians, curators, and critics.

SUZANNE LACY: In 1970 I met Judy Chicago at Fresno State while I was a graduate student in psychology. At first, Judy thought I would never be an artist because I was so far along in premedical studies. If it were not for that meeting, I probably would be a doctor today.

I joined the Fresno Feminist Art Program and the next year followed it to California Institute of the Arts. At CalArts, thanks to a confluence of artists and writers and scholars, there was an explosion of feminist culture. Along with Judy, there was painter Miriam Schapiro, graphic designer Sheila de Bretteville, poet Deena Metzger, historians Arlene Raven, Ruth Iskin, and Paula Harper, with painter Faith Wilding and myself as graduate assistants. There, within the Los Angeles landscape, feminist art education went public, with CalArts programs in literature,

96

Martha Rosler, *Vital Statistics
of a Citizen, Simply Obtained*,
1977. Still from the color video.
Photo: Marita Sturkin, Electronic
Arts Intermix. Courtesy of the
artist.

Guillermo Gómez-Peña and Mike Kelley was created within this context, and to some extent
reflected and reacted to this prevalent feminist
discourse.

Leaving CalArts, we developed the Feminist
Studio Workshop—begun in 1971 by de Bretteville, Chicago, and Raven—which served as a
central focus in the national feminist movement.
The Woman's Building was founded in 1973 in
an old building in downtown Los Angeles, collecting several feminist institutions and businesses, including the Feminist Studio Workshop,
under one roof. A veritable Who's Who of women
artists, writers, musicians, and critics from
around the world came to visit the Woman's
Building—Yvonne Rainer, Martha Wilson, Lucy
Lippard, Mary Daly, Susan Griffin, Bonnie Sherk,
Linda Montano, Pauline Oliveros, Mary Beth
Edelson, Holly Near, Joan Jonas, Judy Baca, Kate
Millett, Lynn Hershman Leeson, Ulrike Rosenbach, Eleanor Antin, Helen Harrison, Adrienne
Rich, and Martha Rosler.

Our work was based on our experiences and
values, the nature of and need for communication, and aesthetic debates, and it laid the groundwork for many of the themes prevalent in contemporary art. Our performances consciously
explored the boundaries between women: the
space between self and other, between races and
to some degree across classes. I explored poverty
(*The Bag Lady*), prostitution (*Prostitution Notes*),

painting and sculpture, sociology, creative writing, and design and with publications, art historical forays, and national gatherings.

New work from these programs reflected
women's life experiences, bodies, poverty, the
nature of identity, relationships, and violence.
Judy Chicago, Aviva Rahmani, Sandra Orgel, and I
produced *Ablutions* in 1972, the first contemporary feminist artwork on rape. This profusion
of women's work created a strong and visible
impact, both at CalArts and in the Los Angeles art
scene. The work of then-students such as David
Salle, James Welling, Chris Burden, and later,

and cross-racial friendship's strengths and perils (*Evalina and I*; *Crimes, Quilts, and Art*; and *The Life and Times of Donaldina Cameron*).

Toward the end of that decade, collaboration became the central work strategy, based on the need to communicate essential information about women's experiences to larger and larger numbers of people. Leslie Labowitz and I, influenced by our teachers, Joseph Beuys and Allan Kaprow, invented the large-scale performance framework—a structure of multiple interdisciplinary collaborations which used life-like activities, public institutional interventions, and mass media (*Three Weeks in May*, *In Mourning and in Rage*, *From Reverence to Rape to Respect*, and *Take Back the Night*).

Lacy and Roth meet in the mid-1970s and for the next several years (both are based in Southern California), their lives and work overlap considerably, as do their communities and friends. They organize and participate in projects together, including a panel at the College Art Association conference in New York; a Women's Caucus for Art "boycott" conference in New Orleans with Lucy Lippard, Lee Ann Miller, and Mary Jane Jacob; an exhibition and performance series at Franklin Furnace in New York City as an exchange between Los Angeles and London women artists; and they critique and support each other's writings.

The 1980s

SUZANNE LACY: I was in an aesthetic conundrum. In the '70s, political and public processes became part of art making. The theoretical basis for this work was not visual, but conceptual. Such processes—for example, eating dinner, producing news, organizing communities, and even making quilts (in Watts)—were difficult to convey visually. This was generally true of art at the time, when artists like Mierle Ukeles, Helen and Newton Harrison, and the collective Group Material were struggling with the visual representation of daily lives, interdisciplinary research, and community processes. Many art critics had difficulties knowing how to evaluate this form of public art.

At the beginning of 1980, public art was still quite object-oriented, but as the decade progressed artists increasingly explored the political, temporal, and conceptual ideas that were the legacy of the '70s—Martha Rosler, Fred Lonidier, and Alan Sekula in San Diego, working on a Marxist analysis for art; Judy Baca and Faith Ringgold organizing around race and culture; the many women, former students and present colleagues, from the Woman's Building, including Jerri Allyn, Cheri Gaulke, and Nancy Angelo, prodigiously exploring collaborative performance art and video; and critics and theorists like yourself, and Lucy Lippard, Mary Jane Jacob, and

Arlene Raven responding to and analyzing those developments as they occurred.

By then, we had formulated an extensive body of inquiry that was activist-based. Our ideas revolved around the relationship between artist and audience; work strategies that had both political and formal implications, such as collaboration; the use of the everyday object or action; local community and media contexts; the effect of art on viewers; and social change. These concerns seemed to put us at odds with "Theory" with a capital "T" that was inspired by French psychoanalysis and linguistics. In the beginning these theories seemed to lead to a rupture of relationships between activists and theorists, women inside and outside academia, and between those committed to populist communication and those whose language was densely theoretical.

Influenced by my teachers Judy Chicago and Allan Kaprow, I theorized my work as a combination of feminist activism and the conceptually oriented avant-garde, beginning with the futurists and constructivists, through happenings, to the present time. I was always concerned with how the shape and formal language of the work communicated, both within the terms of performance art and in a language that was equally accessible to large audiences. Diane Gelon, art historian and the director of Judy Chicago's *Dinner Party* project, gave me an article on turn-of-the-century pageants, part of a grassroots

and community-based theater movement that included large numbers of people working toward political and/or social ends. Adopting the form of tableau, or performative installation, I was soon working in a more visual and expansive, activist, public mode (*Whisper the Waves, the Wind; The Crystal Quilt*; and *The Dark Madonna*).

MOIRA ROTH: In the '80s, my whole notion of "the woman's movement" fractured, as did my understanding of its chronology and geography. I began to think in terms of multiple histories, sites, and identities, and I grappled with notions of "construction" and "deconstruction." Like many of us in the early Californian feminist art movement, I began to analyze and act differently. I thought in terms of strategies and alliances, rather than utopian visions of unity. We attempted to form alliances between diverse women in the hope of creating what Gayatri Spivak has brilliantly described as "strategic essentialism." In private and public, I experienced the pleasures and problems of an immersion in an increasingly diverse world.

New friendships with Faith Ringgold, Margo Machida, Yong Soon Min, Betty Kano, Theresa Harlan, Lucy Lippard, Mary Jane Jacob, Hulleah Tsinhnahjinnie, Howardena Pindell, Judy Baca, and Whitney Chadwick influenced my work; for many of us there was an indecipherable web of connectedness between our lives and our work. I became more and more aware of how many

97
Suzanne Lacy, *Whisper
the Waves, the Wind*, 1984.
Performance with 150 older
women, La Jolla, Calif.
Photo: G. Pasha Turley.

different sorts of audiences existed in response to different kinds of art. My students at Mills College and I explored various art communities in the Bay Area and published a paperback, *Connecting Conversations: Interviews with 28 Bay Area Women Artists*, in 1988.

I became part of a broad multicultural coalition including whites, and I worked with men as well as women. Many of us met in the ambiance of a series of seven wonderful symposia at the San Francisco Art Institute, orchestrated by Carlos Villa, in which women had central roles in the organization and the events. Later, in my foreword to his book, *Worlds in Collision: Dialogues on Multicultural Art Issues*, I wrote, "Collaboration, friendship and trust have made this book possible," and characterized the symposia aims as attempts to create "alliances between individuals, between communities of different ethnicities and cultures, and between people of different classes, ages and sexual orientations." Among our topics were the institutional power of museums and universities, and the controlling role of traditional art history and criticism. These weren't merely abstract debates. For example, we analyzed and created strategies to alter exhibition practices at local museums, instigate the hiring of more artists of color and women artists at local colleges and art schools, and develop a more culturally inclusive art education at both high school and college levels.

All in all, I experienced a new sort of creative and political freedom in the 1980s. A few years ago, I had a most illuminating discussion with Valerie Matsumoto, a friend and UCLA historian, who helped me analyze my cross-cultural (class and ethnic) background as a child in terms of my later attraction to, as well as comfort with, California's shifting, restless, often friction-fraught, mixing of cultures.

The 1990s

SUZANNE LACY: Mid-decade in Monterey, on the site of the former Fort Ord military base, Luis Valdez, filmmaker and founder of Teatro Campesino, Judy Baca and I, later joined by theorist and artist Amalia Mesa-Bains and musician Richard Bains, designed art programs at the California State University at Monterey Bay that reflected our values about the importance of this changing demography. At this new institution, we were able to operate without the givens of tradition, tenure, and turf. Judy and I developed the Institute for Visual and Public Art, a fine arts undergraduate program that turned traditional art curriculum on its head. Our cornerstone courses were not drawing and painting, but Ethics, Diverse Histories, and Community Practice.

After a decade of work that had focused on models for cross-cultural and intergenerational communication, I finally "settled" into Oakland, California. I began to work there, and elsewhere,

Intersections: Themes and Practices

too. I traveled to Finland, where I collaborated with Judy Baca, Allan Kaprow, Pirrko Kurika, Tuula Linsio, and Arthur Strimling on a series of events about borders called "Meeting of the Worlds"; to Chicago for Mary Jane Jacob's project *Culture in Action*, where we installed a series of boulder/monuments to women around the downtown Loop; to Ireland, where I wrote *Mapping the Terrain* (1995) and interviewed northern and southern Irish women; to Medellin, Colombia, where anthropologist Pilar Riaño and I created an installation on memories of loss in a small barrio; and to various sites across the U.S.—including Bedford Hills State Prison in New York—to collaborate on a series of installations using the metaphor of wrecked cars for family violence. The themes of these works oscillated between hope for a community in which people are treated equally and the exposure of forces that prevent such a community. Race was one of the most difficult and explosive aspects of these extensive collaborations, and it is a major subtext in my Oakland work.

Cultural diversity is the signature of Oakland, a city with a rich history of activism that includes the Black Panther movement. It is also a young city, with one-quarter of its population under the age of 18. The population of Oakland's public schools is 55 percent African American, 20 percent Latino, 20 percent Asian American, and 5 percent white and Native American. In 1991,

Chris Johnson, photographer and colleague at California College of Arts and Crafts, and I found ourselves discussing how little we knew about these youth, apart from their media portrayal. The divide was at least in part generational, though Chris himself is African American from Bedford-Stuyvesant and I, white working class, had a lifelong familiarity with many aspects of black culture, neither of us felt we really knew young African Americans.

We volunteered to teach a yearlong class in media literacy at Oakland Technical High School. Over the next few years, Chris and I, working with others, explored the effectiveness of art as a strategy for institutional intervention (*Roof Is on Fire*, a performance with 220 youth in cars on a rooftop garage; *Youth, Cops, and Videotape*, a training tape for police; *No Blood/No Foul*, a basketball game between officers and youth to announce the formation of the Oakland Youth Policy Initiative; and *Expectations*, a summer school class for pregnant and parenting teens and a subsequent installation at Capp Street Gallery in San Francisco).

For many years my work with Oakland youth has taken me into City Hall, the Police Department, the Health Department, and educational institutions. Changes here are slow, and part of a much larger movement where artists work alongside activists from many other disciplines. This work has been as perplexing as the decade

Kano, Brian Tripp, Carlos Villa, and Flo Oy Wong. In 1994, Yolanda Lopez and I co-authored "Social Protest Racism and Sexism," in *The Power of Feminist Art*. In 1998, Jonathan D. Katz, the San Francisco gay activist—art historian, and I collaborated on a collection of my writings, *Difference/ Indifference: Musings on Postmodernism, Marcel Duchamp and John Cage*. I am a founding member of the now ten-year-old Asian American Women Artists Association, and recently a group of us from this organization, including Lenore Chinn, Kim Anno, and Flo Oy Wong, organized a retrospective exhibition and symposium on the brilliant Chinese American abstract painter Bernice Bing, who had died in 1998.

Relationships and conversations in private as well as on panels are central to my life, and I learn from them as much as from reading. International and national exchanges on feminism and multiculturalism continue to preoccupy me. These have included conferences, research, and frequent travel abroad—to the Soviet Union, North Africa, and Asia—as well as maintaining my lifelong connection with Europe. For me, the decade began with a conference in Venice, "Expanding Internationalism," and "A Meeting of the Worlds, " in Joensuu, Finland, in which you also participated.

itself. Speeded up by technology and information, increasingly engaged with very complicated political forces, and more and more expansive—each project was a collaboration with a large and diverse group of artists—we consistently put ourselves into compromising situations, caught between radical politics and the institutions we wanted to change.

MOIRA ROTH: Collaboration, not only a creative pleasure, but also a most appropriate mode for cross-cultural exchange and analysis, has become second nature to me these days.

In the early 1990s, Diane Tani and I created Visibility Press in order to publish a series of catalogues on Bay Area artists Bernice Bing, Betty

It is only last year that I have come up with a shape, a vehicle, for trying to connect poetically these interests and experiences of mine. I am now in the midst of writing a series of essays collectively entitled "Traveling Companions/ Fractured Worlds," which are being published by the *Art Journal*, which are drawn from my reading in fiction, travel, and my reactions to public events.

At the Time of Writing

MOIRA ROTH: In 1999, I saw your *Code 33* performance, which involved 100 police and 150 youth, together with neighborhood representatives and dancers and took place in a multistory Oakland garage. It was a visually stunning performance, composed in colors (red, white, and black cars) and geometry (circles of participants). There were dramatic stage sets on the various floors of the garage and projections of videos along the walls overlooking the city. The performance was illuminated by flood, car, and helicopter lights, and the changing natural light from sunset to darkness—all seen against the background of the Bay Bridge and a distant San Francisco. Everything was choreographed in terms of the timing and movement of hundreds of participants, and watched by a circulating audience.

SUZANNE LACY: Although still recent, I think *Code 33* will prove to be pivotal for me. Since working in Oakland, I have become more alert to the possibilities and pitfalls of working within institutions. It's a treacherous terrain, one filled

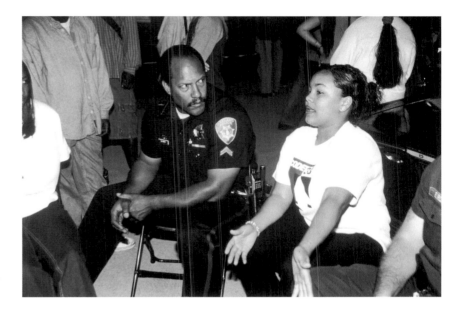

with opportunities for imperfection. But it is an inevitable trajectory for public/political artists. If we look at efficacy as one component of evaluating public art, then eventually we have to take on the institutionalization of change. When we do, we run the risk of the art disappearing altogether.

In the case of *Code 33*, I spent so much time on the institutional relationships and community building that laid the foundation for the performance, that I often wondered if there would be any art left. Conversely, the extravagance of the final performance and the economic expenditures in making it aesthetically powerful made it questionable to some community activists, although their political goals were similar to ours.

99
Suzanne Lacy, *Code 33*, 1999. Performance with 150 youth and 100 police officers, Oakland, Calif. Photo: Amy Sayder.

MOIRA ROTH: There were, of course, many levels to the reading of the piece. I wondered, as I so often do with your large performances, what would happen (could happen?) after the event itself? Does one judge such a performance, as *Code 33*, a year or so later, in terms of political change in the city of Oakland? No. But is this inevitably a question that surfaces? Yes.

You asked yourself if there would be "any art left in the project." My answer would be a resounding yes. *Code 33* was grand public art yet with many opportunities during the process for intimacy and an odd sort of privacy of exchange. (For example, there was a haunting moment before the public performance began in which, as a response to a group warm-up exercise, a tough policeman and a young fragile girl laughingly mimicked each other's movements.) The frequency and evocative quality of those moments always amaze me in your work, given its quality of spectacle.

SUZANNE LACY: Yes, in *Code 33*, there were intense and highly symbolic public relationships as well as intimate and private ones—between the youth and police, artists and activists, youth and adults, and people of different races. The process created its own rather extensive community of collaborators, including Julio Morales, the installation artist; Anne Maria Hardeman, Jose Marquez, and Sheva Gross, artists and Web designers; Oakland police sergeant Jeff Israel; Jacques Bronson, the videographer; and Unique Holland, the young woman artist who has collaborated with me since she was 16, and is now graduating from college.

MOIRA ROTH: In such performances, myriad questions always surface about the difficulty of bringing diverse people together, in circumstances that often reflect unequal balances in power and money—diversities based on race, national origin, class, and political agendas. Once people come together, do they share or differ over strategies, agendas. and expectations? Who speaks? Who is the audience(s)? And how does one (and should one?) sustain relationships once the specific organizing unity, be it performance, exhibition, conference, or political goal, ends?

SUZANNE LACY: Ironically, the contradictions of this decade are no more or less than those of the '70s: interracial collaboration is inherently problematic/oppressive; the Left has difficulty understanding art that does not "look" like traditional modes of resistance; critical discourse in the fine arts continually lags behind that of cultural politics; and educational preparation for community art is insufficiently rigorous. There is a direct relationship between the public art of the '90s and the feminist and community-based art of the '70s in California. Feminist art, no less than feminism itself, is at heart a social justice movement.

MOIRA ROTH: In the '70s, Los Angeles had been a

pivotal site for U.S. feminist art activities; in the 1990s, San Francisco and Oakland played a similar role in multicultural politics.

As I write this, I have in front of me a clipping from over a year ago of the *San Francisco Chronicle* (December 12, 1998), in which a headline states: "In a State of Change Minorities will predominate, push California to 60 million [by the year 2040]." In 2001 it is projected that California will be the first state "in which whites are not the majority."

SUZANNE LACY: Where better to explore, through art, the meanings of our problematized and com-plex identities, the urban, technological, and media contexts we live in, and the hybrid cultural milieu of a clearly inevitable future?

Lacy plans to write a book, "Imperfect Art Working in Public." Roth envisions her series of essays, "Traveling Companions/Fractured Worlds," will be published as a book; she also plans to publish the second anthology of her writings on feminist and multicultural art. Most likely they will continue to draw on each other's work, and that of their wide and often overlapping friendship network for inspiration and support.

JOANN HANLEY

WOMEN, ART, AND TECHNOLOGY
A Brief History

When video equipment first became available to artists in the mid-1960s there was no such thing as "video art"—there were no artists making art with video, no media art centers, no museums or galleries exhibiting video art, no university art departments teaching the history or practice of video art, no audience for or collectors of video art. Perhaps most significantly, there were no established canons or hierarchies. No one had any idea what video's potential might be. The field was wide open to anyone and everyone.

The first portable video equipment, known as portapaks, arrived on the scene in 1965—a particularly advantageous moment in both art history and the women's movement. During the late 1960s and early 1970s, the art world, like the world at large, was in a state of flux. Process art, earthworks, happenings, performance, and conceptual art all challenged modernism's hegemony in the art world while feminism, student uprisings, the sexual revolution, and the Civil Rights movement attacked the political status quo. Women were becoming more vocal and women artists more visible, as they began to create and claim images of themselves that challenged traditional stereotypes.

During the 1970s, video, unlike the tradition-bound, male-dominated fields of painting and sculpture, offered women artists an opportunity, perhaps for the first time, to work on an equal footing with their male counterparts. In general, they were

311

attracted to video for the same reasons as male artists—the immediate feedback, the opportunity to work with the elements of time and sound, and the relative flexibility and low cost compared to film. They were also concerned with many of the same issues—manipulation of time and space; experimentation with genres such as narrative, diary, documentary, essay/personal statement; image processing and abstraction; and articulation of the self through video and performance.

Where women artists differed, however, from their male counterparts and where they greatly impacted future video art practice was in their return to content and their embrace of subjectivity. Free to use the medium in any way that interested them, women from around the world and from many disciplines—social scientists, historians, political activists, as well as artists—used video in surprisingly similar ways to investigate personal and political issues relating to gender and sexuality. Women artists ventured outside the prevailing modernist interest in material and form to infuse their works with personal history and social and cultural criticism, thereby laying the groundwork for much of the art, including video art, that would follow in the 1980s and 1990s.

In the early 1970s, artists everywhere were eager to use not only video, but also new electronic and telecommunications technologies such as fax machines, video phones, computers, lasers, holograms, xerography, and satellite transmission. In California, home to institutions such as Lockheed, McDonnell Douglas, Xerox-PARC, the California Institute of Technology, and the Jet Propulsion Laboratory, new technologies originally developed for defense and aerospace purposes were starting to find their way into everyday life. Silicon Valley was on the verge of becoming a rich technological resource for Bay Area artists. Concurrently, women artists were eager to access the knowledge and facilities housed in the halls of these venerated (and primarily male) bastions of invention and innovation. During the 1970s California-based artists such as Sherrie Rabinowitz and Sharon Grace envisioned using these technologies to create real-time networked environments for collaboration among artists in far-flung locations.

In September 1977, Sharon Grace played a key role in the creation of "SEND/RECEIVE"—one of the first interactive satellite events involving artists' participation. This pioneering telecommunication project was organized by Carl Loeffler of La Mamelle Art Center in San Francisco and Liza Bear and Keith Sonnier of Send/Receive in New York. Working with NASA engineers and artists at NASA's Mountain View, California, facility (where she was employed as an artist/technician), Grace produced three days of live interactive programming which was transmitted by the NASA satellite and broadcast on cable television throughout the New York and San Francisco communities. Concerts, performances, and interactive conversations took place between musicians, dancers, conceptual artists, and philosophers on opposite sides of the country. Grace, working with NASA engineer Skip Gross, successfully created a split screen joining the two coasts in "cyberspace." While attending CalArts in the early 1970s, Grace was the only woman in an apprenticeship program founded by Nam June Paik. Today, she continues her investigative work with interactive video installations, focusing on grammar-guided speech recognition technology.

From 1975 through 1977 Sherrie Rabinowitz with her partner Kit Galloway developed a series of projects called *Aesthetic Research in Telecommunications*. Among these was the *Satellite Arts Project—A Space with No Geographical Boundaries*. Central to the project was research that would use the performing arts as a mode of investigating the possibilities and limitations of technologies to create and augment new contexts and environments for telecollaborative arts. In a time when satellites were the only viable means of transmitting live TV-quality video across oceans, Rabinowitz and her team focused on transmission delays over long-distance networks. Her activities later on (with Galloway) include the creation of the mother of all cybercafes and the world's first cybercafe network—the Electronic

Cafe International. ECI was originally commissioned in 1984 as part of the L.A. Olympics Arts Festival by the Los Angeles Museum of Contemporary Art. Groundbreaking activities, such as a networked cultural research lab, continue today at the cafe's headquarters in Santa Monica— now a unique international network of multimedia telecommunications venues with over forty affiliates around the globe.

By the 1980s California-based women artists such as Vibeke Sorensen and Margaret Crane were also actively investigating the possibilities of computers and the newly available Internet. Vibeke Sorensen's interest in moving beyond video (she began working with it in the early 1970s) was prompted by her realization that the signals of the video camera, audio and electronic music world, video synthesizer, and 3-D computer graphics would converge and that digital networked telecommunications would connect them together. In the early 1980s she became the director of the Computer Graphics Program at Pasadena's Art Center College of Design and a visiting associate instructor in computer science at Cal Tech, an unpaid position which gave her access to the facilities. Subsequently she established the Computer Animation Laboratory at the California Institute of the Arts, where she was a faculty member in the Experimental Animation Program. During this time a grant from the National Science Foundation enabled her to work with scientists on "interactive stereoscopic animation"—known today as virtual reality. She also gained access to the renowned Jet Propulsion Laboratory, where she consulted as a computer animator on a number of space missions. She continues her activities today at the University of Southern California's Division of Animation and Digital Arts.

Since 1984, San Francisco-based artist and writer Margaret Crane, with her collaborator Jon Winet, has been conjoining art and technology to produce work which revolves around the language and images of the information age. From 1997 to 1998, they were artists in residence with the short-lived Xerox-PARC PAIR program. The program paired artists with scientists and researchers working at Xerox's Palo Alto think tank and attempted to bridge the gap between artists and scientists by using technology as a common language. The artists all lived in the San Francisco Bay Area and were already using technology in an advanced and interesting way. (Other women artists with PARC PAIR included Jeanne C. Finley and Pamela Z.) Crane worked with researchers exploring the intersection of art and technology and the impact of the Internet and interactive media on public space. Crane and Winet went on to work on "Democracy—The Last Campaign," a multimedia project focusing on the year 2000 presidential elections.

Technologically based art made its first major museum appearance in California in 1969 when *The Machine as Seen at the End of the Mechanical Age*, curated by Pontus Hulten for New York's Museum of Modern Art, traveled to the San Francisco Museum of Art. Many of the works were kinetic but there was a video sculpture by Nam June Paik as well as works by a handful of women—notably Lillian Schwartz, Lucy Jackson Young, and Marian Zazeela. One year later, curator Maurice Tuchman presented the exhibition *Art and Technology* at the Los Angeles County Museum of Art. Tuchman matched a number of artists, including Claes Oldenburg, Andy Warhol, James Turrell, and Robert Irwin, with engineers and resources from major technology corporations in the United States. Not one woman was asked to participate in the *Art and Technology* show. The Los Angeles Council of Women Artists demonstrated against the museum.

During the 1970s, video art in California, as elsewhere, developed within an alternative infrastructure nurtured by the parallel growth of public arts funding (the National Endowment for the Arts, state and local arts councils, and private funding such as the Rockefeller Foundation). Early video makers found that keeping up with the quickly evolving, high-end consumer tools of electronic media was expensive. As a result, artists would often form informal collectives to share equipment and serve as crew members for each other. For example, in Los Angeles there was the Venice Beach scene, home to the Environmental Communications group and the Video Venice News collective, where the casual visitor might discover video in a storefront on the boardwalk. Artists gathered at informal salons in Venice studios on Friday nights to view work. In Pasadena and Highland Park another group centered around Pasadena's very supportive public-access cable channel, while African American artists such as Barbara McCullough, Senga Nengudi, and Maren Hassinger gathered at Studio Z.

By the mid-1970s video art's funding had developed into programs for both individual artists and a nationwide system of regional media arts centers. These emerging sites of alternative cultural activity typically offered production facilities, training workshops, and active exhibition programs that positioned video within a critical environment of other disciplines that often included film, music, performance, photography, and the visual arts. Screenings by visiting artists were common and were often accompanied by discussions with local audiences about the work and news from the growing field.

Women artists in the Bay Area and Southern California were especially active. In 1976, the Los Angeles Women's Video Center was established at the Woman's Building. Founded by Annette Hunt, Candace Compton, Nancy Angelo, and Jerri Allyn, the Center supported the work of, among others, Nancy Buchanan, Cheri Gaulke, Susan Mogul, Suzanne Lacy, Sheila Ruth, Judith Barry, and Vanalyne Green. An impressive 350 videotapes were produced, many of them during the first decade of the Women's Video Center's existence.

The inauguration of a video department at the Long Beach Museum of Art in 1974 led to the establishment of the museum's unique Video Annex, an internationally known video program which provided not only exhibition opportunities, but also much needed low-cost production and post-production facilities for artists. Thanks to the leadership of adventurous and forward-thinking female curators Nancy Drew (1978–79), Kathy Huffman (1979–84), Jackie Kain (1984–85), and Carole Ann Klonarides (1991–95), the Long Beach Museum of Art forged ahead, making certain that work by California video artists made its way into the world and that the world of video made its way to California. In 1980, Kathy Huffman, in response to an invitation to participate in an international tape exchange with the American Center in Paris, organized an exhibition of work by California artists that included Hildegarde Duane, Sherrie Rabinowitz, Nancy Buchanan, Branda Miller, Patti Podesta, and Ilene Segalove. For many of these artists it was the first time their work had been shown outside the United States—possibly even outside of California. Huffman also played a key role in attempting to establish a venue for video arts on cable television—an idea so far ahead of its time that it has yet to happen. An artist-in-residence program was also established at the museum's Video Annex. The museum's extensive and rich collection of videotapes (all of which were either produced or screened at Long Beach) continues to be one of the largest archives of artists' videotapes in the country and houses the entire collection of tapes made at the Los Angeles Woman's Building.

Several other alternative spaces were also established in Los Angeles during the 1970s. Los Angeles Contemporary Exhibitions (LACE) showed video from its inception in 1979. However, it wasn't until LACE moved to its new facilities on Industrial Street in 1986 that, under the leadership of director Joy Silverman and video curator/artist Anne Bray, a room specifically designed for viewing video was created, as well as VideoLACE, the video programming committee. Bray also created and administered an online video editing program, which provided access at reduced rates for artists at Hollywood post-production facilities, as well as workshops and referral services. Like her counterparts at the Long Beach Museum of Art, Bray was instrumental in getting work created in California out into the world via touring exhibitions, a small distribution program, and a tape archive. During the 1980s, visiting curators always made it a point to stop both at LACE and in Long Beach to

find out what was happening with video in California.

Other pioneering Los Angeles media arts organizations include Visual Communications (founded in 1970), still active today and considered by many to be the premier Asian Pacific media arts center in the United States. Through its production, exhibition, and editing facilities, EZTV (founded in 1979) provided one of the few outlets for moving-image makers who found (or deliberately placed) themselves outside not only the Hollywood mainstream, but the art world as well. EZTV has expanded to include multimedia production and a cybergallery in its continuing support of the media arts community. Active exhibition programs also existed at the Los Angeles Institute of Contemporary Art (LAICA, founded in 1973) and the Los Angeles Center for Photographic Studies (LACPS, founded in 1974).

A number of video-friendly organizations also flourished in the Bay Area. San Francisco organizations such as Video Free America (founded in 1970 by artists Skip Sweeney and JoAnne Kelly), the Film Arts Foundation (founded in 1976 and still going strong), and the Bay Area Video Coalition (BAVC, founded in 1976) supported video artists via workshops, screenings, and production and post-production facilities. Today, under the leadership of Sally Jo Fifer, BAVC is still one of the best regional media arts centers in the country and an invaluable resource for Bay

Area artists. New Langton Arts was founded in 1975 by a coalition of artists, performers, and arts professionals who wanted a center for research and experimentation in performance, visual arts, music, media arts, literature, and cross-disciplinary works. Early New Langton Arts co-director Judy Moran (1970s) and board member, curator, and artist Jeanne C. Finley (1980s) made certain video was an integral part of New Langton's programming. Artspace, founded by Anne MacDonald in 1984 as an exhibition space for explorative and edgy work, also gave grants to writers and was one of the first organizations to provide a free video editing facility. Today the office has moved to New York, where it focuses on publishing original texts and illustrations under the name of Artspace Books. Nancy Frank and Darlene Tong were equally supportive of video at La Mamelle, an art space created specifically to support new, "non-commercial" art forms such as performance, conceptual art, and video. The winter 1976 edition of *La Mamelle Magazine: Art Contemporary* was devoted to video art. Exhibitions in the late 1960s and early 1970s at the DeSaisset Museum in Santa Clara (under curator Lydia Modi-Vitale) and at the University of California, Berkeley Art Museum helped to legitimize video art within established art institutions. The Bay Area also had its share of video collectives—among them Ant Farm, T. R. Uthco, and Optic Nerve. With the exception of Optic Nerve (where

Lynn Adler and Sherrie Rabinowitz did some work), the San Francisco groups had few, if any, women members.

By the end of the 1970s video art had been integrated into California academia through art, media art, and communications departments whose faculty members included early video practitioners. Among them were such California-based artists as Nancy Buchanan, Theresa Hak Kyung Cha, Janice Tanaka, Suzanne Lacy, Susan Mogul, Lynn Hershman Leeson, Eleanor Antin, Shirley Clarke, Martha Rosler, and in later years, Jeanne C. Finley, Max Almy, Vibeke Sorensen, Valerie Soe, Meena Nanji, Jennifer Steinkamp, Diana Thater, Sara Roberts, Erika Suderberg, Victoria Vesna, Tran T. Kim-Trang, and the list goes on. These women taught at places like the California Institute of the Arts (which by 1971 had established a film/video degree program), the University of California at Los Angeles, the University of California at San Diego, the Otis Art Institute, the Art Center of Design Pasadena, San Francisco Art Institute, Mills College, San Francisco State University, and the California College of Arts and Crafts. The emerging California art video community was further enriched by faculty and student contact with internationally respected visiting artists such as Joan Jonas, Steina, Ulrike Rosenbach, Valie Export, Shigeko Kubota, Mary Lucier, and Mako Idemitsu, to name but a few.

By the 1980s most alternative art spaces in California were regularly exhibiting video, both as single-channel tapes and installations. When the Los Angeles Museum of Contemporary Art opened in 1983, a video and performance curator, Julie Lazar, was already in place. In 1988 a media arts department was established at the San Francisco Museum of Modern Art.

The 1980s was also the decade of the video festival and California was home to two of the most prestigious. The short-lived but influential San Francisco Video Festival debuted in 1980 and ended in 1986. Tapes from all over the world were screened, as well as work by such California-based artists as Max Almy, Judith Barry, Ilene Segalove, Susan Mogul, Branda Miller, and Patti Podesta. A San Francisco magazine with an international circulation, *Video 80*, published a festival issue each year.

In 1981 the American Film Institute (AFI) established the National Video Festival. During the festival's most exciting and vibrant years (from 1981 to 1989), hundreds of curators and artists from around the world ventured to the AFI's Los Angeles campus for several days of intense video immersion. Festivalgoers could see everything from demonstrations of the newest technology (high-definition television in 1986, virtual reality in 1987, interactive videodiscs in 1988) to programs devoted to such diverse topics as early television, Japanese video art, student

work from the former Yugoslavia, and world premieres of artist tapes and installations.

During the 1990s, as California entered a recession, monies for video (and most art) began to diminish. The American Film Institute's attempts to keep the video festival alive by making it part of its annual international film festival were unsuccessful. However, a new and important Los Angeles-based festival and organization, L.A. Freewaves, founded by Anne Bray, debuted at the 1989 AFI Festival. Under Bray's leadership and in an unprecedented collaborative effort, more than thirty L.A.-area media and arts organizations presented a three-week celebration of independent video; the festival programs traveled to fifteen sites and included screenings, exhibitions, installations, panel presentations, and cablecasts that reached audiences across Southern California. Through the production of multi-location, citywide festivals, L.A. Freewaves continues to nurture and expand the Southern California video arts community. Selected programs from its festivals are distributed free of charge to area high schools and public libraries and are available for distribution throughout the world.

As we enter the twenty-first century, it appears that video has finally been accepted as a legitimate means for making art. Advances in video, computer, and digital technologies make exhibiting easier for artists, museums, and galleries.

Equipment access is not the problem it once was. The increased popularity of the installation form—which often incorporates video and was pioneered by many video artists (most notably in California by Lynn Hershman Leeson) and the incorporation of video into sculptural forms now offers galleries and museums new ways of exhibiting video. Visitors are no longer required to sit in chairs and watch a television set to experience video art. The art world's recent renewed interest in the artists and genres of the 1970s—performance, conceptual art, and video—has also helped video's cause. California has become an acknowledged international art center in recent years, with an exciting and influential community of contemporary artists who use video and who are becoming well known internationally. On the down side, it continues to be difficult for emerging artists to find funding and a place to exhibit their work. Mounting large-scale exhibitions involving technology continues to be extremely expensive and sponsors hard to find.

Video's acceptance in the art world over the relatively short span of thirty years (compare this to how long it took photography to come into its own as an art form) is directly related to the speed with which technology in general has developed. We presently encounter video technology in our everyday lives with a familiarity and frequency heretofore unknown—and consequently are more open to its presence as an art form. The good news is that we are now dealing with generations of both artists and audiences who have never known a world without television or computers or artists who use technology to make art. Best of all, thanks to the efforts of the pioneering women artists and art professionals clustered in California, the notion that women can make art with video—or any other electronic technology—comes as no surprise to anyone.

NANCY BUCHANAN

WHAT DO WE WANT?

The Subject Behind the Camera:
Women Video Artists and Self-Articulation

The figures sigh and bow, their arms tremble as scenes of murder play across their satin skirts, in slow motion, repeating backwards and forwards. The inflated sculptures seem full of grace, suffering these images. Anne Bray and Molly Cleator first installed their video piece, Double Burning Jagged Extremities *(1998), in a warehouse adjacent to a movie theater in Pasadena—which, appropriately enough, shows mainstream films whose images often resemble the artists' video projections. Their work brings to mind earlier black-veiled, witnessing figures from Suzanne Lacy and Leslie Labowitz's* In Mourning and in Rage, *a performance that took place at Los Angeles City Hall in 1976. Confronting violence against women, specifically television's shrill presentation which seemed to insist on the inevitability of women as victims of the notorious "Hillside Strangler," the artists created a media event, seizing the opportunity to present their own perspective to the public. They framed the performance, including subsequent TV coverage of it, within their own video production (directed and edited by Annette Hunt and Sheila Ruth). Subsequently, a measurable result was publication of rape hotline crisis center numbers by the telephone company.*

Merging art and political power was a central goal of the 1970s women's movement. Women artists both here and abroad recognized their objectification and sought a new language with which to portray themselves as human subjects. And, what better medium to use in attempting this than video, the preeminent tool for creating endless

100
Anne Bray and Molly Cleator,
*Double Burning Jagged
Extremities*, 1998. Pasadena,
Calif. Video projections on three
kinetic figures, 15 × 8 × 8 ft.
each. Collection of the artist.

Intersections: Themes and Practices

desire and objectification? The very different yet somehow parallel figures in the two video pieces/performances described above serve as markers for both the early and late histories of California video art, and epitomize this quest.

Nell Tenhaaf has identified a central contradiction in women's use of electronic tools, in that the technological realm has long been deemed a "masculine" world; in order to claim our own space there, new methods of representation are necessary.[1] However, especially in California, women eagerly grabbed the first clunky portapaks

to use in creating their own videos, and many immersed themselves in understanding the electronic signal itself. This took place both within and outside of newly formed women artists' groups. Having acquired a black-and-white portapak in the mid-1970s, Cynthia Maughan developed her own humorous yet chilling response to oppression, making short works in which torn clothing, bandaged scars, and ironic texts compressed horrific histories into a very few minutes. In *Thank You, Jesus* (1981), Maughan matter-of-factly recounts waking up in heaven following a car accident. Garish 1950s "moderne" magazine-photo interiors and a vibraphone Quiet Village-like music track are a tortuous accompaniment; heaven ultimately provides no relief from the sexist demands of a horny, macho Jesus.

Ilene Segalove created a series of tapes starring her own mother, who dispensed commonsense advice, foregrounding Segalove's ambivalent attitude toward her mother as role model. Both Maughan and Segalove worked largely alone, whereas Nina Sobell's *Interactive Electroencephalographic Video Drawings* (1973, and ongoing) involved work with technical assistants to create graphic displays of couples' emotional relationships. Participants' brain-wave activity was keyed (the bright area of electrographics appears as linear patterns) over their camera images in a real-time graphic EEG display. The resulting design might be interpreted as compatibility—are the brain waves of the partners similar to each other? In this work, Sobell pushed the technological envelope of video application in equal proportion to her focus on emotional space.

Despite the relative affordability of portable equipment, many artists could neither afford their own, nor desired the responsibility of maintenance. Also, many saw the natural bridge to collaborative work, which was already taking place in other media, particularly installation works. When Judy Chicago brought her Feminist Art Program to the California Institute of the Arts

101
Nina Sobell, *Interactive Electroencephalographic Video Drawings*, 1973. Sepulveda Veterans Administration Neuropsychology Laboratory, Sepulveda, Calif. Still from video. Collection of the artist. Photo: Wayne McCall. Collection of the artist, courtesy Sean Kelly, New York.

in 1971, video was a key element within its design program. Susan Mogul spent most of her time with the video equipment, and crafted her own version of the consciousness-raising/confessional mode of 1970s feminism, but transformed it into a mature documentary style which resonates within her work of the 1990s. *Take Off* (1974), Mogul's answer to Vito Acconci's aggressively masturbatory videotape *Undertone*, transformed a confrontation with the viewer into a frank, girlfriend-to-girlfriend discussion of the benefits of vibrators.

Mogul continued to work with the Feminist Art Program when it broke with CalArts, and became independent of outside academic oversight in its consolidation at the Woman's Building. Video was omnipresent, preserving the voices of women who had dropped everything to be part of the Feminist Studio Workshop. Among these were lesbian students seeking role models, black women writers, and incest survivors who shared their experiences long before such speaking out became acceptable. Matriarchs and relatives were honored in many videotaped performances, and the everyday labor of carpentry was recorded lovingly by Sheila Ruth in *Constructing the Woman's Building* (1973), her documentary of repairing the old industrial building in Los Angeles. In fact, emphasis on process fostered many works which might never have been made had they depended on storyboarding and conventional pre-visual-ization. One priceless video document reveals how Nancy Angelo and Candace Compton developed personas on a trip to San Francisco. Using a still camera, the "deviant" and the "nun" photographed one another in various public and semi-public places. The video shows them compiling these photos, discussing them almost as if they were Kirilian documents of ghosts. Their subsequent *Nun and Deviant* tape (1976) enables a process of first articulating the mask one has been given (nun/good girl–deviant/bad girl), then allowing it to crumble as one finds within oneself the contradictions of its repressive boundaries. Such a self-reflective process underscores the influence of Feminist Art Program founders Judy Chicago, Arlene Raven, and Sheila Levrant de Bretteville. A 1979 video interview with Raven, in particular, is as revolutionary today—perhaps more so—as when it was recorded. Raven espouses the validity of Sapphic education—the reciprocal shared learning. Raven's notion was that if explorations and growth are undertaken by both teacher and student, the results of their interaction will be far more profound than those generated within a hierarchical model.

Martha Rosler's *Vital Statistics of a Citizen, Simply Obtained* (1977) is a landmark tape that plays out the struggle with rules, norms and perfection, as she allows each part of her body to be measured and recorded as to its achievement of an ideal average. Rosler's examination of

102
Barbara McCullough, *Shopping Bag Spirits and Freeway Fetishes: Reflections on Ritual Space*, 1981. Still from video. Photo: Roderick Kwaku Young.

women's often obsessional relationship with food was explored both within her postcard series as well as with such videotapes as *Semiotics of the Kitchen* (1975), in which she demonstrated an arsenal of ordinary utensils that could perhaps be used as weapons, and *Losing: A Conversation with the Parents* (1977), a staged "interview" with the parents of a deceased anorexic as well as a discussion of the politics of hunger. While Rosler pursued a unique form of docudrama, soap operas and melodramas were employed by Eleanor Antin, who allowed her characters (such as Ballerina, King, Nurse) to dictate their own stories. Staged

as performances, installations, and for videotapes, a work such as *The Nurse and the Hijacker* (1977), in which brave Nurse Eleanor saved the day (while pursued by numerous lovers), evolved into Antin's portrayal of Florence Nightingale and the real-life drama of nursing's dangers and achievements.

At UCLA, Shirley Clarke stood out from her (mostly male) colleagues on the film school faculty for daring to encourage creativity and personal expression, and was a mentor for Barbara Mc-Cullough and O. Funmilayo Makarah. In her hourlong *Shopping Bag Spirits and Freeway Fetishes:*

Women Video Artists and Self-Articulation

Valerie Soe, *All Orientals Look the Same,* 1986. Still from video. Collection of the artist.

Intersections: Themes and Practices

Reflections on Ritual Space (1981), McCullough interviewed other African American artists about their use of ritual. Visual/performance artists Betye Saar and Senga Nengudi discussed their assemblages of charged objects and imagery. McCullough also included a colorized video version of her own film, *Water Ritual #1: An Urban Rite of Purification* (1979). *Water Ritual* involved stylistically based actions at a charged site where an entire neighborhood in Los Angeles had been razed to accommodate the Century Freeway. A young woman employs water, including that which passes through her own body, to sanctify two remaining ruins. Makarah was also attending UCLA, and had amassed a number of valuable community interviews and other works which she stored in the archives when she decided to study

and work in Germany at the close of the 1970s—tragically, these tapes have been lost. But, returning to UCLA and finding herself still isolated as a woman of color, Makarah's response was *Define* (1988). While the tape's performance segment of Kelly Hashimoto hanging by her long hair at a campus quadrangle was shocking, the tape's central image was artist Yreina Cervantez, wearing bright Central American garments and blindfolded with a swath of African kinte cloth, scattering words written on strips of paper while Makarah and Hashimoto reassuringly called her name. The three artists enacted a bond of shared understanding, resulting from yet also moving beyond their individual identities.

Clarke's daughter, Wendy Clarke, displayed a generosity similar to her mother's. With her *Love Tapes* project, spanning many years and continents, Clarke supplied the bare bones of consciousness-raising techniques to participants whom she invited to enter a private space, select a three-minute background music tape, and talk to the camera about their experiences of love. Rather than being intimidated by the camera's presence, which might have resulted in the stunted responses we see regularly on broadcast television wherein a speaker either reiterates a cliché or perhaps appears incoherent, Clarke's environment allowed participants to control their situation and to express opinions privately, knowing they would have the power to erase their own tape. Indeed, video offered perhaps the single most powerful tool for insisting on the dialogic voice. As soon as inexpensive camcorders and VHS home tape decks became available in the 1980s, an explosion of expression resulted within independent media and art venues.

A concurrent theoretical challenge has been to address "difference" adequately, and video artists tackled that problem in their earliest works.[2] The delicate balance of group and individual identity is framed more negatively in Valerie Soe's *All Orientals Look the Same* (1986), in which successive faces belie the endless repetition of the cliché title on the soundtrack. In 1998, Janice Tanaka completed *No Hop Sing, No Bruce Lee: What Do You Do When None of Your Heroes Look Like You?* a work for her son that questions visible role models for young, heterosexual Asian men, and forms a trilogy with earlier video portraits of her mother (*Memories from the Department of Amnesia*, 1990) and her father—whose mental health was permanently affected by his experience of internment (*Who's Going to Pay for These Donuts, Anyhow?* 1992).

Analogously, Jeanne C. Finley's *Conversations Across the Bosphorus* (1995) examined ways in which Muslim women share questions of faith, but also how communication outside one's cultural group is possible. Meena Nanji poetically interpreted continuing restrictions imposed on women from traditional Islamic backgrounds

(*Voices of the Morning*, 1992). Jane Cottis's humorous *War on Lesbians* (1992) literalizes the media's "demonization" of gay culture, while the collaborative *Dry Kisses Only*, produced with Kaucylia Brooke, offered a re-reading of classic films that foregrounded lesbian subtexts. In her book *The Third Eye: Race, Cinema, and Ethnographic Spectacle*, Fatimah Tobing Rony scrutinizes the elements of the original *King Kong*, proposing its ethnographic representation as "teratological," that is, related to the study of monstrosity. But, as she herself is of Indonesian descent, her scholarly investigation of the movie's portrayal of Skull Islanders "as the most savage" natives and "coded as black [but] also explicitly geographically situated off the coast of Sumatra, in what today is called Indonesia," led her to produce *On*

105
Meena Nanji, *Voices of the
Morning,* 1992. Still from video.
Collection of the artist.

Cannibalism (1994), her personal video response to this material. Tran T. Kim-Trang's *Blindness* series, consisting of eight tapes (1991–), encompasses ideas about physical and metaphorical lack of sight. *Operculum* examines the look of the eye itself. Tran recorded her visits to eight plastic surgeons who offered free consultations on what might be entailed in cosmetic surgery to "correct" her Vietnamese eyelids. Also part of this

same project, *ekleipsis* recreates the experiences of a group of hysterically blind Cambodian women living in Long Beach, replicating the process by which they gradually regained their sight as they replaced the trauma of war with glimpses of a safer life. In *El Espejo/The Mirror* (1991), Frances Salomé España dreamed of crossing the border, but poetically positioned herself in the nowhere-land of East L.A. The curator and cultural historian Chon Noriega pointed out that slippage between English and Spanish opened up this video to historical/cultural readings: "España refers to the bees as moscas, which means flies and is slang for the helicopters that search for undocumented workers."[3] Sixteen-year-old Kimiko Roberts made *Cultural Identity Crisis of an All-American Girl* in a 1992 Youth Production Workshop taught by Martha Chono-Helsley at the Long Beach Museum Video Annex. She used the opportunity to eloquently face recurrent queries as to her ethnicity, which is African American and Japanese, and to affirm her uniqueness. For Chono-Helsley and other media artists such as Gina Lamb, Cheri Gaulke, Eve Luckring, Jessica Irish, and Greta Snider, mentoring young women and men is an extremely important part of carrying forward the task of subject-to-subject recognition, replacing the old subject-object relationship. Bicoastal educator-producer DeeDee Halleck's establishment of Paper Tiger TV on the West Coast also has been most influential for a

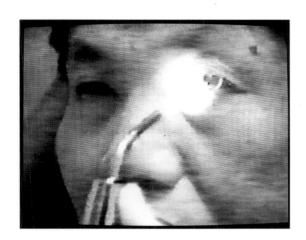

younger generation of artist-activists, who have produced shows both for this Manhattan-based cable series as well as for the satellite-distributed DeepDish TV. Following the 1992–93 Los Angeles uprising, Julia Meltzer and Liz Canner compiled a program entitled *Hands on the Verdict*, and later researched and produced a documentary about the Los Angeles police department, *State of Emergency* (1993).

While many of the foregoing examples positively emphasize women speaking for themselves, artist-critic Christine Tamblyn always cautioned that we do not make our stories just as we might like, for we have no language other than the given—usually defined as patriarchal. She demonstrated this by enacting the construction of herself as a "speaking subject" who analyzed her own sexual fantasies (*As the Worm Turns*, 1988). Both humorous and discomforting, Tamblyn's

direct address invoked the tension between voyeur and exhibitionist, while questioning the origins and legitimacy of women's desires. Throughout her career, she merged her identities of critic and artist, producing scandalous conference lectures and theoretical performance tapes. She also produced three feminist CD-ROMs before her untimely death in 1998.

Interactive technology has provided tools for new ways of writing, allowing experiments in reading. Adriene Jenik used the CD-ROM format to offer video as well as Spanish and English translations of the French-language novel *Mauve Désert* by Canadian writer Nicole Brossard, engaging various and sometimes simultaneous levels of the text. The Internet continues its rapid evolution, and many artists are posting clips of their tapes or films, as has veteran Nancy Cain, who originally worked with the Videofreeks in upstate New York in the early 1970s and later with the infamous video collective TVTV—which gained access to broadcast television largely on its own terms.[4]

Lynn Hershman Leeson pioneered interactivity with her laser disk creation *Lorna* (1979), whose fate was determined by viewers—would Lorna break out of her agoraphobia and leave her apartment? or would she shoot herself? Sara Roberts (*Early Programming*, 1988) devised an "emotional engine" program to convey a child's perspective. An angry, somewhat unpredictable mother could

Jennifer Steinkamp, *The TV Room*, 1998. Audio collaboration with Andrew Bucksbarg, Video installation, 18 × 13 × 60 ft. Photo: Alex Slade. Collection of the artist, distributed by ACME, Los Angeles.

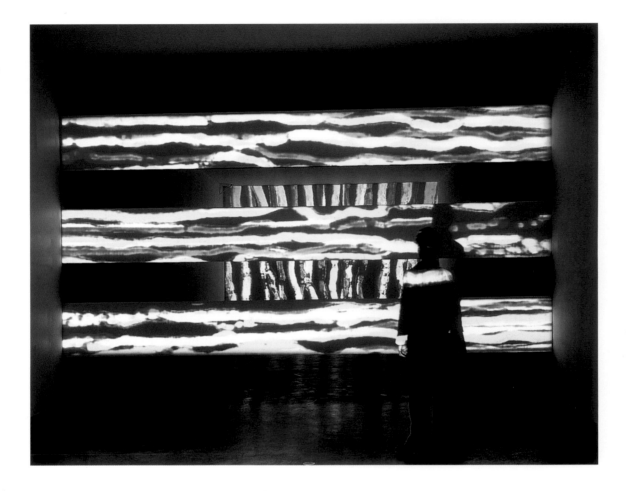

be provoked by computer menu choices. For example, as the pleasurable experience of wind on skin is recalled during a video view out a car window, a computer-generated voice scolds, "You-could-get-your-arm-cut-off-that-way." Such a piece exemplifies a lighter approach to the dynamics of familial power relations.

Other artists confront technology and posi-tion the spectator in subtle ways. Jennifer Stein-kamp uses computer 3-D animation software to create nonrepresentational imagery which she projects within a predetermined architectural space. As the viewers pass through the video pro-jector's throw of light, their shadows become part of the image; artist/curator Carole Ann Klo-narides argues that the viewer thus "become[s]

108
Diana Thater, *Electric Mind*,
1996. Video installation,
Portland Art Museum. Photo:
Fredrik Nilsen. Collection of
the artist.

part of the work and enter[s] a more feminized space than is normally experienced in the museum or gallery." Likewise, Diana Thater puts the viewer in the center of her projections, and works with and against the notion of what is "natural," refusing to hide any equipment in her installation pieces, sometimes additionally revealing the apparatus within the footage. In her work *China* (1995), a recording of two trained wolves shot by six cameras encompasses a 360-degree perspective. The longtime linking of "woman" to "nature" is no accidental reference in Thater's work, yet is interrogated with vigilant sophistication.

Given the strength of the works described here, one might be tempted to conclude that the "work" of women artists to establish their self-articulation is complete, but such a thought would be delusionary. Assumptions are still made based on coded (negative) attributes and behaviors. For example, the author of an art textbook[5] interpreted the collaborative tape Barbara Smith and I made (*With Love from A to B*, 1977) as a male-female romance. Strange to us, since only our hands were shown—one pair giving, the other receiving; in our minds, we illustrated any and all gender combinations. Comparative statistics for male-female representation in gallery and museum exhibitions—as well as regularized teaching jobs—are still unbalanced. And, upon viewing San Francisco video collective Optic Nerve's *50 Wonderful Years*, which covered the 1973 Miss California pageant, a CalArts graduate student who had entered the 1998 Miss Santa Clarita event, spontaneously commented that the tape might have been a recording of her own recent experience. Undoubtedly, women videomakers will continue to employ technological advancements in the ongoing project of what far exceeds autobiography or self-portraiture, but which constitutes the ground of the self.

Notes

Special thanks are due Carole Ann Klonarides for inviting me to join her and JoAnn Hanley in dialogue about the current state of women and video, and for their keen insights.

1 Nell Tenhaaf, "Of Monitors and Men and Other Unsolved Feminist Mysteries: Video Technology and the Feminine," in *Critical Issues in Electronic Media*, ed. Simon Penny, pp. 219–323 (Albany: State University of New York Press, 1995). Tenhaaf concludes her essay by remarking that "Through strategic self-representation, certain video works by women producers have documented the feminist project of freeing the female body from its status as a reflection to be looked upon."

2 See Cecelia Dougherty, "Early Video at the L.A. Woman's Building," *Afterimage* 26, no. 1 (July–August 1998).

3 Chon Noriega, "Talking Heads, Body Politic," in *Resolutions: Contemporary Video Practices*, ed. Michael Renov and Erika Suderburg (Minneapolis: University of Minnesota Press, 1996).

4 One can browse through a list of Nancy Cain's offerings at *http//www.nancysnetwork.com*.

5 Lois Fichner-Rathus, *Understanding Art*, 4th ed. (Englewood Cliffs, N.J.: Paramount Publishing/Prentice Hall, 1995).

Some References on Women/Video

At Home (exhibition catalogue). Text by Arlene Raven. Long Beach, Calif.: Long Beach Museum of Art, 1983.

Cottingham, Laura. *Not for Sale: Feminism and Art in the USA during the 1970s* (video). New York: Hawkeye Productions, 1998.

Dougherty, Cecelia. "Early Video at the L.A. Woman's Building." *Afterimage* 26, no. 1 (July–August 1998).

The First Generation: Women and Video, 1970–75 (video). Curated by JoAnn Hanley, 1993. Independent Curators, New York.

Intersections: Themes and Practices

Fox, Howard N., ed. *Eleanor Antin.* Los Angeles County Museum of Art, 1999.

Gever, Martha. "Video Politics, Early Feminist Projects." *Afterimage* (Summer 1983); reprinted in *Cultures in Contention*, ed. Doug Kahn and Diane Neumaier. Seattle: Real Comet Press, 1984.

Grubb, Nancy, ed. *Making Their Mark: Women Artists Move into the Mainstream, 1970–85.* New York: Abbeville Press, 1989.

Mellencamp, Patricia. *Indiscretions: Avant-Garde Film, Video, and Feminism.* Bloomington and Indianapolis: Indiana University Press, 1990.

Pribram, E. Deidre, ed. *Female Spectators: Looking at Film and Television.* New York: Verso, 1988.

Straayer, Chris. "I Say I Am Feminist: Performance Video in the 70s." *Afterimage* (November 1985).

Sturken, Marita. "Feminist Video: Reiterating the Difference." *Afterimage* (April 1985).

A Survey of American Video: The First Decade (video, eight programs). Produced by Kate Horsfield, 1976. See specifically "Feminist Gendered Confrontations" (program 4). Video Data Bank, Chicago.

Tamblyn, Christine. "Significant Others: Social Documentary as Personal Portraiture in Women's Video of the 1980s." In *Illuminating Video: An Essential Guide to Video Art*, ed. Doug Hall and Sally Jo Fifer. New York: Aperture/BAVC, 1991.

——. "Spectacular Visions Video Art." In *Yesterday and Tomorrow: California Women Artists*, ed. Sylvia Moore. New York: Midmarch Arts Press, 1989.

Trinh T. Minh-ha. *When the Moon Waxes Red: Representation, Gender and Cultural Politics.* New York: Routledge, 1991.

What Does She Want (video, five programs). Conceived and produced by Lyn Blumenthal, 1987. Video Data Bank, Chicago.

Wilding, Faith. *By Our Own Hands.* Los Angeles: Double X/Peace Press, 1977.

Young and Restless (performance-based work by New York video artists). Curated by Stephen Vitiello and co-organized by Barbara London, associate curator, and Sally Berger, curatorial assistant, Department of Film and Video, Museum of Modern Art, New York, 1997. Distributed by Electronic Arts Intermix.

Zegher, Catherine de, ed. *Martha Rosler: Positions in the Real World.* Birmingham, England; Vienna; and Cambridge, Mass.: Ikon Gallery, Generali Foundation, and MIT Press, 1999.

ALLUCQUERE ROSANNE STONE

EPILOGUE

The Baby or the Bath Water; Being an Inquiry into the Nature of Woman, Womyn, Art, Time, and Timing in Five Thousand Words or Less

I confess to being a member of a top secret, elite, strike force, the existence of which is hotly denied by the very society within which we operate. I can reveal it to you because no one other than yourself will ever read about it. By now every copy of the book containing the essay you are now reading was pulled from bookstores' shelves and destroyed. How you came into possession of this, possibly the last remaining copy, I can only imagine. Perhaps you found it misfiled, spine facing inward, in a sec-ondhand bookstore. Or maybe you noticed it wedged up underneath your commuter train seat. However it made its way to you, you and I are alone with each other, sole survivors of the wreck of a discourse, bound irrevocably by the life preserver of our mutual secret.

And so I can speak freely. Come a little closer . . . there, that's better.

Here Beginneth the Tale

Barely seventy years have passed (she said in a conspiratorial whisper, drawing her shawl more snugly about her) since the great brain surgeon James G. Fitzsimmons first published his study, but its importance went unremarked until your Uncle Nilsson stumbled upon it during a literature search in 1983. Most medical imaging researchers recall the work, because likely they read it in freshman radiology, just as your grandfather and I did. The gist of it, as they say, is that in the course of an otherwise routine paper for the *Journal of Phrenological Studies*, Fitzsimmons mentioned an anomaly in one of the X-ray plates in his series on the brain: an odd thickening about the size of an almond, just dorsal to the hippocampus and proximal to Wernicke's area. Fitzsimmons mentioned—almost as an afterthought, it seemed to me—that the odd structure happened to be in the only image of a female brain in his study. But sixty more years would have to pass before your uncle, during a routine archive search, would stumble upon the tiny, dense area of the emulsion on Fitzsimmons's original plate and name it the *bilateral vernix*, by which it is still known. The bilateral vernix is of interest to us now because it is, like your black sheep cousin LeVay's "gay brain," a physical marker of a hotly contested and even (here a wan smile touched the corners of her mouth) culturally constructed category: *It is only found in women artists.*

No one has studied how Jesse Helms came to possess this esoteric bit of information. However, it explains Helms's actions in the spring of 1998, when he quietly acquired a controlling interest in Chromo-Tech LLP, a genetic engineering startup specializing in areas of the Y chromosome that code for cerebral development. Most of this was made public earlier this year (she added) in the

form of addenda to a report of the activities of archconservative senators by the independent watchdog group Senate Watch, but it was largely overlooked because the bulk of the report dealt with (she shook her head dismissively) alleged smut peddling on Capitol Hill.

That much is public knowledge; what was not known at the time the report was first published was that Helms was backed by a hastily organized consortium of religious groups, public agencies, and at least two large media conglomerates.

No wonder they were interested. They correctly perceive that if the genes that code for the bilateral vernix can be precisely identified, that part of the chromosome can, with a little more research, be inactivated or excised—a far more cost-effective solution to the problem of women artists than selective prosecution or the gutting of public funding for the arts. (Shaking her finger, she added) And Chromo-Tech is barely getting warmed up.

Unusual structures in the brain are merely the latest addition to what we might call an alternative history of the female body, for the truth is that history is full of accounts of odd traffic within women's bodies. Everyone in critical studies knows the ancient Greeks believed that the womb could wander among the other organs, providing an explanatory framework for women's otherwise unaccountable emotional states. Such passages in old texts have been used to show how women's internal structure was interpretable at whim to satisfy ideas (usually male, she added, rolling her eyes) of how the body worked. Once modern medical science was firmly established, it was beyond question that the wandering womb conjecture was insupportable by any modern observation or diagnostic technique, not to mention the subjective experiences of millions of women—to the point that when, in 1949, Melba Jackson was admitted to Roosevelt Memorial Hospital in Grand Forks, Idaho with unexplained shoulder pain and the attending doctors were startled to discover that her womb had wandered up into her neck, nobody cared—(here she gave a deep sigh) which leads, not to questions of how psychology influences representation, but instead to ask what happened to women's bodies in the intervening two thousand years to cause their internal organs to settle into fixed locations, and what could that outcome mean to philosophy and medicine.[1]

The rest of the story is almost incomprehensibly terrifying.

So let me introduce myself. I'm in some senses the least likely choice to write this essay that the editors could have made, and in other senses the inevitable outcome of our hesitant but energetic progresses toward the millennium and what it signifies. Call me the token cyborg. Firstly, I got this gig because my students (and I) live at the intersections of a dense tangle of late twentieth-century discourses of art, technology, and the human body. This problematic locus, or maybe better to say moving target, has no name. In part, at least, it has no name because we work hard to keep it that way. A while back I was called upon by the Yale architecture school to go out there and tell them what the name was for what we were doing. Back in the actlab we obediently wrote down syllables on scraps of paper, put them in an oatmeal container, shook it up, and drew out two. From this procedure we determined that the name of our nascent discipline was Fu Qui. I dutifully conveyed this information to Yale. The casual observer would probably be inclined to call Fu Qui by the currently fashionable euphemism "New Media," so to save time and thought I'll do that too for the remainder of the discussion.

It's possible that I came to this work because of a fortuitous association with Cynbe ru Taren, the man who is now my partner in life. Mentioning my husband is not gratuitous, and I'll return to the reasons presently. Cynbe's work involves writing computer code that turns digital scans of the human body into three-dimensional color images. Over time that research became what is now known as the Visible Human project. A brief word about how that works is in order. It involves a partnership between the University of Washington, the University of Colorado, and the State of Texas. U. Washington has, among other researchers, Cynbe;

U. Colorado has a very large vibrating cryogenic microtome, that is, a high-tech meat slicer; and the Great State of Texas has death by lethal injection. A partnership made in heaven. Texas kills and chills; U. Colorado slices and dices; and the digitized result, transmitted from Denver to Seattle through that policy-neutral medium known as the Internet, winds up on Cynbe's desk, where gigabytes of information about a convicted and executed murderer's most intimate anatomy get converted into a cute, blood-free virtual doll with great tattoos, and that any school kid can play with.[2]

When I first heard about the project I immediately thought of Foucault's riff on "The Anatomy Lesson." Wow, I said, here it is updated to the digital age, the sovereign's ultimate power not merely to punish criminals but to atomize their bodies after death. I set about producing a paper on this, but when I discovered that the criminal in question had been delighted at the prospect of being atomized and in fact had volunteered (I'm gonna be in every database in the world? Sign me up, yup, yup), my enthusiasm cooled. So instead I got married. (Some of you, who understand that in some cultures the things I do are considered normal, may recognize this as a logical progression.)[3]

The Author Situates Hirself

But back to the second of my two reasons for writing this. It also, somehow, seems right and meet that the person chosen to close a collection of essays about twentieth-century women artists should be an UnWoman—a member of the female culture club by virtue of another dense and problematic tangle of discourses: the medical, legal, psychological, and political discourses of Transgender. Depending upon whom you ask, I'm either just another gal; woman by choice; born in the wrong body; alien nutcase; sick pretender; tool of the masculinist conspiracy; or the female Prometheus. There's nothing quite like literally embodying controversy.

Without bearing down too hard on the point—that comes later—the message I bring is that it is not only art that is changing, and not only understandings of gender and ethnicity and their relationships to situated art practices and women practitioners; but the foundation of the entire study upon which this book is based. To be precise, it's the concept of Woman that's changing, and it's my considered observation that the issues Transgender raises—what does it mean to say "woman," and how do we know that—are calling into question the ontology of gender as we now understand it; and thus what it means to produce a book that claims to be about women (artists).

Even as I write those words they sound odd, look odd on the page. After all, everyone who reads this knows there is something absolutely grounded about what it means to be called woman. We have a long history of specific oppressions, and attempts at redress, to prove it. Yes, but: Societal needs and societal inertia can preserve irreality for an indefinite time. Witness the report, done for the Nixon administration by (you should excuse the expression) unimpeachable medical and legal authorities, that showed marijuana to be essentially harmless and possibly beneficial. Buried too deep to even find the body, that one was, because society—which is to say, the power structure that gets to say what society means—refused to hear it. It's barely possible, though, that we may be learning to listen.

Perforce I live narrowly and firmly in the Now. This is because the women I teach, or whom I like to think I teach, keep me very much that way. To the best of my knowledge and understanding the beliefs and practices to which they subscribe are grounded in no historical tradition and are realized through no historical praxis. They are the final product of the devaluation of any serious historicity in the U.S., and spiritual heirs of the Hundredth Monkey hypothesis: that lovely and appealing conceit that social phenomena need only achieve a critical mass in one locality to change the entire world.

On the other hand, they may simply know something I don't. After all, they grew up immersed in the densest networks of electronic communication since the beginning of time, and ghu knows how they get their information. In Finland we're observing the emergence of flock-ing and schooling behavior in teens, an unprecedented phenomenon in homo sapiens, a species which has always exhibited pack behavior like primates or wolves. Teen flocking behavior is mediated by cell phones, which in Finland are ubiquitous. Most teens in Helsinki carry them constantly and call each other to report anything interesting taking place on the street. Many use the phone's auto dial function to call a programmed list of friends in rapid-fire succession. The result is that masses of teens coalesce at locations where interesting things are happening, then melt away again to coalesce somewhere else. The electronic prosthesis changes behavior patterns in deep and unforeseen ways. Technology has a way of doing that, most noticeably with young people; just as, though futurists predicted that the automobile would lead to highways, gas stations, and motels, nobody foresaw how the back seat would cause profound changes in teen courtship behavior.

New Media Replicates Early Feminism, maybe

How do women relate to this New Media-fu? Suddenly. Though the form and context may differ, some of you may have experienced this riff: When the actlab started up, its inhabitants were all men, or at least people who had chosen to perform man. The lack of women in this hot new mix of art and technology had been noted long since, usually in the dry, vaguely anxious way of social studies, sometimes in the more fiery manner of political action. The reasons, so they said, were well known. Veterans of some of the battles over this state of affairs try, in their individual manner, to encourage change: For years Brenda Laurel (and occasionally Yours Truly) would make the thankless trek to the Computer Game Developers' Conference and harangue the assembled multitudes about the need to not simply be open to the idea of women in the field, but to actively seek and recruit women. This was particularly poignant, and a particularly vicious sticking point, because of its chicken-and-egg hopelessness: Without women game developers there would be no games for women, and without a sizable women's game market there would be no women developers.

There's an obvious and prickly knot of assumptions in there, starting with the idea that women can't (or worse, shouldn't) write the kinds of violent games in which young men seem to revel; proceeding through the idea that women are better at cooperative, networking, touchy-feely sorts of things, and that society would be better if we could involve women in more of those activities, adding to the mix the Magic of Computer-Mediated-fu; and winding up in the Tarpits of Doom where women teach men how to be kinder and gentler, to give up violence and learn to stroke their inner child instead of their outer member.

Geeks Speak

The first clue we had of the magnitude and shape of the problem, really, came while Brenda was addressing, or possibly yelling at, a group of the Usual Geeks at the Hackers' Conference. Somewhere in the back of the room a hand went up, and a nerdly geek unfolded himself from his chair. "Um," he said, "with all due respect, you've got to realize that some of us went into this field to get away from you."

Could the problem have been better stated? Which is why when the change came, it wasn't incremental, it didn't follow any identifiable cause and effect relationship, and even with the perspective of almost ten years' time I think that attempts to determine such a relationship obscure rather than reveal whatever happened. But anyway: Put briefly, one minute there were no women hackers, and the next minute we were hip deep in young women—kids, really—who wanted to hack. One might have expected them to approach the temple of technology tentatively, with reverence and circumspection. They didn't. They showed up, elbowed the boys aside, and fell to. Some were starting from absolute nada, with no skills at all; at least one had never even been close to a computer. They descended like locusts, and like locusts they chomped up whatever they could find. When they needed help they asked for it, or rather extracted it.

At first the things they made were rough, clumsy, frequently primitive. Left to themselves, what they chose to do bore no relation to any curriculum, real or imagined. But they learned what they needed to know with lightning speed. Given the opportunity, they chose the implements of their emergent culture with discrimination and care. Most interesting, I think, was that they seemed utterly ignorant of history, but—*pace* Santayana—to the best of my knowledge they managed not to relive it. You who were there at the tail end of second wave American feminism may recall many of the same things: The new kids' disregard of and disrespect for their elders, who, rightly or wrongly, felt that they had dug the trenches and deserved consideration for it. In a nation increasingly without any semblance of historical consciousness, it shouldn't be surprising to note the egregious absence in young people of a grasp of history in relation to women's struggle—no, maybe not *absence*, exactly, but more as if what we thought was important in that common history wasn't what they thought was important. The outcome was nearly the same, though: Suddenly we were surrounded by a brand new crop of riot grrrls who took the hard-won freedoms of those who fought for them in the '60s and '70s for granted, and whose summary of those years of work went something like "Thanks a lot, but now would you mind getting out of the way so we can get on with changing the world?" Not the way *we*

wanted to see the world change, mind you; but the way *they* wanted it to.[4]

In relation to women and Fu Qui in the late '90s, why did this happen? What set it off?

Where do Geekgrrls Come From

1. It's possible that Fu Qui—excuse me, New Media—really was and is an emergent phenomenon, an unforeseeable consequence of collisions between complex discourses of art, technology, pedagogy, and gender. Emergent phenomena, almost by definition, at first escape customary regimes of surveillance and control. If you've met a geekgrrl or two, you know why this would have considerable appeal.

2. The actlab was, and to a great extent is, constructed as a TAZ—Hakim Bey's Temporary Autonomous Zone, loose and nomadic but internally cohesive, whose discursive qualities preserve its dynamic structure as it moves. A TAZ is another discursive formation which, for a time, escapes surveillance and control.

3. Many universities and the societies in which they were embedded had only the fuzziest of ideas about what New Media was. In the early '90s even the term didn't exist; what the Fu Qui geeks were doing was labeled, insofar as it was labeled, as "Interactive Multimedia": an expression coined before the century's halfway mark to mean slide projectors used with phonographs. (And yes, it was developed for the military.) Yet every geekly

artist knew something was happening that deserved its own definition. And since at such moments it behooves one to be very careful how one defines the territory, there was a rare window of opportunity to postpone definition and consequently defer closure on the meaning structure of whatever it was they were doing.

Because they were able to defer closure on meanings associated with New Media work, the young women laboring in the art-and-tech vineyard didn't simply define New Media within the university, they were New Media—and so to an extent free of the institutional agendas and expectations that would in all likelihood have been incumbent upon either a center or institute which grew naturally out of its existing surrounds, or one which had been started by older academics more thoroughly grounded in institutional beliefs and procedures. The actlab is merely a perspicuous example: Its manner of arrival was like an eruption within the institution, in the sense of a zit or boil. It followed no traditions, owed no allegiances. Its curriculum was a bricolage of everything and anything that looked like it might bear on any of the topics within the loose purview of what was not yet called Fu . . . uh, New Media. Its classes were free for alls in which a few words about the reading of the day might lead straight to total unabashed weirdness. Its students came from every department in the huge, sprawling

university, drawn by some amazing extrasensory message that Things Happened over here.

Out of this regime of experimentation (or pit of license, choose one or both) emerged a loose constellation of practices which I consider useful to women artists who may be setting out on the road to pedagogy or practice—hard to tell the difference—in a similar unnameable discourse. I recommend them as points of departure, and keep in mind that they are descriptive rather than proscriptive. It's likely, though by no means certain, that they owe their beginnings to three suggestions from deep in the mists of time: Refuse closure; Insist on situation; Seek multiplicity. I won't burden you by spinning them out; use your imagination. From them, maybe, in not too clear a cause-effect progression, come some other practices that I may elaborate on a bit more. Okay, here we go: Teaching women art and technology in the twenty-first century.

Reward risk taking. No elaboration necessary.
Trust subjective criteria. Your own, that is.
　Trust your sense of the value of the work.
　Don't lean on a canon where none exists;
　don't reify a canon simply to have one.
Translate incomprehensible weirdness into institutional clarity. Be a shield and interlocutor for your students against the institution's need for uniformity and predictability.

Make their work appear to embrace order where no order exists.

Finally, by way of A. E. Van Vogt: *Do not ridicule by word or deed any edicts of the institutional empire. Simply disobey them.*

Let's touch on institutional futures for a moment. It may appear that the New Media take on women, art, and technology exists in a vacuum, but in what passes for our minds this is merely a temporary expediency, necessary during the time that institutional structures are catching up. However, they catch up in peculiar times. In Texas, at least, public funding for education is not merely diminishing, but within ten years may have evaporated altogether, in perfect accord with theories of postmodernism and their predictions regarding how late capitalism will squeeze everything that exists into its most efficient shape. That is, the publicly funded university may all but disappear, to be replaced by something else, something perhaps uglier in purpose but no less the place where knowledge workers—we used to call them scholars—go for shelter and to recover a sense of purpose, no matter how tenuous.

In certain respects, the University of the Future looks, oddly enough, much like the more daring New Media teaching labs: Light, reconfigurable, schizoid, partially distributed. The core pedagogical structure consists of a collection of generalists, surrounded by satellite groups of specialists. The core group reconfigures itself in response to funding opportunities, but the funding has also gotten lighter and more configurable and therefore is more frequent but comes in smaller packages. Elsewhere I've called this action drive-by funding and just-in-time theory: a group emerges in response to funding opportunities, swallows the nourishment, digests, burps up a deliverable, and disappears back into the generalist pool. This model, rough though it is, has worked in a few experimental deployments. However, it still suffers from big problems, since the institutional head is still unaware of what the tail is doing; in spite of a push within many universities toward more entrepreneurial notions of research in the arts and humanities, try saying "deliverables" and see what happens.

Meanwhile within the academy, after a long and sleepy periodo flatency, scholars have become alert to the possibilities for new scholarship in relation to New Media; but so far the results have been largely problematic. This is because when you study New Media with the methods of a traditional discipline—anthropology, say, or sociology—the result is always Old Media. For rather than generating new understandings of nontraditional work, any account from within a traditional discipline merely reifies the epistemological and methodological constructs of that discipline. To study New Media with the quality of attention it deserves, and to produce intelligible results, requires a radical break with past and present theories and methods, and the creation—sans tradition, sans expectation—of a wholly new constellation of theories and methods. This bunch of tools for studying New Media—call it New Studies—requires a disciplinary language which, rather than emerging from existing languages, constitutes a radical break from existing languages. This is our brief for the next hundred years.

With that, let's put a cap on the background material. I've related it simply as prelude and introduction to the following question: At an unprecedented confluence of emerging technologies whose impact can only be compared to the dawn of the machine age, and in what might arguably be called a magic window of time within that confluence, and in a temporary autonomous zone isolated from cultural, societal, or institutional definitions—a ragtag, brilliant, self-selecting group of women were free to be . . . *what?*

Insofar as women, as a cultural concept, are called into being by that culture, to what extent do they escape naming and surveillance by entering something like the actlab—in the sense that the actlab provides an epistemic Faraday cage in which the usual tensions of power are momentarily nulled? More urgently, perhaps, insofar as they do escape that naming and surveillance, *to what extent are they then women?*

Most of us have lived most of our lives in a time of relatively stable definitions of body and gender. The advent of Queer discourse may have revealed some new possibilities, but while the possibility of new categories has been raised, the preexisting definitions remain unchanged. I want to approach this predicament not from the standpoint of the freak outsider chanting "we're Un, we're fun, get used to it," but rather as a respectful interlocutor who perceives an opportunity to code-switch, to translate, between the gendered language we all understand and which ineluctably and unconsciously shapes us, and the coming language whose outline we may be able to see in the behavior of those actlab artists who are—for want of a better term—women. For if anyone is going to figure out how to produce a radical break between the regimes of language and power, it's likely to be these Fu Qui women: women without history, without precedent, without fear. It's to them I speak now. Listen up, you freaks.

Originally we were drawn together because we were all exiles. But exile in itself does not a community make. The message the UnWomen bring is that "Ain't I a woman," brave and empowering a statement though it is, reifies oppression every bit as much as any description of one's place in a regime of power. Speaking under the sign of Woman is to always already be interpellated as oppressed. Salvaging freedom through affirming the power of the already-named is a doomed enterprise. It signifies that one has already accepted the definitions imposed by a regime of power so pervasive that its existence is assumed, given, invisible. The foremothers, struggling for freedom, still saw themselves as women . . . and by that interaction with their society, perforce constructed themselves as women.

When Queer activists re-appropriated "Queer" as a mark of pride, the reversal of meaning was total, since Queer had been a term that society despised. Its use as affirmation marked a rupture with the regime of power in which it was situated. The situation is different with "Woman." Our society has warped the term beyond recuperation. Quantum-like, its meanings are simultaneously positive and perverse, echoing the way women are perceived in predominantly masculinist discourses. Since in mainstream American culture its meanings are both vaunted and despised, its potential for rupture is foreclosed. One could say the term is spoiled, in the way contaminated food is spoiled. The contamination can't be scraped off. It runs too deep.

How are we to move beyond continually redefining ourselves within the prison of the conditional—"women artists"? Of course it was important to make the contributions of women artists visible in a society that rendered women invisible from the very dawn of history. And in the century just past we have made enormous strides toward accomplishing that task. But, as Joanna Russ pointed out, along with all these accomplish-

ments, *we have still not lost our femininity*—weiblichheit, womanitude, whatever you call that complex of aperçu and appearance which we continually recreate in interaction with the silent expectations of society, and therefore by which we continually recreate the vexed identity which, by society's rules, we must both affirm and escape.[5]

Which brings us, finally, to the UnWoman.

In her capacity as identity artist, it is the Un-Woman's task here to quietly remind us that speaking of, and of necessity from, a discourse of power within which one is already spoken is a tricky business. If we're going to turn that trick successfully, likely we'll do it out of the struggle for voice, in answer to the need for voice. And the trick will be turned not by linguists or politicians but by artists. I mean art beyond the millennium just ended; art created with "unnameable" media, made by "women" in the age of the UnWoman—for whom Woman is not a discursive formation which exists only over against its enantiomorph "Man," but which continually rearticulates itself through time in dynamic interaction with a web of discourses unimaginably large and incomprehensibly complex; for whom the cultural sign of Woman has ceased to be sovereign and for whom the definition of woman means, red-queen-like, just what we choose it to mean—nothing more and nothing less.

Living, as we do, deep in the past, it's sometimes hard to appreciate the incongruity of our headlong fall beyond the end of the categories we've defended so stoutly for an entire century and countless centuries before it, and the gains we've made while still managing to speak from within that category. Suffrage, equal pay for equal work, a scintilla of control over our bodies, glass ceilings . . . and then to suddenly notice that we're running, like Wile E. Coyote, across thin air, with nothing supporting us but our crazy belief in our own existence.

And so finally, you and I are alone with each other, sole survivors of the wreck of a mighty discourse. What have we learned about how that discourse flourished and faded in the century now dead? The UnWoman says: identity politics had

limits; although we can try awfully damn hard and turn the language this way and that, we can't have our biology-is-destiny cake without eating our socially constructed icing too—and not without acknowledging that in art as elsewhere, such a feast signals the end of binarism as an investigational tool. Beyond binarisms lie more complex methods, vexed discourses, harder choices; all of which require more subtle tools than those to which, perforce, we've been accustomed. And speaking of harder choices . . . from beyond the end of easy identity the UnWoman extends her hand, palm up in the ancient gesture, catches your gaze, and in a quiet voice asks: *Exactly what you mean "we," womyn-born-womyn?*[6]

Notes

1 For openers, let's all get on the same page here. The preceding paragraphs are fiction, that's spelled F-I-C-T-I-O-N. After them comes discussion. I call your attention to this obvious fact in the same way Harvey Kurtzman found it necessary to spell out that the stories in the original *Mad* magazine were l-a-m-p-o-o-n-s, lest some frantic and overworked publisher mistake them for plagiarism. After *The War of Desire and Technology* was published, I received several frantic calls from sociologists begging me to repudiate the book because of the damage it was doing to the credibility of the field. It turned out that they hadn't read the footnotes, which spelled out as clearly as possible the experimental mix of fact, fiction, and fantasy deployed there in the interests of producing not a traditional sociological or even academic text but something, shall we say, completely different. RTFN, Y'all.

2 Artistic license has been liberally taken here. Colorado and UW would be interested to hear they are partners: The usual interpretation vis-à-vis the Visible Human project is that Colorado intercepted the contract intended for the UW by claiming UW's preliminary dataset as its own. Some observers believe Colorado had leverage because UW got all the sectional data it used from the Swedish researcher Wolfgang Rauschning, almost certainly the best in the world at vibrating cryomicrotome sectioning. So the first round of kill, chill, slice, and dice occurred offshore. The Colorado group, using a much coarser microtome, created the current dataset. Using Rauschning's methods the full dataset would likely have run to terabytes of data, yielding a reconstruction with much higher resolution; in the current version the full dataset runs to no more than tens of gigabytes. Still, that's

huge, so pulling more than boiled-down abstracts of it through the Internet is unusual. In practice it travels on sets of CD-ROMs or DLT tapes.

3 Obviously there's a whole raft of issues in there that I don't have space to unpack in this essay. To mention a few, the default choice for the Visible Human was—you guessed it—male. This decision is justified by all the usual means, including one that does have a reality factor attached: Fresh bodies of young women executed by lethal injection are harder to come by than those of young men. Part of being a digital anatomy researcher involves being a ghoul—hanging around emergency rooms, always having your cell phone turned on, massaging a network of contacts and informants who work in places where fresh corpses are likely to turn up. Competition for intact young corpses in prime condition is fierce among researchers from medical schools and experimental labs such as the Digital Anatomist project, and the facts are that males die violently in far greater numbers than females do.

4 I don't want to imply that the ways they wanted things to change were always for what I thought would be the better. In theory a lot of young women get their ideas of goodness and badness from mass media, though on close observation this is true to a lesser extent than is generally believed.

5 A fine irony here for those who may have followed the Trans Wars: a Trans quoting the notorious Trans basher Joanna Russ, who once halted a conference on women writers to eject a Trans participant. To my knowledge no one has surpassed her ironic declaration (in *The Female Man*) that, with all the progress Woman has made, she has still "not lost her femininity."

6 Let's dispose of one issue that, quite logically, arises at this point: In view of the problematic state of societal definitions of Woman, to ask why, then, M2F Transsexuals still want their membership cards stamped is beyond the scope of this discussion. Buy me a beer sometime and we'll talk about it.

CONTRIBUTORS

NANCY BUCHANAN currently teaches Video Production and Video Art History at the California Institute of the Arts. Her own work has encompassed performance, drawing, installation, and computer works in addition to video. Her most recent work is a CD-ROM entitled *Developing: The Idea of Home* (1999).

WHITNEY CHADWICK is professor of Art at San Francisco State University. She has published widely on surrealism, feminism, and contemporary art. Her books include the widely acclaimed *Women, Art and Society* (1990, 1996); *Women Artists and the Surrealist Movement* (1985); and the novel *Framed* (1998).

ANGELA Y. DAVIS is professor in the History of Consciousness Department at the University of California, Santa Cruz. Her most recent book is *Blues Legacies and Black Feminism: Gertrude "Ma" Rainey, Bessie Smith and Billie Holiday* (1998).

ROSA LINDA FREGOSO is professor of Women and Gender Studies at the University of California, Davis. She has been a producer and critic for National Public Radio. Her many articles and books include *The Bronze Screen: Chicana and Chicano Film Culture* (1993).

DIANA BURGESS FULLER has been an activist, curator, producer, gallerist, and administrator in fine arts and film arts for over 30 years.

JENNIFER GONZALEZ is assistant professor in the Art History Department at the University of California, Santa Cruz. Her most recent publication is "The Appended Subject: Race and Identity as Digital Assemblage," in the forthcoming *Race and Space: Politics, Identity and Cyberspace* (Routledge).

JOANN HANLEY is an independent media arts curator who has been working with artists and independent film and video makers since 1978. Her writings and exhibitions include *The First Generation: Women and Video, 1970–1975* (1993).

THERESA HARLAN is Program Administrator at the California Arts Council and formerly the Director/Curator of the Gorman Museum, Native American Studies, University of California, Davis. Her most recent publication is "Adjusting the Focus for an Indigenous Presence," in *Critical Image* (1998).

KARIN HIGA is Senior Curator of Art and Director of the Curatorial and Exhibitions Department at the Japanese American National Museum in Los Angeles. She is the author of *The View from Within: Japanese American Art from the Internment Camps, 1942–1945* (1992).

PHYLLIS J. JACKSON is assistant professor of Art and Art History at Pomona College and the Intercollegiate Department of Black Studies of the Claremont Colleges. Her publications include "(in)FORMING the Visual (re)PRESENTING Women of African Descent," in *International Review of African American Art* (1997).

AMELIA JONES is professor of Contemporary Art and Theory at the University of California, Riverside. She is the author of numerous articles and books, including *Body Art /Performing the Subject* (1998).

SUZANNE LACY is Director of the Center for Art, Design and Social Responsibility at the California College of Arts and Crafts. She is a public artist on political themes and editor of *Mapping the Terrain: New Genre Public Art* (1995).

PAMELA LEE is assistant professor in late twentieth-century art, theory and criticism at Stanford University. Her publications include the forthcoming book *Object to be Destroyed: The Work of Gordon Matta-Clark* (MIT Press).

AMALIA MESA-BAINS is Director of the Visual/Public Art Institute at California State University, Monterey. She is an internationally recognized artist, cultural critic, lecturer, and author, and her awards include the distinguished MacArthur Fellowship Award in 1992.

LAURA MEYER is a doctoral candidate in the Department of Art History at the University of California, Los Angeles. She is the author of several essays on the feminist art movement, including "A Feminist Chronology, 1945–1995," in *Sexual Politics: Judy Chicago's Dinner Party in Feminist Art History* (1996).

SANDRA S. PHILLIPS is Senior Curator of Photography at the San Francisco Museum of Modern Art. She is a scholar, lecturer, and critic and has organized numerous critically acclaimed exhibitions of modern and contemporary photography, including *Crossing the Frontier: Photographs of the Developing West, 1849 to the Present* (1997).

JOLENE RICKARD is assistant professor at the University of Buffalo in the Art and Art History departments and focuses on American Studies. Rickard writes, lectures, and makes work about the issues of indigenous peoples. She was the keynote speaker at the British Museum's Northeast Native American Conference in 1999.

TEREZITA ROMO is Senior Curator at the Mexican Museum in San Francisco and formerly the Arts Director of the Mexican Fine Arts Center Museum in Chicago. She is an art historian, curator, and writer. She curated and edited the catalogue for *Patssi Valdez: A Precarious Comfort* in 1999.

MOIRA ROTH is the Trefethen Professor of Art History at Mills College in Oakland, California. She is a feminist art historian, critic, activist, and curator and has lectured extensively. In 2000, she won the Frank Jewlett Mather Award for lifetime achievement in criticism. Her most recent publication, co-authored with Jonathan D. Katz, is *Difference/Indifference: Musings on Postmodernism* (1998).

DANIELA SALVIONI has been a curator and critic for sixteen years and her writings have been included in major art publications and international exhibition catalogues.

ALLUCQUERE ROSANNE STONE is the director of the Interactive Multimedia Laboratory and assistant professor in the Department of Radio, TV and Film at the University of Texas, Austin. She is also founder and director of the Group for the Study of Virtual Systems at the Center for Cultural Studies at University of California, Santa Cruz.

GAIL TSUKIYAMA is an author, educator, and lecturer in the Creative Writing Department at San Francisco State University and a founding judge for the Pacific Rim-based Kuryama Awards. She is the author of four novels to date, *Women of Silk* (1991), *The Samurai's Garden* (1995), *Night of Many Dreams* (1998), and *The Language of Threads* (1999).

JUDITH WILSON is assistant professor of the History of Art and African and African-American Studies at the University of California at Irvine. Her critical writing includes "Critical Issues in American Art" (1997) and "Bearing Witness: Contemporary Art by African-American Women" (1996).

ILLUSTRATIONS

Illustrations

INDEX

Note: Italicized page numbers indicate illustrations.

of, 107, 298; teaching of, 297, 317; Woman's Building and, 300; works: *Blood of a Poet Box*, 244–45; *California Lives*, 22, *23*, 24–26; *The Nurse and the Hijacker*, 325; *100 Boots* series, *244*, 245

antiwar movement, 179

Antoine, Janeen, 144, 193

Antoni, Janine, 168

apartheid, protest of, 64, *65*

Aphrodite of Cnidus (sculpture), 76–77

Applebroog, Ida (Horowitz), 25

Appleby, Anne, 115

Arai, Tomie, 84

architecture: African American in, 206, 214n24; documenting construction of, 252; highways as, 235–36; students of, 207. *See also* space

Argentina, disappeared in, 264–65

Armstrong, Gloria, 198

Arroyo Seco River, 232

art: as activism, 4–5, 7–8, 172–73, 232, 246–47, 249–51, 255; "American" type of, 204, 213n13; as commodity, 85 (*See also* art market); content vs. abstraction in, 5; current diversity in, 97; definitions and redefinitions of, 4, 8, 72–73, 103, 151–52, 171; as educational, 207, 209, 216n42 (*See also* art education); everyday life fused with, 129, 168, 243–46; female sensibility in, 103, 111–12; fine vs. applied, 205–6; hierarchical categories in, 98, 151, 152, 158–59, 179, 190, 192, 207, 247; politicization of, 98, 103–4, 165, 178, 180, 321–22; as process and object, 86; role of, 67; space shaped by, 277; video as legitimate, 318–19

Art and Technology (exhibition), 109, 296, 314

Artaud, Antonin, 107

Art Center College of Design (Pasadena), 313, 317

art education: changing demographics of, 304; "drive-by" funding for, 343; GI Bill and, 4, 21, 203; in internment camps, 87; mentoring in, 328–29; racial tolerance in, 204; suggestions for, 342–43. *See also specific institutions*

"art for art's sake," idea of, 36

Artforum (journal), 29

art historical criteria: approach to, 11–13; documents necessary in, 73–74

Art in America (journal), 212

Art Institute of Chicago, 88

art institutions: critique of, 8, 246; cultural challenges in, 22; denunciation of, 67; future of, 343; normalization of whiteness in, 71; power of, 304; racial discrimination of, 201, 210; role of, 20–21; subversion of, 245. *See also* exhibition venues; publications; *specific institutions*

artists: defining self as, 66–67; use of term, 45–46. *See also* women artists

artist's books (Ruscha), 246–47

Art Journal, 307

art market: diffusion of feminism and, 173; lack of development of, 2; subversion of, 246; women marginalized in, 102

Artspace, 317

Artweek (journal), 109

Art West Associated (Los Angeles), 210

Art West Associated—North (San Francisco), 210

Art Workers Coalition (New York), 21, 165

art world (Calif.): amnesia in, 77; Native art's function in, 143, 146–48, 150; politics of, 70–74; specificity of, 2–3

Arzner, Dorothy, 259

Asawa, Ruth: as Asian American woman artist, 92–93; background of, 21, 85–86; exhibitions of, 94n16; focus of, 86–87; influences on, 94n14; works: *Group of Architectural Works*, 87

ASCO (collective), 136, 168

Ashton, Dore, 119n2

Asian American movement: description of, 82; strategies of, 83–85; visual art and, 85–93

Asian American women: labor activism of, 48–49; marginalization of, 84, 93n9

Asian American women artists: absence of, 84–85; definition of, 81–82, 92–93; diversity of, 90–92; use of term, 85–86

Asian American Women Artists Association, 306